I am most impressed with this collection of thoughtful essays from Notre Dame's distinguished faculty to help us think about the impact of marketing and its contributions to society.
Philip Kotler, S.C. Johnson & Son Distinguished Professor of International Marketing, Kellogg Graduate School of Management, Northwestern University, USA

Most insightful and comprehensive collection of essays on marketing and society authored by scholars from diverse disciplines and perspectives! Each essay in *Marketing and the Common Good* is thought-provoking and challenges the existing dogma in marketing.
Jagdish N. Sheth, Charles H. Kellstadt Professor of Marketing, Emory University, USA

The Fighting Irish beat their scholarly swords into societal ploughshares with a collection that is catholic in scope and Catholic in spirit. Ecumenical and enlightening, *Marketing and the Common Good* is a Notre Dame antidote to the B-school diseases of devil-take-the-hindmost and sin-to-win. This book is better than brilliant, it's uncommonly good!
Stephen Brown, Professor of Marketing Research, University of Ulster, UK

In a world where there is so much vanilla writing on marketing, this book adds welcome flavor. Issues about ethics, society, sustainability, Catholic social thought, public policy: all these have been sidelined in academic marketing too long. Using a cast of leading voices, *Marketing and the Common Good* tells a compelling story about why values matter, even when those values reach beyond consumer taste.
Thomas Donaldson, Mark O. Winkelman Endowed Professor, Wharton School, University of Pennsylvania, USA

With the increased attention in our field of Marketing to issues related to ethics, macromarketing, and transformative consumer research, this book about societal impacts on the Common Good offers timely insights into topics of increasing urgency. In short, the book provides required reading for both academics and practitioners concerned with the problem of contributing to the moral and spiritual elevation of our market-driven economy.
Morris B. Holbrook, W. T. Dillard Professor Emeritus of Marketing, Graduate School of Business, Columbia University, USA

This book is a manifesto for stakeholder-centric marketing. The essays focus on how marketing serves the common good and specifically addresses major dimensions of social responsibility, including social issues, sustainability, planned obsolescence, childhood obesity, firearms, personal selling issues, as well as many other dimensions.
O.C. Ferrell, Professor of Marketing, University Distinguished Professor and Bill Daniels Professor of Business Ethics, University of New Mexico, USA

An impassioned plea for the re-enchantment of Marketing by targeting fairness, social justice and sustainability. An exciting and persuasive collection of essays which argue that Marketing can make a major contribution to the common good.
Richard Elliott, Dean, School of Management, University of Bath, UK

This volume is a remarkable and demanding book. It is distinguished by its positive intentions, its largeness of view, and immense thoughtfulness. It confronts and stimulates the reader to ruminate about the marketing system. Ever since I read it I have been obsessively brooding about a profound question: Is there such a thing as the common good?
Sidney J. Levy, Coca-Cola Distinguished Professor of Marketing, Eller College of Management, University of Arizona, and Charles H. Kellstadt Professor *Emeritus* of Marketing, Kellogg Graduate School of Management, Northwestern University, USA

I can't envision a more thoughtful set of essays about the interface of marketing and the common good of the planet than these. They are both immediately actionable and deeply philosophic. They are historical, contemporary, and forward looking. They will comprise a valuable asset for anyone interested in human development, sustainability, global inequality, social marketing, transformational consumer research, quality of life, or business and consumer ethics. And they showcase the intellectually powerful and spiritually profound group of marketing scholars that Notre Dame has attracted and produced. This is a timely and compelling book.
Russell Belk, Kraft Foods Canada Chair in Marketing, Schulich School of Business, York University, Canada

The University of Notre Dame has long been a towering lighthouse of guidance across the turbulent sea of inevitable moral dilemmas in social and economic life. This new volume from its Mendoza College of Business reaffirms the continuing leadership of its marketing faculty in advancing profound and lasting knowledge about the nature and the necessity of virtues, values, and ethics in the practice of business today, and beyond.
David Glen Mick, Robert Hill Carter Professor of Commerce, McIntire School of Commerce, University of Virginia, USA

Combining marketing and the common good may seem implausible to some, but the Notre Dame faculty has a longstanding history of recognizing that our profession not only can but should be concerned with our larger societal impact. As a community of scholars they have celebrated the ways in which marketing has contributed to the common good, while fully recognizing the downside of our actions and the role of government to rectify resulting problems. This volume is a must-read for executives and students alike who wish to understand and advocate for the common good in ways that can truly make the world a better place.
Ronald Hill, Richard J. and Barbara Naclerio Chairholder in Business, Villanova University, USA

This is a pioneering and significant contribution shaped by institutional context and the visible hand of moral sentiment. The authors assemble the thoughtful work of a cohort of scholars that is truly unique in key regards: unique not only in terms of the stature of their contribution to the evolving moral tone of the discipline over the last 50 years; nor in their in penetrating accounts of the knots of ethical construct and social justice that frame the marketing gaze on societal impact; but in their virtually unprecedented return to discourse of the 'commons' and the 'common good' to suggest pathways towards the moral turn in marketing studies.

Douglas Brownlie, Professor of Marketing, University of Stirling, UK

I heartily recommend *Marketing and the Common Good*. This provocative collection of essays, written by prominent researchers in the field, provides a critical assessment of marketing and its role in some of the most pressing social problems facing humanity. Ultimately, their message is hopeful as readers are challenged to imagine a world where we are citizens first, and business and marketing practices serve our collective interests.

Julie L. Ozanne, Sonny Merryman Professor of Marketing, Virginia Tech University, USA and Chair, Advisory Committee on Transformative Consumer Research (ACR)

At a time when turning on the news frequently yields a new crop of corporate scandals, it is clearly appropriate that the scholarly community reflect on their role in affirming the present economic system. This collection is an admirable response to such a task. It scrutinizes the role of marketing in society, looking at its contribution to social justice and environmental sustainability. For those who require an introduction to the many complex debates surrounding the relationship between marketing and society, Murphy and Sherry's volume is essential reading.

Mark Tadajewski, Professor of Marketing, Durham University, UK

While marketing journals and textbooks overflow with a firm-centric and customer-centric micro lens on marketing, the Notre Dame marketing faculty for over five decades have telescoped out with a macro lens to debate and engage in dialogue about the social impact of marketing. This book celebrates that continuing dialogue and will benefit all that read and reflect upon the insights shared in this book.

Robert Lusch, James and Pamela Muzzy Chair in Entrepreneurship and Executive Director of the McGuire Center for Entrepreneurship, University of Arizona, USA

As modern Business Schools grapple with how to best embed ethics in the curriculum, Notre Dame showcases its prowess and long-standing interest in this area in this collection of thought-provoking and enlightening essays. Covering a diverse and comprehensive range of topics, the essays invite us to contemplate both specific consumption-related problems, such as obesity and firearms, and general marketing

system issues. This volume is a worthy addition to the limited but growing body of work addressing the role of marketing in a fair and just society.
Simone Pettigrew, Professor of Marketing and Director of the Health Evaluation Unit, University of Western Australia, Australia

Marketing so often seems at odds with the common good, not least given some of the unintended consequences of marketing activities. However, as this wide-ranging and thought-provoking collection of essays shows, marketing can be conceived and practiced in ways that promote the common good as well. It offers insight for marketing practitioners and scholars alike. It is also testament to the long-standing commitment of marketing faculty at Notre Dame to scholarship on issues of marketing and society, marketing ethics, and marketing and public policy—in short, to marketing and the common good.
N. Craig Smith, INSEAD Chaired Professor of Ethics and Social Responsibility, France

Marketing is widely demonized as being synonymous with egocentric materialism, a shallow consumer culture, broken promises, intrusiveness and other ills. The collection of essays now published by two of the most eminent marketing scholars and business ethics researchers, John F. Sherry, Jr. and Patrick E. Murphy, provides a welcome antidote to these prejudices. The contributions demonstrate that the field of marketing has substantially more intellectual gravitas than is commonly assumed. Illustrating the interconnectedness of marketing to ethics, moral economy and public policy, this book is a must read for anyone who is interested in societal aspects of marketing and in the fundamental question of how we all want to live together.
Bodo Schlegelmilch, Professor of International Marketing and Management, and Dean, Executive Academy, Vienna University of Economics and Business, Austria

A unique and important collection of essays join together in a coherent whole to make a powerful case for marketing's role in strongly influencing the common good. The common thread that underlies a multitude of specific marketing and society issues (ethical practices, sustainability, guns, childhood obesity, and et. al.) is revealed, placed in its historical and intellectual context, and even debated. Reading this volume will give many marketing scholars and students a far better understanding and perspective of our field's future.
Josh Wiener, Professor of Marketing, Carson Professor of Business Administration, and Director of the center for Social and Services Marketing, Oklahoma State University, USA

This book is a remarkable collective effort to re-imagine marketing as a means of identifying and achieving the common good. It provides a post-postmodern perspective of the intersection between marketing and society and paves the way for the remaking of marketing as 'societing'.
Bernard Cova, Professor of Marketing, Euromed Management and Visiting Professor, Bocconi University, Italy

This book is a must read for anyone who is interested in consumerism, marketing and society, marketing ethics or stewardship. Notre Dame has been at the forefront of research and thinking in these areas for decades. The authors are luminaries in the field.

Cornelia Pechmann, Professor of Marketing, Paul Merage School of Business, University of California, Irvine, USA, and Editor of *Journal of Consumer Research*

For more than three decades, the Marketing Department at the University of Notre Dame has served as both thought leader and social conscience of the marketing discipline. While others in our field have focused on publishing in significant journals, the Notre Dame faculty have focused on publishing significant work – work that makes the world a better place (much of which appears in significant journals). This focus reflects their individual, collective and institutional orientations that marketing should serve a high purpose, that it should make a world a better place, and that it should empower people to think and act beyond their personal interest. If, as a marketing manager, you strive to improve the lives of your customers and community, as well as your firm, then your decisions are likely shaped by the thinking and teaching of Notre Dame. If, as a marketing scholar, you can articulate to others how marketing can make the world a better place, your argument almost certainly includes the thinking and teaching of the faculty of Notre Dame.

John Mittelstaedt, Professor and Chair, Department of Management and Marketing, University of Wyoming College of Business, USA

Drawing on the interdisciplinary concept of "the common good" as its central motif, this inspiring collection from Notre Dame scholars focuses our attention on the complex and powerful role that marketing and consumption play in contemporary society. Together the provocative chapters leave the reader with a much keener appreciation of the many ethical and moral ramifications of marketing activities and their societal impact, taking us through a wide range of pressing issues that cover topics as diverse as firearms, kidney donations and childhood obesity. This book is essential reading for all current and future marketers to understand the broader implications of their actions and how the discipline can affect the common good in positive as well as negative ways.

Pauline Maclaran, Professor of Marketing & Consumer Research, Royal Holloway, University of London, UK

The authors included in this volume are among some of the most respected in the marketing discipline. It is hard to imagine that they all have some connection to one school (Notre Dame). Personally, I was especially attracted by the fact that, E.J. McCarthy, professor of the very first marketing course I ever enrolled in, was included in this volume. I believe that the topics covered should be useful to marketing students, academic researchers and business leaders alike.

Scott J. Vitell, Hardin Professor of Marketing, University of Mississippi, USA and Marketing and Consumer Behavior Section Editor for the *Journal of Business Ethics*

Not only does this text pay tribute to the continued voice and multifarious contributions of the Mendoza College of Business at Notre Dame in helping us understand what marketing can do to help us realize the common good but also provides another important part, alongside scholarship in macromarketing and public policy, of a collective cornerstone for enlightened marketing. This should be essential reading for all business school students across our world!

Pierre McDonagh, Dublin City University Business School, Ireland and Associate Editor, *Journal of Macromarketing*

I applaud this important effort at scholarly reflection on how marketing can serve the common good. It brings together serious scholarship on marketing with consideration of our obligation to serve society.

Rev. John Jenkins, President, University of Notre Dame

MARKETING AND THE COMMON GOOD

Marketing is among the most powerful cultural forces at work in the contemporary world, affecting not merely consumer behaviour, but almost every aspect of human behaviour. While the potential for marketing both to promote and threaten societal well-being has been a perennial focus of inquiry, the current global intellectual and political climate has lent this topic extra gravitas.

Through original research and scholarship from the influential Mendoza College of Business, this book looks at marketing's ramifications far beyond simple economic exchange. It addresses four major topic areas: societal aspects of marketing and consumption; the social and ethical thought; sustainability; and public policy issues, in order to explore the wider relationship of marketing within the ethical and moral economy and its implications for the common good.

By bringing together the wide-ranging and interdisciplinary contributions, it provides a uniquely comprehensive and challenging exploration of some of the most pressing themes for business and society today.

Patrick E. Murphy is Professor of Marketing at the Mendoza College of Business, University of Notre Dame, USA. Pat specializes in marketing and business ethics issues and his recent work has focused on normative perspectives for ethical and socially responsible marketing, distributive justice as it relates to marketing decision making, emerging ethical concerns in advertising, stakeholder theory, and marketing as well as ethics and corporate social responsibility for marketing in a global marketplace.

John F. Sherry, Jr. is Herrick Professor of Marketing and Chairman of the Department of Marketing at the Mendoza College of Business, University of Notre Dame, USA. John is an anthropologist who studies the sociocultural and symbolic dimensions of consumption, and the cultural ecology of marketing. His recent work has focused on experiential retailing, holistic branding, and consumption aesthetics. Among his current project is a study of the social rituals involved in tailgating during football games.

MARKETING AND THE COMMON GOOD

Essays from Notre Dame on Societal Impact

Edited by
Patrick E. Murphy and John F. Sherry, Jr.

Routledge
Taylor & Francis Group

LONDON AND NEW YORK

First published 2014
by Routledge
2 Park Square, Milton Park, Abingdon, Oxon OX14 4RN

Simultaneously published in the USA and Canada
by Routledge
711 Third Avenue, New York, NY 10017

Routledge is an imprint of the Taylor & Francis Group, an informa business

British Library Cataloguing in Publication Data
A catalogue record for this book is available from the British Library

Library of Congress Cataloging in Publication Data
Marketing and the common good: essays from Notre Dame on societal
impact/edited by Patrick E. Murphy and John F. Sherry, Jr.
pages cm
Includes bibliographical references and index.
1. Marketing—Moral and ethical aspects. 2. Social marketing. I. Murphy,
Patrick E., 1948– II. Sherry, John F.
HF5415.M2186 2013
306.3'4—dc23
2013002577

L0074о7825
ISBN: 978-0-415-82882-6 (hbk)
ISBN: 978-0-415-82883-3 (pbk)
ISBN: 978-0-203-36630-1 (ebk)

Typeset in Bembo
by Book Now Ltd, London

To our colleagues who set us on the path toward the common good:
David L. Appel
Wesley C. Bender
Yusaku Furuhashi
John R. Malone

CONTENTS

ILLUSTRATIONS

Figures

Tables

Boxes

CONTRIBUTORS

Unless otherwise specified, all contributors are Notre Dame faculty members.

Kevin D. Bradford is an Associate Professional Specialist in Marketing whose research addresses significant issues within the marketing system (marketers, customers, and public policymakers) and its relationship to society. His recent work has centered on sales management and the development of relationships, firearm diversion, and distribution channel responsibility.

Tonya Williams Bradford, Assistant Professor of Marketing, is pursuing two research streams: gift-giving and relationships. Some of the projects included in these streams are dispositions of gifted assets, intergenerational reciprocity, charitable gifting, gift registry, brand loyalty transitions, cross-cultural consumption of voluntary migrants, and service providers as family members.

Georges Enderle, John T. Ryan Jr. Professor of International Business Ethics, conducts research on the ethics of globalization, wealth creation, and corporate responsibilities of large and small companies, with a view on developments in China. He has investigated the ethics and corporate responsibilities for marketing in the global marketplace; the potential of the Golden Rule for a globalizing world; and Muslim, Christian, and Jewish views on wealth creation.

Michael J. Etzel, Emeritus Professor of Marketing, specializes in the study of consumer decision making, services marketing, and sales force management. He is a past Chair of the Board for the American Marketing Association. He also served as Chair of the Department of Marketing at Notre Dame from 1980 to 1987 and from 1993 to 1994 and is viewed as the "architect" of the current department.

Y. Hugh Furuhashi was Professor Emeritus of Marketing, and a former Dean, on multiple occasions, of Notre Dame's College of Business, where his research focused on international marketing, and in particular on American–Japanese relations. He was instrumental in setting up summer internships for ND MBA students in Japan and a summer program at Notre Dame for Japanese executives.

John F. Gaski, Associate Professor of Marketing, treats issues of larger significance in his research, such as social power – in this context, that which prevails among firms in a distribution channel. His primary current emphasis is the macroscopic societal impact of marketing activity, that is, how marketing impinges on human welfare.

Timothy J. Gilbride, Associate Professor of Marketing, investigates empirical methods applied to marketing problems. He specializes in Bayesian statistics developing new methodologies and models to describe consumer and firm behavior. Current projects include modeling shoppers' unplanned purchasing behavior, consumer decision-making under risk, and advertising and channel management.

Joseph P. Guiltinan, Emeritus Professor of Marketing, researches the management of a firm's product line, including product line pricing, bundling of products, and product obsolescence. His recent projects include: framing of price discounts in bundling; pricing strategies for durable replacement products; environmental ethics and planned obsolescence of durable goods.

John J. Kennedy, Professor of Marketing, studies both quantitative and behavioral dimensions of marketing, and is especially interested in gender issues. He is currently examining chaos theory for its relevance to management. He has served on the marketing faculty at Notre Dame for nearly 50 years.

Thomas A. Klein, Emeritus Professor of Marketing from the University of Toledo, where he served as Dean and in other administrative positions, specializes in the areas of macromarketing, ethics and Catholic Social Teaching. He served as a visiting professor at Notre Dame during the 2001–02 and 2002–03 academic years teaching marketing as well as ethics courses.

Gene R. Laczniak, Emeritus Professor of Marketing at Marquette University, researches marketing ethics, marketing strategy, business ethics, corporate social responsibility, and marketing in society. He and Pat Murphy have collaborated on ethics articles and books for over 35 years beginning when they were colleagues at Marquette.

E. Jerome McCarthy is Professor Emeritus at Michigan State University, and introduced the concept of the four Ps into the marketing literature. His research interests centered on marketing strategy. He and Yu Furuhasi co-authored an innovative book on social issues in marketing and recognized the larger societal role of marketing to the larger society 40 years ago.

Alexandria Miller, a Notre Dame BBA and MBA alumna, is a research associate at Bovitz, Inc., a design-driven research and strategy firm. Her primary interests include consumer information processing, sociocultural influences on consumption, and the emotional dimension of consumer–product relationships.

Jenny Mish was an Assistant Professor of Marketing whose research focus is the development of sustainable markets. Her recent work includes a study of exemplary triple-bottom-line firms and another of the role of sustainability-related product standards in the US food system. She pursues understanding of stakeholder marketing, the role of meanings in value creation, multi-stakeholder market self-regulation, and co-creation and decentralized diffusion of innovations.

Elizabeth S. Moore, Associate Professor of Marketing, studies the effects of advertising on children, intergenerational family studies, and the impacts of marketing in society. She is currently investigating public policy issues related to the online marketing of food to children, the impacts of recent self-regulatory advertising initiatives, family impacts on childhood obesity, and the relationship between childhood obesity and the functioning of the aggregate marketing system.

Patrick E. Murphy, Professor of Marketing, specializes in marketing and business ethics issues. His recent work has focused on normative perspectives for ethical and socially responsible marketing, distributive justice as it relates to marketing decision-making, emerging ethical concerns in advertising, stakeholder theory and marketing, as well as ethics and corporate social responsibility for marketing in a global marketplace.

F. Byron (Ron) Nahser, is currently a Senior Wicklander Fellow at DePaul University's Institute for Business and Professional Ethics, and also Provost Emeritus of Presidio School of Management, San Francisco. His research interests include business values, vision, marketing strategy, branding, social responsibility, and integrative sustainable management. He is a Notre Dame alumnus and has spoken in classes and participated in conferences on the ND campus for over four decades.

Qibin Niu, a Professor at China University of Petroleum, Beijing, studies challenges for marketing in China and strategic management of Chinese corporations going global, particularly in the oil industry. He has published numerous case studies on corporate behavior in China and in other countries. He spent the 2009–10 academic year as a visiting professor in the Department of Marketing working on ethics projects and attending a number of classes in ethics.

John F. Sherry, Jr., Herrick Professor of Marketing and Chairman of the Department, is an anthropologist who studies the sociocultural and symbolic dimensions of consumption, and the cultural ecology of marketing. His recent work has focused on experiential retailing, holistic branding, and consumption aesthetics. Among his current project is a study of the social rituals involved in tailgating during football games.

Joel E. Urbany, Professor of Marketing, explores consumer and managerial decision-making around issues of information, values, and decision-making. Current projects include how a firm's clarity in designing, pricing, and presenting products and services influence customer choice and assessment of value, and how/why managers' beliefs about customer needs/requirements frequently vary from actual customer beliefs.

John A. Weber, Emeritus Associate Professor of Marketing, researches both professional sellers and customers to assess comparative attitudes regarding the integrity of specific selling practices and is attempting to uncover creative alternative strategies and tactics that professional sellers can use to avoid compromising selling integrity, without compromising sales performance.

William L. Wilkie, Nathe Professor of Marketing, studies marketing's impacts on consumers and society in general, the topic of his latest book. He has recently been active in revising the American Marketing Association's official definition of the field, and on research projects involving (1) stemming the illicit diversion of firearms from legal channels of distribution, and (2) exploring the epidemic of childhood obesity in the United States and elsewhere.

ACKNOWLEDGMENTS

We are indebted to numerous colleagues who contributed the many selections in this book. We thank each of them for (mostly) meeting our deadlines and responding in a good-spirited manner to our incessant requests.

We gratefully acknowledge the funding provided by the Dean's Office of the Mendoza College of Business that allowed us to host the 2011 Notre Dame Symposium on Marketing and the Common Good that became the platform for this volume.

In addition to the publishers who permitted us to reprint articles in this text, we are especially grateful to Jerry McCarthy and Mitsuko Furuhashi for allowing us to reprint work from a book that Jerry and Yu Furuhashi published over 40 years ago.

Assembling, editing, and formatting material for this volume posed particular challenges. Two individuals at the University of Notre Dame assisted in this endeavor. Diane Stauffer, of the Faculty Support Office in the Mendoza College of Business was indispensable in taking many disparate chapters and transforming them into the coherent and editorially consistent contributions that you see here. Sandy Palmer, long-time Administrative Assistant for the Department of Marketing, worked meticulously to seek permission for reprinted chapters and figures included in this book, and supervised some of the research assistants that supported contributors' efforts. We are indebted to Diane and Sandy for their fine work.

We thank Jacqueline Curthoys, Alex Krause, and Emily Senior at Routledge, who commissioned and shaped the initial project, and Richard Cook and his associates at Book Now for guiding the volume through production.

Despite the efforts of these individuals, errors may always occur. We take full responsibility for them (as we should, as editors of an ethics book!).

Patrick E. Murphy
John F. Sherry, Jr.

PART I
Introduction

1

THE COMMON GOOD

The enduring effort to re-center marketing

Patrick E. Murphy

The genesis for this book outlining the contributions of the Marketing faculty members in the Mendoza College of Business at the University of Notre Dame came in a conversation that John Sherry and I had about similar books in which he had been involved at another university. These texts promoted the wide-ranging interests of the marketing faculty at that school. What we discussed was the unique positioning and longstanding commitment of Notre Dame's Department of Marketing to the general area of marketing and society, including ethics, public policy, and a number of societal issues.

This conversation led to a symposium entitled "Marketing and the Common Good" (MCG) in April 2011 held on the Notre Dame campus. The common good was the university-wide theme of a year-long set of discussions, presentations, and symposia on the topic. The MCG symposium explored the tendency of marketing to ramify far beyond simple economic exchange, into the realms of ethics and moral economy, issues of public policy, and practices of accommodation and resistance to consumer culture. Early versions of most of the chapters in this book were presented at that time.

The ensuing period has been one of revising, polishing, and in some instances, generating new manuscripts that fill the pages of this volume. The contributions fall into one of five general parts – societal aspects of marketing and consumption, Catholic Social Thought (CST) issues, sustainability issues, public policy issues, and ethical issues. The book ends with a concluding chapter and an afterword. At the end of this introductory essay, I offer a preview about each of the seventeen chapters that make up the text.

Origins of the common good

The concept of the common good has many parents. The disciplines of political science, ecology, education, philosophy, and theology all have contributed to our understanding of the concept.

The study of ecology examines the inter-relationships between people and nature. Two significant articles appeared in the 1960s that argued against a selfish view of humanity. In "The Tragedy of the Commons," Garrett Hardin (1968) persuasively argued that individuals pursuing narrow self-interest would use up the commons and leave few resources for the future. This theme ties in with the common good in that the "commons" must be protected. About the same time, Kenneth Boulding (1966), a Nobel laureate, coined the phrase "spaceship earth" and contrasted it with the prevailing cowboy economy which looked at natural resources as being unlimited. Although he did not use the common good to bolster his position, his view of the limitations of a resource-depleting economy flies in the face of what most would view as being good for others.

Within the philosophical literature, the common good is thought to have originated over two thousand years ago from the classic writings of Plato, Aristotle, and Cicero. One more recent conception of the common good follows the utilitarian theory which examines outcomes of decisions that maximize the happiness or utility of individuals within a society (Mill 1979). Some call it "the greatest good for the greatest number" and thus would state that such an ideal would lead to the common good since most are better off. Critics might argue that utilitarianism does not account for distributive justice (e.g., some individuals are harmed significantly while the majority may benefit moderately) and within the business sector, the concept of "economic utilitarianism" may mean that the common good could be reduced to whatever decision leads to the most profit or financial return for the company.

The late contemporary ethicist, John Rawls, offers a complete account of the basic structure of society and provides a more robust definition of the common good as "certain general conditions that are . . . equally to everyone's advantage" (1971, p. 246). In fact, he makes the distinction between the "good," actively creating a better world, and the "just," which creates a fair, liberal social infrastructure. In taking a bit of poetic license with his theoretical and much acclaimed position, we might argue that the "common" good would be a society with both (the) good and just characteristics.

Within theological circles, a general position that is advanced is that the "Golden Rule" promotes the common good. In what is not a surprising finding, the Golden Rule is present in virtually all organized religions (Murphy et al. 2005). Some would criticize this position in that such a rule leaves much open to interpretation and the common good goes beyond what one would consider as his/her duties to others.

The most extensive theological treatment of the common good is found in Catholic Social Teaching. Several of the Papal encyclicals make reference to the common good and this ideal is considered one of the major principles of CST that is not only followed by Catholics but many other faith-centered individuals. Although there are many references to the common good within these documents, one of the best summaries of what the common good entails is captured by the following passage:

> Because of the increasingly close interdependence which is gradually extending to the entire world, we are today witnessing an extension of the role of the common good, which is the sum total of social conditions which allow people, either as groups or as individuals, to reach their fulfillment more fully and more easily. The resulting rights and obligations are consequently the concern of the entire human race. Every group must take into account the needs and legitimate aspirations of every other group, and even those of the human family as a whole.
>
> *(Paul VI 1965)*

The common good and contemporary society

In the late twentieth and early twenty-first century, further discussion of the common good has occurred by a number of observers. They come from a variety of perspectives:

> We face a choice between a society where people accept modest sacrifices for a common good or a more contentious society where groups selfishly protect their own benefits.
>
> *(Robert Samuelson, Newsweek writer,*
> *quoted in Velazquez et al. undated)*

> Solving the current crisis in our health care system – rapidly rising costs and dwindling access – requires replacing the current "ethic of individual rights" with an "ethic of the common good."
>
> *(Daniel Callahan, bioethics expert, quoted in Velasquez et al. undated)*

> This kind of constructive, enlarging experience with the other counters the tribal fear of the outsider and tills the ground in which a seed of commitment – not just to me and mine, but to a larger, more inclusive *common good* – can be planted.
>
> *(Parks et al. 1996, p. 65, emphasis in the original)*

These quotations place the common good in a larger context than mere individual selfish interests. Furthermore, the seeds and planting analogy in the Parks quote underscores the importance of commitment to the common good. In the business and marketing, the stakeholder orientation presupposes that a broader view of the firm is necessary in today's complicated and interconnected world (Laczniak and Murphy 2012). In fact, the emphasis on sustainable marketing practices views future generations, or even the environment itself, as a stakeholder. Similarly, discussions of corporate social responsibility highlight the necessity of taking into consideration the needs of society beyond just those of customers, employees, and stockholders.

Common good in marketing presupposes a broader context than just consumers buying products from marketers. Many other stakeholders must be drawn into the discussion. In an article entitled, "The Stakeholder Theory and the Common Good," Argandona (1998) argues that the common good should serve as one of the foundations of stakeholder theory. Within a particular company, the common good is the fulfillment of the company's purpose to create the conditions where all participants in the firm can accomplish personal goals. Thus, there can be a common good both inside and outside the firm. This foundation for stakeholder theory in the common good is not to say that the common good can be translated into a list of rights and duties for a company. Rather, Argandona explains what these two concepts mean in practice:

> However, the theory of the common good introduces a major change in the traditional approach to stakeholders. The approach identifies stakeholders as being those who have an "interest" in the company (so that the firm, in turn, may have an "interest" in satisfying their demands) and this may provide a sufficient basis for a positive theory of the organization (although, probably, incomplete). The theory of the common good is based on the classic concept of "good": the company does "good" to many people, to some by obligation and to others more or less involuntarily. And "it must do good" to certain groups by virtue of its obligation to contribute to the common good, which goes from the common good of the company itself to that of the local community, the country and all humankind, including future generations. In any case, the concept of good seems to provide a more appropriate foundation for an ethical theory than the concept of interest.
>
> *(Argandona 1998, p. 1099)*

In a recent influential book (*What Money Can't Buy*), Michael Sandel, a Harvard government professor, takes aim at what he calls the "era of market triumphalism" by persuasively advocating that there are many things in life that money cannot buy. He criticizes the commodification of blood donorship, using the criteria of fairness and corruption. By fairness Sandel means that some individuals in society can readily afford to pay a financial price for virtually anything, but the poor, uneducated, and vulnerable will be left out. The corrosive tendency of markets means putting a price on the good things in life can corrupt them. In his chapter on "Naming Rights" he notes that the corrosive effects of advertising matters less in the grocery aisle than it does in the public square, where naming rights and corporate sponsorships are becoming widespread (p. 189). These naming rights have become pervasive, going beyond ballparks and skyboxes to police cars and school buses with corporate logos on them.

In the last few pages of his book, he takes aim at our consumer culture dominated by marketing, but concludes with a call for the common good:

> It isn't easy to teach students to be citizens, capable of thinking critically about the world around them, when so much of childhood consists of basic training for a consumer society. At a time when many children come to school as walking billboards of logos and labels and licensed apparel, it is all the more difficult – and all the more important – for schools to create some distance from a popular culture steeped in the ethos of consumerism ....
>
> Democracy does not require perfect equality, but it does require that citizens share in a common life. What matters is that people of different backgrounds and social positions encounter one another, and bump up against one another, in the course of everyday life. For this is how we learn to negotiate and abide our differences, and how we come to care for the common good.
>
> And so, in the end, the question of markets is really a question about how we want to live together. Do we want a society where everything is up for sale? Or are there certain moral and civic goods that markets do not honor and money cannot buy?
>
> *(Sandel 2012, pp. 200–201)*

Another recent text (Skidelsky and Skidelsky 2012) outlines what the authors indicate is the "good life" and their description is very similar to what we are calling the common good in this volume. Their contention is that almost all things are viewed as marketable and this detracts from a larger vision of society:

> The continued pursuit of growth is not only unnecessary to realizing the basic goods; it may actually damage them. The basic goods are essentially non-marketable: they cannot properly be bought or sold. An economy geared to maximizing market value will tend to crowd them out or to replace them with marketable surrogates. The result is a familiar kind of corruption. Personality becomes part of the jargon of advertising, with consumers of the most everyday products said to be "expressing" or "defining" themselves. Friendship is no longer the ethically serious relationship it was for Aristotle but an intrigue for the enjoyment of leisure. Meanwhile, leisure itself is subject to the same economizing logic that governs production, with sports, games and nightclubs striving to pack

the maximum of excitement into the minimum of time. "The market penetrates areas of life which had stayed outside the realm of monetary exchange until recently," writes sociologist Zygmunt Bauman (2005, p. 88). "It relentlessly hammers home the message that everything is or could be a commodity, or if it is still short of becoming a commodity, that it should be handled *like* a commodity."

(Skidelsky and Skidelsky 2012, pp. 170–71)

In the concluding page of this influential book, Skidelsky and Skidelsky (2012, p. 218) make the following statement: "Could a society entirely devoid of the religious impulse stir itself to pursuit of the common good? We doubt it." This philosophy is echoed in Part II of our book and is an undercurrent of many of the other selections.

Overview of the book

Part I contains this chapter and the next by William Wilkie and Elizabeth Moore. Their chapter is adapted from an influential *Journal of Marketing* article. This selection presents a comprehensive examination of marketing's contribution to society. It outlines both marketing's positive aspects and several criticisms and problems with the aggregate marketing system. The chapter concludes with six lessons learned and the final one speaks directly to the common good.

Part II includes four chapters. In the initial one, John Sherry outlines the intersection between marketing and society from several perspectives. His chapter firmly positions the topic of the common good as a central one for all who are interested in the societal aspects of marketing. Joe Urbany examines the issue of clarity and how commercial marketers have until recently obfuscated the information that they made available to consumers. He proposes a model that places a premium on transparency and clarity as a marketing strategy. He sees this approach as quite consonant with the common good. The third selection is co-authored by John Gaski and our emeritus colleague, Mike Etzel. These authors propose the narrowest conception of the common good as only pertaining to fair relationships with consumers. They reject the notion of taking a broader stance where both unintended consequences from marketing activity and marketers' assuming some social responsibility might occur. Readers will be reminded of Milton Friedman's words that they only social responsibility of marketing is to maximize profits. The fourth selection in Part II is a reprint from the first chapter of a book co-authored by our late colleague, Yusaku Furuhashi, and a former Notre Dame faculty member, E. Jerome McCarthy. Although their book was published over 40 years ago, the chapter has a timeless quality to it in that many of the issues they identified back then remain with marketing well into the twenty-first century.

Part III features only two chapters. Laczniak, Klein, and Murphy examine the last encyclical by Pope Benedict and its relevant passages for marketing.

They identify nine specific paragraphs in the document that have application for marketing. Some of the topics are ethical issues in business, the stakeholder concept and the importance of stewardship for the natural environment. They conclude by tying these paragraphs to the theological conception of the common good. Tim Gilbride offers additional insight into CST and its relevance to marketing as well as its acceptance as a normative ethical theory.

Part IV focuses on sustainability issues in marketing. Ron Nahser provides a broad discussion of the essential nature of markets, commons, and marketing to better understand the sustainability challenges that the marketplace faces now and into the future. As a native Chicagoan, he examines a number of sustainability initiatives undertaken in the Chicago area both recently and historically. Jenny Mish and Alexandria Miller use the familiar 4 P's conception of marketing to examine sustainability. Their approach contains both micro- or firm-level suggestions as well as macro/societal perspectives as well. Joe Guiltinan's contribution was originally published as an article in the *Journal of Business Ethics*. He has long studied the concept of planned obsolescence and in this chapter he firmly grounds the issues surrounding this controversial marketing tactic to the ethics of sustainability.

Part V explores several public policy issues facing marketing. Betsy Moore examines the important societal issue of childhood obesity. She contends that manufacturers of food and beverages as well as food retailers all have contributed to growth of this issue (pun intended). If the larger society is to help alleviate this problem, the lens of the common good is a proper paradigm to better understand the scope of the obesity epidemic. Kevin Bradford chronicles the societal issues that have arisen in the distribution of firearms in the United States. Many of the problems arise from the "diversion" of guns from traditional retail channels to unregulated sales through gun shows, back of trucks, and cars. Bill Wilkie and I are both "alums" of the Federal Trade Commission. Our chapter traces the rich intertwined history of Notre Dame's link to the FTC. It started with Edward Hurley, the benefactor of the first College of Foreign and Domestic Commerce building on Notre Dame's campus and has continued with the five current and former faculty members in the Department of Marketing who spent time working at the agency.

Part VI touches on several ethical issues associated with marketing. Tonya Bradford discusses the complicated process associated with kidney donation and why much of the enterprise is fraught with ethical implications. She identifies a recent matching procedure that helps both donors and recipients and is a very good application of the common good. John Weber examines selling activity and the multiple ethical problems associated with it. He proposes a stakeholder-based approach to alleviating, if not solving, a number of these issues. He sees a central role for ethics training to better sensitize salespeople to the ethical challenges they may face. Georges Enderle and Qibin Niu discuss several case studies of ethics in global marketing with a focus on China. Because the regulatory framework is not nearly as advanced in the Chinese economy, they see an expanding role for companies in raising the ethical standards for marketing in that country and around the world.

Part VII consists of a concluding essay by John Sherry which shows that CST is a relevant concept for much of contemporary marketing and challenges the discipline's thought leaders to re-imagine marketing as a means of identifying and achieving the common good. John Kennedy's afterword ruminates on the history of the Notre Dame Marketing Department and its contributions to the common good over the past half century.

Urgency and relevance of perspective: Some recent illustrations

The events of 2012 have added great impetus to the notion of the common good and the selections in this volume. Some of the most significant are illustrated below.

- The horrific shootings at Sandy Hook Elementary School in Newtown, Connecticut on December 14, with the deaths of 20 children and six adults have led to increased pressure for more stringent gun control laws in the United States. (For a summary of the news accounts of this tragedy, see Cooper 2012; Friedman 2012; Nagourney 2012; and Shear 2012 on Sandy Hook and the episode's implications for gun control.) The chapter by Kevin Bradford could help to inform these deliberations.
- The findings that Walmart was involved in bribing government officials in Mexico (Barstow and von Bertrab 2012) and the fact that Foxconn (Mozer 2012) remains in the news adds credence to the chapters by Enderle and Niu and Weber on the importance of ethics in marketing both at national and international levels.
- The Pontifical Council for Justice and Peace (2012) published *Vocation of a Business Leader: A Reflection* that outlined how business leaders can contribute to the common good. While some of the responsibilities noted in this recent document are slightly different, they echo the contributions of Laczniak, Klein, and Murphy as well as Gilbride in the chapters on Catholic Social Teaching and its relationship to the common good.
- *The Economist* (2012) published a special section to its magazine in December on obesity. The adjoining editorial and six articles focused on food companies and fast food in particular and their responsibilities to alleviating this problem. The chapter by Moore in this volume indicates that special efforts should focus on the young so as to reduce the likelihood of a lifelong battle on containing one's weight. *The Wall Street Journal* also reported on the fact that food companies are trying to hook kids into mobile games that are linked to company promotions (Troianovski 2012). This issue is one that is central to the common good ideal and is growing in importance.
- The United States Federal Trade Commission (2012; Wyatt 2012) promulgated a new set of "Green Guides" in October. These guides updated earlier

ones and set new rules for marketers that are advertising sustainability efforts. This guidance lends further urgency to the chapters by Nahser, Mish, and Miller and Guiltinan. Furthermore, the FTC has been increasingly active in the children's online privacy issue (Singer 2012). This renewed activity by the FTC shows that this matter is a complex problem that warrants close study by observers concerned with the common good, as noted in the Murphy and Wilkie chapter.

These events, and a host of others, draw attention to the many ways that the role of marketing is intertwined with the quality of life in contemporary society. The contributors to this volume have described the societal impact of marketing, and outlined ways in which the discipline can, and should, affect the common good. We invite our readers to join in this critical assessment as they ponder the following pages.

References

Argandona, A. (1998) "The stakeholder theory and the common good," *Journal of Business Ethics*, 17: 1093–1101.

Barstow, D. and von Bertrab, A. (2012) "The bribery aisle: How Wal-Mart used payoffs to get its way in Mexico," *The New York Times* (December 18): A1 and B6–8.

Bauman, Z. (2005) *Liquid Life*, Cambridge: Polity.

Boulding, K. (1966) "The economics of the coming spaceship earth," in H. Jarrett (ed.) *Environmental Quality in a Growing Economy*, Baltimore, MD: Resources for the Future/ Johns Hopkins University Press, pp. 3–14.

Cooper, M. (2012) "Debate on gun control is revived, amid a trend toward fewer restrictions," *The New York Times* (December 15).

Economist, The (2012) "Special report: Obesity" (December 15): 1–16.

Friedman, R. (2012) "In gun debate, a misguided focus on mental illness," *The New York Times* (December 17).

Hardin, G. (1968) "The tragedy of the commons," *Science*, 162 (3859, December 13): 1243–48.

Laczniak, G. and Murphy, P. (2012) "Stakeholder theory and marketing: Moving from a firm-centric to a societal perspective," *Journal of Public Policy & Marketing*, 31 (2): 284–92.

Mill, J. (1979) *Utilitarianism*, Indianapolis, IN: Hackett.

Mozer, P. (2012) "Foxconn workers: Keep our overtime," *The Wall Street Journal* (December 18): B1 and B2.

Murphy, P., Laczniak, G., Bowie, N., and Klein, T. (2005) *Ethical Marketing*, Upper Saddle River, NJ: Pearson Prentice Hall.

Nagourney, A. (2012) "States' leaders proposing steps to control guns," *The New York Times* (December 18).

Parks Daloz, L., Keen, C., Keen, J., and Parks Daloz, S. (1996) *Common Fire: Leading Lives of Commitment in a Complex World*, Boston: Beacon Press.

Paul VI (1965), *Gaudium et Spes*, paragraph 26. Reprinted in A. Flannery (1996), *Vatican Council II: Constitutions, Decrees and Declarations,* Northport, NY: Costello Publishing, p. 191.

Pontifical Council for Peace and Justice (2012) *Vocation of the Business Leader: A Reflection*, Vatican City: Pontifical Council.

Rawls, J. (1971) *A Theory of Justice*, Cambridge, MA: Belknap Press of Harvard University Press.

Sandel, M. (2012) *What Money Can't Buy: The Moral Limits of Markets*, New York: Farrar, Strauss and Giroux.

Shear, M. (2012) "Obama promises fast action pressing for gun control," *The New York Times* (December 19).

Singer, N. (2012) "U.S. tightening web privacy rule to shield young," *The New York Times* (September 28): A1 and A3.

Skidelsky, R. and Skidelsky, E. (2012) *How Much is Enough?* New York: Other Press.

Troianovski, A. (2012) "Child's play: Food makers hook kids on mobile games," *The Wall Street Journal* (September 18): A1 and A14.

United States Federal Trade Commission (2012) *Revised Green Guides*, accessed at: www.ftc.gov/os/fedreg/2012/10/greenguidesfrn.pdf (May 30, 2013).

Velasquez, M., Andre, C., Shanks, S.J., and Meyer, M. (undated) "The common good," Markkula Center for Applied Ethics, Santa Clara University, accessed at: www.scu.edu/ethics/practicing/decision/commongood.html (February 5, 2013).

Wyatt, E. (2012) "F.T.C. issues guidelines for 'eco-friendly' labels," *The New York Times* (October 2): B4.

2

A LARGER VIEW OF MARKETING

Marketing's contributions to society

William L. Wilkie and Elizabeth S. Moore

Introduction

Our goals for this chapter

This chapter is an adapted version of a journal article[1] summarizing the results of a major project we undertook to address the topic: "What does marketing contribute to society?" We originally chose to study the field of marketing because we found it to be among the most stimulating, complex, and intellectually challenging of academic areas in a university. In contrast to its general reputation as a "soft" area, we have found that the marketing field welcomes insights from many disciplines, including economics, psychology, history, mathematics, sociology, law, political science, communications, anthropology, and the creative arts. It combines objectivity and subjectivity, demands both quantitative and qualitative insights, requires persistence yet rewards creative leaps, and allows imaginative freedom yet grounds its efforts in actions with measured consequences.

In the spirit of the special "Millennium Issue" of the *Journal of Marketing*, we view this article as an effort to clarify, illustrate, and celebrate some special aspects of our field and its relationship to society. As the academic field of marketing nears its 100th birthday, its focus is squarely on firms, markets, and household consumers – few persons are examining marketing's contributions to society. However, the subject is well worthy of consideration (likely why the Marketing Science Institute named it a key topic for this Special Issue). Thus, our purpose here is to provide a *different* look at marketing, one that engages thoughtful deliberation on the larger system and its contributions to the common good.

One hundred years of academic marketing

Three early insights we've gained are that marketing's contributions (1) *accumulate over time*, (2) *diffuse through a society*, and (3) *occur within the context of everyday life*.

This makes them hard to discern at a given time. Thus we begin with a look over a very long period.

A view across time: Marketing's impact on daily life in the United States, or "it's a wonderful life"

Here we join Mary Bailey as she reads a diary her mother recently had given her as a family heirloom. It had been written by Mary's great-grandmother Anne at the turn of the century, 100 years ago. As she settles under a lamp on a cold winter's evening in Bedford Falls, Mary is imagining her ancestor's times and how much life has changed.

(*Daily activities*) As she reads, Mary is surprised to discover how Anne spent her days.[2] Largely dependent on walking or horses, families centered on the home and local community. Daily life meant physical labor. Equipped with only a scrub board, the typical housewife spent 7 hours a week doing laundry and carried 9,000 gallons of water into the house each year, which she then had to boil before using (only 25 percent of homes had running water). Cooking, baking, and food preservation required substantial time, some 42 hours per week! Products that now routinely are bought, such as clothing, often were produced in the home. Central heating would not arrive until the 1920s; Anne's family heated only the kitchen for the winter, using fuel hauled in daily by family members. Only 3 percent of households had electrical lighting, so most families relied on coal, kerosene, or oil to light their homes. As she reads on under her bright lamp, Mary wonders how bright the lighting had been for the author whose words she was reading.

(*Health and safety improvements*) Mary is reading deeply as Anne described relief that her baby Aaron had survived; infant mortality was common in Bedford Falls at the time (about one in every ten births). In checking the family tree, Mary finds that Anne herself had died at a relatively young age (life expectancy in 1900 was only 47 years of age). In contrast, life expectancy today is nearly 80 years of age, and Mary has not had to worry seriously about infant mortality (now significantly less than 1 percent) or death from infectious disease. Thinking more about this, Mary realizes that her family's health, safety, and ability to enjoy life have been assisted by the fruits of advances in diagnostic equipment, pharmaceuticals to combat disease, pain relievers, bacteria-safe foods, safety-tested products, and so forth.

(*Impacts of technology and growth of the marketing system*) The academic field of "marketing" began about the time Anne was writing her diary. During the ensuing century, we have experienced many changes in daily life in the United States. The aggregate marketing system, in conjunction with the other aggregate systems with which it interacts (e.g., technology, finance, production) has delivered most of these changes to society. For example, the availability of home electricity was followed by the creation of many new appliances – clothes washers and dryers, vacuum cleaners, air conditioners, dishwashers, music systems, television, and so on – that bring efficiency and enjoyment to homes today. Home refrigeration and supermarkets mean fewer trips to the store; together with appliances, this has allowed the average time spent on food preparation to fall from 42 hours to less than 10 hours per week! With economic growth (gross national product is 400 times greater than a century ago), higher incomes, and technological innovations new opportunities arise. A vast array of goods and services is now available. Moreover, real prices for many goods (e.g., television, autos) have fallen to the point that they are accessible to almost every member of US society today.

Mary Bailey closes her diary and begins to think about other changes as well. She and her family are informed readily about national and global events and can travel from Bedford Falls to anywhere in the world. Her family's daily life is far, far removed from that of her ancestor's. As she ponders this, she realizes that the world for her children will be different from hers today, in as yet unknown ways, as the aggregate marketing system continues to deliver change to their society in the future . . . .

The importance of perspective

Viewing a topic from a single perspective highlights certain characteristics but can hide other aspects that also may be important: for example, a person looks different from the front than from the back and different again if viewed from the side. To understand a topic well, it is helpful to walk around it mentally, adopting different perspectives on it. Four perceptual barriers in this topic involve *time, system limits, culture,* and *personal experience.* The Mary Bailey illustration addresses the slow diffusion of marketing's contributions over time by contrasting two extremes, and when viewed in this way the contributions the marketing system has delivered to Americans today are clarified. With respect to system limits, not only is the marketing system vast (as we shall demonstrate shortly), but *its operations converge and coordinate with* the operations of other aggregate systems within a society's larger economic system. (In a Venn diagram, we might conceive of aggregate systems in marketing, finance, technology, production, and so forth as partially overlapping large circles that reflect areas in which activities are in common and those in which activities lie only in that field.)

With respect to culture, marketing is a social institution that is highly adaptive to its cultural and political context. Thus, we can move easily around the world to locate societies with very different marketing systems. In some global locations, we would find rudimentary marketing systems offering none of the conveniences Mary Bailey is enjoying; people there may be living as Anne did a century ago. Elsewhere, as in parts of Brazil, we would find people just discovering installment credit and using it to obtain the first home conveniences they have ever enjoyed. In parts of China, we would find incredible levels of investment – one of every five construction cranes in the world is reportedly at work just in Shanghai – to bring modern elevators, air conditioners, and other conveniences to the citizenry. Thus, coverage of aggregate marketing systems is culture-bound. We must take care to distinguish which lessons are generalizable and which are not. With regard to personal experience, many marketing contributions are "behind the scenes," unseen by those not directly involved. It is thus important that we remain mentally open to discovery of new possibilities about marketing.

We have come away from this project with a new, richer view of our field and hope that readers will as well. There are four sections to the chapter. First is an overview of the aggregate marketing system (AGMS), which provides a "larger view" of the field of marketing. We then draw upon the AGMS to profile the range of benefits marketing offers to society in the second section. Our third section adds balance, as we summarize criticisms of the marketing field, and our fourth section provides a brief summary of the lessons we've learned in this undertaking.

The aggregate marketing system

Studies have shown that the less familiar a person is with the marketing field, the more likely he or she is to equate marketing with advertising or selling. As a person learns more, the view broadens, and the richness of the marketing field emerges (Kasper 1993). We now turn to the aggregate marketing system (although marketing systems used to be a central topic, the current emphasis on managerial decisions). If marketing thinkers are to appreciate the range of contributions of our field, it is good to remind ourselves about the scope of its work.

The system at work

The idea for the following illustration is based on a longer discussion used by Vaile *et al.* (1952) to begin their classic textbook on marketing. We have updated and changed the description, here opting to join Tiffany Jones and her family in New York, as Tiffany reaches for her breakfast pastry and blows softly across her cup of coffee. . . .

"Breakfast at Tiffany's"

(*A cup of coffee*) Although a commonplace event, the breakfast setting also represents the confluence of a powerful set of forces from the AGMS. Let us first consider how her coffee arrived at this morning's meal. Tiffany has chosen a leading brand, one that delivers a consistent color, scent, and taste favored by its many customers. The marketing system for this brand reflects considerable attention to achieving efficiencies as well as a continuing emphasis on quality control. How exactly does this system operate? The major steps are shown in Figure 2.1.

First, the coffee that Tiffany has prepared is actually a combination of beans grown in a number of different countries, then brought to the United States and blended into a prespecified mixture to deliver the unique qualities associated with this brand (because of different geographic growing seasons and inherent product characteristics, the source countries for the beans will change as the year progresses: coffee is grown in some fifty nations around the world). As shown in Figure 2.1, let us assume that some of the beans in this cup began their journey on a Colombian hillside, hand-picked (to ensure ripeness) in the grower's field. The process from field was highly structured: from basket, to tractor, to truck, the beans were transported to the coffee grower's de-pulping mill, where the inner beans were separated from their cherries. Still "wet" and protected by a parchment-like cellulose shell, the beans were spread on a sun-filled patio to dry for several days. The beans were then milled (a process of removing the parchment

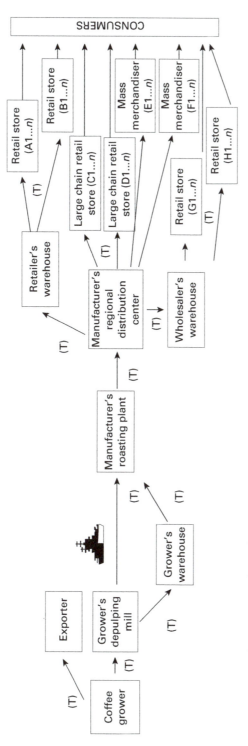

FIGURE 2.1 Marketing system for coffee (T = transport).

sheath to produce a "green" bean), then graded according to established national coffee standards. Samples of the beans were forwarded to both buyers and the government coffee board to allow checking of the grading process. The green beans were then placed into 60-kilo (132-pound) burlap or polyester bags, which were marked with the grower's name and assured quality level, and warehoused at the grower's facility. Either at this point, or earlier, exporters and large buyers were contacted by the grower to arrange for sale and delivery. In the case of Tiffany's major coffee brand, this purchase was made on the basis of a long-standing business relationship with this grower, built on trust in both the quality and grading accuracy of his beans, his capability to deliver agreed-upon quantities at agreed-upon times, and his willingness to stand behind his agreements. The seller holds similar views about potential buyers, and will only deal with certain firms in his form of "relationship marketing."

Continuing with Figure 2.1, once the buyer was determined, the beans were loaded on trucks and driven from the mountains down to the port city (humidity levels near the ocean could damage the beans had they been warehoused there). There they were loaded directly into 20-ton "piggyback" containers designed to transport seamlessly amongst ships, trains, and trucks. After 4 or 5 days at sea, the beans arrived at the port of New Orleans, again sampled for quality, and turned over to the care of a warehouse service retained by the purchasing firm. This service handled custom's clearance and unloaded the bags into hopper trucks destined for the coffee firm's "silo" facility, in which loads of different beans are stored, then blended together into 20-ton hopper trucks and taken to the firm's New Orleans roasting plant (alternatively, the beans might have been directed to the firm's Midwest or Southwest roasting plants in 80-ton hopper cars). Here the final coffee is carefully prepared, tested for quality, and packaged into the familiar red cans or "bricks." As indicated in Figure 2.1, from this point the exact route of the finished product is a function of the type of purchaser: it may be shipped in large volumes to one of the firm's seven regional distribution centers, thence to be sold to wholesalers, then to retail outlets, or – in the case of very large national accounts – delivered directly from the plant in entire 40,000-pound truckloads. As Tiffany had purchased her coffee from the neighborhood IGA store, it had traveled along the longer route. Even so, the vacuum-pack containers had kept it quite fresh through the distribution channel, and lent pleasure to her cup this morning.

Thus we see how a marketing system has operated to provide a simple cup of coffee to one American consumer on one typical morning. This provides us with some useful insights, particularly those associated with physical flows. Coffee is, however, a relatively simple product, and the AGMS deals with much greater levels of complexity than this. Let us move along one further level, therefore, by considering another item in Tiffany's breakfast: a breakfast pastry.

(*A breakfast pastry*) This product is a new entrant produced by a major food marketer to compete in the fast-growing "premium" breakfast segment. Although still a relatively simple product, the operation of its marketing system surpasses that for coffee in several significant respects. We do not depict the system here, but in comparison with Figure 2.1 we would see much greater complexity at the left side, since each unit of pastry comprises 15 ingredients. Each of these basic ingredients has its own system, similar to coffee, for collection, processing, and transport to the ingredient processors, who then create and deliver the final ingredients to the manufacturer. The pre-production marketing system here, therefore, is substantially more involved than is the relatively linear system for coffee. The pastry brand is similar to the coffee brand, however, in that both will fail if their quality control procedures do not operate at a very high level of consistency. Thus we find exacting product specifications for each ingredient, with careful attention by buyers and sellers to product quality standards, delivery dates, and so forth.

This is a new product introduction, which allows us to consider its product management and marketing-mix decisions. Stimulated by the success of competitors' new entries, growth in the category, and consumer research indicating emerging unmet demand for bakery-fresh quality with the convenience of home storage, the firm initiated a major new product development process. Experts in food science, nutrition, and related technologies were challenged to translate the benefit concept into an actual food to meet all the criteria for marketplace success. A lengthy, iterative process ensued, as a number of attributes – size, icing, taste, consistency, flavoring, shelf-life, preparation mode, packaging, acceptable costs for pricing, production feasibility, and so forth – had to be brought to acceptable levels. Numerous consumer tests were run during this process, including reactions to prototypes, in-home use tests of alternative product forms, and BehaviorScan controlled-store market tests of alternative prices, promotional vehicles, and effects on consumers' purchase substitution patterns. Based upon these tests and financial projections, the firm's Board of Directors faced a decision whether or not to launch the product. Key factors in this decision were the internal rate of return over a six-year time frame, capital equipment requirements (new plant vs. conversion), possibilities for co-packing or outsourcing production, and implications for other offerings in the firm's product line. Because the new entry would be directly positioned as a "bakery quality" item, the Board was quite concerned that the ingredient sources of supply – the marketing system to the left of the producer – would be regularly available, cost-controlled, and precisely geared to meeting the approved recipe quality. Given the green light, the pastry brand's entire marketing mix was then finalized and implemented. To the right side, the distribution system was similar to that for the coffee brand. Tiffany had, in fact, purchased both at the same market.

(*Further considerations*) Although our illustration is getting long, we are still only a little way along toward capturing the true immensity of the AGMS (thankfully, however, we will dispense with further details here, and simply point to major issues for consideration). For example, we have only discussed two of the items available for the Jones' breakfast. Tiffany and Robert have two children, and the family members have some different taste preferences. The AGMS is easily able to accommodate these, so that a variety of products and formulations are available for the meal. Finally, the breakfast meal actually depends upon much more than simply the food: an entire kitchen support system – appliances, utilities, and accouterments – is available to assist this consumption episode. We should take special care to notice that all aspects of the kitchen system have been brought to the Jones household through the workings of the AGMS, some many years ago (e.g., the plumbing and the furniture), others more recently (e.g., the new dishwasher bought on sale last week), and others just yesterday, including the coffee, pastry, and fruit for this morning's meal. We should further recognize that each element listed has had its own complex marketing system. Global sourcing was involved for some – the mug from England, the coffeemaker from Germany, microwave from Japan, and so forth. In every case, a system had been planned, created, and run for the purpose of delivering these products and services to households like Tiffany's. In most cases the provider was a competitor who had to win out over others to gain Tiffany's attention, then win her patronage. In summary, if we were to analyze each element of this breakfast setting as we have the coffee and the pastry, many pages would be used – the total number of system interactions needed to create this breakfast is impressive! When we then realize that the system routinely provides, in one fashion or another, breakfast for some 100 million American households every morning – and that this is only a trivial element of its total activity – we can further sense its immensity and significance in our daily lives.

(*Marketing-system activities*) Figure 2.2 provides a partial listing of system activities that enabled this breakfast to occur. Several points emerge:

- There are a surprisingly large number of entries; the AGMS undertakes a wide range of activities to provide for a simple breakfast meal.
- There are participants other than marketers in the AGMS. Business customers and ultimate consumers are key players (buying is crucial at each stage), and governments provide services to facilitate system operations (shown at the right in Figure 2.2, these cross all stages).
- As indicated by the keyed entries in Figure 2.2, marketing managers only control ("1") some of the activities of the AGMS. Other necessary activities are carried out by persons who do not consider themselves marketers. In most of these cases, marketing managers serve as influences ("2") on these actions, whereas in some cases ("3"), necessary system activities are carried out with little or no direct influence from marketers (this is particularly apparent in the consumer realm). Note that this property of the system calls for a perspective on marketing that reaches beyond a sole focus on a manager's controllable decisions. (Also, the numbers assigned to each activity are generalized, and readers may wish to consider whether they would agree.)
- The three classes of participants all engage in activities apart from the AGMS: the system is very broad but not entirely dense. Some parts of virtually every organization work on tasks only indirectly related to the marketing activities listed and carry these out independently (shown as "n" in the bottom flight of Figure 2.2). We would not define these as AGMS activities, nor would we include government agencies' or consumers' activities that are directed entirely toward other sectors of society and life. Thus, our visual conception of the AGMS would resemble a cross-section of fine swiss cheese or steel mesh, similar to Figure 2.1, with linkages between organizations as we move across to the right, but with holes inside each organization to represent parts where the work arguably is outside the marketing system.

FIGURE 2.2 — Selected marketing system activities (present in the coffee and breakfast pastry examples).

Sales and delivery

The classic functions of distribution

Organizations:
- Transportation (2)
- Storage (2)
- Financing (2)
- Risk-bearing (2)
- Assembly (1)
- Selling (1)
- Standardization (2)
- Market information (1)

N.B. Detailed levels of activities exist (e.g., transport activities):
- Truck to depulping mill
- Beans to drying area
- Ship to New Orleans
- Hopper truck to roasting plant
- Truck to retail store ...
- additional steps in text

Purchasing and use

Organizations:
- Sourcing raw material supply (2)
- Quality specifications (2)
- Purchase of capital equipment (2)
- Outsourcing: specialist/expert services (3)
- Purchase for resale (1)
- Assortment building (2)
- Bulk breaking (1)
- Order processing (1)
- Negotiation: terms of sale (2)
- Transfer of ownership (2)

Consumers
- Product acquisition (2)
- Product preparation (3)
- Product consumption (3)
- Product maintenance/repair (2)
- Product disposition (2)

Knowledge development/intelligence

Organizations:
- Market analysis (1)
- Market demand assessment (1)
- Analysis of competitive strategies (1)
- Market segmentation (1)
- Market forecasts (1)
- Performance monitoring (1)
- Program evaluation (1)

Consumers:
- Consumer education (2)
- Information search (2)
- Word of mouth (3)
- Store visits (2)
- Post-purchase analysis (3)

Marketing plans and programs/government actions

Organizations:
- Financial projections (2)
- Board of directors approval (2)
- Product design (2)
- Product line decisions (1)
- Budget setting (2)
- Distribution planning (1)
- Brand name selection (1)
- Packaging (1)
- Market testing (1)
- Positioning strategy (1)
- Pricing decisions (1)
- National advertising (1)
- Direct marketing (1)
- Consumer promotion (1)
- Trade promotion (1)
- Trade advertising (1)
- Communication to sales force (1)
- Point of purchase materials (1)
- Publicity (2)
- Warranty terms (2)
- Customer service (2)
- Retailer assortment (1)
- Merchandising (1)
- Retail advertising (1)
- Inventory management (2)

Government agencies:
- Standard setting (2)
- Export/import controls (2)
- Trademark protection (2)
- Financing arrangements (2)
- Nutritional labeling (2)
- Inspections (3)
- Regulatory rules and guidelines (2)

Centers of little or no marketing involvement

Organizations:
- Internal management of work force (n)
- Management of plant and equipment (n)
- Financial mgmt., accounting and control (n)
- Basic research, etc. (n)

Government:
- All non-commerce/non-consumer sectors (n)

Consumers:
- All non-consumer aspects of daily life (n)

Numerical key:

(1) = Largely or entirely controlled by marketing managers
(2) = Largely controlled by others, but influenced by or coordinated with marketing managers
(3) = Little or no influence by marketing managers
(n) = Activity does not involve marketing

FIGURE 2.2 Selected marketing system activities (present in the coffee and breakfast pastry examples).

- Finally, Figure 2.2 significantly *understates* system activity. Each listing may have many detailed steps (consider, for example, advertising, merchandising, or transportation, in the leftmost column).

(*Estimating the scope of the AGMS*) Box 2.1 also helps us to begin to assess the scope of the US aggregate marketing system. Horizontally, note that the AGMS extends from extraction of raw materials/crops at the left through many levels of value creation to end consumption and disposition in far-off locales at the right. (Again, the preceding Venn diagram analogy should clarify our conception that some of these activities are regarded properly as also belonging to other intersecting aggregate systems, not just marketing.) Vertically, we first add all competing coffee and pastry systems, then add all other food systems, followed by all other goods and services. In concept, this process will include all organizations that engage in marketing system activities, all levels of government activities that affect this system, and all forms of consumer participation by all societal members. Our next illustration provides some estimates from 1999 of the magnitudes involved.

The huge size and scope of the AGMS

Probably the most difficult-to-grasp characteristics of the aggregate system are its size and complexity, which we now explore in more detail. There are the three key actors in the system: marketers, consumers, and public policymakers (government). Marketers and consumers are active on a daily basis, each approaching the marketplace for the purpose of making transactions. The transactions themselves, however, involve quite different tasks for the two parties, in that marketers are selling, while consumers are buying. Public policymakers, meanwhile, are to represent society's interests: they are charged with maintaining the most desirable AGMS for that society. Here are some size estimates from 1999 for the US AGMS.

"From here to eternity"

The AGMS is immense and growing rapidly. As we move past the Year 2000, in the United States alone we find some 275 million consumers arrayed in 100 million households, all participating on the consumption side of the system. They are spending five trillion dollars each year, or about two-thirds of the nation's Gross Domestic Product. To place this spending in perspective, we may recall that the distance from the Earth to the Sun is about 93 million miles. The spending by US consumers each year – if five trillion dollar bills were placed end to end – would stretch from the Earth to the Sun, around the Sun (ignoring the scorching factor!), back to the Earth, back to the Sun, back again to the Earth, and back yet again to the Sun. Viewed another way consumer spending is such a huge number that if we were to try to count it at the rate of one dollar per second, it would take us over 150,000 years, or much longer than the history of civilization. While the aggregate marketing system may not stretch quite to "eternity," it certainly does stretch a very long way!

BOX 2.1 PROPOSITIONS ON THE AGGREGATE MARKETING SYSTEM

The aggregate marketing system:

1 *incorporates many activities,* including the classic distribution functions, marketers' plans and programs, and actions by consumers and government;
2 *is composed of planned and continuous flows* among participants, including flows of goods and materials, service deliveries, dollar payments, and flows of information and influence;
3 *is extensive, in several respects,*

   (a) extending all the way from the collection of raw materials through multiple intermediate
        processes to use and disposition at each individual household,
   (b) combining materials/goods from around the globe into market offerings,
   (c) with multiple sets of marketers, acting as competitors, performing activities in parallel, and
   (d) in its geometric exchange activity, with multiple producers selling to multiple purchasers and multiple buyers purchasing from multiple sellers;

4 *is sophisticated structurally,* relying on a massive physical and communications infrastructure that regularly and routinely creates and delivers goods and services across the society;
5 *is a key basis for resource allocation in a market economy,* because consumer responses to market offerings determine which goods and services are created in the future;
6 *is governed by forces for efficiency,* most notably self-interest, competition, and characteristics of market demand;
7 *is constrained by social forces,* including laws, government regulations, cultural norms, and ethical codes of business and consumer conduct;
8 *relies on coordinated processes,* with producers and resellers seeking interdependent purchases to fit pre-specified standards with the later expectation of purchase by consumers;
9 *operates through human interactions, experience and trust* as participants develop and maintain marketplace relationships as a basis for conducting their system activities; and
10 *is an open system, geared toward growth and innovation,* as participants seek to solve problems and pursue opportunities, investing with faith in the future operations of the market.

To further appreciate the immensity of the system, we might recall that annual data are actually done for convenience purposes, which can understate true performance and impacts. As we saw in our analysis of the breakfast at Tiffany's, households accumulate stocks of consumer durables through the marketing system, and these continue to provide benefits through all the years they are in use. As one estimate of this phenomenon, consider that about 200 million motor vehicles are currently registered for road use in the United States: all of these have been provided through the marketing system, and many are used to carry out its functions on a daily basis. Also, in terms of the work of marketing, a significant portion of Americans are employed either entirely or in part in assisting the system to perform its functions. While exact figures are elusive because of categorization problems, it appears that *over 30 million Americans work directly within the AGMS*, with salespersons accounting for the largest portion. There are almost 20 million businesses as buyers: three million of these are retailers that resell to consumers, with another one-half million wholesaling firms (interestingly, because of multiple steps in the wholesale channel, total sales of wholesalers are larger than those of retailers). Advertising spending is huge and growing, now some $200 billion per year: other areas of recent growth include services (now over half of all consumer spending) and direct marketing, which has doubled in recent years.

Even though the numbers above are huge, still we have understated the true scope and involvement of the aggregate marketing system in the daily life of society. For example, the AGMS of the United States does not stand alone in the world: by not including other nations' systems we have understated by many times the actual impacts of marketing around the globe. Even within the United States, we have likely under-represented marketing's actual presence with respect to employment. Consider the many professional practices (attorneys, accountants, architects) that were not included in these counts, but that must engage in accepted marketing actions in building and maintaining clientele. Further, numerous persons in not-for profit groups and agencies, also not included in our formal numbers, must frequently employ marketing actions, on the one hand to garner resources and on the other to reach and satisfy the clients they are serving. Also, government workers at local, state, and federal levels are involved in negotiating contracts, purchasing goods and services, and monitoring marketing performance. Finally, because marketing is intrinsic to the operations of 20 million business firms, a portion of the responsibilities of many positions – from Chief Executive Officer to plant quality inspector to billing and receivables clerk – are involved with improving the organization's performance within the system. Overall then, the AGMS is surely a ubiquitous presence in our society.

Characteristics of the aggregate marketing system

Box 2.1 completes our background on the AGMS with a summary of its key properties. Propositions 1, 3, and 4 have been discussed at length, but the others deserve brief comment. Proposition 2 provides a system perspective that we long have perceived as powerful: the concept of continuous flows in various modalities, including physical, persuasive, informational, and monetary. Flows occur in both directions (e.g., money flows backward in the system in payment for goods; information and influence flow forward from advertising and sales efforts but also backward with marketing research). Some are simultaneous, but many are not; for example, the investment flow forward (in plant, labor, production, and promotion in advance of sales) represents levels of risk-taking and confidence in marketing activity.[3] Meanwhile, Proposition 5 reflects that, in a market-based system, consumers' responses to marketers' offerings drive supply allocations and prices. Depending on a society's decisions on public versus private ownership, the aggregate marketing system plays a greater or lesser role in allocating national resources. The United States has given substantial freedoms to its aggregate marketing system. Apart from certain restrictions, a person may choose to produce almost any good or service he or she desires, in any form and name; offer it for sale at places, prices, and terms of his or her choosing; and advertise it or not, using virtually any appeal believed to be effective. Although restrictions exist in each of these areas, they are primarily to protect the rights of competing marketers or consumers.

Proposition 6 reflects that the AGMS does more than physically deliver goods and services; it also works to bring a *dynamism* to society that encourages continual growth and progress (Vaile *et al.* 1952). Marketers know that observed demand is not really fixed and that consumers can be highly responsive to different marketing programs. Thus, competition is the main driving force, leading marketers to search for areas of comparative advantage that will lead to greater financial success. New competitors are attracted to areas of opportunity; over time, prices can be adjusted downward through competition and/or production efficiencies. New buyers join in buying the favored offerings, and some markets grow while others wither away. Not all marketing system programs are successful; the effort to support dynamism can lead to excesses, failures, and sometimes unforeseen consequences.

Proposition 7 illustrates this underlying tension by reflecting the need for controls. A market system needs a legal infrastructure for property rights, performance of contracts, freedom of choice, and so forth. The role of government as society's representative is thus central, though this can be contravened if politicians allow cynical, self-seeking interests to circumvent either competition or desirable restraints. Thus, the issue of government achieving a proper balance to serve a society's goals becomes a key issue for aggregate marketing systems.

Propositions 8 and 9, meanwhile, refer to the bonding forces that constitute the heart of the marketing effort. The existing infrastructure requires coordination in space, time, and fit, because offerings require intermarriage of components within a context of high efficiency. We have been impressed by the serious attention given to process quality control within this system. Furthermore, we have been reminded that, at its roots, this is a human institution in which both experience and trust play major roles, a point that also has emerged recently in relationship marketing thought. Even economists have recognized the role of trust within the system. As Kenneth Arrow (1972), Nobel Laureate in Economics, explained, "virtually every commercial transaction has within itself an element of trust . . . much of the economic backwardness in the world can be explained by the lack of mutual confidence" (p. 357). Finally, Proposition 10 notes that this "open system" stresses achievement, growth, and progress. These are the elements of the US aggregate marketing system that have brought huge, positive changes to the daily lives of its society's members, as indicated in our first illustration, "It's a wonderful life."

Marketing's contributions

Contributions to the larger economic system

Whatever the political choices, an aggregate marketing system is integral to a society's economic system. We attend to ten areas in which marketing contributes to the larger economic system. (1) The AGMS offers *employment and incomes* for the millions of persons engaged in this field. (2) That consumers can exercise of freedom of choice means that the preferences of society's members largely are reflected in the system's goods and services, which should mean that *aggregate satisfaction is enhanced*. (3) The AGMS is *delivering the standard of living* enjoyed by society's members. (4) Investments for the AGMS have *assisted national infrastructure development* in such areas as distribution facilities, transportation, communication, medical care, and the financial sector. (5) Related to this, *monies for governments* (sales and excise taxes) are gathered by the AGMS. (6) With respect to consumption, the system's *mass-market efficiencies* have led to lower costs, lower prices, and increased total consumption for citizens. (7) The system's dynamic character also *fosters the diffusion of innovations*, bringing new benefits to consumption. (8) Internationally, the AGMS is a *crucial contributor to the nation's balance of trade* and (9), in seeking new areas of opportunity, is a *force for international development*. (10) Overall, then, in many ways, the AGMS is an integral part of the economic prosperity of the United States.

(Our discussion of classical theories that explain the functions performed within marketing systems, and the benefits (utilities) they provide, has been omitted from this chapter due to space constraints; interested readers can access these in the original article cited in note 1.)

Marketing and economic development

The societal benefits that flow from the aggregate marketing system are nowhere more apparent than in the area of economic development. Nations with higher proportions of their populations in marketing also have higher GDPs – development of the marketing system is necessary for this to occur (Wood and Vitell 1986). However, specific roles for marketing differ by stage of economic development. In early urbanization, for example, priorities are to develop distribution infrastructure (i.e., transport, storage, and selling networks). In advanced systems, all marketing functions are important, with investment financing and consumer credit as key tools for growth. Marketing's roles are also dependent on the host government's policies (e.g., Thorelli 1996) – the AGMS is thus part of a complex political context. As a social institution, the marketing system must be embedded in the society's culture, and this can be problematic in some societies (for example, if aspects of a culture do not welcome some features of the US marketing system). Even if a US-style system is desired, moreover, certain consumer behaviors (e.g., handling of finances, planned saving and choice processes, defenses to persuasion) must be learned for the system to work well. Marketing experts working in the "transitional economies" (i.e., those moving from centralized planning to market-based systems) of Eastern Europe, the former Soviet Union, and China note that entrepreneurial risk-taking, marketing management expertise, and the use of strong business planning and control systems are crucial in determining success (e.g., Batra 1997). These experts differ as to ease of transfer of such knowledge, but the large number of international students educated in business schools in recent years does provide cause for optimism. For more basic economic settings, "Marketing's Development Functions" are relevant (Moyer 1965). Here marketing encourages increased production by organizing networks for communication and exchange. Speculation across time is needed to bring future production and consumption using entrepreneurial risk of capital and effort. Equalization of supply and demand occurs across distance (transport), time (storage), and quantity (price), while spatial connectivity joins diverse locales into a larger marketplace for efficiencies of scale and lower prices. Over time, these can grow into a center for capital accumulation (investment) and serve as a springboard for marketing entrepreneurs' entry as industrialists. For example, some years after its nationhood, nearly half the leading industrialists of Pakistan were found to have come from the marketing sector (Papenek 1962).

Contributions to buyers from specific marketing activities

We now focus on marketers' actions that benefit buyers. Because there are millions of competing firms in the AGMS, at any time a huge number of these benefits are being offered in parallel. Across time, these benefits accumulate through billions of purchase and use occasions.

Benefits from product and service offerings

A marketing exchange relies on both transacting parties' expecting to be better off, with benefits for customers accruing from use or consumption. Thus each use occasion creates an opportunity for another benefit delivery from the AGMS. Further, because products are "benefit bundles," users are actually deriving multiple benefits (e.g., Green *et al*. 1972). For example, a toothpaste that combines attributes such as decay prevention, whitening, tartar control, and good taste is delivering multiple sources of value each day. Extensive product variation enables closer fits with users' preferences, and new offerings and improvements to current offerings assist in this regard. Further, we should note that much of the care taken by marketers in design, creation, and delivery of offerings remains unseen, and is likely underappreciated by the general public. This care aids a brand's competitive success by providing an intended, identical service or use experience expected by loyal customers. Finally, the marketing system generally stands behind its offerings, with buyers often protected by guarantees or warranties. To verify our impression of this system stress on quality, we checked *Consumer Reports*' ratings in some 200 product/service classes. Our tabulations showed that, of 3,028 ratings, only 51 items (1.7 percent) were rated as "poor" in quality. Including "fair" as a passing grade, 98 percent of marketers' offerings received satisfactory ratings; 88 percent received ratings of "good," "very good," or "excellent." Clearly the US AGMS is delivering quality offerings to its public.

Benefits of branding/trademarks

Unique identification (branding) benefits buyers in four ways (Aaker 1991):

- In organizing future behaviors: if problems ensue the source can be notified.
- Efficiency in locating favored sellers (summed across products, time, and competing demands, this efficiency actually is quite significant in total).
- Rapid, confident choices in self-service settings (the average time for a single choice in a US supermarket aisle is only a few seconds: again a massive plus in the aggregate).
- Help in deriving symbolic benefits from purchase, ownership, or use.

Benefits from market distribution

The distribution functions are performed largely out of sight of nonparticipants, so the performance of distribution easily can be underappreciated. As noted in Tiffany's coffee example, the AGMS performs these functions repetitively and routinely, millions of times daily, each time offering benefits to receivers. Beyond this, wholesale and retail activities offer additional benefits. Some of these are well known, but four deserve mention:

- One powerful aspect of the US marketing system is *facilitating the transaction process*, which saves consumers time and effort, maximizing purchase opportunities. Consider, for example, the benefits of extended store hours, convenient locations, free parking, stocked shelves, posted prices, displays, fast and smooth checkout, advertising price specials, salespersons' pleasant and efficient completion of transactions, and so forth. (Consumers from some other cultures express surprise and delight on this discovery of the US retailing system.)
- *Processes for extending consumer credit* enable some expensive purchases to occur that otherwise would have been delayed, and bank credit cards have eased transaction processes for buyers and sellers alike. That stores pay significant fees, approximately 3 percent, for bank card charges is a good indicator of how much the system desires to facilitate purchase transactions.
- When a durable-good purchase is made, the marketing system offers a *postpurchase support structure* with benefits such as delivery, installation, repair services, and liberal return policies.
- Channels of distribution serve as the entry point *(gatekeeper) for new products and services*. Receptivity by wholesalers and retailers to offerings that provide better value, or new benefits, has made this dynamic work for societal gain. Similarly, government actions to reduce barriers to entry serve to enable innovations and price competition to work to benefit consumers.

Benefits from salespersons and representatives

Sales representatives facilitate flows within the AGMS. An estimated 20 million sales representatives are at work daily, 9 million in business-to-business selling, and 11 million others dealing directly with consumers. In business-to-business sales we often see a salesperson as a professional representative dealing with generally well-informed buyers who have problems needing resolution. To start, salespersons may be called on to consult on large programs (e.g., plant construction, advertising campaigns), often as part of account teams that include specialists. Here he or she may help crystallize client needs, educate about alternatives, introduce new entries, and customize the offering when feasible. He or she further works to facilitate the entire transaction, payment, and product delivery or project completion. During this process, which could extend for years, the sales representative provides access to technical support and offers personal service to ensure customer satisfaction and a continuing relationship. Finally, the salesperson may report back to the firm about opportunities to enhance its future benefits.

Benefits from advertising and promotion

Each year, an incredible amount of money is spent on advertising and sales promotion, accounting for approximately 3 percent of US GDP. Due to high visibility, advertising is the most criticized facet of the AGMS, though it does provide some key benefits as well:

- Consumers often appreciate *the information advertising provides* on products and prices.
- They may not recognize that advertising can enhance consumer decisions through *lower search costs* (product proliferation, however, raises search costs).
- Advertising can *enlarge market demand and contribute to lowering prices*. Less obvious are three related benefits in this category: reducing distribution cost per unit, aiding entry by new competitors, and fostering acceptance of new innovations by a society.
- Consumers do at times applaud advertising's role in *subsidizing media*, and also at times express pleasure with advertising's *creative offerings*.

Two broader views of benefits

Contributions from improvements in marketing system activities

It is clear that the AGMS's current level of performance has resulted from its emphasis on a continual search for improvement. Thus, our interest is in not only *kinds* of benefits but also *increased levels* of benefits, emanating daily from individual firms and people.

"Back to the future"

The constant press for improvements characterizes the world of the AGMS. Many efforts do not work out, some yield minor advances, and a few lead to norms of the future. For example, trucking firms now combine onboard computers and satellite tracking systems – one firm uses this system to coordinate routes and communicate with all 10,000 trucks in its fleet, thereby adapting instantly to weather or traffic delays. The result is better delivery service with lower costs for the firm. Similarly, containerization has added efficiency in shipping and handling; our coffee beans, for example, shifted easily from ocean to ground transport and were less susceptible to damage, spoilage, and theft. As distribution channels have embraced relationship marketing, order processing systems have saved time and costs. For example, two firms may use electronic data interchange, in which inventories (e.g., a drugstore's entire stock in a line) automatically are replenished as sales movement data are transmitted to the wholesaler; people are limited to oversight of the system. Also, improvements in communications, transport, and technology have enabled marketers to move increasingly worldwide to obtain materials at much lower costs. Although global sourcing has generated legitimate criticisms, it also has provided consumers with quality goods at lower prices and added to the AGMS's of other societies as well. In retailing, checkout scanners and computerized pricing enabled stores to lower labor costs, better manage inventory, and promote more effectively through information on the tastes of each store's customers. For food-makers, this technology also speeds adjustments to consumers' preferences.

In product development, "match or better" means a search for value parity on most key attributes, and advantage on the others. For example, in the early 1980s, Ford Motor Company had just lost $3 billion when it created "Team Taurus," a group of marketers, designers, engineers, and plant personnel charged with developing a new car to rescue the firm. The team relied on consumer research, choosing 700 features for the new car from this source. In addition, the team bought models of popular competing cars, then tore them apart to analyze their best features (over 400 features were "borrowed" in this process). The net result of Team Taurus's efforts? One of the most popular cars ever produced and a turnaround for Ford, whose market share rose from 16 percent to 29 percent (Wilkie 1994). The general lesson? Marketers know that demand is highly responsive to advantages consumers perceive a product to have (or lack) and can be quite responsive to price as well. In sum, pressures for improvements in the AGMS are relentless, and the positive benefits of this force should be appreciated.

Contributions to quality of life

In this final section on contributions we examine briefly the AGMS as a human institution composed of people. Our effort is illustrative, intended to raise this topic as worthy of further attention. We first examine benefits offered to the many workers in marketing.

Social/psychological benefits to marketing participants

Our first set of entries reflects several social and psychological benefits we believe are offered to persons who work in marketing. Drawing on the system's stress on competition, *achievement is highly rewarded* in this field. This is one reason for steep increases in marketers' incomes, in contrast to accounting or engineering, in which salaries begin at higher levels but increase much more slowly. Because of the marketing system's openness to change, opportunities abound for *feelings of personal growth and individual autonomy*. Whether pursuing clearer understanding of the consumer marketplace, creating a new advertising campaign, managing a retail store, closing an important sale, or planning a new product launch, marketing offers *challenges to creativity and ingenuity*, as well as *opportunities to influence others*. Marketers in many areas can *offer service to others*, and those in the arts can *foster aesthetic values* within society. Many marketing positions require teamwork to achieve a common goal, which can provide *valued group affiliations*. It is common for sellers to develop *friendly relationships* with their clients as a consequence of ongoing exchange activities (in our breakfast illustration, for example, the large transaction between the coffee buyer and major grower was sealed with a handshake).

Social/psychological benefits created by consumers

Since the study of consumer behavior entered marketing's mainstream during the 1950s and 1960s, consumers' goals and motivations have been studied extensively. Most research has been instrumental (e.g., what can we learn about consumers so that we can sell more effectively to them?), but some reveals interest in deeper human issues. Examples include two older books by well-known marketing consultants, Daniel Yankelovich (1981), who revealed concerns about society's direction at the time, and Arnold Mitchell (1983), who designed the VALS (values and lifestyles) system using Maslow's humanistic need theory. More recently, the interpretivist orientation (e.g., Sherry 1991) has honed our appreciation of goods' meanings in consumers' lives. A carefully cultivated lawn and flower garden can give a homeowner a sense of accomplishment, or a parent may derive special satisfaction from selecting food, clothing, or furniture for a safe, healthy home. Gift-giving can involve significant emotional and symbolic dimensions. Movies, sporting events, or theatrical productions can lead to feelings of belonging, prestige, escape, or excitement. Consumer activities enable learning, socializing, and self-enhancement (listening to music, playing tennis); benefits are emotional, subjective, and experiential (Holbrook and Hirschman 1982). Spending money can bring feelings of achievement, status, control, and even play. Shopping is an enjoyable activity for many. Although intangible and difficult to express, our treatment of the marketing system's contributions to consumers would be incomplete without discussion of these sometimes meaningful consequences.

Two emerging areas of study on marketing's broader contributions

During the 1960s and 1970s, literature on marketing and society raised questions about (1) how well society itself was faring and (2) how it might be improved. These questions spawned two different subareas: research on "quality of life" (QOL) and "social marketing." Marketers interested in QOL faced three special issues: (1) the fact that marketing is only one of many forces that combine to yield overall lifestyles; (2) daunting conceptualization and measurement issues on exactly what QOL is; and (3) difficulty in communicating across fields. Economists defined issues to fit their terms and research forms, as did psychologists, sociologists, ecologists, and political scientists. The International Society for Quality of Life Studies now carries on this work. Recent work on the American Customer Satisfaction Index shows promise in reflecting market-based performance of the system at various levels of aggregation (Fornell *et al.* 1996), as does work on the Index of Consumer Sentiment Toward Marketing (Etzel and Gaski 1999).

Social marketing differs from traditional marketing by aiming to benefit the target audience directly (e.g., AIDS awareness or childhood immunization) or society as a whole (e.g., recycling programs, blood donations) rather than the firm sponsoring the program (Andreasen 1991). It has, however, faced academic difficulties on two fronts: (1) it has tended to be an "action" field in which primary emphasis is on successful intervention and (2) value judgments are made on desirable behavioral changes, so the area is also "activist" in this sense. Useful field work has been progressing for some time, applying marketing tools to health, education, charitable giving, politics, the arts, and the environment.

These two fields of study highlight that the AGMS is composed of more participants than just business marketers. Private marketing is the mainstay of the system in the United States, but government, the entire consumer sector, and many individuals in the not-for-profit sector are also participants. The system's issues extend to societal concerns and, in turn, are affected by them as well.

Criticisms and problems of the aggregate marketing system

Our focus in this chapter has been on accomplishments, but balance calls on us to acknowledge that the AGMS long has been controversial in some respects. In Figure 2.3 we summarize many of the most prominent criticisms, controversies, and problems that have been raised. We begin with *critiques of system values*. These usually are made by persons speaking from vantage points outside the system and raising philosophical points about its nature. These criticisms tend to say little directly about the practice of marketing but instead focus on broader issues such as the "consumer culture" and the economic system that sustains it. Political theory is the root of some of these critiques, but not all. These are not simplistic arguments, and we do not wish to do them an injustice in such a brief summary.

Readers will find writings by Galbraith (1958) of interest, as well as the Pollay (1986, 1987) versus Holbrook (1987) advertising debate and the collection by Goodwin *et al.* (1997).

Classic social and economic debates are next in Figure 2.3. These have a long history, though they have evolved over time. For example, the distribution cost debate of the early 1900s had farmers questioning why they received only a low percentage of the consumer's food dollar; today, buyers (and farmers) ask why cereal brands are priced so high relative to ingredient costs. Also, much attention has been given to advertising, as in four of the eight debates. These debates likely persist because (1) strong proponents on each side will not concede; (2) generalizations are, at times, based on episodes; (3) decisive empirical evidence has not been available because of severe measurement difficulties; and (4) the underlying issues actually are complex.

The second column of Figure 2.3 reflects the views of the consumer movement. These tend not to be antagonistic to the AGMS itself (recall the high ratings in *Consumer Reports*), but are aimed at having the system serve consumers' interests. Thus, President John F. Kennedy's 1962 proclamation of the "Consumer Bill of Rights" was regarded as crucial in placing the power of government squarely on the side of consumers in the four basic ways listed (that is, it affirmed that US society would pass laws, restricting marketers if necessary, to ensure consumers received their rights). During the past century, there have been three eras (Mayer 1989) of high public receptivity to consumer movement issues. Consumer issues have shifted over time as early concerns largely have been attained (e.g., food processing safety). A root belief sustaining the consumer movement, however, is that major economic imperfections persist within the system, especially reflecting pricing and value received per dollar. These are listed in the next entries of this section (Maynes 1997). Again, our treatment here cannot do justice to the arguments' sophistication, but excellent readings are available, including Aaker and Day (1982), Maynes and colleagues (1988), Mayer (1989), and Brobeck (1997).

The third column of Figure 2.3 highlights difficult issues that arise naturally in marketing and must be addressed. Handling by some marketers may spark legitimate criticisms, whereas others' efforts may merit commendation. Also, problems may arise in balancing goals of different stakeholders. Illustrative issues are organized in three topics. First, limits for persuasive influence arise in both advertising and selling; a firm must focus on both policy and daily control levels to address these. Second, specific problems arise from certain products or from markets that pose societal externalities if only short-term sales and profits are pursued. We expect increasing conflict here if societies' controls of marketer actions are challenged by further globalization. Third, consistently responsible actions by all members of an organization are needed. Efforts here include design of systems to assist customers with problems and formalization of the presence of influential "voices" for all stakeholders, including employees, consumers, and the broader society. The right-hand column of Figure 2.3 then shifts to deliberate problem behaviors, as in our final illustration.

Broad social and economic concerns	Views of the consumer movement	Continuing challenges for marketing practice	Problem episodes through deliberate behaviors
Critiques of system values Promotes materialism – Stresses conformity – Social competitiveness, envy – Exacerbates pain of poverty Negatively affects cultural values – Creates insidious cycle of work and spend – Discourages participation in noneconomic activities (e.g., arts, community, leisure) – Undermines families, alters socialization Is fundamentally persuasive/manipulative in character – Creates artificial wants and needs – Invokes imbalance between marketer and consumer Cultural imperialism – Cultural impacts – Natural resource depletion – Global warming	**The Consumer Bill of Rights** – The right of safety – The right to be informed – The right to choose – The right to be heard **Consumerism's three major eras: key issues** I. Turn of the century – Food and drug safety – Regulation of competition II. 1920s and 1930s – Objective information – Consumer representation III. 1960s and 1970s – Product safety – Advertising's social impact – Avenues for redress **Economic imperfections: the asymmetric power of marketing** – Difficult product quality assessment – Incomplete or biased information	Limits to information and persuasion Advertising content – Limits to persuasion – Themes, executions, and copy – Intrusiveness: environmental clutter – Ad approval processes – Sales, pricing, and after-sales practices – Limits to persuasion – Control of sales abuses – Warranties and guarantees – Retailer and distributor pricing Practices Information disclosure – Limits to disclosure – Effective warning labels – Use of disclaimers **The broader environment** Environmental concerns – Natural resource depletion – Threats to ecology – Reusability and disposition	**Marketing sector** – Deceptive advertising – High-pressure sales techniques – Misrepresentations of sales intent – Inferior products and services – Bait and switch – Price fairness: high–low pricing – Price fixing – Predatory pricing – Franchise abuses – International: Bribery – Gray-market goods – Counterfeit goods – Internet fraud **Consumer sector** – Uninformed decisions – Consumer fraud (e.g., shoplifting, credit abuse)

Broad social and economic concerns	Views of the consumer movement	Continuing challenges for marketing practice	Problem episodes through deliberate behaviors

Proposes limitless, unsustainable aggregate consumption levels
Capitalist system promotes inequality in benefit distribution (fairness versus allocative efficiency)
Emphasis on private consumption leads to deterioration in quality of public goods
Pervasive commercialism
System is inherently self-serving, directed toward no broader social purpose
 	
"Classic" social and economic debates
 	
  – Does distribution cost too much?
  – Is there too much advertising? Is it wasteful?
  – Advertising: information or market power?
  – Advertising: good taste and morality?
  – Subliminal advertising?
  – Is price related to quality?
  – Is deliberate product obsolescence good?
	– Too few sellers in some local markets
	  – Uncaring civil servants
	  – Too little time for considered decisions
	  – Underrepresentation of consumer interest
	  – Ineffective regulatory agencies
	  – Consumers' deficiencies
	
	Some continuing controversies
	
	  – Dangerous products (e.g., cigarettes)
	  – Vulnerable groups (e.g., children, elderly)
	  – Emerging problems with marketplace encroachment
	  – Intrusiveness of advertising
	  – Concerns regarding invasion of privacy
	  – Restrictions on database usage
	  – Selling as marketing research
	  – Exploitation by price discrimination
		Product safety
		  – Hazardous products
		  – Regulatory approval processes
		  – Product failure and liability
		Anticompetitive practices
		  – Effects of quotas/trade barriers
		  – Antitrust issues
		
		Responsible corporate citizenship
		
		Consumer dissatisfaction
		  – Rumors and negative word of mouth
		  – Complaint handling
		  – Problem resolution systems
		Corporate actions
		  – Incorporating ethical concerns
		  – Role of consumer affairs departments
		  – Criteria for evaluating business performance
		  – Industry self-regulation
		  – Community involvement
			– Bankruptcy
			  – Product liability: frivolous lawsuits
			  – Compulsive consumption
			
			Government sector
			
			  – Errors of omission
			  – Errors of commission

FIGURE 2.3 Criticisms and problems of the aggregate marketing system.

"Ruthless people"

On rare occasions, a participant in the AGMS chooses to act in ways that injure others. This occurs in all system sectors, as indicated in the following reports (Wilkie 1994).

(*Marketing slippage*) "Creating a consumer want" has a cynical meaning among a certain stratum of marketers who first alter a consumer's product, then point out the problem to gain a sale. Gas stations on interstate highways, for example, have been caught plunging ice picks into tires and placing chemicals into batteries to cause adverse reactions. "Termite inspectors" have been caught placing the bugs in houses, then informing frightened residents of an imminent home collapse unless repaired immediately. Some traveling "tree surgeons" thrive by pointing out imagined diseases in large trees over a house, then removing the trees at high prices. A classic case of this fear selling, however, was used by the Holland Furnace Company, which employed 5,000 persons in its 500 US offices. Its sellers were to introduce themselves as "safety inspectors," go down to the furnace and dismantle it, and then condemn it as "so hazardous that I must refuse to put it back together. I can't let myself be an accessory to murder!" Senator Warren Magnuson (Washington) called the selling "merciless." One elderly woman was sold nine new Holland furnaces in six years, which cost more than $18,000 at the time.

(*Consumer slippage*) We have pointed out that one hallmark of the marketing system is emphasis on providing satisfaction after sale, including liberal return policies. Some consumers abuse this service, as this quote shows:

> Mark is a soccer player who needs new shoes frequently. He has developed a system to get them from a local store that takes back defective shoes. Once or twice a year, Mark removes the sole, slices off a cleat, or places a rip in the tongue, each in a way that is hard to detect. He then brings the shoes to the store to exchange . . . at last count he'd received eight new pairs this way. Mark is sure to go to a different clerk on each visit, and . . . probably won't get caught.

(*Government sector*) Government abuses are harder to identify because of the few legal cases and difficulty in observation. Errors of omission (failure to act when warranted) may be more common than errors of commission because of the incentive structure of a bureaucratic system. For example, New York City's health department discovered that a dispute between two laboratory managers had led to delays of up to one year in reading cancer test results for women using city clinics. Of 3,000 delayed Pap smear readings, 500 abnormalities called for immediate follow-up, 93 more appeared malignant, and 11 were clearly malignant. On discovery, the commissioner denounced his department for "betrayal of the public trust" as he demoted four people (evidently, none could be fired).

Several points remain. This is a complex area involving the law; it may not be clear that an act was deliberate or that a certain party was responsible. Also, criticisms usually are aimed at marketers, but all system participants have responsibilities, including public policymakers and consumers, and negative acts occur in each sector regularly. In addition, some acts deserve to be criticized by all participants. The

US system is designed for dealings to be open, honest, and well-informed. Deceptive and irresponsible behaviors injure honest competitors or consumers. Thus, it is disingenuous to simply defend actions of fellow marketers or consumers because system roles are shared. It is not clear why anyone would want disreputable persons' actions to define either the standards or image for the system overall.

Conclusions and implications

Our goal has been to stop at this unique point in time, consider the larger picture of the marketing field, then fairly portray its structure, activities, and benefits to society. The system is huge and dynamic. Its imperfections stand as challenges for improvement, and it is appropriate for participants to work to rectify them. Beyond this, the AGMS offers much that is impressive.

In summary

This chapter began by comparing daily life today with that at the turn of the last century. It is evident that the AGMS has brought many improvements to society. An illustration of a breakfast then showed the confluence of marketing systems, which highlighted the physical side of marketing and the wide range of system activities. Together, these explain why the AGMS is so ubiquitous within US society: It employs approximately one in five adults and includes several million firms, several hundred million consumers, and many others who deal with marketing in their work in government, the professions, services, and not-for-profit sector. In the next section of the chapter, we summarized a three-set series of contributions the AGMS offers to society: (1) benefits to the overall economy and economic development; (2) an impressive array of direct benefits to buyers; and (3) continuous enhancements in system performance plus an array of noneconomic contributions to the quality of life to members of a society. We followed this with a summary of criticisms of the system. The AGMS emerged from this overall analysis as a worthy testament to those who have shaped it over time.

Six lessons learned from the project

This project has been illuminating, and six "lessons learned" stand out for us:

- *The size, power, and practiced performance of the AGMS have emerged in this project.* Several points are key here: (1) There is a real need to appreciate the magnitudes involved in this system; (2) many "hidden aspects of marketing" are being excluded in thinking about the field; and (3) the marketing elements the public experiences directly, such as advertising and retail selling, are receiving disproportionate weight in its view of the field.
- *Not all lessons are entirely positive; future developments likely will place marketers at the center of further controversies.* "Society," as referenced in the chapter's title, may be losing cohesion, and global marketers can be described as assisting this process

(though this might not be intentional). Consider challenges to ethical systems (e.g., bribery), religious beliefs and customs (e.g., interest rates), or government protections for home industries and workers (trade barriers) and growing needs for adaptations in national antitrust policies (Federal Trade Commission [FTC] 1996). Not only does the Internet seamlessly cross societal boundaries, but the incredible efficiency of its reach offers huge potentials for marketing fraud. In one recent FTC (1997) case, an Internet pyramid scam promised investors $60,000 per year for an initial investment of $250: 15,000 consumers had bought in before it was stopped. Overall, concerns are increasing about marketer intrusions in privacy of records, security of financial resources, and selling to children.

- *This chapter has concentrated on benefits and system potentials. However, at this special point in time, it is reasonable for every marketing person to ask whether the current AGMS actually represents "the best of all worlds."* Our emphasis here is not critical but philosophical. The system is very powerful, and marketers are at work to help it achieve its ends. That society has granted marketers substantial freedoms, and that these serve to allocate much of the nation's resources, is a key statement about a societal purpose of the AGMS. To what extent do marketing managers view themselves as having responsibility for improving the public interest or acting as stewards of a society's resources? What implications do these views have for the field as presently constituted?

- *The central role for innovation in improving a society's quality of life became more evident to us.* The contributions from innovations and improvements are striking. Conceptually, this underscores the value of dynamism in an AGMS, and the key role of competition in providing impetus. In turn, the societal importance of a government's policies to foster and protect both innovation and competition – antitrust, patents, trademarks, and so forth – become clearly apparent, but global differences may impede future progress. We also find the system's twin reliance on competition as a driver and trust as a bonding agent to be impactful yet somehow paradoxical. Finally, success in discovering, developing, and managing new products is a central issue, calling for closer ties with other areas, such as science and marketing.

- *Tremendous potentials exist for marketing contributions to economic development, which can literally "change the world" for citizens of developing nations.* Each AGMS is specific to its own society and time. Although a society's choices will constrain options, development also proceeds in identifiable stages. Thus, it is possible to transfer knowledge, products, and methods found useful in prior stages of advanced systems. AGMS's are in flux daily across the globe. Will "transitional" nations trying to move from command to free-market systems be successful? Strong linkages between public policy and AGMS performance are starkly clear in these cases.

- *The aggregate perspective of marketing enriches consideration of "Marketing and the Common Good."* Finally, with respect to the emphasis of this book, it is our view that adopting an aggregate perspective on marketing holds considerable potential to advance considerations of the common good. First, it provides us with a much fuller, more sophisticated view of "Marketing," showing it to be a massive, powerful force in our world, with much potential for positive contributions to a society. It also allows us to move beyond a simplistic focus on either advertising or selling when examining both contributions and problems. Further, the systemic nature of this perspective provides an excellent basis from which to examine the dynamics of major problems, searching for positive options for alleviating these. For example, Kevin Bradford's excellent contribution (Chapter 13) on the illegal diversion of firearms reports how their study of distribution channel safeguards (reflecting a marketing systems approach) provides empirical verification that voluntary adoption of increased safeguards across the industry would be an effective means of deterring crime. In another societal problem sphere, the authors of this piece are currently applying an aggregate marketing system approach in a large-scale study of what has now become an epidemic of childhood obesity (see Moore, Chapter 12). We are optimistic that this will afford a comprehensive examination of key institutional factors at work. This in turn may help to identify especially effective options for addressing the problem, which would certainly improve the lives of many children, and thus contribute to the common good.

Notes

1   In 1997 the *Journal of Marketing* (since its inception in 1936, a premier publication for the field) announced that it would publish a "Special Millennium Issue" to commemorate the coming new century. This issue would address just four questions, identified by the special issue's editors as the most pressing facing the field of marketing. Only papers addressing these questions would be considered for inclusion, and these were to be "developmental" in nature – new, major, groundbreaking efforts. A series of successive competitions were designed to winnow the original candidate field (of some 170 proposals) down to a final 12 articles, while also providing feedback for those surviving into the next round. We decided to address the question, "What Does Marketing Contribute to Society?" and launched into work. Our project benefited greatly from the unique competitive process, grew considerably across the several years of development, and emerged as a much respected article in the Millennium Issue in November 1999. We believe that the article, entitled "Marketing's Contributions to Society," is a useful inclusion for this book, as it provides readers with a broader look at marketing, one that is useful for recognizing the contributions that the marketing system is making to our daily lives.

   The original article is too long for this book's parameters, so we have created an abstracted version here (we have maintained the original language and numbers, except where there was a need for change to have a smooth flow): readers who wish to locate fuller discussion may obtain a free download of the original article at: http://business. nd.edu/Faculty/wilkie.html.
2   Comparative numbers are from a variety of sources, especially Lebergott (1993) and *U.S. News and World Report* (1995).
3   This analysis also highlights marketing's contributions at the firm level by demonstrating marketing to be the function that reaches out from a firm to the outside world (marketplace) with flows of products, information, and promotion activity and further shows marketing as using its learning about that world (through an inward flow of research) to influence decisions within the firm. Finally, marketing generates an inward flow of dollars to sustain the firm's continued existence, which earns it our title of "Lifeblood of the Business."

References

Aaker, D.A. (1991) *Managing Brand Equity*, New York: The Free Press.
—— and Day, G.S. (1982) *Consumerism: Search for the Public Interest*, 4th edn. New York: The Free Press.

Andreasen, A.R. (1991) "Consumer behavior research and social policy," in T.S. Robertson and H.H. Kassarjian (eds) *Handbook of Consumer Behavior*, Englewood Cliffs, NJ: Prentice Hall, pp. 459–506.

Arrow, K. (1972) "Gifts and exchanges," *Philosophy and Public Affairs*, 1 (4): 343–61.

Batra, R. (1997) "Executive insights: marketing issues and challenges in transitional economies," *Journal of International Marketing*, 5 (4): 95–114.

Brobeck, S. (ed.) (1997) *Encyclopedia of the Consumer Movement*, Santa Barbara, CA: ABC-Clio.

Etzel, M.J. and Gaski, J.F. (1999) "A report on consumer sentiment toward marketing," working paper, Graduate School of Business, University of Notre Dame.

Federal Trade Commission (1996) *Anticipating the 21st Century: Competition Policy in the New High-Tech, Global Marketplace*, Washington, DC: US Government Printing Office.

—— (1997) *Anticipating the 21st Century*, Washington, DC: US Government Printing Office.

Fornell, C., Johnson, M.D., Anderson, E. W., Cha, J., and Everitt, B. (1996) "The American customer satisfaction index: Nature, purpose, and findings," *Journal of Marketing*, 60 (October): 7–18.

Galbraith, J.K. (1958) *The Affluent Society*, Boston, MA: Houghton Mifflin.

Goodwin, N.R., Ackerman, F., and Kiron, D. (1997) *The Consumer Society*, Washington, DC: Island Press.

Green, P.E., Wind, Y., and Jain, A.K. (1972) "Benefit bundle analysis," *Journal of Advertising Research*, 12 (April): 31–36.

Holbrook, M.B. (1987) "Mirror, mirror, on the wall, what's unfair in the reflections on advertising?" *Journal of Marketing*, 51 (July): 95–103.

—— and Hirschman, E.C. (1982) "The experiential aspects of consumption: consumer fantasies, feelings and fun," *Journal of Consumer Research*, 9 (September): 132–140.

Kasper, H (1993) "The images of marketing: facts, speculations, and implications," working paper 93-015, Maastricht, Netherlands: University of Limburg.

Lebergott, S. (1993) *Pursuing Happiness*, Princeton, NJ: Princeton University Press.

Mayer, R.N. (1989) *The Consumer Movement: Guardians of the Marketplace*, Boston, MA: Twayne.

Maynes, E.S. (1997) "Consumer problems in market economies," in S. Brobeck (ed.) *Encyclopedia of the Consumer Movement*, Santa Barbara, CA: ABC-Clio, pp. 158–64.

—— and ACCI Research Committee (eds) (1988) *The Frontier of Research in the Consumer Interest*, Columbia, MO: American Council on Consumer Interests.

Mitchell, A. (1983) *The Nine American Lifestyles*, New York: Macmillan.

Moyer, R. (1965) "Marketing in economic development," working paper, Graduate School of Business, Michigan State University.

Papenek, G.F. (1962) "The development of entrepreneurship," *American Economic Review*, 52 (2): 46–58.

Pollay, R.W. (1986) "The distorted mirror: reflections on the unintended consequences of advertising," *Journal of Marketing*, 50 (April): 18–36.

—— (1987) "On the value of reflections on the values in the distorted mirror," *Journal of Marketing*, 51 (July): 104–110.

Sherry, J.F., Jr. (1991) "Postmodern alternatives: the interpretive turn in consumer research," in T.S. Robertson and H.H. Kassarjian (eds) *Handbook of Consumer Behavior*, Englewood Cliffs, NJ: Prentice Hall, pp. 548–91.

Thorelli, H.B. (1996) "Marketing open markets and political democracy: the experience of the PACRIM countries," *Advances in International Marketing*, 7: 33–46.

U.S. News and World Report (1995) "By the numbers," August 28, 83.

Vaile, R.S., Grether, E.T., and Cox, R. (1952) *Marketing in the American Economy*, New York: The Ronald Press Co.

Wilkie, W.L. (1994) *Consumer Behavior*, 3d edn, New York: John Wiley & Sons.

Wood, V.P. and Vitell, S. (1986) "Marketing and economic development: review, synthesis and evaluation," *Journal of Macromarketing*, 6 (1): 28–48.

Yankelovich, D (1981) *New Rules: Searching for Fulfillment in a World Turned Upside Down*, New York: Random House.

PART II

Societal aspects of marketing and consumption

3

SLOUCHING TOWARD UTOPIA

When marketing *is* society

John F. Sherry, Jr.

Introduction

While Oscar Wilde has provided our discipline a plethora of aphorisms for reflection – who among us has not potted his pithy observation of cynicism as the knowledge of the price of everything but the value of nothing in our quest to articulate an ethics of marketing? – his meditation on Utopia is the platform for my essay:

> A map of the world that does not include Utopia is not worth even glancing at, for it leaves out the one country at which Humanity is always landing. And when Humanity lands there, it looks out, and seeing a better country, sets sail. Progress is the realization of Utopias.
>
> *(Wilde 1891: 303–4)*

Whether we consider it as a field of pure inquiry or as the application of management principles derived from that inquiry to business problems, marketing is the imagination and pursuit of Utopia (Maclaran and Brown 2005). I have posited (Sherry 2011) that marketing may be the foremost Utopian influence abroad in the contemporary world, and, that a moral toll may be exacted if marketers become the principal cartographers of this journey. I build on this position in this chapter, and advocate a role for marketing in cultural reformation.

As an orienting example, I cite a snippet of conversation purportedly overheard at Starbucks, sent to me for enjoyment and redistribution, by a like-minded meme monitor: "Nonfat half-caff-triple-grande quarter-sweet sugar-free vanilla nonfat-lactaid extra-hot extra-foamy caramel macchiato." My reaction to this request for product remains an invocation of the wonderment of comedian Yakov Smirnoff: "What a country!" The phrase, at once a celebration of the miracle of hyper-customized instant gratification and an indictment of misplaced consumer priority, arouses an ambivalence in me that I struggle to unpack (Sherry 2008), self-consciously immersed as I am in consumer culture.

The choice seems to represent both the zenith and the nadir of our culture, and directs our contemplation from the sublime to the ridiculous. That the apotheosis and trivialization of choice can reside in the same example is an outcome of the anthropological sensibility that governs my marketing imagination. From my perspective (Sherry 2008),

> For better and for worse, marketing has become perhaps the greatest force of cultural stability and change at work in the contemporary world (Sherry 1995). Elsewhere (Sherry 2000) I have claimed that the problems caused by marketing are best solved by marketing, and that such mitigation might be well informed by ethnography. This is a minority viewpoint in my tribe. A tribe that rightly fears abetting the rise of a "great imperium with the outlook of a great emporium".
>
> *(de Grazia 2006: 3)*

This position stems from my belief that an imperfectly understood shadowland surrounds the aggregate marketing system (Wilkie and Moore 1999) that my colleagues have labored to describe. By shadowland, I mean a world that has arisen in response to our managerial activity, but which has been obscurely rendered by our disciplinary focus and left relatively unexplored by marketers. This shadowland has been called the culture of consumption by our discipline's critics, and cited (Sherry 2008) as a global threat to the common good:

> Encouraging us to imagine ever fewer opportunities to escape the market, producing local cultural dislocation in the wake of its adoption, and inviting marketers, consumers and activists alike to conflate consumption, politics and identity, consumer culture is alleged to efface anything that stands in its path.
>
> *(p. 88)*

Consumption pervades everything we do. It is the idiom in which our most important considerations are discussed. It has become a measure of moral development, in that the level of one's ability to consume often determines self-worth, not merely fiscal worth, rendering some lives perceptually more valuable than others. With marketing as its engine, consumption pits the forces of destructive creation against those of creative destruction (Sherry 2008), to drastic effect:

> A short laundry list of grievances would include the following indictments. Contemporary capitalisms are hegemonic in nature, and promote cultural homogenization (Greider 1997; Wallace 2005); this massive reduction of diversity is considered both morally reprehensible and evolutionarily maladaptive. Globalization constitutes the enrichment of the core and the immiseration of

the periphery (Kinzer 2006; Sherry 1983). Ethnocide is waged via systematic cultural dislocation, and the spread of iatrogenic diseases integral to development (Appadurai 2006). Ecocide is perpetuated through pollution and climate change (Ridgeway 2004). Materialism elevates acquisitiveness to a cultural syndrome, and the continued democratization of luxury promotes the endless escalation of insatiable want (Farrell 2003; Rosenblatt 1999; Whybrow 2005). Spectacle fosters distraction and complacency, encouraging a compliant citizenry (DeZengotita 2005). Consumer debt arises through and reinforces dysfunctional socialization and promotes a kind of indentured servitude (Williams 2004). And so forth.

(p. 89)

The moral gravity of consumption, whether considered in critique or defense (Livingston 2011; Potter 2010), and its sociocultural consequences, have increasingly exercised researchers (Schor *et al.* 2010) as the exploration of consumer behavior has grown beyond the field of marketing.

In the next sections of this chapter, I detail the evolution of our understanding of the societal impact of marketing. The stages I describe are all currently under active construction, even though I array them along a developmental continuum. I depict them graphically in Figure 3.1. I speculate on the prospects of harnessing the discipline to the task of achieving the common good. Finally, I offer some directives for negotiating the shadowland we have created.

FIGURE 3.1   The three evolutionary stages of our understanding of the societal impact of marketing.

Marketing *and* society

The marketing *and* society orientation, as the conjunction in the label suggests, connotes a simple combination or co-occurrence of areas, such that each domain is at best semi-autonomous and reciprocally influential. These domains are usefully considered together, in light of one another, and doing so produces mutual illumination. This view typically privileges the perspective of the firm, despite the attention given to societal impact.

The marketing *and* society orientation has been succinctly summarized into a set of six principal concerns by Gundlach *et al.* (2007). The macromarketing area is characterized by a focus on the aggregate marketing system and its societal impact. The public policy and marketing area has been largely attuned to domestic regulatory and legislative issues. The international consumer policy area has addressed analogous foreign regulatory and legislative issues. The social marketing area has addressed the topic of social change. The marketing ethics area has treated the challenge of corporate morality. Finally, the consumer interest economics area has been the platform for stand-alone sorties by researchers into a number of siloed fields. While there is some overlap among these six areas, it is reasonable to view their projects as exercises in discrete inquiry, with little effort devoted to integration across focal concerns.

Marketing *in* society

The marketing *in* society orientation, as the preposition in the label suggests, connotes a more complex situating or nesting of areas, such that the former domain is included in the latter, engulfed or incorporated in a way that allows for symbiosis to occur. This arrangement implies that society is the structure (and structuring agent) within which marketing acts. Society governs marketing even as the governance is influenced by its subject. Marketing is contained by society, much as religion, politics, and other institutions that shape and reflect the polity have been throughout time.

The marketing *in* society orientation provides us with the earliest intimations of the shadowland I have just described. Using the same six domains identified by Gundlach *et al.* (2007) that I've just employed, and inserting a seventh diagnostic dimension, let me unpack this orientation at greater length, from the perspective of the shadowland.

The macromarketing area is the most apparent portal to the culture of consumption, revealing the complications and sequelae of the marketing ethos to analysts probing beyond the managerial imperative. If we understand marketing as a realm of fascination for the culture itself, and not simply as an efficient means of need detection and benefit distribution, the extra-economic importance of consumption swiftly becomes apparent. By treating marketing as a cultural cynosure, we understand managers as behavioral architects and moral actors that profoundly shape not only the quality of life, but the continued viability of life itself.

The public policy and marketing area provides a window onto a fundamental principle of regulation, beyond the conventional controls established by governmental authority, which is often labeled appropriation, or co-optation (Holt 2004; Sherry 1995). This principle refers to the tendency of the market to commoditize (and often thence to brand) any sphere of experience with which it comes into contact. This tendency extends equally and vitally to spheres that actively resist or creatively redirect the hegemonic forces of the market. For brevity's sake, let me refer collectively to these spheres as the countercultural. Counterculture is a critical source of anti-structure that fosters cultural stability and change. Counterculture is the wellspring of creativity, and a font of generativity. Marketing routinely engages in countercultural co-optation, appropriating novelty and resistance in the service of spectacle. What now goes by the name of co-creation and prosumption masks this inexorable incorporation of distinctiveness into the evolution of marketing.

The international consumer policy area is a vantage point onto the globalization of this tendency of marketing to assimilate anything in its path, and alter everything in its wake. In particular, Scandinavian researchers have argued for a thorough (and long overdue) exploration of the moral geography of consumption, whose intricate complexity has yet to be satisfactorily charted (Bostrom *et al.* 2005). Further, Nordic researchers have championed a social movement described as political consumerism (Jensen 2005), which advocates the reappropriation of culture through the redirection of the very practices of marketing that produced the original disenchantment. The dream of effecting an emancipatory transformation of consumer culture through an enlightened practice of marketing is certainly one that the academy might embrace.

The social marketing area affords a view of our enterprise that just begins to broach the nature of our complicity in the creation of dissatisfaction on a grand scale. I find it instructive to contemplate an early medical definition of consumption as a wasting disease. Just as medicine has had to grapple with so-called iatrogenic (doctor-caused) disease, so also will marketing need to address mercarigenic (marketer-caused) syndromes, those biocultural disorders whose etiologies lie in the inexorable stimulation and ineffective resolution of desire. For example, analysts now refer to our contemporary culture as "obesogenic," and recognize that what marketing has helped to create, marketing must help to abate.

The marketing ethics area opens up the prospect of developing a philosophy of conscientious consumption, complete with undergirding practices. This enterprise would begin with the recognition that consumption is still incompletely understood, and that, despite the intensity of its critique, it not only embodies and supports numerous prosocial conditions, but also may be the occasion of spiritually uplifting experience as well. To the extent that consumer culture depends upon dissatisfaction for its sustenance, our ability to deflect what Bauman (2008: 173) views as our "nowist" individualistic "discard and replace" focus on disposition toward a systemic appreciation of the consequences of disposition that trains dissatisfaction on the societal impact of our consumer behavior will be paramount. Understanding that consumption is socially embedded, that it consists of linked streams of decisions, and that it exists at all stages of economic activity will help us avoid overshooting the biophysical and sociopsychological limits of sustainability (Princen *et al.* 2002: 14). Replacing the doctrine of consumer sovereignty with an ethic of sustainable "cautious consuming" – or balanced consumption (Dauvergne 2008) – will require the engagement of many disciplines and stakeholders in a creative act of rethinking (Princen *et al.* 2002: 326). Indeed, the "practices and politics of ethical consumption" should cause us to re-examine "the good life" in ways that "challenge the logics of consumer culture itself" (Lewis and Potter 2011: 18). Penaloza (2012: 512) has proposed a cultural approach to ethics that is relational, dialogic and negotiated, a nesting of micro and macro factors. That ethical consumption is a profoundly political practice akin to a social movement (Barnett *et al.* 2011) should not be overlooked or underestimated by marketers.

The consumer interest economics area is poised to shift from an assemblage of silos to an integrative network of hybrids and creoles. We are currently witnessing an unprecedented interest in the multidisciplinary study of the culture of consumption. This fluorescence can be tracked in the rise of professional societies, conferences and scholarly journals devoted to this inquiry. For purposes of concision, I note just a few of the developments emerging from within my own narrow circles of interest as a reflection of the larger trend afoot. In the past decade, two groups have evolved from the Association for Consumer Research. The first is the Transformative Consumer Research (TCR) movement. The second is the Consumer Culture Theory (CCT) Consortium. Through conferences and publications, the former association has focused on consumer welfare and quality of life issues, and the latter on macro, critical, and interpretive approaches to consumption. Because consumption is such a fundamental, rich, and cross-cultural phenomenon, its study virtually begs for collaborative ventures, and its allure has drawn a wide spectrum of consumer researchers into the fold. What started in the early 1980s as a piecemeal migration of solitary scholars into consumer research (itself an emerging field newly differentiated from marketing proper in the mid-1970s) promises to become a comprehensive field-based inquiry as we move into the new millennium's second decade. Just as CCT and TCR researchers have imported the insights of other disciplines into our field, so also are the basic disciplines beginning to discover the work in marketing that would allow them to probe consumption more effectively.

I've added a seventh domain to the marketing *in* society orientation, which I've borrowed from the literary world (Sherry 1991), called K-Mart Realism, to draw attention to the rapidly proliferating trend of artists imbricating marketing into their work. K-Mart realism is a genre of American fiction that is characterized, among other things, by a fascination with consumption venues and brand names. Writers, musicians, painters, performance artists, film makers, and others use marketing as a medium and source of content, as well as interpret, criticize, and celebrate consumption in the bargain. This is a time-honored aesthetic tradition (Outka 2009). Some recent examples include Alex Shakar's *The Savage Girl*, William Gibson's *Pattern Recognition*, Viktor Pelevin's *Homo Zapiens*, Max Barry's *Jennifer*

Government and *Company*, Christopher Buckley's *Boomsday*, Jonathan Dees' *Palladio*, Colson Whitehead's *Apex Hides the Hurt*, James Othmer's *The Futurist*, Romuald Hazoume's *Ear Splitting*, Stephen Colbert's *Colbert Report*, and Morgan Spurlock's *Pom Wonderful Presents the Greatest Movie Ever Sold*, to name just a few. This trend is mirrored in the academic realm by the crisis of representation, which finds marketing scholars conveying their understanding of marketplace phenomena in vehicles beyond articles, chapters, and books. Novels, poems, films, and paintings are among the genres currently being exploited, and forays into creative nonfiction grow increasingly common. These trends represent both the increasing interpenetration of marketing and society, and analysts' determination to represent this phenomenon evocatively for their audiences. Whether personnel committees can be persuaded to accept these new genres as evidence of scholarship is a challenge facing senior scholars eager to speed diffusion of marketing thought across disciplinary boundaries (Sherry 2004).

Marketing *is* society

The marketing *is* society orientation has arisen over the past decade in recognition of the subsumption (or, perhaps more precisely, sublation) of culture by marketing, propounded by theorists who claim the two domains have become coterminous. This orientation is associated in particular with the maturation of the CCT tradition (Arnould and Thompson 2005; 2007) of interdisciplinary inquiry into marketplace behavior. The marketing *is* society orientation, as the verb in the label suggests, connotes not just an integration of areas, but their fundamental identity. From this perspective, marketing has so thoroughly pervaded the cultural ethos that the two are indistinguishable from one another. Society and marketing have become coextensive.

This position is a strong-form argument of the type that has previously attached to the critique of mass culture and to the co-optation of counterculture by commerce (Heath and Potter 2004). The position is breathtaking: "Marketing has simply become so diffuse as to be a social activity" (Moore 2007: 86), engaged in by managers, consumers, citizens, consumerists and stakeholders of every conceivable stripe. The position is the culmination of the episodically hotly debated "broadening" of the marketing concept initiated by Kotler and Levy (1969) over four decades ago. The inexorable commodification of formerly (semi-autonomous and (semi-) discrete spheres of cultural production, and the diffusion of marketing philosophy and technique across the domains of everyday practice, not only abet this subsumption of society by marketing, but also mute the expression (or even the possibility) of criticism.

The marketing-is-society perspective derives from a world view of capitalist realism (Fisher 2009) which construes capitalism not just as the only viable political-economic system, but as a way of perceiving that thwarts the mere imagining of viable alternatives. Consumer culture preemptively formats desire and hope, installing a "business ontology" in which "it is simply obvious" that society should be run as a business, rendering "reflexive impotence" a self-fulfilling prophecy (Fisher 2009: 9; 17; 21). The recent economic meltdown (Tett 2009; McLean and Nocera 2010; Roubini and Mihm 2010) actually suggests that we are not smart enough to "leave things to the market," and that markets need to become less efficient (Chang 2010: 168; 231); in short, many of the economic assumptions undergirding our beliefs are faulty. These current beliefs will not help us avert future financial or environmental disaster (Fisher 2009; Chang 2010). Some finance scholars (Shiller 2012) have begun rethinking their concept of the "good society" to take these matters into account.

As the shadowland engulfs the aggregate marketing system, the components of the former nether region have invited exploration by consumer cultural theorists. These researchers have chronicled the global diffusion and local individuation of the culture of consumption, examining the myriad acts of accommodation and resistance this evolution has encouraged. Let me use the same seven shadowland domains I extrapolated from Gundlach et al.'s (2007) analysis to unpack the marketing is society orientation.

The area of countercultural co-optation has given rise to the study of numerous heterotopias, such as the Burning Man Project (Kozinets 2002; Sherry and Kozinets 2007), the Mountain Man Rendezvous (Belk and Costa 1998), the Rainbow Gathering (Niman 1997) and the Civil War Reenactment (Mottner and Bryce 2003). Forays into the virtual cyberias and cyburbias of Web 2.0 grow increasingly common, with such alternative metaverses as Second Life (Boellstorf 2010) providing irresistible challenges to researchers interested in the cultural practice of worlding. Kozinets and Handelman (2004) have sought to understand anti-consumption activism as a subversive movement springing in part from religious ideologies that attempts to sacralize collectivist values devoted to realizing the common good over more individualistic goals that enshrine a problematic acquisitiveness. In their introduction to the special issue of *Consumption Markets and Culture* on anti-consumption, Kozinets et al. (2010) examine the threat to societal welfare that the individualistic orientation to culture (whether embracing or renouncing of rampant consumption) poses. Further, they consider the prospect of an engaged scholarship that harnesses research to activist ends, implicitly challenging colleagues to descend from the ivory tower to practice espoused values (much as our managerial brethren have done for decades).

The political consumerism area has proved an exceptionally fertile field for inquiry into the common good. Researchers in this area have been especially interested in public goods. Critical theorists and participatory action researchers (Saren et al. 2007; Tadajewski and Brownlie 2008; Zwick and Cayla 2011) have considered ways of restoring stakeholder equity in marketing transactions. Development studies have also flourished, with inquiries into non-ethnocentric development (Dholakia and Sherry 1987) and sustainable development (Fuller 1999; Dauvergne 2008; Martin and Schouten 2012) broadening and humanizing our conception of the field. Interest in public goods and the reclamation of public space is being renewed (Visconti et al. 2010). The emergent field of transformative consumer research (Mick *et al.* 2012) promises to become a revitalization movement, restoring the common good to a focal position in scholarly consciousness.

The mercarigenic syndromes area has witnessed efforts to redress some of the excesses that have resulted from the neglect and unsophisticated treatment of the wants vs. needs debate within our discipline. The consequences of affluenza (de Graaf *et al.* 2001) are gradually being identified and addressed. The morality of pursuing niche therapies – for example, the treatment of middle-class ailments such as erectile dysfunction or social anxiety to the neglect of more widespread problems associated with lower socioeconomic status, such as tuberculosis, malaria, bilharzia, or various waterborne illnesses – is slowly being questioned (Bodley 2007, 2008; Economist 2012; Inhorn and Brown 1997; McElroy and Townsend 2008). Studies of medical and sexual tourism (Brennan 2004; Hall 2012; Perfetto and Dholakia 2010; Ryan and Hall 2001; Seabrook 2001) are illuminating the dark side of one of commercial colonialism's greatest growth markets. Carbon offset complacency, debt-credit crises and other dysfunctions of an evolving capitalism are currently being explored. Each of these issues speaks directly to the realization of the common good.

The conscientious consumption area has encouraged investigation into a number of alternative forms of capitalism that treat stakeholders more equitably. Schumacher's (1973) early call for a Buddhist economics set the tone for this field, and Payne's (2010) recent updating reinforces the contemporary relevance of Buddhism to the reformation of consumer culture. Voluntary simplicity (Elgin 1981) and bioregionalism (Thayer 2003) are promising and provocative challenges to the status quo. Ecofeminism (Dobscha 1993; Dobscha and Ozanne 2001; Warren 2000) and ecotheology (Berry 2006; Kearns and Keller 2007; Fox 1988) are also emerging contenders. Hartman (2011) has advanced the case for a consumption ethic grounded in Christian tradition. Inquiry into the lifestyles of the so-called cultural creatives (Florida 2003) is likely to produce additional insight into enlightened consumer behavior, as these individuals are context-sensitive trendsetters.

The area of hybrids and creoles is becoming a hot-house of interdisciplinary possibility, as multidisciplinary inquiries start to converge. Recall that this area is a mélange of fusions and hyphenates, organizations that have managed to blend previously discrete realms of interest into insightful new combinations. Scholarly societies and professional associations are rapidly spawning structures (such as interest groups) devoted to understanding contemporary marketing and consumer behavior. These pods are gradually colliding, even as their denizens travel between them. Again, in the interest of space, I identify just a few of these groups in my own area of interest to illustrate the potential of this awakening in contiguous disciplines. The American Anthropological Association has groups devoted to public policy and government regulation, managerial practice, and economic behavior. Further, the Society for Applied Anthropology and the Society for Economic Anthropology are each concerned with issues of consumption worldwide. The American Sociological Association has recently launched a Consumer Studies Research Network; the European Sociological Association has an analogous

Consumer Research Network. The Association of American Geographers also has an Economic Geography Specialty group. Finally, Charisma (charisma-network. net) is a web-based interdisciplinary consortium of international researchers focused on consumer market studies, both theoretical and applied. As bridges are forged between groups, and as marketing and consumer research literatures diffuse across boundaries, convergence will become the order of the day. This local snapshot of the cross-disciplinary fervor afoot in the academic world mirrors the diversification of interest at work in our own field. The proliferation of newsletters, and of interdisciplinary journals such as *Culture, Markets & Consumption*, the *Journal of Consumer Culture, Cultural Geographies, Space and Culture*, and the *Journal of Material Culture*, to name just a few, is also a harbinger of a more comprehensive and nuanced understanding of marketplace behavior awaiting development.

The crisis of representation area holds out the hope that our scholarly understanding of marketing and consumption can be deepened, humanized, and communicated beyond our conventional academic boundaries. Researchers are increasingly employing the very media that their artistic brethren have developed both to dimensionalize insight and render it evocatively, to promote a visceral comprehension of marketing and consumption. For example, scholarly poetry has appeared in the *Journal of Consumer Research*, the *Journal of Advertising*, the *Journal of Business Research*, and *Consumption Markets & Culture*, as well as in chapbooks (Wijland *et al.* 2010; Wijland 2011). Stephen Brown's (2006, 2008, 2009) trilogy of marketing novels is another engaging example. Ronald Hill's (2001) evocative collection of short stories on homelessness is yet another. As the volume of this artistic activity increases, our theoretical and practical insight into consumption and marketing will deepen.

Reflection

In his study of emancipatory consumption, Kozinets (2002) asks a provocative question: Can consumers escape the market? In response to the commercialization of civic life, which countercultures have arguably abetted, some critics (Heath and Potter 2004: 333) have suggested that we "make the best of global capitalism" by "searching high and low for market failures and, when we find them, thinking creatively about how they can be resolved". Heath and Potter (2004: 8) advocate "measured reform from within the system." Activists collectively described as "culture jammers" have tried to sabotage, appropriate, and even intensify the marketing ethos in their effort to offer resistance; none of these strategies is predicated on attaining independence from the market (Harold 2007). The "pervasive ubiquity of late capital" seems to limit resistance to "[valuable] incremental reform" (Harold 2007: 26, 68). The inability to extricate ourselves completely from consumer culture is mitigated by the rise of open source and open content movements; that intensifies market logics (in effect co-opting them) to create consuming publics capable of generating the common good, largely by shifting our conception of property from the proprietary to propriety (Harold 2007: 145, 157). These groups are able to focus on issues important to the community rather than to marketers, and engage in empowering cocreation rather than passively outsourcing agentic faculties. Ownership in this context becomes less important than sharing, on many dimensions.

The conflation of consumption and our culturally mandated quest for authenticity (Heath and Potter 2004: 185) is one of the principal drivers of the culture of consumption, and an anchor of the marketing-*is*-society world view. Market mediation is an invaluable component of contemporary authenticity (Outka 2009; Beverland 2009; Gilmore and Pine 2007), for better and for worse. For that quest to evolve beyond a simple status competition (Potter 2010), and for marketers to assist consumers in realizing the common good, some metamarketing might be in order. If marketing's technology of influence (from the mythological to the logistical) were to be redeployed in the service of redirecting our quest for authenticity from a materialist to an ecological plane – to an ecocentric enterprise that reinvested our animistic impulse back into the natural world from its current materialist moorings – the spiritual ends of immanence and transcendence might be subversively realized (Sherry 2000).

If, as Hardt and Negri (2009: 377) assert, happiness is "perhaps the ultimate collective good," requiring an "institutional character to guarantee its longevity," the creation of a durable happiness seems an appropriate Utopian project for marketers to undertake. This would be a deep or serious happiness, a kind of balanced, harmonious contentment, which would remake consumption as a means of re-enchanting the world. This happiness would be contingent upon the recognition of the marketing *is* society position as a calamitous overshooting of the marketing *in* society orientation, and a course correction that realigned marketing with culturally sacrosanct values. The early intimations of Marketing 3.0 – discernible in the practices of collaborative, cultural and human spirit marketing – suggest that managers may be growing more receptive to a transformation in their activity that might better shape the common good (Kotler *et al.* 2010).

Utopia and the common good

I began this chapter by invoking Oscar Wilde. I conclude by evoking William Butler Yeats (1921: 19):

> Surely some revelation is at hand;
>
> Surely the Second Coming is at hand.
>
> The Second Coming!

That rough beast Yeats imagines slouching toward Bethlehem might well be understood as the reimagined marketing I have long espoused (Sherry 2000). The breathless awe the poet intones might be inspired by the diversion of the marketing imagination from the pursuit of a fracturing, egocentric (and inexorably totalizing) You-topia to a quest for a unifying Utopia focused squarely on the common good. This transformation implies a shift from a stakeholder-centric (or even a socio-entric) view of marketing to one that is more properly geo- or eco-centric, one that exalts systemic good above mere individual satisfaction (and the hegemony the ego-centric approach has produced). Ironically, perversely – as my friend Kal Applbaum (2004) chides me – and inevitably, the reclamation of culture from marketing is best accomplished with the assistance of marketers (Sherry 2008). The Second Coming of marketing will be a social movement focused on the common good.

In a provocative, if curiously reasoned, defense of consumer culture, Livingston (2011: 42-44) asserts that, since consumption rather than private investment has driven economic growth since 1919, and since household savings are not needed to fund growth through private investment, deferred gratification fosters neither public good nor private character. Consumer culture enables a "politics of more" to flourish, whose pleasures elude us to the extent that we are haunted by the Protestant work ethic, whose "pathos of productivity" interferes with the self-love we express in our embrace of extravagance (Livingston 2011: 77, 165, 179).

In place of the "metapolitical discourse" of the critique of consumer culture, Livingston (2011: 74, 89) proposes that the consumption ethos (whose dysfunctions he cursorily catalogues and dismisses with a minimum of counterargumentation) be used to forge a metapolitical critique of the ethos of economic growth. In short, he advocates the use of consumption as a vehicle for re-examining the kinds of individuals – and, by extension, society – we want to become. For Livingston (2011: 179), the goal is to work less and consume more, with the expectation that consumption can create a more hospitable, equitable and ecologically considerate culture. Regrettably, he offers no blueprint or action plans for the achievement of this alternative Utopia. While a close reading of consumer behavior (of the type espoused by CCT researchers) may, and, I believe, should, be used to inform a reformation of contemporary cultural values, it does not in itself mitigate the blow-back that the culture has generated. It will take a transfiguration of consumer culture to produce the Utopia that Livingston envisions.

Keat (2000) construes consumer sovereignty as a threat to practices – after MacIntyre (1981), social activities with internal standards of excellence that are supraordinate to external goods such as power, status, or money – as the former is based on preferences that may be inimical to the internal standards of the latter. Cultural practices embody (in the form of values), varying conceptions of "the good" that contribute to people's well-being (Keat 2000: 47). In the face of the "colonizing tendencies" of the market, consumer preferences can trump values, rendering cultural institutions ineffective in complementing the market's ability to generate the conditions of its own continued success. Keat (2000: 152, 156-57, 162) places these cultural goods (or metagoods) beyond the market, and regards them as necessary to ensuring that the market contributes to human welfare: cultural goods help us assess the value of consumer goods to our well-being. The CCT tradition has long maintained that the rhetoric of the market has masked more than a few problematic assumptions, beginning with foundational vocabulary. Consumer "goods" are more accurately understood as "neutrals" susceptible to cultural valence, and are as often better construed as "bads" that work against essential interests of stakeholders.

Keat (2000: 167) calls for a "democratic debate" about the market under the aegis of a "politics of common goods." I have asserted that this debate has begun within our discipline, and that marketers need to be among the vanguard of reformers in re-establishing a conception of the common good. Moral evaluation and critique have long been staples in consumer studies outside the field of marketing (Schor *et al*. 2010). It is time for such values-based assessment to take root in our own field as well.

New York mayor Michael Bloomberg's recent proposal that the city ban the sale of sugary soft drinks in containers larger than 16 ounces has generated great controversy in many quarters (Saul and Grossman 2012), and has spawned a number of full-page ads in the *New York Times* lashing out at the nanny state. The Disney Corporation's recent decisions to alter its advertising in child-centric media to conform to strict nutritional standards, and to reduce sodium levels of foods served in its parks, has also been criticized by some consumerists (Barnes 2012). The difficulty of creating consensual solutions even to widely recognized problems is an indication of the urgent need for immediate and enlightened discussion of the kind of society we wish to inhabit. Deshpande's recent work on customer-centric marketing (e.g., Deshpande and Raina 2011; Deshpande *et al*. 2012), in which he examines some of the specific practices undertaken and resulting challenges encountered by managers seeking to contribute to the common good, might be a useful primer for pragmatists and idealists to consult as a prelude to such discussion.

The question of whether or not it is possible to reconcile markets and morals (Friedman 2008) is at the heart of our quest for the common good, especially in this era of looming sociocultural, geopolitical, and ecological degradation. Satz's (2010) analysis of noxious markets is one potent example of the urgent need to address this question in a public forum. Sandel's (2012) call for a civic discussion of the moral limits of markets – and a rethinking of the moral assumptions that have guided economic reasoning about the polity – is a timely prompt for a rethinking of our conceptions of the good life. This discussion should involve all stakeholders, and focus on the common good. This civic conversation can become the platform for the launch of Capitalism 4.0 (Kaletsky 2010). Coyle's (2011) recent manifesto for a rethinking of capitalism, and the consequences of reconsidering happiness, nature, posterity, fairness, and trust, is a provocative first step in this direction. Challenges facing consumers committed to overhauling contemporary culture, such as the insatiability of want (Gagnier 2000), extreme conservation (Hengeveld 2012), sharing (Belk 2010), and collaborative consumption (Botsman and Rogers 2010), to name just a few, remain to be enumerated and operationalized.

The emergence of a rationale mobilizing an ethical, sustainable consumption, described as "alternative hedonism" – the tendency of affluence to give rise to revised conceptions of individual and common good – is a hopeful contemporary utopian impulse, to the extent that the "pleasures of affluence" are recognized as "both *compromised* by their negative by-products, and as *pre-emptive* of other enjoyments" (Soper 2007: 210-212). The civic rethinking of consumption and its relation to the common good is a vision quest in which our field must fully participate if the "good life" is to be justly distributed.

Millenarian marketers will help us temper materialism with a sensitivity to materiality, an appreciation of the animate vibrancy of matter (Bennett 2010; Ingold 2000), that will allow us to re-enchant the natural world and avoid ecological collapse (Sherry 2000). As guerrilla semioticians, they will help us deconstruct, desacralize, and decommission fetishes, allowing us to concentrate on communal quality of life. They will practice demarketing, hell yes, demarketing (Kotler and Levy 1971), and not merely clean up the problems they create, but successfully ferret out unanticipated and unintended consequences of their prospective decisions. They will homestead the frontiers of disciplinary research. They will seek generativity in new genres, using our encounters with art as teaching moments to help us contemplate, discern and feel the goodness of fit of wants with needs. They will encourage us to understand the directions in which our consumer behaviors ramify, just as they have meditated on the ramifications of their own teaching, research, and consulting to produce an engaged scholarship. They will forge an alliance between managers, policymakers, consumers, and citizens in an effort to negotiate and implement the common good. They will help us steer between the Scylla of the free market and the Charybdis of state capitalism as we navigate the next Utopia.

Acknowledgments

I thank Laurel Anderson, Robert Kozinets, Thomas O'Guinn, Julie Ozanne, and Patrick Murphy for their constructive comments on earlier drafts of this chapter.

References

Appadurai, A. (2006) *Fear of Small Numbers: An Essay on the Geography of Anger*, Durham, NC: Duke University Press.

Applbaum, K. (2004) *The Marketing Era: From Professional Practice to Global Provisioning*, New York: Routledge.

Arnould, E. and Thompson, C. (2005) "Consumer Culture Theory (CCT): Twenty years of research," *Journal of Consumer Research* 31 (4): 868–82.

—— (2007) "Consumer culture theory (and we really mean theoretics): Dilemmas and opportunities posed by an academic branding strategy," in R. Belk and J.F. Sherry, Jr. (eds) *Consumer Culture Theory*, Vol. 11 of *Research in Consumer Behavior*, Oxford: Elsevier, pp. 119–47.

Barnes, B. (2012) "Promoting nutrition, Disney to restrict junk-food ads," *New York Times*, June 5: B1.

Barnett, C., Cloke, P., Clarke, N., and Malpass, A. (2011) *Globalizing Responsibility: The Political Rationalities of Ethical Consumption*, Chichester, UK: John Wiley.

Bauman, Z. (2008) *Does Ethics Have a Chance in a World of Consumers?* Cambridge, MA: Harvard University Press.

Belk, R. (2010) "Sharing," *Journal of Consumer Research*, 36 (5): 715–34.

—— and Costa, J. (1998) "The mountain man myth: a contemporary consumer fantasy," *Journal of Consumer Research*, 25 (3): 218–40.

Bennett, J. (2010) *Vibrant Matter: A Political Ecology of Things*, Durham, NC: Duke University Press.

Berry, T. (2006), *Evening Thoughts: Reflecting on Earth as a Sacred Community*, San Francisco: Sierra Club Books.

Beverland, M. (2009) *Building Brand Authenticity: 7 Habits of Iconic Brands*, New York: Palgrave.

Bodley, J. (2008) *Victims of Progress*, Walnut Creek, CA: Alta Mira Press.

—— (2007) *Anthropology and Contemporary Human Problems*, Walnut Creek, CA: Alta Mira Press.

Boellstorf, T. (2010) *Coming of Age in Second Life: An Anthropologist Explores the Virtually Human*, Princeton, NJ: Princeton University Press.

Botsman, R. and Rogers, R. (2010) *What's Mine Is Yours: The Rise of Collaborative Consumption*, New York: Harper Collins.

Bostrom, M., Follesdal, A., Klintman, M., Micheletti, M., and Sorenson, M. (eds) (2005) *Political Consumerism: Its Motivation, Power and Conditions in the Nordic Countries and Elsewhere*, Copenhagen: Norden.

Brennan, D. (ed.) (2004) *What's Love Got to Do With It?* Durham, NC: Duke University Press.

Brown, S. (2006) *The Marketing Code*, London: Marshall Cavendish.

—— (2008) *Agents and Dealers*, London: Marshall Cavendish.

—— (2009) *The Lost Logo*, London: Marshall Cavendish.

Chang, H. (2010) *23 Things They Don't Tell You About Capitalism*, New York: Bloomsbury Press.

Coyle, D. (2011) *The Economics of Enough: How to Run the Economy as If the Future Matters*, Princeton, NJ: Princeton University Press.

Dauvergne, P. (2008) *The Shadows of Consumption: Consequences for the Global Environment*, Cambridge, MA: MIT Press.

de Graaf, J., Wann, D., and Naylor, T. (2001) *Affluenza: The All-Consuming Epidemic*, San Francisco: Behrett-Kohler.

de Grazia, V. (2006) *Irresistible Empire: America's Advance Through 20th Century Europe*, Cambridge, MA: Belknap Press.

Deshpande, R. and Raina, A. (2011) "The ordinary heroes of the Taj," *Harvard Business Review*, December, 119–23.

——, Sucher, S., and Winig, L. (2012) "Cipla 2011," Harvard Business School Case 9-511-050. Boston, MA: Harvard Business School Publishing.

de Zengotita, T. (2005) *Mediated: How the Media Shapes Your World and the Way You Live In It*, New York: Bloomsbury.

Dholakia, N. and Sherry, J.F., Jr. (1987) "Marketing and development: A resynthesis of knowledge," in J. Sheth (ed.) *Research in Marketing*, Vol. 9, Greenwich, CT: JAI Press, pp. 119–43.

Dobscha, S. (1993) "Women and the environment: Applying ecofeminism to environmentally related consumption," in L. McAlister and M. L. Rothschild (eds), *Advances in Consumer Research*, Volume 20, Provo, UT: Association for Consumer Research, pp. 36–40.

—— and Ozanne, J. (2001) "An ecofeminist analysis of environmentally sensitive women: Qualitative findings on the emancipatory potential of an ecological life," *Journal of Public Policy and Marketing*, 20 (2): 201–14.

Economist, The (2012) "Hot Tropic," February 4, p. 65.

Elgin, D. (1981) *Voluntary Simplicity: Toward a Way of Life That Is Outwardly Simple, Inwardly Rich*, New York: Morrow.

Farrell, J. (2003) *One Nation, Under Goods: Malls and the Seductions of American Shopping*, Washington, DC: Smithsonian Books.

Fisher, M. (2009) *Capitalist Realism: Is There No Alternative?* Ropley, Hants, UK: Zero Books.

Florida, R. (2003) *The Rise of the Creative Class*, New York: Basic Books.

Fox, M. (1988) *The Coming of the Cosmic Christ*, San Francisco: Harper and Row.

Friedman, D. (2008) *Morals and Markets*, New York: Palgrave MacMillan.

Fuller, D. (1999) *Sustainable Marketing: Managerial-Ecological Issues*, Thousand Oaks, CA: Sage Press.

Gagnier, R. (2000) *The Insatiability of Human Wants*, Chicago: University of Chicago Press.

Gilmore, J. and Pine, J. (2007) *Authenticity: What Consumers Really Want*, Cambridge, MA: Harvard Business School Press.

Greider, W. (1997) *One World Ready or Not: The Manic Logic of Global. Capitalism*, New York: Simon & Schuster.

Gundlach, G., Block, L., and Wilkie, W. (eds) (2007) *Explorations of Marketing in Society*, Mason, OH: Thomson.

Hall, C.M. (ed.) (2012) *Medical Tourism: The Ethics, Regulation and Marketing of Health Mobility*, London: Routledge.

Hardt, M. and Negri, A. (2009) *Commonwealth*, Cambridge, MA: Belknap Press.

Harold, C. (2007) *Ourspace: Resisting the Corporate Control of Culture*, Minneapolis: University of Minnesota Press.

Hartman, L. (2011) *The Christian Consumer: Living Faithfully in a Fragile World*, Oxford: Oxford University Press.

Heath, J. and Potter, A. (2004) *Nation of Rebels: Why Counterculture Became Consumer Culture*, New York: Harper Collins.

Hengeveld, R. (2012) *Wasted World: How Our Consumption Challenges the Planet*, Chicago: University of Chicago Press.

Hill, R. (2001) *Surviving in a Material World: The Lived Experience of People in Poverty*, Notre Dame: University of Notre Dame Press.

Holt, D. (2004) *How Brands Become Icons: The Principles of Cultural Branding*, Cambridge, MA: Harvard Business School Press.

Ingold, T. (2000) *The Perception of the Environment: Essays in Livelihood, Dwelling and Skill*, New York: Routledge.

Inhorn, M. and Brown, P. (eds) (1997) *The Anthropology of Infectious Diseases*, New York: Routledge.

Jensen, H. (2005) "What does political consumerism mean for marketers?," in M. Bostrom, A. Follesdal, M. Klintman, M. Micheletti, and M. Sorenson (eds) *Political Consumerism: Its Motivation, Power and Conditions in the Nordic Countries and Elsewhere*, Copenhagen: Norden, pp. 439–54.

Kaletsky, A. (2010) *Capitalism 4.0: The Birth of a New Economy in the Aftermath of Crisis*, New York: Public Affairs.

Kearns, L. and Keller, C. (eds) (2007) *Ecospirit: Religions and Philosophies of the Earth*, New York: Fordham University Press.

Keat, R. (2000) *Cultural Goods and the Limits of the Market*, London: Macmillan Press.

Kinzer, S. (2006) *Overthrow: America's Century of Regime Change from Hawaii to Iraq*, New York: Times Books.

Kotler, P. and Levy, S.J. (1969) "Broadening the concept of marketing," *Journal of Marketing*, 33 (January): 10–15.

—— and Levy, S.J. (1971) "Demarketing, Yes, Demarketing," *Harvard Business Review* (November–December): 74–80.

——, Kartajaya, H., and Setiawan, I. (2010) *Marketing 3.0: From Products to Customers to the Human Spirit*, New York: Wiley.

Kozinets, R.V. (2002) "Can consumers escape the market? Emancipatory illuminations from burning man," *Journal of Consumer Research*, 28 (June): 67–88.

—— and Handelman, J.M. (2004) "Adversaries of consumption: consumer movements, activism, and ideology," *Journal of Consumer Research*, 31 (December): 691–704.

——, Handelman, J.M., and Shyue Lee, M. (2010) "Don't read this: or who cares what the hell anti-consumption is, anyways," *Consumption, Markets, and Culture*, 13 (September): 225–33.

Lewis, T. and Potter, E. (eds) (2011) *Ethical Consumption: A Critical Introduction*, New York: Routledge.

Livingston, J. (2011) *Against Thrift: Why Consumer Culture is Good for the Economy, the Environment, and Your Soul*, New York: Perseus.

McElroy, A. and Townsend, P. (2008) *Medical Anthropology in Ecological Perspective*, Boulder, CO: Westview Press.

McLean, B. and Nocera, J. (2010) *All the Devils Are Here: The Hidden History of the Financial Crisis*, New York: Penguin.

MacIntyre, A. (1981) *After Virtue: A Study in Moral Theory*, Notre Dame, IN: University of Notre Dame Press.

Maclaran, P. and Brown, S. (2005) "The center cannot hold: consuming the Utopian marketplace," *Journal of Consumer Research*, 32 (September): 311–23.

Martin, D. and Schouten, J. (2012) *Sustainable Marketing*, Upper Saddle River, NJ: Prentice Hall.

Mick, D., Pettigrew, S., Pechmann, C., and Ozanne, J. (eds) (2012) *Transformative Consumer Research for Personal and Collective Well-Being*, New York: Routledge.

Moore, E. (2007) *Unmarketable: Brandalism, Copyfighting, Mocketing and the Erosion of Integrity*, New York: New Press.

Mottner, S. and Bryce, W. (2003) *An Honorable Calling: The 15th Alabama Reenacting Company in the Pacific Northwest*, a videography abstracted in P. Anand Keller and D. W. Rook (eds) *Advances in Consumer Research*, Volume 30, Valdosta, GA: Association for Consumer Research, pp. 2–10.

Niman, M. I. (1997) *People of the Rainbow: A Nomadic Utopia*, Knoxville, TN: University of Tennessee Press.

Outka, E. (2009) *Consuming Traditions: Modernity, Modernism, and the Commodified Authentic*, London: Oxford University Press.

Payne, R. (ed.) (2010) *How Much Is Enough? Buddhism, Consumerism and the Human Environment*, Somerville, MA: Wisdom Publications.

Penaloza, L. (2012) "Ethics," in *Marketing Management: A Cultural Perspective*, in L. Penaloza, N. Toulouse, and L. Visconti (eds) New York: Routledge, pp. 505–23.

Perfetto, R. and Dholakia, N. (2010) "Exploring the cultural contradictions of medical tourism," *Culture Consumption and Markets*, 13 (4): 399–417.

Potter, A. (2010), *The Authenticity Hoax: How We Get Lost Finding Ourselves*, New York: Harper.

Princen, T., Maniates, M., and Conca, K. (eds) (2002) *Confronting Consumption*, Cambridge, MA: MIT Press.

Ritzer, G. (1995) *The McDonaldization of Society: An Investigation into the Changing Character of Contemporary Social Life*, Thousand Oaks, CA: Pine Forge Press.

Rosenblatt, R. (ed.) (1999) *Consuming Desires: Consumption, Culture and the Pursuit of Happiness*, Washington, DC: Island Press.

Roubini, N. and Mihm, S. (2010) *Crisis Economics: A Crash Course in the Future of Finance*, New York: Penguin.

Ryan, C. and Hall, C. M. (2001) *Sex Tourism: Marginal People and Liminalities*, London: Routledge.

Sandel, M. (2012) *What Money Can't Buy: The Moral Limits of Markets*, New York: Farrar, Straus and Giroux.

Saren, M., Maclaran, P., Golding, C., Elliott, R., Shankar, A., and Catterall, M. (eds) (2007) *Critical Marketing: Defining the Field*, New York: Elsevier.

Satz, D. (2010) *Why Some Things Should Not Be for Sale*, New York: Oxford University Press.

Saul, M. and Grossman, A. (2012) "Sugar ban stirs up New York," *The Wall Street Journal*, June 1: A3.

Schor, J., Slater, D., Zukin, S., and Zelizer, V. (2010) "Critical and moral stances in consumer studies," *Journal of Consumer Culture*, 10 (2): 274–91.

Schumacher, E. F. (1973) *Small Is Beautiful: Economics as if People Mattered*, New York: Harper and Row.

Seabrook, J. (2001) *Travels in the Skin Trade: Tourism and the Sex Industry*, London: Pluto Press.

Sherry, J. F., Jr. (1983) "Business in anthropological perspective," *Florida Journal of Anthropology*, 8(6): 15–36, Pt. 2.

—— (1991) "Postmodern alternatives: The interpretive turn in consumer research," in T. Robertson and H. Kassarjian (eds) *Handbook of Consumer Behavior*, Englewood Cliffs, NJ: Prentice Hall, pp. 548–91.

—— (1995) *Contemporary Marketing and Consumer Behavior: An Anthropological Sourcebook*, Thousand Oaks, CA: Sage.

—— (2000) "Distraction, destruction, deliverance: The presence of mindscape in marketing's new millennium," *Marketing Intelligence and Planning*, 18 (6–7): 328–36.

—— (2004) "Culture, consumption and marketing: Retrospect and prospect," in K. Ekstrom and H. Brembeck (eds) *Elusive Consumption: Tracking New Research Perspectives*, New York: Berg, pp. 45–64.

—— (2008) "The ethnographer's apprentice: trying consumer culture from the outside in," *Journal of Business Ethics*, 80: 85–95.

—— (2011) "The marketing reformation redux," in J. Cayla and D. Zwick (eds) *Inside Marketing: Cultures, Ideologies and Practices*, London: Oxford University Press, pp. 343–50.

—— and Kozinets, R. V. (2007) "Comedy of the commons: Nomadic spirituality at Burning Man," in R. Belk and J. F. Sherry, Jr. (eds) *Consumer Culture Theory*, Vol. 11 of *Research in Consumer Behavior*, Oxford: Elsevier, pp. 119–47.

Shiller, R. (2012) *Finance and the Good Society*, Princeton, NJ: Princeton University Press.

Soper, K. (2007) "Rethinking the good life," *Journal of Consumer Culture*, 7: 205–24.

Tadajewski, M. and Brownlie, D. (2008) *Critical Marketing: Issues in Contemporary Marketing*, Chichester, UK: John Wiley.

Tett, G. (2009) *Fool's Gold*, New York: Free Press.

Thayer, R., Jr. (2003) *Lifeplace: Bioregional Thought and Practice*, Berkeley, CA: University of California Press.

Visconti, L., Sherry, J. F., Jr., Borghini, S., and Anderson, L. (2010) "Street art, sweet art: The reclamation of public place," *Journal of Consumer Research*, 37 (3): 511–29.

Wallace, T. (ed.) (2005) *Tourism and Applied Anthropology: Linking Theory and Practice*, NAPA Bulletin 23, Berkeley, CA: University of California Press.

Warren, K. (2000) *Ecofeminist Philosophy*, Lanham, MD: Rowman and Littlefield.

Whybrow, P. (2005) *American Mania: When More Is Not Enough*, New York: W.W. Norton.

Wijland, R. (ed.) (2011) *Coyotes Confessions Totems*, St. Bathans, New Zealand: University of St. Bathans Press.

——, Sherry, J. F., Jr., and Schouten, J. (eds) (2010) *Canaries Coalmines Thunderstones*, St. Bathans, New Zealand: University of St. Bathans Press.

Wilde, O. (1891) "The soul of man under socialism," *Fortnightly Review*, 291 (February): 292–319.

Wilkie, W. L. and Moore, E. S. (1999) "Marketing's contributions to society," *Journal of Marketing*, 63 (10/02): 198–218.

Williams, B. (2004) *Debt for Sale: A Social History of the Credit Trap*, Philadelphia: University of Pennsylvania Press.

Yeats, W.B. (1921/2003) *Michael Robartes and the Dancer*, Whitefish, MT: Kessinger.

Zwick, D. and Cayla, J. (2012) *Inside Marketing: Practices, Ideologies, Devices*, Oxford: Oxford University Press.

4

THE CASE FOR CLARITY

Joel E. Urbany

Introduction

Consumers face a great deal of complexity today. Expanding variety, innovation, and changing regulation have made complicated markets like banking, insurance, healthcare, and technology even more challenging to navigate. Rankin (2004) notes substantially rising consumer complaints about banking services and suggests that in considering investments, "decision-making is confusing and stressful (and) customers are often later surprised by the penalties incurred" (see also Scott 2004). Two-thirds of commercial insurance buyers seek "better information on prices and terms being transacted" in the insurance markets (Bradford 2005). Markard and Holt (2003) similarly report that consumers express a significant concern for additional information in energy provider decisions. Likewise, the biggest obstacle to an effective healthcare market " that information on cost and quality are complex, problematic, and often difficult to understand" (Bennett 2009). Finally, a recent *Wall Street Journal* article highlights the vast complexity of modern-day contracts:

> [I]n one recent study, 61 percent of consumers reported that they didn't read all the terms of contracts before agreeing to them. (And those are just the ones who will admit to it.) "Laid edge to edge, they're impossible to stay on top of," says New York-based plaintiffs' attorney James Denlea. "It would be a full-time job."
>
> *(Sullivan 2012)*

Such conditions only make our limited decision skills more of a handicap. Consumer decision-making is often incomplete and biased, a finding established with such empirical certainty that a current crop of books summarizing these problems have topped best-seller lists providing advice on how to cope (see Thaler and Sunstein 2008; Ariely 2009; Heath and Heath 2007, 2010). However, the advice in these volumes for dealing with irrationality and complexity – as it relates to the working of competitive markets – tends to focus more on regulatory interventions than on how individual firms might positively address these consumer challenges. This shifts the burden of forging the common good away from firms to the government, presuming little incentive for individual firms to enhance consumer decision-making.

The goal of this chapter is to suggest that the consumer's problem in dealing with market complexity and the social disutility resulting from this problem may actually represent a significant growth opportunity for firms. Generally speaking, individuals prefer less uncertainty to more. However, managerial instincts in competitive markets are not naturally responsive to consumer preference for greater certainty. In fact, one school of thought in economics holds that firms instead seek to strategically confuse consumers, explicitly managing the complexity in their products (Gabaix and Laibson 2004) or pricing (Carlin 2006) to increase profitability. While acknowledging that such behavior exists in certain contexts, I argue that complexity is much more likely to result from firms' natural pursuit of volume growth and incentives to generate variety, as well as managerial gaps in understanding what consumers' value. Given these tendencies, there are several reasons why an untapped demand for what I will label *clarity* is not being leveraged. That demand is driven in large part by the fact that clarity touches important consumer values around respect, empathy, and confidence in value, very much in keeping with principles of the common good.

Here, I'll first consider how firms create confusion, both intentionally and without realizing it. I'll review the developing school of thought that complexity is intentional – i.e., that firms purposely seek to build profitability by confusing consumers. I will then consider that complexity may be less a function of that intentional obfuscation and more the result of two things: (a) the natural competitive evolution of markets, and (b) the fact that many firms have a limited understanding of the value that consumers place on less over more uncertainty. The second section of the chapter explores marketing and clarity production, considering the factors that drive demand for clarity and organizational examples of clarity production. The final section of the chapter explores the relationship between clarity and the common good.

Marketing as confusion

In both the academic literature and in conventional business thinking, the last fifteen years have seen increasing attention to the idea that complexity is purposeful (cf. Spiegler 2006). One of earliest mentions of "confusion marketing" (Banyard 2001) defines a particular aspect of the concept but also suggests it predates the twenty-first century:

> I am not sure whether the mobile phone sector actually pioneered the technique, but I suspect that it has been around since the first barrow boy[1] . . . . instead of competing head-on over pricing of nearly identical

products, you throw up a storm of niche offers . . . the intended result is to keep overall *profit margins* high because a direct comparison between competitors is too difficult.

It seems indisputable that consumer confusion is under certain circumstances intentionally created by firms. This notion is documented not only in trade press accounts like the one above but is also now formalized in economic models of confusion and rigorous evidence that examines various pricing and communications practices (Gabaix and Laibson 2004, 2006; Ellison and Ellison 2009), which provide an important starting point for this discussion.

Obfuscation

The notion that firms seek to manage or even increase consumer confusion has recently been formalized in economics, initially in the work of Gabaix and Laibson (GL) (2004, 2006). GL seek to explain firm behavior in light of the complexity and confusion that consumers experience in their decision-making and consumption. In GL's model, goods are valued by consumers to be a function of both an offering's true value and a component representing "noise":

$$U_{ia} = \underbrace{v_i - p_i}_{\text{true value}} + \underbrace{\sigma_{ia}\varepsilon_{ia}}_{\text{noise}}$$

where

U_{ia} = overall utility of good i;
v_i = true value of good i;
p_i = true price of good i;
σ_{ia} = complexity of good i (as determined by the firm);
ε_{ia} = an error term.

In this model, the firm strategically chooses its level of complexity. The market is "noisy" in the sense that the consumer knows neither the true expected value of the good nor its true expected cost. In the model, noise comes from product complexity, marketing campaigns, the difficulty of anticipating future needs and use, evaluating financing options, and so on. The firm sets price and its level of complexity σ_i to maximize profits. Complexity actually produces positive value to a certain point, as it reflects more sophisticated products, but ultimately becomes dysfunctional for consumers. Essential to the model is the notion that firms understand and strategically manage the confusion they can create:

- Increasing complexity σ_i (also referred to as confusion) can increase a firm's market share.

- When there is noise (i.e., uncertainty about quality) in the market, the forces of competition do not work effectively. For example, new competitive entry does *not* drive down mark-ups as classic theory would expect.
- Increasing competition "tends to exacerbate the production of excess complexity" (p. 20). In other words, as more competitors enter, existing firms benefit from creating more confusion.
- However, the best firms produce the least confusion (and vice versa).
- Returns to a strategy to "educate consumers" are observed to be weak – as GL note, "education greatly benefits consumers (who can better pick out the best deals), but only moderately benefits the firm who invests in the education."

All of this leads to the conclusion that the majority of firms will seek to "make their own products excessively complex" (GL: 25) and do not have strong incentives to invest in educating consumers.

GL's model is an interesting account of a firm's incentives in a competitive market where consumer evaluations are noisy. More importantly, it represents an institutionalization of the notion that "marketing = confusion." There is little doubt that under certain circumstances, firms seek to make competitive comparisons intentionally difficult. Such behaviors may range from the relatively innocuous – e.g., competing retailers carrying slightly different product assortments apparently to make price comparison difficult for consumers (Shugan 1992) – to efforts to hide fees or even engage in bait-and-switch advertising (Ellison and Ellison 2009; Gabaix and Laibson 2006). However, I propose that complexity (and consumer confusion) is much more likely to be explained by three prominent factors that have nothing to do with the deceptive practices discussed in the contexts studied above. We'll consider these next.

Complexity without intent of confusion

In the contexts modeled in the last section, confusion appears to have purposeful intent and might well be a focus of regulatory attention. It is important to note here that complexity in the marketplace has other, likely more significant explanations.

1   *Errors.* Decision-making in organizations is complex, with time and resource constraints, many people involved, and at times inadequate oversight (often attributed to managerial biases and organizational/human inertia; see Goddard and Eccles 2012; Boulding *et al.* 1994; Miller and Friesen 1980). Apple is currently dealing with a significant number of complaints from both regulators and consumers in Australia for their apparently misleading claims that their phones are "4G capable" when, given technology definition differences in the Australian 4G network owned by Telstra, the devices cannot work on the network. The error is attributed to "commercial myopia" – in this case, the launch of a global marketing campaign that was focused on US and Canadian providers (Huang 2012). Similarly, Vodafone's recent mislabeling of a potentially costly

add-on feature as free created significant consumer dissatisfaction and regulatory intervention, but was found to be inadvertent (Nordqvist and Gay 2011).
While such errors (assuming they are one-offs) would not provide a broad,
systematic explanation of tactics that increase complexity for consumers, they
contribute to confusion frequently.

2   *Natural evolution toward variety.* Work in strategy over the last 20 years has
    established the dynamic forces that drive competitive markets today (Dickson
    1992; D'Aveni 1995). Rapid *innovation–imitation cycles* in almost all industries
    have led to a proliferation of assortments almost universally. The Food
    Marketing Institute estimates the number of new consumer packaged-goods
    products introduced jumped from around 10,000 in 1980 to over 18,000 in
    2005 (Martinez 2007), with estimates going upwards of 30,000 (Christensen
    et al. 2005), while Hübner and Kuhn (2012) report a 30 percent increase in the
    average number of items in overall store assortments in 2000 and 2009.
    The same sort of proliferation is taking place in the insurance and investment
    industries, where "complexity is often justified by market demand and the
    strategic value generated by a large product portfolio" (Van Weegan *et al.*
    2012). Firms will see this proliferation as a natural result of their growth strat-
    egies and to some degree as defensive strategy, as opposed to the strategic
    effort to confuse consumers.

3   *Buyer–seller goal and differences in perspective.* What is good for the buyer
    (e.g., lower prices) is not always good for the seller. Buyers are motivated to
    compare competitive offerings to get the best deal. Generally speaking, sellers
    would prefer buyers *not* compare. In this self-interested view, any form of
    uncertainty reduction that risks or initiates exposure to other brands won't
    likely even be considered for many firms. The motivation to "sell my product"
    rather than stand up to a careful assessment against competitors is likely to be
    a strong, natural instinct. This mindset leads managers to focus consumer
    attention on selling and defending the features of their own products or ser-
    vices, and downplaying and ignoring those of competitors (unless there are
    competitor deficiencies). Day and Moorman (2010) make a compelling case
    that such an inside-out view of the world holds many organizations back from
    growth. This constraint on growth is broadly due to an internal and product/
    service attribute-focus leads to "talking about us," rather than listening for real
    needs in the market. Ironically, while the motivation to tout the current
    product and avoid competitive comparison is natural and instinctive, it may
    significantly limit exposure to longer-term opportunities for growth.

The latter point from Day and Moorman is very important. The natural instinct
to prevent closer scrutiny (and just sell) is powerful, but it may be another factor
that distracts managerial attention away from a true understanding of the real
value that customers seek. The next section of the chapter makes the case that,
in fact, reducing uncertainty may be a significant part of the value that attracts
customers to the firm.

Marketing as clarity production

Defining clarity

Clarity is defined here as an incremental change in uncertainty that creates positive value for consumers.[2] There are many different ways that uncertainty might be reduced: the consumer gets an explanation from a friend about the most important attributes to consider in purchasing a laptop; they read a *Consumer Reports* article that identifies the best brands of refrigerators; or they find a manufacturer's website very helpful in explaining a new technology that has improved the performance of room air conditioners. We'll specify particular sources of uncertainty below, but suffice to say that clarity is produced for consumers *by a firm* when uncertainty (in any form) is reduced by an action attributable to that firm.

Sources of uncertainty

Consumption and the choices that surround it are inherently uncertain (Bettman 1979; Hansen 1972) and there are several sources of the uncertainty that consumers may experience (cf. Lipshitz and Strauss 1997). First, there is uncertainty due to *inadequate understanding*, which reflects the fact that information may have multiple meanings or interpretations (Daft and Weick 1984). Alternatively, inadequate understanding may result from complex concepts which may be difficult to learn or communicate (Babrow 1992; Babrow *et al.* 1998). Second, there is uncertainty in *how to choose*. Even if consumers have full information about competitive options, they still experience preference or choice uncertainty (Wang *et al.* 2007; Urbany *et al.* 1989) which could emerge from different sources, e.g., *conflict in attribute levels between-alternatives* (cf. Tversky and Shafir 1992), *limited differentiation between options* (Lanzetta 1963; Kahn and Sarin 1988); or an inability to *assign a value to an alternative* (Fischer *et al.* 2000; Luce *et al.* 2003). Finally, there is uncertainty due to *incomplete information* (cf. Ross and Creyer 1992; Gunasti and Ross 2009; Wang *et al.* 2007: 202).

Uncertainty is common in all phases of the consumption process. Figure 4.1 presents one way to depict those stages, along with typical kinds of uncertainty experienced. There is no shortage of opportunities for a firm to reduce uncertainty in consumption. But why does that create value for consumers?

The demand for clarity

A commodity is valuable when a consumer perceives important benefits associated with it. At its root, such value is defined by whether the commodity is believed to serve and resolve a deeper need or personal value. Some of those needs may be functional in nature (e.g., a diet soda quenches my thirst) and some may be deeper, tied to emotions (e.g., I used to drink Coke at fun family outings). Clarity may play both roles.

To explore this, 60 adult Executive MBAs at a major Midwestern university – averaging 36.5 years of age and 15 years work experience – each read two scenarios

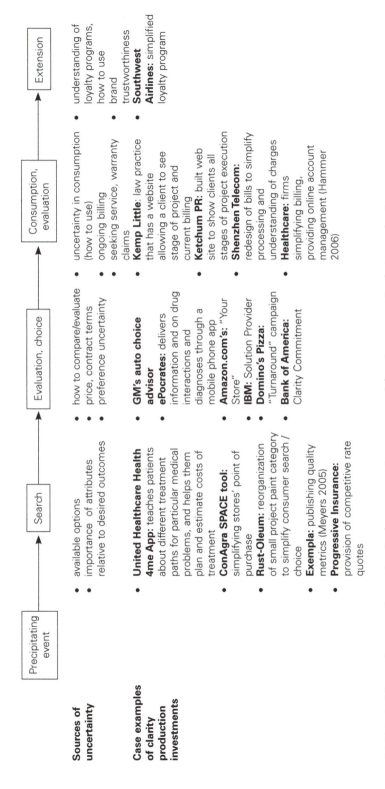

	Precipitating event	Search	Evaluation, choice	Consumption, evaluation	Extension
Sources of uncertainty		• available options • importance of attributes relative to desired outcomes	• how to compare/evaluate • price, contract terms • preference uncertainty	• uncertainty in consumption (how to use) • ongoing billing • seeking service, warranty claims	• understanding of loyalty programs, how to use • brand trustworthiness
Case examples of clarity production investments		• **United Healthcare Health 4me App:** teaches patients about different treatment paths for particular medical problems, and helps them plan and estimate costs of treatment • **ConAgra SPACE tool:** simplifying stores' point of purchase • **Rust-Oleum:** reorganization of small project paint category to simplify consumer search / choice • **Exempla:** publishing quality metrics (Meyers 2005) • **Progressive Insurance:** provision of competitive rate quotes	• **GM's auto choice advisor** • **ePocrates:** delivers information and on drug interactions and diagnoses through a mobile phone app • **Amazon.com's:** "Your Store" • **IBM:** Solution Provider • **Domino's Pizza:** "Turnaround" campaign • **Bank of America:** Clarity Commitment	• **Kemp Little:** law practice that has a website allowing a client to see stage of project and current billing • **Ketchum PR:** built web site to show clients all stages of project execution • **Shenzhen Telecom:** redesign of bills to simplify processing and understanding of charges • **Healthcare:** firms simplifying billing, providing online account management (Hammer 2006)	• **Southwest Airlines:** simplified loyalty program

FIGURE 4.1 Uncertainty at various points in the consumption process and firm investments in clarity production.

designed to reflect firms' efforts to reduce consumer uncertainty in specific stages of the consumption process. The goal was to obtain a conservative estimate of the importance of clarity and, more significantly, *why* clarity might be important to consumers. Four scenarios were used in total, each involving cases in which a consumer was considering a choice between two firms. The following clarity-producing behaviors of one of the firms were described:

- a retailer who provided customers with competitors' prices for similar goods;
- an insurance company who did a thorough job of explaining to consumers why their rates have gone up in correspondence;
- a mobile phone company which had "an exceptionally clear and even interesting billing statement" relative to its competitors;
- a plumber who called ahead to let customers know that he's on his way and then called back after the job to see if the problem had been fixed.

Based upon a laddering exercise (cf. Reynolds and Gutman 1988; Wansik 2003), we found a strong linkage between each of these customer scenarios and deeper consumer values. Respondents were asked to consider whether and why that firm's clarity-producing action might be important to them in comparing two different competitive options, and then sequentially asked why they saw value in each of the answers they gave about that value. They appeared to find the deeper values associated with each firm action fairly easily. The dominant value path for the pricing explanation and billing clarity centered on feeling *confident in the financial value* the one is getting. This sense of certainty came out consistently across these two scenarios. That almost half of all respondents mention this factor suggests strongly that *confidence* is an important driver of value. Providing competitive prices had a time-saving value that laddered up most frequently to a sense of *control*. Calling ahead on service delivery was most strongly associated with personal value coming from the belief that the service-provider is considerate and cares, ultimately associated with a sense of *respect* and *trust*. Interestingly, these values are intrinsically related to ethical marketing and, subsequently, the common good (Murphy *et al.* 2012).

For each scenario, deeper values emerged relatively simply and naturally. While based upon a small sample and an exploratory method, this evidence reinforces a simple point – there is value in clarity because it touches basic human instinct and needs. We might summarize a broader array of reasons why consumers respond positively to clarity as follows.

Cognitive value

The most robust finding concerning the value of clarity production is that people generally prefer less ambiguity and complexity to more (Acquisti and Grossklags 2005; Becker and Brownson 1964; Einhorn and Hogarth 1985). While most of these studies deal with ambiguity about gambles, there are many contexts in consumer search and decision-making in which uncertainty-reduction can produce value that has a basis in knowledge and understanding. If a firm were to provide competitive price or quality information for consumers engaged in pre-purchase search, for example, this essentially *reduces search costs* by substituting the firm's effort for search that might otherwise be undertaken by the consumer (Urbany 1986; Trifts and Häubl 2003). Beyond search efficiency, however, cognitive returns to clarity production may best be captured in *understanding*, a core human value. Providing people the reasons behind requests or actions (and, therefore, clarifying *the firm's intent*) enhances understanding and has a substantial impact on compliance (Taylor and Bower 2004; Kwong and Soman 2007; Kahneman *et al.* 1986a,b). Another explanation offered for ambiguity avoidance is that people may anticipate a *need to justify* their decisions to others or to themselves (Ellsberg 1961). The need to justify (i.e., have reasons for) decisions places a similar emphasis on the desire for understanding and being able to convey understanding to others. Further, reducing consumer uncertainty may impart a sense of *control*, which is a powerful driver of human behavior in general (cf. Langer 1975; Parker 1993; Hui and Zhou 1996) and, more specifically, in explaining ambiguity avoidance (Curley *et al.* 1986). Finally, it is possible that significant effort in seeking to provide clarity may be seen by consumers as a *signal of the firm's quality*, provided it reflects a distinctive effort relative to competitors and that the signal is bonded (Ippolito 1990; Kirmani and Rao 2000; Kirmani and Wright 1989; Kirmani 1990).

Affective value

Greater clarity may produce a sense of *empathy* and appreciation that the firm cares. Second, though, is the firm's *willingness to be open* to customers about issues and concerns, some of which may not always be flattering. There is a substantial literature in psychology regarding "self-disclosure," suggesting that even among strangers in a laboratory setting, greater disclosure of personal information produces greater liking (Collins and Miller 1994). Similarly, the willingness to share information, not all of which reflects positively on the firm has been found to positively affect trust (e.g., Anderson and Narus 1990; Anderson and Weitz 1989). It is in part this relational dimension of value that Eggert and Helm (2002) argue explains the positive impact of relationship transparency on customer satisfaction and value in business markets that they observe.

Limits on the supply of clarity

So, there are a substantial number of hard-wired forces that drive consumer interest in and perceived value of a firm's clarity production. Why, then, is the supply apparently limited? As noted at the outset, there are many markets in which the demand for clarity seems to far exceed supply. Earlier we discussed the fact that some complexity emerges naturally, out of the firm's efforts to grow. In addition, there may be a separation between firm's management and customers (and an associated limited or outdated understanding of customer needs/values). Let's consider specific aspects of how a firm may evaluate the benefits and costs of clarity production:

1   *Low expected returns from clarity production (based upon expected consumer benefits).* Managers may not see consumer uncertainty to be a problem because they don't understand decision-making effectively from the consumer's perspective. There is a fair amount of evidence that managerial estimates of customer needs and beliefs may vary significantly from true customer beliefs (Parasuraman *et al.* 1985; Hoch 1988; Davis *et al.* 1986; Urbany *et al.* 2000) due to motivational or projective biases. Camerer *et al.* (1989) find in experimental studies a "curse of knowledge" in which agents in a market who are better-informed tend to infer that less informed agents are more knowledgeable than they truly are. Camerer *et al.*, for example, find in their experiments that when traders with knowledge of market outcomes are asked to estimate the previous forecasts of less informed traders, those estimates are significantly biased by the estimators' own superior knowledge. In sum, firms may fail to appreciate consumer uncertainty because they tend to project their own knowledge on those consumers.

We should also note that the likely returns from clarity production may be discounted by two other factors. First, the firm may conjecture that any clarity-producing technology will be *imitated by competitors*, therefore neutralizing any competitive advantage. Such projections are likely the result of hindsight following a scenario in which fast competitive imitation eliminated a firm's gains from imitation, as occurred with Duracell's innovation of on-battery charge testing (Day and Reibstein 1997). Second, and consistent with GL's model described earlier, some managers may look at clarity production as a proposition in which the *consumer gains at the educating firm's expense*. In other words, it is possible that consumers take what they learn from the firm's efforts to educate them and simply use this knowledge to go out and find the best deal (see Stone and Welch 2012 for a description of this in the current case of Best Buy).

2   *High expected costs of clarity production.* It is important to note that efforts to produce clarity of the types above are costly, in part because they require investment in customer research and education, information acquisition, and technology development that are likely to be outside many firms' core competency sets. At the same time, such costs are measured and estimated with relative ease compared with measuring projected consumer benefit and response. Costs have a straightforward interpretation within the income statement and are quite vivid and concrete in decision-making. In contrast, as noted above, in executives' minds, estimates of consumer response may be fuzzy and uncertain at best (Adams *et al.* 1998; Montgomery *et al.* 2005). Further, there are costs other than financial costs at stake. In some cases, efforts to increase clarity (again, defined broadly) may actually put the firm at risk for

exposing information that reveals competitive inferiority. Such inferences may be more likely if the stated motives do not match the motives actually implied by the action (Forehand and Grier 2003). In any case, the risk of being exposed as a weaker option may be given very heavy weight in (and may prevent) the consideration of greater clarity production.

Firm investment in clarity production: Examples

Recalling Figure 4.1, many firms have undertaken significant investments in helping reduce consumer uncertainty in either providing information (e.g., United Healthcare, Progressive Insurance, Ketchum), improving the clarity of billing (Shenzhen Telecom), helping to simplify assortments (ConAgra, Rust-Oleum), or actually helping the consumer to better understand and make choices (e.g., GM's auto choice advisor, IBM/s solution provider). Further there are growing accounts of firms willing to take the risk of opening up and communicating about mistakes they have made and how they are correcting them. A case-in-point is the turnaround of Domino's Pizza after making public via You Tube customers' critical commentary about the poor quality of its pizzas and building a new strategy to successfully re-energize the business around that criticism (Restaurant Hospitality 2010). Bank of America created a new approach to communication of mortgage loan commitments with its "Clarity Commitment" in 2010. This program involves presenting mortgage terms in a simple one-page summary to ensure that the consumer receives the right loan with no surprises. The company has since extended this concept "to small business credit card accounts and Bank of America Home Loans customers, AND developing 'Investor Education' fact sheets for wealth management customers that describe investment solutions in plain language" (*Investment Weekly News* 2011).

In sum, this section has considered the value of marketing as a clarity-producing – rather than obfuscating – discipline. Consumers experience uncertainty in many stages of the consumption process. Reducing that uncertainty holds significant value for them. Despite the natural biases that firms have against clarity production (i.e., emphasizing low returns and high costs), there are numerous examples of firms in complex industries who are pursuing a clarity strategy as a way of building customer relationships and competitive advantage. The final section of the chapter considers how clarity production interacts with the common good.

Clarity and the common good

This chapter considers a paradox in the marketplace – that consumers value greater confidence and certainty, but it appears that firms often create complexity instead. While clarity production results in significant value to consumers – that value is not being translated into incentives for the firm to produce greater clarity around their products and services.[3]

In this final section, I'll consider clarity production as it relates to the common good. There are three points. First, I briefly review principles of Catholic Social

Teaching (CST) as they relate to the common good. What emerges there is the straightforward point that clarity production – in producing greater honesty and dignity in the firm–customer relationship – provides value in a way that is quite consistent with the common good. Related to this is the fact that such production requires thinking that extends beyond the firm's short-term profit objective, which many managers may not be inclined or even able to do. The second point is that there is agreement in economics and marketing about one thing: clarity production is most likely among those firms who are already judged to be superior in their categories and have the courage to put themselves up for evaluation and continuously improve to stay at the top. However, the third point raises the possibility that – like any competitive innovation that moves a market successfully – the production of clarity may be imitated.

The common good and judging the value of clarity

In a business or entrepreneurial sense, the concept of the common good encourages management to think beyond the firm's own income statement. It reflects the idea that there is not only merit and honor, but also obligation in a business' playing a part in creating a better world and society. Summarized in the principle of munificence, firms should foster a generosity of spirit in building not only value for its shareholders but also for the larger society. In their account of the virtues of work, Naughton and Laczniak (1993) quote Oswald von Nell-Breuning in articulating how the common good is reflected in the behavior of the entrepreneur who

> employs his working men for the creation of goods of true worth; . . . who offers to the consumer nothing but useful goods and services rather than, taking advantage of the latter's inexperience or weakness, betrays him into spending his money for things he does not need, or that are not only useless but even injurious to him.
>
> *(p. 988)*

Within the context of CST, the production of clarity is similarly both virtuous and an obligation. Vaccaro and Sison's (2011) recent consideration of Pope Benedict XVI's *Caritas in Veritate* notes an association "disclosing the information necessary to provide a truthful representation of a product or a service" and "respect for human dignity." These authors argue both ethical and instrumental dimensions of the importance of transparency in business, the latter capturing a firm's responsibilities to treat customers with respect, to provide information to which customers have a right, and to withhold information in the interest of privacy.

Business with an eye toward the common good requires taking a larger view of the purpose – considering not only the impact of the business on society but also how the business can participate in making a better society (Sagawa and Segal 2000; Spence and Schmidpeter 2003). This places a significant priority on respecting the dignity and fostering the development of all agents to enable them to make effective decisions. I would offer that designing the marketing mix with clarity in mind – i.e., with attention to the customer's frustrations, anxieties, and uncertainty – is very much consistent with these principles of the common good.

Yet what may be remarkable is that doing *the right thing* as an organization – i.e., behaving in a manner consistent with the common good principles of openness, respect, and preserving the dignity of others – can translate into doing *the profitable thing*. Consider three other case study examples (see Cristol and Sealey 2000; Karolefski 2010). Acura has simplified its product line by replacing fictitious sub-brand names with a more straightforward numbering system. Procter and Gamble has cut its number of hair-care stock-keeping units in half in order to simplify consumer search. ConAgra has implemented an in-store space management system based largely on making it easier for consumers to shop and choose in categories with large and complex brand assortments. Each of these efforts are variations around a theme of creating clarity for consumers by simplifying or better communicating the product line structure and enhancing their ability to choose effectively. For the various reasons reviewed earlier, such simplification creates value for consumers. Each strategy has significant risk, not the least of which is creating vulnerability to the poaching of competitors who *do not* trim their product or service lines. Yet in each case market shares and category revenues jumped, while in at least two of the cases costs went down due to smaller product lines.

So, for many reasons, clarity may have a tangible effect on consumer evaluation, choice, and, as a result, firms' outcomes. Yet, the mechanisms by which these effects occur may be quite intangible, steeped in deeper, more ephemeral consumer values. As such, the value of clarity production is difficult for managers to see and touch. As noted, there are a number of reasons why managers may be unlikely to believe that such value either exists or would influence choice/willingness-to-pay were considered. First, there is little systematic evidence regarding consumer response to organizational efforts to produce clarity. I have discussed a number of case scenarios in which firms have undertaken investments in clarity production, many with positive returns. There is a need for systematic research on how various forms of clarity production (e.g., simplifying product/service usage; billing communication, pricing presentation, openness of competitive comparisons) influence consumers' attitudinal and behavioral responses, particularly the incremental impact of these clarity dimensions on choice behavior. Second, we don't know with any rigor how executives evaluate the notion of clarity production (Vaccaro and Sison 2011; Laud and Schepers 2009). The current literature is absent evidence of managers' beliefs about consumer uncertainty when making decisions related to product variety, pricing, communications, and information disclosure.

Clarity as good strategy, but are only the best firms incented?

Clarity production can provide significant incremental gains to individual brands. Astellas' incontinence drug Vesicare experienced a significant improvement in market share in 2008 when research discovered that urologists had two misperceptions about the drug: they believed that Vesicare had equal efficacy with market leader Detrol and that Detrol had a superior program for managed care. The reality was Vesicare had *superior* efficacy (NewsRx 2008) and its managed care program was equivalent to Detrol's. An aggressive branding and communications program attacked these misperceptions and was associated with significant improvements in sales. In sum, the branding program represented the production of clarity, bringing new life to a product that in fact was the most effective on the market, and enhancing the common good.

The Vesicare case illustrates the idea that every brand has incentives to be clear about its positioning and value proposition. In fact, *that* is the goal of marketing. An exceptional product (i.e., of "true worth") that is not articulated effectively for the marketplace can be argued to be a net loss to society. Are there, however, limits to the gains that might be produced for brands from clarity production?

On this matter, an interesting parallel exists between the modeling of consumer confusion from the economists (e.g., Gabaix and Laibson 2004 (GL)) and the work more recently of the advocates for consumer advocacy in helping consumer decision-making (Urban 2004, 2005; Cristol and Sealey 2000). Recall that GL conclude that firms have no long-term incentive to reduce complexity – i.e., it is optimal to create some level of confusion among consumers. At the other extreme is Urban's work (2005) which suggests just the opposite – i.e., that in the forthcoming age of open information-sharing and comparison via the internet, firms should seek to be completely open and helpful to consumers in facilitating their decision-making. While these perspectives are diametrically opposed, Urban and GL have complete agreement on one thing: there is or will be a strong association between being the best in your category and driving out complexity (with slightly different causal logics). GL suggest that being the best creates incentives for the firm to keep complexity low. In their words, the model leads to the conclusion that "the firms with the highest extrinsic quality choose to produce the least excess confusion" (p. 22). Urban's (2005) conclusion is the same, but presumes a dynamic that is put into motion once a firm *commits to* a policy of clarity and openness. Urban notes that "If a company embraces honesty, it must have good, if not the best, products. With transparency, this is the only way to earn the customer's purchase" (p. 157).

In testament to the expectations of both GL and Urban, Eskildsen and Kristensen (2007) explore the role of transparency in explaining patterns in the satisfaction index managed by several European agencies (EPSI). The model for EPSI holds that consumer perceived value is driven by four dimensions of satisfaction (image, expectations, product quality, service quality), and that *perceived value drives overall satisfaction*, which then determines *customer loyalty*. The authors suggest that transparency (the perceived openness of the firm in sharing information with consumers) may add significantly to the explanation of perceived value. Eskildsen and Kristensen (2007) find a very strong effect of their transparency measure on perceived value, after accounting for the effects of the other predictors. More importantly, the analysis for both banks and mobile phones revealed in each industry a single firm which anchored the "high transparency, high perceived quality" position in the industry, with all other firms clustered at lower combinations of the two variables (in the supermarket industry, the firms were less clustered and more evenly distributed). The study indicates both a strong effect of transparency on value and the fact that there does appear to be a clear incentive for only the best firm in a market to be differentially open and transparent. The implications for the common good are mixed. All consumers benefit when firms collectively pursue to produce effective products/services and seek to be open about it. Once one firm consciously decides to emphasize clarity production, one of two outcomes is plausible: (a) a competitive dynamic may occur in which all firms are compelled to both improve quality and be more open, or (b) a distribution of quality forms, where different quality levels appeal to different consumer segments who vary both in their attentiveness to quality and information and their desire to pay lower prices (as a trade-off for more uncertain quality). The common good is well-served by outcome (a); whether outcome (b) is problematic depends upon whether the leading firms' efforts to be more open affect the average level of quality in the market.

In sum, the question for the common good is whether efforts to produce clarity have the potential to become competitively contagious. Some casual empiricism in the auto insurance industry gives an indication of how this issue might be examined. In 1995, the property and casualty industry's score on the American Customer Satisfaction Index was 75. Progressive Insurance's rise to national prominence began shortly before that time, as it began providing competitive price quotes to customers initially by phone and then via its web page. Today, the industry's ACSI score is 83. That 8-point rise is exceeded only by the 10-point rise in limited service restaurants (McDonald's, Subway, etc.) for industries represented in the full 1995–2012 period.[4] While there is no way of knowing how much of that effect is attributable to Progressive's competitive price clarity strategy, there is other research which suggests it was likely significant. In other contexts there has been observed a move to more competitive industry outcomes in which firms give in to a certain momentum caused by better consumer information (or at least caused by their expectations). This occurred in response to the Nutritional Labeling and Education Act (NLEA) (see Moorman 1998), as well as in response to several studies examining the effects of the publishing of competitive retail grocery store prices (exemplified by Boynton *et al.* 1983). It is possible that such momentum is starting to surface in several industries, leading some to foretell a coming "age of transparency."

Conclusion

[I]n this age of transparency . . . organizations must tell the truth, be considerate of the interests of others and be willing to be held accountable for delivering against their commitments.

(Tapscott and Williams 2011, p. 36)

This chapter is the start of a conversation about the tension between consumers' drive for greater confidence and certainty in their consumption lives and firms' incentives to act in a way that creates complexity and confusion at times (whether intentional or not). It is not easy for an individual firm or brand manager to snap fingers and commence a program to reduce complexity – it goes against a very strong tide of instinctive growth through variety and price differentiation. At some point, however, that tide goes against both firm and societal interest. The world is changing, and consumer demand for clarity is beginning to reveal itself. Interestingly, the quote immediately above was not pulled from a Papal Encyclical or an academic treatise in an ethics journal. It came from a trade publication in which a couple of practitioners were urging financial executives to mend their confusing ways. These authors made no mention of the common good; we can be sure that they were cheerleading the target audience to greater profitability. But this is a very clear example of a coming age in which the inherent bond between doing what's right and being profitable is itself gaining clarity.

Notes

1 The term barrow boy refers to a peddler of fruits and vegetables from a wheelbarrow in English villages. Source: *Cambridge Dictionary Online*, http://dictionary.cambridge.org/dictionary/british/barrow-boy.
2 Our focus here is on the value to consumers of *reducing* their uncertainty. We should note, however, current literature which finds that consumers under some circumstances place positive value when firms increase uncertainty (see Brashers 2001; Goldsmith and Amir 2010; Lee and Qiu 2009).
3 It is instructive to note that a brilliant book called *Simplicity Marketing* (Cristol and Sealey 2000) lays out a very interesting framework for precisely how organizations can simplify by replacing simpler for more complex marketing mixes. It is noteworthy that the book was published over 10 years ago and appears to have had limited impact on firm practice.
4 Other industries in the survey for the entire 17-year period include airlines (score of 67 in 2012, −2 points vs. 1995), consumer shipping (82, +1), fixed-line telephone service (70, −11), hospitals (76, +2), motion pictures (76, −1), US Postal Service (75, +6).

References

Acquisti, A. and Grossklags, J. (2005) "Uncertainty, ambiguity and privacy," working paper: Heinz School of Public Policy and Management, Carnegie-Mellon University, pp. 1–21.

Adams, M., Day, G.S., and Dougherty, D. (1998) "Enhancing new product development performance: an organizational learning perspective," *Journal of Product Innovation Management*, 15: 403–22.

Anderson, E. and Weitz, B. (1989) "Determinants of continuity in conventional industrial channel dyads," *Marketing Science*, 4 (Fall): 310–24.

Anderson, J.C. and Narus, J.A. (1990) "A model of distributor firm and manufacturer firm working partnerships," *Journal of Marketing*, 54 (January), 42–58.

Ariely, D. (2009) *Predictably Irrational, Revised and Expanded Edition: The Hidden Forces That Shape Our Decisions*, New York: Harper Collins.

Babrow, A.S. (1992) "Communication and problematic integration: understanding diverging probability and value, ambiguity, ambivalence, and impossibility," *Communication Theory*, 2 (May): 95–130.

——, Kasch, C., and Ford, L. (1998) "The many meanings of uncertainty in illness: towards a systematic accounting," *Health Communication*, 10, 1–23.

Banyard, P. (2001) "Confusion marketing," *Credit Management*, (April), 32–33.

Becker S.W. and Brownson, F.O. (1964) "What price ambiguity? Or the role of ambiguity in decision making," *Journal of Political Economy*, 72: 62–73.

Bennett, D. (2009) "Transparency efforts evolve to include total cost of services," *Managed Healthcare Executive*, 19 (February), 27–28.

Bettman, J.R. (1979) *An Information Processing Theory of Choice*, New York: Addison-Wesley Publishing Company.

Boulding, W., Chapman Moore, M., Staelin, R., Corfman, K.P., Dickson, P.R., Fitzsimons, G. (1994) "Understanding managers' strategic decision-making process," *Marketing Letters*, 5 (4), 413–26.

Boynton, R.D., Blake, B.F., and Uhl, J.N. (1983) "Retail price reporting effects in local food markets," *American Journal of Agricultural Economics*, (February), 20–29.

Bradford, D.K. (2005) "Information and insurance: The power of transparency," *Financial Executive,* (January/February): 40–41.

Brashers, D. (2001) "Communication and uncertainty management," *Journal of Communication*, (September): 477–97.

Camerer, C.F., Lowenstein, G., and Weber, M. (1989) "The curse of knowledge in economic settings: experimental analysis," *Journal of Political Economy*, 97 (5): 1232–54.

Carlin, B. (2006) "Strategic price complexity in retail financial markets," *Journal of Financial Economics*, 91 (March): 278–87.

Christensen, C.M., Cook, S., and Hall, T. (2005) "It's the purpose brand, stupid," *The Wall Street Journal*, (November 29): B2.

Collins, N.L. and Miller, L.C. (1994) "Self-disclosure and liking: A meta-analytic review," *Psychological Bulletin*, 116 (3): 457–75.

Cristol, S.M. and Sealey, P. (2000) *Simplicity Marketing: End Brand Complexity, Clutter, and Confusion*, New York: Free Press.

Crosetto, P. and Gaudeul, A. (2012) "Do consumers prefer offers that are easy to compare? An experimental investigation," working paper: Friedrich Schiller University.

Curley, S.P., Yates, F., and Abrams, R.A. (1986) "Psychological sources of ambiguity avoidance," *Organizational Behavior and Human Decision Processes*, 38, 230–56.

Daft, R.L. and Weick, K.E. (1984) "Toward a model of organizations as interpretation systems," *Academy of Management Review*, 9 (2), 284–95.

D'Aveni, R.A. (1995) *Hypercompetition*, New York: The Free Press.

Davis, H.L., Hoch, S.J., and Easton Ragsdale, E.K. (1986) "An anchoring and adjustment model of spousal predictions," *Journal of Consumer Research*, 13 (1), 25.

Day, G.S. and Moorman, C. (2010), *Strategy from the Outside In*, New York: McGraw-Hill.

—— and Nedungadi, P. (1994) "Managerial representations of competitive advantage," *Journal of Marketing*, 58 (2): 31–44.

—— and Reibstein, D.J. (1997) "The dynamic challenges for theory and practice," in *Wharton on Dynamic Competitive Strategy*, New York: John Wiley & Sons, pp. 1–18.

Dickson, P.R. (1992) "Toward a general theory of competitive rationality," *Journal of Marketing*, 56 (1), 69–83.

—— (1997) "Positioning strategy," in *Marketing Management*, Fort Worth, TX: Dryden.

Eggert, A. and Helm, S. (2002) "Exploring the impact of relationship transparency on business relationships: A cross-sectional study among purchasing managers in Germany," *Industrial Marketing Management*, 32: 101–08.

Einhorn, H.J. and Hogarth, R.M. (1985) "Ambiguity and uncertainty in probabilistic inference," *Psychological Review*, 92 (4): 433–61.

Ellison, G. and Ellison, S.F. (2009) "Search, obfuscation, and price elasticities on the internet," *Econometrica*, 77: 427.

Ellsberg, D. (1961) "Risk, ambiguity and the savage axioms," *Quarterly Journal of Economics*, LXXV: 643–69.

Eskildsen, J. and Kristensen, K. (2007) "Customer satisfaction – the role of transparency," *Total Quality Management*, 18 (January-March): 39–47.

Fischer, G.W., Luce, M.F., and Jia, J. (2000) "Attribute conflict and preference uncertainty: effects on judgment time and error," *Management Science*, 46 (January): 88–103.

Forehand, M.R. and Grier, S. (2003) "When is honesty the best policy? The effect of stated company intent on consumer skepticism," *Journal of Consumer Psychology*, 13 (3): 349–56.

Gabaix, X. and Laibson, D. (2004) "Competition and consumer confusion," working paper, Cambridge: Harvard Business School.

—— (2006) "Shrouded attributes, consumer myopia, and information suppression in competitive markets," *The Quarterly Journal of Economics*, 121 (2): 505–40.

Goddard, J. and Eccles, T. (2012) *Uncommon Sense; Common Nonsense*, London: Profile Books.

Goldsmith, K. and Amir, O. (2010) "Can uncertainty improve promotions?" *Journal of Marketing Research*, XLVII (December): 1070–77.

Gunasti, K. and Ross, W.T., Jr. (2009) "How inferences about missing attributes decrease the tendency to defer choice and increase purchase probability," *Journal of Consumer Research*, 35 (5), 823.

Hammer, D.C. (2006) "Adapting customer service to consumer-directed health care," *Healthcare Financial Management*, 60 (September) (9): 118–22.

Hansen, F. (1972) *Consumer Choice Behavior: A Cognitive Theory*, New York: Free Press.

Häubl, G., Benedict, G.C.D., and Usta, M. (2007) "Ironic effects of personalized product recommendations on subjective consumer decision outcomes," working paper, School of Business, University of Alberta.

Heath, C. and Heath, D. (2007) *Made to Stick: Why Some Ideas Survive and Others Die*, New York: Random House.

—— (2010) *Switch: How to Change Things When Change Is Hard*, New York: Broadway Books.

Hoch, S.J. (1988) "Who do we know: predicting the interests and opinions of the American consumer," *Journal of Consumer Research*, 15 (December), 315–24.

—— and Ha, Y.W. (1986) "Consumer learning: advertising and the ambiguity of product experience," *Journal of Consumer Research*, 13 (September): 221–32.

Huang, R. (2012) "'Confusion marketing' prevalent in some IT sales," online: www.zdnet.com/ confusion-marketing-prevalent-in-some-it-sales-2062304362/ (accessed October 17, 2012).

Huber, G.P. (1991) "Organizational learning: The contributing processes and the literatures," *Organization Science*, 2 (1): 88–115.

Hübner, A.H. and Kuhn, H. (2012) "Retail category management: state-of-the-art review of quantitative research and software applications in assortment and shelf space management," *Omega*, 40 (2): 199–209.

Hui, M.K and Zhou, L. (1996) "How does waiting duration information influence customers' reactions to waiting for services?" *Journal of Applied Social Psychology*, 26 (19): 1702–17.

Investment Weekly News (2011) "Bank of America releases first corporate social responsibility report," July 30.

Ippolito, P.M. (1990) "Bonding and nonbonding signals of product quality," *Journal of Business*, 63 (1): 41–60.

Jolly, J.P., Reynolds, T.J., and Slocum, J.W., Jr., (1988) "Application of the means-end theoretic for understanding the cognitive bases of performance appraisal," *Organizational Behavior and Human Decision Processes*, 41: 153–79.

Jonas, E., Schulz-Hardt, S. Frey, D., and Thelen, N. (2001) "Confirmation bias in sequential information search after preliminary decisions: An expansion of dissonance theoretical research on selective exposure to information," *Journal of Personality and Social Psychology*, 80 (4): 557–71.

Kahn, B.E. and Sarin, R.K. (1988), "Modeling ambiguity in decisions under uncertainty," *Journal of Consumer Research*, 15 (2), 265–65.

Kahneman, D., Knetsch, J.L., and Thaler, R.H. (1986a) "Fairness and the assumptions of economics," *The Journal of Business*, 4 (October): IS285.

—— (1986b) "Fairness as a constraint on profit seeking: Entitlements in the market," *American Economic Review*, 76 (September): 728–41.

Kaiser Network Daily Reports (2005) "Los Angeles Times examines consumer-driven plans' lack of information on prices," December 13.

Kalayci, K. and Potters, J. (2011) "Buyer confusion and market prices," *International Journal of Industrial Organization*, 29 (January): 14–22.

Karolefski, J. (2010) "Simplifying product assortment leads to more efficiency, sales for Conagra Foods," *CPG Matters*, online: www.cpgmatters.com/CategoryManagement0410.html (accessed October 17, 2012).

Kirmani, A. (1990) "The effect of perceived advertising costs on brand perceptions," *Journal of Consumer Research*, 17 (September): 160–71.

—— and Wright, P. (1989) "Money talks: Perceived advertising expense and expected product quality," *Journal of Consumer Research*, 16 (December): 344–53.

Kocyigit, O. and Ringle, C. (2011) "The impact of brand confusion on sustainable brand satisfaction and private label proneness: a subtle decay of brand equity," *Journal of Brand Management*, 3 (December): 195–212.

Kwong, J. and Soman, D. (2007) "Processing fluency and the decision to spend loyalty program points," Hong Kong: The Chinese University of Hong Kong.

Langer, E.J. (1975) "The illusion of control," *Journal of Personality and Social Psychology*, 32: 311–28.

Lanzetta, J.T. (1963) "Information acquisition in decision-making," in O.J. Harvey (ed.) *Motivation and Social Interaction-Cognitive Determinants*, New York: Ronald Press, pp. 239–65.

Laud, R.L. and Schepers, D.H. (2009) "Beyond transparency: information overload and a model for intelligibility," *Business and Society Review*, 114: 365–91.

Lee, Y.H. and Qiu, C. (2009) "When uncertainty brings pleasure: The role of prospect imageability and mental imagery," *Journal of Consumer Research*, 36 (4): 624.

Lipshitz, R. and Strauss, O. (1997) "Coping with uncertainty: a naturalistic decision-making analysis," *Organizational Behavior and Human Decision Processes*, 69 (February): 149–63.

Luce, M.F., Jia, J., and Fischer, G.W. (2003) "How much do you like it? Within alternative conflict and subjective confidence in consumer judgments," *Journal of Consumer Research*, 3 (December): 464–72.

Markard, J. and Holt, E. (2003) "Disclosure of electricity products – lessons from consumer research as guidance for energy policy," *Energy Policy*, 31: 1459–74.

Martinez, S. (2007) "The U.S. food marketing system: Recent developments, 1997–2006," Washington, DC: United States Department of Agriculture Economic Research Service.

Meyers, S. (2005) "The road to transparency," *Trustee*, 58 (5): 18–22.

Miller, D. and Friesen, P.H. (1980) "Momentum and revolution in organizational adaptation," *Academy of Management Journal*, 23 (December): 591–614.

Montgomery, D.B., Moore, M.C., and Urbany, J.E. (2005) "Reasoning about competitive reactions: Evidence from executives," *Marketing Science*, 24 (1): 138–49.

Moorman, C. (1998) "Market-level effects of information: competitive responses and consumer dynamics," *Journal of Marketing Research*, 35 (February), 82–98.

Murphy, P.E., Laczniak, G.R., and Prothero, A. (2012) *Ethics in Marketing: International Cases and Perspectives*, London: Routledge.

Naughton, M. and Laczniak, G.R. (1993) "A theological context of work from the Catholic social encyclical tradition," *Journal of Business Ethics*, 12 (December): 981–94.

NewsRx (2008) "Incontinence; Astellas/GlaxoSmithKline's Vesicare has advantages over Pfizer's Detrol LA/Detrusitol XL in reducing episodes of urge urinary incontinence," *Drug Week* (April 18), online: http://www.newsrx.com/health-articles/934342.html (accessed October 17, 2012).

Nordqvist, S. and Gay, E. (2011) "Vodafone 'sorry' for misleading ads," online: www.nzherald.co.nz/technology/news/article.cfm?c_id=5&objectid=10744578 (accessed October 17, 2012).

Parasuraman, A., Zeithaml, V.A., and Berry, L.L. (1985) "A conceptual model of service quality and its implications for future research," *Journal of Marketing*, 49 (Fall): 41–50.

Parker, L. (1993) "When to fix it and when to leave: relationships among perceived control, self-efficacy, dissent, and exit," *Journal of Applied Psychology*, 78 (December): 949–59.

Rankin, D. (2004) "Simplicity and transparency: returning from the land of the bland," *Journal of Financial Services Marketing*, 9 (2): 172–78.

Restaurant Hospitality (2010) "Lessons from the Domino's turnaround," *Restaurant Hospitality*, 94 (6) (June): 30–3.

Reynolds, T.J. and Gutman, J. (1988) "Laddering theory, method, analysis and interpretation," *Journal of Advertising Research*, 28 (1), 445–61.

Ross, W.T., Jr., and Creyer, E.H. (1992) "Making inferences about missing information: the effects of existing information," *Journal of Consumer Research*, 19 (June): 14–25.

Sagawa, S. and Segal, E. (2000) "Common interest, common good: Creating value through business and social sector partnerships," *California Management Review*, 42 (Winter): 105–22.

Scott, J. (2004) "Ethics, governance, trust, transparency, and customer relations," *The Geneva Papers on Risk and Insurance*, 29 (January): 45–51.

Shafir, E., Simonson, I., and Tversky, A. (1993) "Reason-based choice," *Cognition*, 49 (October–November): 11–36.

Sonsino, D., Benzion, U., and Mador, G. (2002) "The complexity effects on choice with uncertainty – experimental evidence," *The Economic Journal*, 112 (October): 936–65.

Spence, L.J. and Schmidpeter, R. (2003) "SMEs, social capital and the common good," *Journal of Business Ethics*, 45 (June): 93–108.

Spiegler, R. (2006) "Competition over agents with boundedly rational expectations," *Theoretical Economics*, 1: 207–31.

Stone, B. and Welch, D. (2012) "The future retail wasteland," *Business Week*, April 12.

Sullivan, M. (2012) "It's not your eyes . . . The fine print is getting really, really small," *The Wall Street Journal*, January 15.

Tapscott, D. and Williams, A.D. (2011) "The age of transparency," *Financial Executive*, 27 (4): 34–40.

Taylor, V.A. and Bower, A. (2004) "Improving product instruction compliance: 'If you tell me why, I might comply'," *Psychology and Marketing*, 21 (March): 229–45.

Thaler, R.H. and Sunstein, C.R. (2008) *Nudge: Improving Decisions About Health, Wealth, and Happiness*, New York: Penguin Books.

Trifts, V. and Häubl, G. (2003) "Information availability and consumer preference: Can online retailers benefit from providing access to competitor price information?" *Journal of Consumer Psychology*, 13 (1&2): 149–59.

Tversky, A. and Shafir, E. (1992) "Choice under conflict: the dynamics of deferred decision," *Psychological Science*, 3 (November), 358–61.

Urban, G.L. (2005) "Customer advocacy: A new era in marketing?" *Journal of Public Policy & Marketing*, 24 (1): 155–59.

—— (2006) "Customer advocacy: A new paradigm for marketing?" in J.N. Sheth and R.S. Sisodia (eds) *Does Marketing Need Reform?* Armonk, NY: M.E. Sharpe, pp. 119–25.

Urbany, J.E. (1986) "An experimental examination of the economics of information," *Journal of Consumer Research*, 13 (September) (2): 257–63.

—— , Dickson, P.R., and Wilkie, W.L. (1989), "Buyer uncertainty and information search," *Journal of Consumer Research*, 16 (September), 208–16.

——, Dickson, P.R., and Sawyer, A.G. (2000) "Insights into cross- and within-store price search: Retailer estimates vs. consumer self-reports," *Journal of Retailing*, 76 (Summer), 243–56.

Vaccaro, A., Sison, A.J.G. (2011) "Transparency in business: The perspective of Catholic Social Teaching and the 'Caritas in Veritate'," *Journal of Business Ethics*, 100 (March): 17–27.

Van Weegen, J., Van den Brande, P., and Verheijden, P. (2012) "The insurance challenge: Managing complexity," online: www.atkearney.com/index.php/Publications/the-insurance-challenge-managing-complexity.html (accessed October 17, 2012).

Wang, T., Venkatesh, R., and Chatterjee, R. (2007) "Reservation price as a range: An incentive-compatible measurement approach," *Journal of Marketing Research*, 44 (May): 200–13.

Wansik, B. (2003) "Using laddering to understand and leverage a brand's equity," *Qualitative Market Research*, 6 (2): 111–118.

5

HOW MARKETING SERVES THE COMMON GOOD

A long-term consumer perspective

John F. Gaski and Michael J. Etzel

This chapter tells the story of a consumer research and data collection odyssey culminating in a satisfaction measure, provided by consumers, representing marketing's overall performance *for* consumers. After the conceptual and methodological essentials of the project are described, a review of over a quarter-century of results yields meaning for the present and future of the institution of marketing. The findings are rather equivocal, but pregnant with societal import. The chapter's concluding section offers these derived implications for the relation between marketing practice and the "common good." One fair interpretation: The field of marketing appears to deserve at least a grade of "I" for improvement.

Virtually every contemporary definition of the institution of marketing incorporates three elements. The first is the function: a system of business activities designed to plan, price, promote, and distribute products. The other two are goals: that the buyers of those products be satisfied, while the objectives of the organization undertaking the marketing are achieved (Etzel *et al.* 2007: 6).

Clearly, if customers are satisfied and organizations are successful, society benefits and the common good, at least as construed within the commercial realm, is accomplished. Although organizational objectives, such as a particular level of sales or profit, may be precisely prescribed and their achievement assessed, the notion of what constitutes customer satisfaction and how it should be determined raises many questions (Oliver 1980). For example, what level of customer satisfaction with marketing is desirable or sufficient? What is the subjective texture of that satisfaction? And, given that marketing consists of several activities, which factors most determine a customer's overall satisfaction?

Occasionally over the decades, the marketing literature has featured reports of panoramic, omnibus studies of the American consumer's collective assessment of the performance of the institution of marketing. Hustad and Pessemier (1973), Lundstrom and Lamont (1976), Barksdale *et al.* (1976), Barksdale and Darden

(1972), and Fornell *et al.* (1996) have produced somewhat mixed indications of the efficacy of marketing practice, mainly in terms of public perception. Despite the uneven findings, the continuing interest in a subject so fundamental to our conceptualization of marketing, as well as our relationship with that business function, is understandable. Gauging an institution's broad impact on the surrounding social milieu is a worthy interpretation of the task of capturing its effects on the common good – and is that not the ultimate societal value for any institution?

Given this background and orientation, our project's objective was to improve on the quality of measurement in this ongoing stream of research into marketing practice. We developed a thoroughly validated multi-item scale designed to measure overall consumer sentiment toward marketing via assessment of the individual outputs of the practice of marketing, i.e., the "four p's" commonly referred to as the marketing mix: product, price, promotion, and distribution.[1] The measure is known as the Notre Dame–Socratic Technologies *Index of Consumer Sentiment toward Marketing* (ICSM). The one minor presumption involved is that consumer sentiment toward these marketing indicia is a fair, rough proxy for the actual performance of marketing in the sense of providing societal outcomes *qua* human satisfaction.

The study has produced results that may disappoint some, especially those who view unalloyed customer satisfaction as the sole hallmark of successful marketing. On the other hand, the results, among their substantive lessons, invite examination of the satisfaction construct beyond simple recognition of its desirability.

Method

Appendix A presents the questionnaire items used to measure the four elements of American consumer sentiment toward marketing. The primary ways consumers come into contact with marketing are experiences with products, prices, advertising, and retailers. These relations correspond – approximately – to the commonly accepted elements of marketing management previously mentioned: product, price, promotion, and distribution. Thus, the ICSM measure is composed of four multi-item Likert scales, each reflecting one of the elements of marketing as it is experienced by consumers.[2]

Item creation, pre-testing, and purification details were reported at the outset of the research (Gaski and Etzel 1986). Substantially expanded validation, employing two decades of data and 27,146 total observations, was reported in Gaski (2008). Calculation of the separate component measures for product, price, promotion, and distribution involves adding the scores within each of the four elements, and weighting each element by a self-reported importance measure (five-point scale, "Not at all important"–"Extremely important" to the consumer respondent). Formally, an individual's consumer sentiment score is determined by summing the four weighted elements, or

$$\sum_{j=1}^{n} \left(w_j \sum_{i=1}^{m} x_{ij} \right)$$

with

x_{ij} = scale item response i in category (marketing element) j,
w_j = importance weight for the marketing element category j,
m = number of items in marketing element category (5), and
n = number of marketing element categories (4).

Individual scores are then summed *across* respondents and averaged to produce a mean for the entire sample. Annual mean scores are converted to index numbers with 1984 serving as the baseline to facilitate longitudinal analysis.[3]
   To illustrate, a hypothetical score of *12* (out of the range of −200 to +200) for an individual might be produced as follows. First, a product component score is calculated: The possible range of scores for product (or any of the four components) is −50 to +50, achieved by initially summing the individual's responses on the five product items, each with a range of −2 to +2. Assume our hypothetical consumer's five product scale responses are 0, 0, 2, 1, and −1. These are summed (2 in this case), and then multiplied by the consumer's reported importance for product, which has a range of 1-5. Assume next that this consumer's importance score for product is 3. The result then is 3 × 2 or 6. This is repeated for the individual's price, promotion, and distribution measures. That is, the scores on the five items for each dimension are summed and then multiplied by that element's importance weight. Assuming scores for price (−8), promotion (4), and distribution (10), when these are added to the product score (6), the individual's overall sentiment or satisfaction score equals 12. (Again, the arithmetic mean of all such individual scores, across respondents from the sample of consumers for a given year, provides the annual raw aggregate number which serves as basis for the year's ICSM index number.)

Data collection: Sampling

Survey administration has taken place every February–March since the pilot pre-test of 1983 and first full sample of 1984, except for a two-year hiatus in 2007–08 when data collection was transitioning from the original to the current professional provider. Since 2009 the ICSM scale has been administered by e-mail to a nation-wide US consumer sample by the San Francisco research firm, Socratic Technologies. Previously, the project used a sample drawn from the national consumer mail panel of Synovate (formerly Market Facts, Inc.), the ninth largest market research organization in the world and fifth largest custom research supplier in the United States. In the initial Socratic data collection, mail survey was also done, so aggregate scores from the different modes of administration could be reconciled to eliminate the presence of a method factor. In other words, post-2008 data have been adjusted to be interpretable on a consistent basis with the previous data set.
   The actual annual sample typically comprises 1,000 male and 1,000 female heads of households, and usable response rates have ranged from 49.5 percent

(Y2004) to 72.2 percent (Y1987). (In addition to the described ingredients of the focal sentiment measure, various demographics were also gathered annually via the questionnaire.) Including the most recent data collection of 2011 and the original pilot study, therefore, a 29-year period, 1983-2011 inclusive, is captured by the study's longitudinal duration. Total number of cases is now over 30,000.

For such an extensive and enduring national polling effort, the long-term *pro bono* involvement of leading research services has been an invaluable asset. The authors express appreciation to steadfast data partners Market Facts, Synovate, and especially now Socratic Technologies for their commitment to the project, as well as to the Mendoza College of Business of the University of Notre Dame for its material support.

Results

The basic trend of the ICSM results, as seen in Table 5.1 and Figure 5.1, is positive. US consumer sentiment toward marketing is improving, having recently inverted from a negative to a slightly positive value. Moreover, the changes over time have generally been found to be statistically significant (Gaski and Etzel 2005: 860; Gaski 2008: 202-204). Table 5.1 reports the annual raw ICSM sentiment scores expressed as mean across respondents for each year, then the same converted to an index number, followed by raw mean scores for each component of the sentiment scale. Figure 5.1 portrays the basic information of the first two columns graphically.

Concerning the absolute level of sentiment revealed, the ICSM annual average score has indeed moved into the positive range. Yet the mean score from the sample surveys has always remained very near the neutral point within the range of possible scores from −200 to +200 on the weighted 20-item instrument. Although this appears to indicate an indifferent or apathetic consumer attitude toward marketing, most psychometricians are skeptical that a subjective human response at the neutral midpoint of a questionnaire scale necessarily represents an exactly neutral feeling. The positive trend is the bigger story, but at least there is no hard evidence from the research project that American consumers presently have a negative view of the practice of marketing as they experience it.

Regarding the four elements of marketing, consumer sentiment is more favorable toward products and the retail service experience (how distribution is typically manifested to the consumer) than it is toward the other two elements, price and advertising (Table 5.1; cf. Gaski and Etzel 2005: 862; Gaski 2008: 203-05). Naturally, it is human nature for no consumer to ever like any price (above zero) very much, and advertising, because of its omnipresent annoyance factor, suffers a predictable fate in terms of negative attitudes. Our results do bolster a prevailing impression of advertising's relatively poor public image, although that, too, is improving.

One other (non-)finding that has remained consistent throughout the term of the project is that demographics do not relate very strongly to the ICSM.

TABLE 5.1 Index of Consumer Sentiment toward Marketing and its components, 1984-2011

Year	ICSM score[a]	Index[b]	Product	Price	Advertising	Retail service
1984	−14.9	100	−5.1	−15.9	−2.0	8.0
1985	−14.3	100.33	−4.6	−14.3	−2.1	6.9
1986	−13.1	100.97	−4.0	−15.0	−1.7	7.3
1987	−11.2	102.03	−3.2	−13.3	−1.2	6.9
1988	−13.1	100.98	−4.2	−13.3	−1.2	5.7
1989	−14.7	100.09	−4.0	−14.2	−2.3	5.3
1990	−14.7	100.14	−3.8	−14.3	−2.5	6.3
1991	−13.6	100.7	−2.9	−14.2	−2.5	5.8
1992	−12.4	101.38	−2.3	−13.7	−3.1	6.3
1993	−8.9	103.26	−1.7	−12.2	−2.3	7.6
1994	−10.3	102.47	−2.2	−12.6	−2.4	7.2
1995	−8	103.76	−0.4	−11.9	−2.7	6.8
1996	−7.5	104.01	−0.8	−12.1	−2.5	7.4
1997	−7.9	103.79	0.0	−12.7	−2.6	7.4
1998	−8	103.75	−0.6	−11.4	−2.4	6.7
1999	−8.4	103.5	−0.4	−10.9	−2.3	5.3
2000	−6.7	104.46	0.6	−11.2	−1.9	5.9
2001	−4.5	105.62	1	−9.6	−2	6.1
2002	−6	104.81	0.2	−9.5	−2.3	5.6
2003	−5.7	104.99	0.9	−9.8	−2.7	5.8
2004	−7.3	104.09	0.5	−10	−2.7	5.1
2005	−5.1	105.29	1.6	−9.9	−2.9	6.1
2006	−7.1	104.18	0.4	−10.5	−3.0	5.6
2007[c]						
2008						
2009	0.4	103.63	0.7	−1.4	−3.6	4.7
2010	4.2	105.60	1.9	−5.4	−0.2	7.9
2011	5.5	106.28	1.9	−5.4	0.01	9.0

Notes:

[a] ICSM score is the raw sum of the four components, each weighted by perceived importance. Possible range is −200 to +200.

[b] Index is a conversion of raw ICSM score based on 1984 = 100.

[c] Data were not collected in 2007 and 2008.

No patterns have been found on the basis of age, income, education, household size, or geographic region (Gaski 2008: 206-10). Males, however, have a slightly more negative reaction to marketing than females do (Gaski and Etzel 1986: 76; Gaski 2008: 206).

A significant and maybe novel finding from supplementary data analysis (not shown) is that the ICSM relates significantly to the US national crime rate

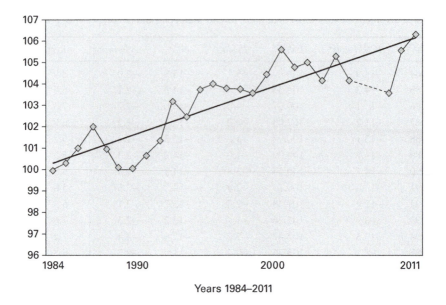

FIGURE 5.1 Index of Consumer Sentiment toward Marketing, 1984–2011.

Note: highest index score, 106.28 in Y2011 (5.5 raw score); lowest index score, 100 in Y1984 (–14.9 raw score).

(Gaski 2008: 210-211). After quasi-testing different causal orderings through various time lags, the ICSM was found to relate as inverse antecedent to the national crime rate ($-.533 \leq r \leq -.454; p \leq .05$). Although one might infer that a better consumer mood about marketing leads to a lesser need for criminal behavior, this result may not be subject to facile explanation.

Finally, two, but only two, macroeconomic variables do seem to have a significant relation with the ICSM: inflation and the national saving rate. With variables lagged appropriately to be consistent with a *macroeconomic conditions → consumer sentiment* causal sequence, we find that more inflation and *higher* saving depress US consumer sentiment (Gaski and Etzel 2005: 862). Evidently, American consumers are happier with the practice of marketing when they are spending, not saving. No wonder the US saving rate is so low! (Economic aggregates and indices not found to relate to the ICSM are real GDP, per capita real GDP, disposable personal income, unemployment, and the S&P 500 index.)

A possible curiosity of note is that the ICSM correlates non-significantly with two other prominent consumer sentiment measures, the University of Michigan Survey Research Center's *Index of Consumer Sentiment* and the Fornell *et al.* (1996) *American Customer Satisfaction Index* (ACSI; see Gaski and Etzel 2005: 862). The former is more of a macroeconomic barometer, of course, so the divergence is not too surprising. The ACSI is a general consumer satisfaction measure, but focuses on product instead of the whole marketing mix, as does the ICSM.

Conclusion

The ICSM project fulfills the authors' original aim of providing the field of marketing with a validated, global, longitudinal indicator of how the institution of marketing is faring in the eyes of the US public. The short answer is: not badly, certainly much better than the negative stereotype and caricature that has been hurled at marketing from some quarters over the years (e.g., Packard 1957). And the degree of improvement in the ICSM score since 1983/84 covers 5.1 percent (20.4 points) of the possible range of the scale, thereby denoting the magnitude of change.[4]

Still, marketing as an institution can be concerned that its popularity is not greater. There is probably a natural limit on the upside of consumer sentiment assessments, given the age-old "economic problem" of unlimited wants and limited resources. That is, consumers inevitably will be dissatisfied to some degree. And some part of the satisfaction shortfall surely is attributable to poor decisions by consumers themselves, or government regulators, for which marketing should not be blamed (but probably is). Yet there remain about 195 available points of ICSM scale latitude – the difference between the most recent aggregate score and the upper limit of 200 – for marketers to aspire to fill in or traverse through positive performance.

Regardless, none of this record would be known if not for the ICSM study undertaken and maintained over the past three decades. Obviously, perseverance has been a factor in continuing to execute data collection at regular intervals throughout such a long period. The authors again are pleased to recognize the project's research partners, currently Socratic Technologies, for their vital role.

Implications

As a work of pure science, this study is not particularly amenable to managerial implications *per se*, i.e., in the sense of actionable guidance for management. Perhaps marketing managers can benefit from awareness that certain macroeconomic conditions can affect aggregate consumer mood. To the extent that marketers adjust strategy, such as promotional content, to customer attitude and mood, this *macro-economy* → *ICSM* empirical finding could be broadly directive. Or marketers might like to know that product and price seem to contribute more heavily to overall consumer satisfaction than distribution/retailing and promotion/advertising do (inferred from higher average importance-weight scores of the former two categories). For the most part, though, the managerial insight yielded here is a converse one: not a matter of what the results imply for managerial practice, but what the practice of marketing management has done for the results. We find an implication *from* the collective performance of America's marketing managers.

What the consumers of marketing's work-product are telling us is that American marketing has performed at least moderately well even from their demanding perspective, probably better than the popular impression, and that the performance is getting better. One implication *for* the field of marketing management after all, therefore, is to take this finding to heart and not tamper too drastically with the favorable trajectory.[5]

Other stakeholders, especially industry "watchdog" groups, regulators, and legislators, also should find the ICSM results informative. Faced with the responsibility to protect consumers from illegal and/or unethical behavior, those oversight groups can take some reassurance from learning that, in general, marketers are seen as behaving in an acceptable fashion.

The ICSM study has now been borrowed and replicated by other researchers on at least five continents (e.g., Boshoff and DuPlessis 1991; Ferdous and Towfique 2008; Peterson *et al.* 2009; Todd and Lawson 2001; Wee and Chan 1989; as might be expected, there is a tendency for consumers in less-developed economies to report lower satisfaction). The scale instrument has been cited as a model in leading research textbooks and handbooks (e.g., Alba 2011: 75-76; Bearden *et al.* 1993; Churchill 1988; Churchill and Iacobucci 2002). Plans are for the project to continue uninterrupted into the future. Marketing and society both need this kind of enduring scorecard.

ICSM and the common good

If contributing to the "common good" is interpreted as acting in a responsible way and in the best interest of society collectively (cf. Rawls 1999: 109, 246), a positive ICSM score would suggest that business firms in the aggregate are conducting themselves reasonably toward consumers in this sense. However, the ICSM historical profile, in the negative range most years and only modestly positive recently, may shed some light on the complexity of the often quoted and seemingly prosaic notion of *satisfying customers* as the avenue to business success. Despite its intuitive appeal, ascribing priority to satisfying customers implies an imbalance of goals, with customer welfare given precedence. That is, if making a firm's customers happy supersedes all other goals of an organization, the orientation is untenable. Although such activity, while it lasts, might result in highly positive ICSM scores, it would also lead to failed businesses because business and marketing are confronted with several often-competing goals.

Providing a high level of customer satisfaction, therefore, must be balanced with the other principal goal, inherent in a free enterprise system, of producing a profit – to justify investment in the firm and enable provision for employees, as well as to allow existential survival. Simply stated, a firm's revenues must exceed its costs in a competitive market environment. As a result, products must be designed with a particular (finite) level of quality or durability, prices must produce a profit, service must be accounted for with revenue, and advertising must gain and hold the customers' attention.

Concordantly, in respect of the common good, firms do have a responsibility to treat customers fairly by maintaining product quality, charging reasonable prices, providing adequate service, and making appropriate, i.e., truthful, claims for their offerings. While this ideal may appear to serve a selective good rather than the common good, it is actually the institution of marketing collectively that makes such a set of economic benefits generally available as a common societal asset. The high living standards in market-oriented nations confirm this as a strong empirical tendency (OECD 2010). Hence, the public good is served in common by marketing system outputs. As Sen concurs (1993: 51), "The over-all success of the firm . . . is really a public good, from which all benefit." Moreover, marketing's *consumer* customers in totality *are* public society.

From the layman's perspective, while some ethics scholars and moral philosophers may appear to complicate the "common good" construct, imbuing with nuanced meaning, it is actually straightforward and largely what the name suggests. Nevertheless, strictest interpretation requires that "common good" benefits be *equally* available to all (Rawls 1999: 246), which would seem to rule out most of economic and commercial life on grounds of unequal resources (even including talent) across a population, all of which implies unequal access. Applying to consumer satisfaction derived from products, pricing, etc., it is questionable whether the "common" condition, so interpreted, could perfectly adhere. License for looser interpretation of common good in this sphere appears necessary and reasonable, therefore. Otherwise, the concept would be difficult to operationalize in a free-market society; even papal encyclicals do not mandate the equal (and stifling) results of true socialism or communism (*Centesimus Annus* 1991, Sec. IV). This alternative manifestation, allowing for unequal distribution, is sometimes called the "collective good" (Dolhenty 2006). Again, however, marketing typically *offers* its satisfying outputs equally to all comers, to anyone's dollars, euros, or shekels indiscriminately.

Finally, if we (1) conclude that most organizations behave legally and ethically (although consumers' general perceptions − positive overall in this study − may be disproportionately distorted by experiences with a relatively few unethical operators), (2) accept the premise that in an advanced society expectations are high, (3) acknowledge the desire of consumers to optimize their utility, and (4) recognize the inescapable tradeoff of interests in free exchange, as described, then a modestly positive ICSM score may not only be reasonable, it may also be desirable or even optimal. In short, business cannot *maximize* customer satisfaction by "giving away the store." A slightly positive ICSM score may therefore be the best that can realistically be expected. The latest ICSM results may very well be the true face of the common good in today's consumer marketing context.

Notes

1   The originator of this "four p's" classification scheme, Jerome McCarthy, a Notre Dame marketing professor, referred to the fourth function as "place," an obvious contrivance to mnemonically use a word beginning with the letter "p" (1964: 38–40). Because "distribution" is the best, most accurate term for the intended marketing function, the classic "four p's" are really three "p's" and a "d"!

2   The scale format is simply named after its inventor, Rensis Likert. The measuring device has been in use in social science research for literally over eight decades. As seen in the appendix, its distinguishing characteristic is the "strongly agree"–"strongly disagree" range of options for each item.
3   Index numbers are calculated as

$$100 \times \text{(raw score difference from measure's lower limit)}/ \\ \text{(1984 raw score difference from lower limit)}.$$

4   The 1983 pre-test ICSM score ($n = 41$) was identical to that of the first full survey of 1984.
5   A symptom of this salutary trend may be the renewed or enhanced primacy of a conscious customer focus in American businesses, manifested in a recognition that all corporate functional areas ultimately exist to serve the customer. A parallel development is the addition of Chief Customer Officer to firms' "C-suites" (Joyner 2012).

References

Alba, J.W. (ed.) (2011) *Consumer Insights: Findings from Behavioral Research*, Cambridge, MA: Marketing Science Institute.

Barksdale, H.C. and Darden, W.R. (1972) "Consumer attitudes toward marketing and consumerism," *Journal of Marketing*, 36 (October): 28–35.

——, ——, and Perreault, W.D., Jr. (1976) "Changes in consumer attitudes toward marketing, consumerism, and government regulation: 1971–1975," *Journal of Consumer Affairs*, 10 (Winter): 117–39.

Bearden, W.O., Netemeyer, R.G., and Mobley, M.F. (eds) (1993) *Handbook of Marketing Scales: Multi-Item Measures for Marketing and Consumer Behavior Research*, Newbury Park, CA: Sage Publications.

Boshoff, C. and DuPlessis, A.P. (1991) "South African consumer sentiment toward marketing," working paper, Port Elizabeth, S.A.: Vista University.

Centesimus Annus (1991) Encyclical Letter of Pope John Paul II (May 1), Rome: The Catholic Church.

Churchill, G.A., Jr. (1988) *Basic Marketing Research*, Chicago: The Dryden Press.

—— and Iacobucci, D. (2002) *Marketing Research: Methodological Foundations*, 8th edn, Mason, OH: South-Western.

Dolhenty, J. (2006) "An overview of natural law theory," *The Jonathan Dolhenty Archive* (November 8), online: http://radicalacademy.com/ philnaturallaw.htm (accessed 5/5/12).

Etzel, M.J., Walker, B.J., and Stanton, W.J. (2007) *Marketing*, 14th edn, New York: McGraw-Hill.

Ferdous, A.S. and Towfique, B. (2008) "Consumer sentiment towards marketing in Bangladesh: The relationship between attitudes to marketing, satisfaction and regulation," *Marketing Intelligence & Planning*, 26 (5): 481–95.

Fornell, C., Johnson, M.D., Anderson, E.W., Cha, J., and Everitt Bryant, B. (1996) "The American customer satisfaction index: Nature, purpose, and findings," *Journal of Marketing*, 60 (October): 7–18.

Gaski, J.F. (2008) "The index of consumer sentiment toward marketing: Validation, updated results, and demographic analysis," *Journal of Consumer Policy*, 31 (June): 195–216.

—— and Etzel, M.J. (1986) "The index of consumer sentiment toward marketing," *Journal of Marketing*, 50 (July): 71–81.

—— and —— (2005) "National aggregate consumer sentiment toward marketing: A thirty-year retrospective and analysis," *Journal of Consumer Research*, 31 (March): 859–67.

Hustad, T.P. and Pessemier, E.A. (1973) "Will the real consumer activist please stand up: an examination of consumers' opinions about marketing practices," *Journal of Marketing Research*, 10 (August): 319–24.

Joyner, A. (2012) "Make room for a new face on your top team: The rise of the chief customer officer," *Inc.*, April: 102–4.

Lundstrom, W.J. and Lamont, L.M. (1976) "The development of a scale to measure consumer discontent," *Journal of Marketing Research*, 13 (November): 373–81.

McCarthy, E.J. (1964) *Basic Marketing: A Managerial Approach*, rev. ed, Homewood, IL: Richard D. Irwin.

OECD [Organization for Economic Co-operation and Development] (2010) OECD. StatExtracts, *Quarterly National Accounts: Quarterly Growth Rates of GDP*, online: http://stats.oecd.org/index.aspx (accessed October 14, 2011).

Oliver, R.L. (1980) "A cognitive model of the antecedents and consequences of satisfaction decisions," *Journal of Consumer Research*, 17 (November): 460–69.

Packard, V. (1957) *The Hidden Persuaders*, New York: D. McKay.

Peterson, M., Ekici, A., and Hunt, D.M. (2009) "How the poor in a developing country view business' contribution to quality-of-life 5 years after a national economic crisis," *Journal of Business Research*, 63 (June): 548–58.

Rawls, J. (1999) *A Theory of Justice*, Cambridge, MA: Belknap Press.

Sen, A. (1993) "Does business ethics make economic sense?" *Business Ethics Quarterly*, 3 (1): 45–54.

Todd, S. and Lawson, R. (2001) "Consumer sentiment: New Zealanders' views on marketing," in S. Chetty and B. Collins (eds) *Bridging Marketing Theory and Practice. Proceedings, ANZMAC Conference*, New Zealand: Massey University.

Wee, C.H. and Chan, M. (1989) "Consumer sentiment toward marketing in Hong Kong," *European Journal of Marketing*, 23 (4): 25–39.

Appendix A: Questionnaire items

Five-point scale response options labeled from "Agree Strongly" to "Disagree Strongly." (R) indicates reverse scored.

Product quality

I am satisfied with most of the products I buy.

Most products I buy wear out too quickly. (R)

Too many of the products I buy are defective in some way. (R)

The companies that make products I buy don't care enough about how well they perform. (R)

The quality of products I buy has consistently improved over the years.

Price

Most products I buy are overpriced. (R)

Businesses could charge lower prices and still be profitable. (R)

Most prices are reasonable considering the high cost of doing business.

Most prices are fair.

In general, I am satisfied with the prices I pay.

Advertising

Most advertising is very annoying. (R)

Most advertising makes false claims. (R)

If most advertising was eliminated, consumers would be better off. (R)
I enjoy most ads.
Most advertising is intended to deceive rather than to inform consumers. (R)

Retailing or selling

Most retail stores serve their customers well.
Because of the way retailers treat me, most of my shopping is unpleasant. (R)
I find most retail salespeople to be very helpful.
When I need assistance in a store, I am usually *not* able to get it. (R)
Most retailers provide adequate service.

6

SOCIAL ISSUES OF MARKETING IN THE AMERICAN ECONOMY

Y. Hugh Furuhashi and E. Jerome McCarthy

The pages below appeared in the Introduction to a seven-chapter book co-authored by our deceased Notre Dame colleague, Yu Furuhashi, and E. Jerome McCarthy (Furuhashi and McCarthy 1971); McCarthy is best known for coining the 4 P's of marketing in his book, *Basic Marketing*, now in its eighteenth edition (Perrault *et al.* 2010). What most recent observers do not know is that McCarthy spent six years on the Notre Dame faculty during the 1960s before moving to Michigan State.

In the material that follows from the Introduction to that book, many of the observations seem timeless, like the opening sentence that indicates there is a "basic dissatisfaction with business ... showing itself in the United States today." It sounds like they are talking about the twenty-first century and not the 1970s. Although the names mentioned in the following paragraphs are dated and Calvin Coolidge has been out of office for 80 years, the sentiment about young people also describes our current time quite well. Both the questions posed by the authors and critics of that era bear further thought in our current uncertain economic times. The fundamental premise of marketing that they describe is the same today.

Some of the discussion about the economic system and the micro and macro issues now differs in degree, but not in kind. The section on the paper manufacturers was purposely retained because many of the pollution problems noted 40 years ago are still troubling manufacturing firms not only in the United States but throughout the world. The micro–macro dilemmas in the political environment seem more insoluble now than they were back then. Given the gridlock in Washington, the last sentence of the micro–macro dilemma seems to suggest an opportunity for business to take the lead in negotiating the common good.

The final section outlines sixteen major "gripes" with business in general and marketing in particular from over 40 years ago. We ask our readers to consider how many of the complaints are still being aired by the critics of marketing. In keeping with the book's theme of the common good, we challenge marketing scholars and practitioners thoughtfully to consider how the "marketing system" could address such grievances to become a more significant contributor to the common good.

Introduction

There is little question that a basic dissatisfaction with business is showing itself in the United States today.

This attitude is especially strong among the young, who consider the "American Dream" of earlier decades a sort of nightmarish joke. They speak disdainfully of the corporate "establishment"; they often repudiate the jobs and material goods which business and our market-directed economic system make available to them. Some refuse to consider working within either the establishment or the military–industrial complex. Many identify with the anti-business and "consumerism" movement. They see men such as Ralph Nader, Robert Choate, Jr., and other defenders of consumer rights as new leaders of a crusade for change. Others look to Marxism or communism for immediate, radical reorganization of the political and economic structure, as the only means to eradicate all the evils of the present system.

It is important to realize that their concerns are heartfelt and sincere, and that their voices may be joined by many others – *soon*. Thus it becomes imperative that responsible citizens and business leaders develop a deeper understanding of the nature of these concerns, what can be done about them (if anything) and possible ways of responding creatively to these challenges.

Do we need a "better" economic system?

Forty years ago, Calvin Coolidge issued his well-known statement: "The business of America is business." In the intervening years, our American economic system has worked extraordinarily well in bringing the United States to the highest standard of living in the world. People in countries of all levels of development envy America's material welfare and seek to emulate it.

There seems little doubt that our economic system has "delivered the goods" and will continue to do so, barring a national catastrophe. However, the extent of our success has led to some serious criticisms of the system.

The most commonly expressed charge is that the United States has delivered an over-abundance of goods, but in so doing has not necessarily improved the quality of people's lives. Such critics feel we have placed an undue emphasis on economic growth, on acquiring material goods for their own sake, but that we have made relatively little progress toward elevating the quality of human life, individual security, and happiness. They ask whether Americans, despite their enjoyment of the highest income in the world, are really better off or happier than the citizens of other countries and systems. These critics also point out that, in the midst of plenty and overabundance, we have a substantial portion of the population under what the President of the United States called the "poverty line."

Some critics condemn our present system out of hand, giving little thought to constructive change that might be achieved within it. Some call for a dramatic shift to an alternative political-economic system, convinced that the inadequacies of the present system would automatically disappear.

Other critics would settle now for change within the present system, but only with sweeping reforms carried out *now*. For example, some feel that the automobile industry should be controlled – to limit its production of socially undesirable products, such as the "over-powered" cars which lead to high accident rates and pollution of the environment. Or, they believe the food industry should be placed on a tighter rein, to offer really nutritious foods, rather than the synthetic products now on the market, with taste and appearance appeal but little nutritional value.

Some critics appear willing to accept the approach and basic goals of the US economic system, but are greatly concerned about the independent, often irresponsible actions of individuals, firms, and government agencies which cause the system to work ineffectively. They see efforts to fix prices, to form monopolies, to use false or deceptive promotional devices; and they feel that the "culprits" ought to be brought to justice. They see the need for wider protection through new laws, or more vigorous enforcement of existing laws.

The American political and economic system is guided by a set of laws which have evolved over time, supposedly in response to the needs and desires of the people. It probably will continue to evolve.[1] But in what direction? What can be considered a "wise" course? Will it lead to a "better" system?

How our market-directed economic system works

To provide some framework for subsequent discussion, let us now briefly examine the way our market-directed economic system works and how it inevitably leads to some of the problems and dilemmas mentioned above. Our Introduction will then close with comments on how to approach the discussion topics raised in subsequent chapters.

The reader needs to understand the functioning of an economic system; it affects him in his roles both as a producer and consumer. As a *producer* (that is, a seller of factors of production), he is primarily concerned with the size of his claim against the output of the total system, since this represents his income. As a consumer, on the other hand, he is concerned with "what" is made available in "what manner" to him, since he is interested in maximizing his satisfaction with this income. These two roles for each individual are inherent in our system, but can lead to difficulties and dilemmas. What is "good" for some producers may not be so "good" for some, or all, consumers – but more on this later.

Satisfying human wants obviously serves as the basis for developing an economic system such as ours and is the end goal of all its activities. The resources of
an economy are the *means* for producing goods and services to achieve the end,
that is, satisfying human wants.

Any economic system must decide *what to produce and in what proportions* – that
is, how to allocate its relatively scarce resources to produce those things which will
best satisfy the varied wants and needs of members of the society. The society must
also decide *how to produce* and *who will produce what*. The state of technology available at a particular time is important because it has a direct bearing on how
effectively a society can organize production in its effort to convert available
resources into want-satisfying forms. Finally, a society must decide *how the producers are to be compensated*, and *who is to get what share* of the output. It is here that the
individual's roles as producer and consumer overlap; how, and how well a producer
is compensated determines what share of the output he will be able to command
and when.

How key economic decisions are made in various economic systems

Over the course of history, various approaches have evolved for making the
key economic decisions regarding production, distribution of income, and
consumption.

Early, relatively static societies (and some less-developed societies still) relied on
customs and *tradition* to solve these economic problems. The assignment of jobs
generally passed from father to son, and from group to group, through time. This
solved not only the production problems, but also regulated the distribution of
income, because the acceptable compensation rate for various jobs was also governed by customs and tradition.

Later, *command-directed* economic systems developed. Here, a king, dictator, or
central planners attempt to coordinate the activities of the various units in the
society and direct the economy toward a specific goal(s). Some parts of the US
economic system regularly are directed by government planners, and in extreme
situations such as national disaster or emergency, all or much of it is government
controlled. This is accomplished by martial law and administrative boards set up to
modify the existing methods of production and consumption. Wartime economies
often must choose between "guns or butter," and a command system may be the
best way to get the job done.

The bulk of the US economy is *market-directed*, i.e., directed by the market
mechanism which relies on a multitude of individual micro-level decisions, in both
producing and consuming units. Each decision may be small in scope, but collectively the individual small decisions determine the macro-level decisions for the
whole economic system.

In a pure market-directed system, people as consumers determine a society's
production decisions when they make their consumption decisions, that is, by their

choices in the marketplace. In this sense, they decide what is to be produced, and by whom. Thus, ideally, the control of the economy is completely democratic, with dispersion of power throughout the economy.

In a pure market-directed society, people have free choice in finding work that is satisfying to them, thereby increasing their sense of responsibility and feeling of contribution to the system. Similarly, by having a free choice as to what they consume, they will, we assume, maximize their own satisfaction.

Presumably, a market-directed economy lets the people in the economy decide for themselves both their role as producers and consumers. Ideally, no one is forced to take a job which he does not want, and no one is forced to buy goods or services he does not want. But he must find something "good" to do if he is to have a claim against the output of the system.

To fully appreciate how a market-directed system works, it is important to understand the role of market price. The prices of consumer goods and services serve roughly as a measure of their social importance. If consumers are willing to pay the market prices, apparently they feel they are getting at least their money's worth. Similarly, the cost of resources is a rough measure of the value of the resources used in the production of these goods and services. In a market-directed system, both the prices in the production sector (for resources) and in the consumption sector (for products and services) fluctuate to allocate resources and distribute income in light of the preferences of consumers. The end result is an equilibrium of demand and supply and the coordination of the economic activity of many people and institutions.

The micro–macro dilemma

Few modern economic systems are pure examples of any type, and the American economy is no exception. But our system probably comes closest to being a market-directed system, with modifications.

Some command-system elements have been added to it in an attempt to remedy seeming "deficiencies" of a pure market-directed system. These "deficiencies" develop for a number of reasons, for example (1) producers and consumers do not always, or are not always able to, make the "best" decision; (2) special interest groups may join forces and exert a greater power than many individuals working alone; (3) income distributions are not always equal, therefore some consumers have more power than others in the marketplace; (4) market structures vary by industry and provide some producers with more market power than others; and (5) the pricing mechanism works effectively for many purposes, but may not be completely adequate for running a whole system.

This movement away from a pure market-directed system towards a mixed system with command elements is caused by our efforts to remedy the *micro–macro dilemma*.

As noted earlier, what seems desirable from the point of view of individual producers or consumers (acting in their own selfish best interests) often turns out to be undesirable for the whole society. Each of the micro-level operators (producers and consumers) may be engaged in some activity which contributes to the operation of the whole system, i.e., to the macro-system. However, the aggregate of the individual efforts may fall considerably short of what the whole society feels it ought to accomplish. In other words, Adam Smith's "invisible hand" may not work as well as some or all of the members of the society would like. Therefore, they are willing to accept some restriction of the free operation of a market-directed system in favor of some command elements, in order to accomplish their desired goals.

The paper manufacturers' problems

The nature of a micro–macro dilemma can be dramatically illustrated in a case involving pollution of a lake by several paper manufacturers. Individual firms have located around the shores of a particular lake to make use of the nearby raw materials, water, and labor. In a micro sense, the manufacturers are doing "good" providing employment to workers, profits to their stockholders, and products for the benefit of interested consumers.

Through the normal production process, however, the various companies may pollute the lake and thereby diminish its usefulness to all other users, including some of the people who have jobs in the factory. Hence, logically there may be a conflict between the workers' interests (micro), as employees of the factory, as well as the consumers of paper products, and their interests (macro), as "consumers" of the local environment that is, clean water for swimming, boating or fishing.

If the paper manufacturers join together in an attempt to solve the problem, they may be blocked by laws which were passed in an attempt to remedy an earlier micro–macro dilemma. Anti-trust officials may charge them with conspiracy under laws which were intended to protect competition, and therefore the operation of the macro-level system.

Ultimately, each manufacturer may decide to do nothing, because unilateral action, while raising the firm's costs and reducing profits, would have little impact on the lake.

If consumers in the aggregate become upset about the producers polluting the economy's resources, laws may be passed to limit the freedom of individual firms, with the result that the firms' profits are reduced and therefore, the income of stockholders who depend on the dividends from these paper companies.

Subsequently, the firms may have to raise their prices, thereby affecting some consumers because rising costs usually must be passed on to consumers. Alternately, the firms may have to close their doors and fire all the workers. The lake will return to its original beauty, but the society must do without the paper products. Former employees may not be able to find other work, and will have to be supported by those still working within the macro-system. And the resources invested in the plants will be wasted.

Our society's problem-coping with micro–macro dilemmas

The moral of this story is that in a modern society composed of a complex interrelated web of micro-operators (producers and consumers), each one's seemingly "good" actions (from a selfish viewpoint) *may or may not* benefit the macro-level system. Further, proposed remedies to a "bad" situation may help that situation, but may or may not improve the overall operation of the macro-level system.

Most of the questions which critics of our economy raise involve a micro–macro dilemma. Finding answers to their questions is not easy. Sometimes it is difficult to decide if a problem even exists. To the corner grocer whose trade has dwindled because a huge supermarket moved in a block away, there certainly is a problem – a "big monopolist" is "driving me out of business." To the president of the supermarket chain, however, there is no problem; in his view: "The name of the free enterprise game is competition, and if we can better serve the market, then consumers are better off, we are better off, and the only person who perceives our move as a problem is the corner grocer, whose own monopoly in the neighborhood has been eliminated." As the supermarket president sees it, the macro-system will work better because of his efforts, i.e., consumers will get more variety at lower prices. Is there a problem, or isn't there? It depends on whom you talk to. Existing US antitrust legislation reflects both "yes" and "no" answers. Some laws are designed to encourage competition, others to protect small competitors.

There may be no "absolutely right" answers to micro–macro type problems, but some answers may be better than others. The point to remember here is that seemingly good answers to micro problems may be bad for the macro-system. A legal requirement that all grocery stores should not exceed five hundred square feet, to protect small food retailers, may be good for small retailers (the micro-level) but bad for all consumers (the macro-level) because food costs probably would be higher. Thus, before we, as a society, take action to remedy some socio-economic problem, it is extremely important that we understand both the micro- and macro-level consequences if we are to be "socially responsible."

Although there may not be many "right answers," there are problems which are asking for solutions. There may be some validity to some of the critics' charges and serious students of business and marketing must understand and be able to answer them.

The role of business is to satisfy consumers. Good business and marketing management makes a difference in the success or failure of an individual firm; the same kind of thinking can be useful in developing a better economic system.

Therefore, it would seem appropriate that business leaders take the initiative in building a better macroeconomic system, while keeping in mind the micro–macro dilemma.

The major anti-business gripes

To organize our discussion, we have isolated sixteen basic "gripes" about business and marketing which seem to be fairly representative of the anti-business, anti-marketing sentiments of a variety of critics:

1   Business provides materialistic quantity in American life, but does not necessarily advance the quality of life.
2   Business appears too impersonal and selfish, and "humanity" is sacrificed to efficiency in the pursuit of profits.
3   Business often fails to meet the basic needs of poor markets, as in ghetto areas, or charges exorbitant prices to these essentially captive markets.
4   The market mechanism is restricted in some cases where the danger to consumers is open to speculation (e.g., marijuana, pornography), but is allowed to function without restraint for many products which do affect the safety of others (e.g., guns and overly powerful cars).
5   The value added by marketing is difficult to justify, both in terms of high markups on many goods, and in exorbitant prices.
6   Marketing misallocates resources by encouraging the consumption of "non-necessities."
7   Marketing breeds contentment with mediocrity (it offers nothing "higher"), and does not serve markets (e.g., ballet, symphony, chamber music, etc.) if they are not directly profitable.
8   Marketing, through restyling and poor quality in production, encourages and engages in planned obsolescence.
9   Many products in an individual product category are not very different, if at all. An excess of products in one product category represents a misallocation of resources and also breeds consumer bewilderment.
10   Consumer recourse for defective products is often sadly lacking.
11   Big business has tremendous power over smaller businesses.
12   The concentration of industrial wealth and power has led to an effective denial of the American Dream (of any individual's right and capability of going into business for himself).
13   Advertising creates false needs and manipulates the consumer.
14   Salesmen are often overly aggressive.
15   Advertising and other promotion efforts, including packaging and labeling, are often deceptive, false, and misleading. Many products are not as distinctive or as differentiated as the promotion implies. Many advertising claims are voided by obsolescence (advertisements induce dissatisfaction with past purchases).
16   Producers foul public resources for private profit. Lumber companies destroy beautiful forests. Firms pollute once beautiful rivers. Neon signs and outdoor advertisements blight once pleasant thoroughfares.

In an effort to face the issues raised in these sixteen gripes, while keeping our discussion manageable, we will focus on seven topics (see Table 6.1 for chapter titles and question headings), all of which are relevant to business decision-making. These topics follow roughly the format of basic marketing texts which focus first on consumers and their buying behavior and then go on to develop marketing mixes to satisfy potential consumers …

TABLE 6.1 Chapter titles and question headings in Furuhashi and McCarthy (1971)

Chapter	Title	Question
1	How Rational Is Consumer Behavior?	Is rational decision making desirable? What is rational purchasing behavior? Is all purchasing behavior rational?
2	How Free Should "Freedom of Choice" Be?	Where should we draw the line in the cigarette controversy? Is some line needed when safety is involved?
3	How Good Should a Product Be?	What should be done about product problems? Is more legislation needed? Would stronger product warranties or guarantees help? Is more legislation the right answer? Are there criteria for specifying "how good a product should be"? Safety of products – how safe is safe enough? Quality of products – what is quality?
4	Who Should Backup Guarantees and Warranties on Products?	What does the warranty really say and mean? Should manufacturers or dealers fulfill the warranty?
5	What is Deceptive Advertising and Promotion?	Is anyone doing anything about deception? Are there criteria for identifying deception in what is said or written? Are there criteria for identifying deception? How much information is in the "consumer interest"?
6	Is it Fair to Discriminate on Price?	What is price discrimination? What is predatory pricing? What is unreasonable low?
7	Should Business Meet Any and All Consumer Demands, Regardless of Profitability?	What about macro versus micro implications of a profit-oriented system? What about food retailing in low-income areas?

Note

1   Some understanding of existing federal legislation is desirable for full appreciation of some of the arguments raised in this book. In particular, you should be aware of the Sherman Antitrust Act, the Clayton Act, the Federal Trade Commission Act, the Robinson–Patman Act, the Miller–Tydings Act, and the Wheeler–Lea Act. Some details are presented in most introductory marketing texts (e.g., McCarthy 1971).

References

Furuhashi, Y. and McCarthy, E.J. (1971) *Social Issues of Marketing in the American Economy*, Columbus, OH: Grid.

McCarthy, E.J. (1971) *Basic Marketing*, 4th edn, Homewood, IL: Richard D. Irwin, Chapter 3.

Perreault, W., Jr., Cannon, J., and McCarthy, E.J. (2010) *Basic Marketing*, 18th edn, New York: McGraw-Hill Companies.

PART III

Catholic Social Thought issues in marketing

7

CARITAS IN VERITATE

Updating Catholic Social Teaching for responsible marketing strategy[1]

Gene R. Laczniak, Thomas A. Klein, and Patrick E. Murphy

Introduction

Two of the authors recently published "Applying Catholic Social Teachings to Ethical Issues in Marketing" (Klein and Laczniak 2009). The objective therein was to provide a perspective on ethical issues in marketing, consumption, and public policy that was novel in terms of its roots in the moral theology of the Roman Catholic Church. At the same time, the authors maintain that these core ethical principles likely could be derived from moral philosophy, that is, have a corresponding root source in some secular rather than religious tradition, thereby enhancing the validity and appeal of application for all business managers. The major purpose in taking on that task was to show that Catholic Social Teaching (CST) could be seen as a useful "principles-based theory of business ethics" rather than a niche in sectarian moral theology.

That presentation was organized around key themes in CST juxtaposed against major areas of ethical concern in marketing, such that the intersection of principle and problem provided guidance for action. The key principles discussed were human dignity, the common good, subsidiarity, preference for the poor and vulnerable, worker rights, solidarity, and stewardship. For summaries of the principles, see Box 7.1. The common good with its emphasis on the societal aspects of marketing is the theme of this book.

In Klein and Laczniak's (2009) article, the marketing issues identified for inclusion were product design and management, promotion and pricing, consumer ethics, public policy and regulation, and globalization. The point of that exposition was to show how one or the other of these key principles could guide ethically inspired action by managers, consumers, or policy makers. For example, the principle of human dignity guides product designers to "place a high priority on safety" (p. 238).

BOX 7.1 KEY PRINCIPLES OF CATHOLIC SOCIAL TEACHING

Human dignity

The most basic and fundamental instruction of CST flows from the idea that *all* persons have inherent worth regardless of race, color, or creed. Dignity is not "earned" but rather it is always a given right to be accorded to all persons in all circumstances. This principle is used to argue that *"The economy exists for the person, not the person for the economy"*[1] and that an excessive focus on profit maximization can be harmful to authentic personal development because rewards and burdens may not be justly distributed. Following this principle, the exploitation of workers in Third-World countries to achieve cost advantage is clearly unethical. Similarly, charging premium credit rates to those least likely to handle their debt load seems an unambiguous violation of this principle.

Common good

This principle flows partly from the idea that persons typically live in community and therefore social rules should contribute to the benefits of the commonwealth. While CST clearly affirms the right of private property, this teaching provides a foundation for the notion that all persons have the right to secure the basic necessities of life (e.g., food, shelter, available work, as well as access to education and affordable healthcare). Following this principle, a marketing firm would assess the impact of its products on multiple stakeholders. A clear violation of this principle would be cigarettes which clearly do harm to consumers, often impact families negatively due to loss of loved ones and also affect society in terms of increased medical costs. The common good should be a consideration in any *outcomes* assessments.

Subsidiarity

This is one of the most basic articulations of rights and responsibilities inherent in CST. Specifically, "It is an injustice ... to assign to a greater or higher association what lesser and subordinate organizations can do."[2] Commentators on this principle also imply that the concept warns about the dangers of over-regulating business activities and, indeed, such an argument can be sustained. However, the same principle is also used in CST to insure that sufficiently powerful parties (including government) weigh in to offset persistently unfair practices in society. Following the subsidiarity principle means that companies would allow marketing departments, product managers, and salespeople to make decisions at the lowest feasible level regarding issues relating to treatment of customers and other stakeholders.

Preference for the poor and vulnerable

This teaching recalls the admonitions of Scripture to "Love thy neighbor" and "What you do for the least of my brethren, you do for me." Here CST argues that the proper end of economic activity is the progress of the entire community, especially the poor. The centrality of the obligation to help the poor is manifest not only in CST, but also in *every* other major religious doctrine – Jewish, Protestant, Islamic, Hindu, and Buddhist. Finance schemes that target the debt-laden or using fear tactics to sell second-rate products to the elderly surely would violate this principle. Securing market research information over the Internet from unsuspecting children is another clear trespass of this doctrine.

Worker rights

This theme advances the idea that work is central to human growth and that workers help to continue the wonder of creation. This is the oldest teaching of modern CST dicta dating back to 1891. A more recent affirmation proclaims: "All people have the right to economic initiative, to productive work, to just wages and benefits, to decent working conditions as well as to organize and join unions or other associations."[3] These writings grant workers the right to organize in unions and contend that past loyalties by workers always need to be recognized by the firm. This principle suggests that managers have a moral obligation to create trusting, nurturing communities in which employees can improve as persons, even as workers should be motivated to provide a productive work for their employer.

Solidarity

This concept recognizes that all people and social groups are united in a brotherhood that seeks common growth and fulfillment, dependent on one another for the support that we require in community. It provides a framework for the idea that "economic life should be shaped by moral principles" because all persons both seek and want a fair opportunity to attain betterment in their lives.[4] This foundational theme of CST is the basis for advocating ethical responsibilities of rich nations to poor as well as the special ethical obligations of multinational businesses operating in developing countries. This means that international marketers should develop products that are economically affordable and appropriate for customers in less affluent markets.

(Continued)

(Continued)

Stewardship

This precept captures the responsibility of every party – including corporations – to contribute to the care of the earth. It is among the newest in the evolution of CST. It calls for economic actions always to "respect the integrity and cycles of nature" and to fastidiously avoid environmental exploitation.[5] It views the physical environment as a common pool of abundant resources not to be exploited for the benefit of only a few or at the expense of future generations. It connects to the "green ethic" and "sustainability" so prominent in current business strategy discussions. Marketers practicing the stewardship principle would likely develop less environmentally harmful versions of their products, never engage in "greenwashing" and would create reverse channels for the disposal of their products.

Source: Adapted from Klein and Laczniak (2009) and Murphy *et al.* (2012).

Notes

1 National Conference of Catholic Bishops, "A Catholic framework for economic life," *U.S. Catholic Conference*, 1997.
2 Pope Pius XI, *Quadragesimo Anno (On Reconstructing the Social Order)*, Vatican City, 1931.
3 National Conference of Catholic Bishops, op. cit.
4 National Conference of Catholic Bishops, op. cit.
5 Pontifical Council for Justice and Peace, *Compendium of the Social Doctrine of the Church*, Rome: Pontifical Council, 2005.

On June 29, 2009, in Vatican City, Pope Benedict XVI released the third encyclical of his papacy, *Caritas in Veritate* (Charity in Truth). Many eagerly awaited this papal letter because Church officials had hinted for some months that aspects of the communication would address the global financial recession. At over 30,000 words – divided into six chapters and 79 organizing paragraphs – the final document is extensive even by standards of previous encyclicals. The letter is certainly sweeping in its scope, touching not only on the publicized topic of the great world recession but also on the role of human solidarity in economic development, the benefits and detriments of new technologies, and the responsibilities of humanity to the physical environment of the planet. In 2010, two of the authors (Laczniak and Klein 2010) updated their previous article on CST to account for some of the new perspectives addressed in the new encyclical. This chapter is an expansion of that note and particularly deals with questions that touch on the broader dimensions of marketing practice. The authors hope this introduction encourages readers to directly examine *Caritas in Veritate* (*CiV*) as well as the abiding principles of CST from other documents (recall Box 7.1). Specifically, we reiterate here that CST can be seen as principles-based, blended ethical philosophy that also can be derived by logical reasoning and that is useful in the normative analysis of macromarketing issues – i.e., the connections of markets, marketing, and society.

Why is this encyclical titled "Truth in Charity"? Such titles traditionally come from the first words of the letter but there is a more important thematic aspect. The name of the document stems, in part, from the centrality of the Christian *virtue of charity* in motivating authentic human development. Charity is portrayed as the uniting force behind CST because humanity is a brotherhood created in the image of God; love of neighbor (broadly speaking) is the greatest commandment because it encompasses the essential nature of the key CST principles: human dignity, solidarity, and so on. In the section below, the authors select nine quotations from the letter (the number in parenthesis indicates the source paragraph) along with a brief comment concerning its possible societal and marketing implications. The authors chose these selections because of their market-centric focus, but there are many other passages as well that hold social and moral implications for the ethical practice of business in a global economy.

Nine excerpts from the letter (*CiV*) with commentaries

On the role of markets, trust, and the importance of distributive justice

> In a climate of mutual trust, the *market* is the economic institution that permits encounter between persons, inasmuch as they are economic subjects who make use of contracts to regulate their relations as they exchange goods and services of equivalent value between them, in order to satisfy their needs and desires. The social doctrine of the Church has unceasingly highlighted the importance of *distributive justice* and *social justice* for the market economy, not only because it belongs within a broader social and political context, but also because of the wider network of relations within which it operates . . . . If the market is governed solely by the principle of the equivalence in value of exchanged goods, it cannot produce the social cohesion that it requires in order to function well. *Without internal forms of solidarity and mutual trust, the market cannot completely fulfill its proper economic function.* And today it is this trust which has ceased to exist, and the loss of trust is a grave loss.
>
> *(35)*

Comment. In these remarks, a historic position of CST is affirmed; that is, the market should be the primary mechanism by which people exchange goods and services. However, the excerpt also implies that markets should be governed by the mutual interests of participants, and result in *fairness* for those interests. In other words, drawing on the concept of distributive justice, market outcomes are judged by fairness, transparency, and cooperation, taking into account differences in power among market participants as well as considering any vulnerabilities that those participants may bring to market transactions (see Laczniak and Murphy 2008). Each of these elements is seen as critical for establishing a just marketplace.

On economic activity and the common good

Economic activity cannot solve all social problems through the simple application of *commercial logic*. This needs to be *directed towards the pursuit of the common good*, for which the political community in particular must also take responsibility. The Church has always held that economic action is not to be regarded as something opposed to society. In and of itself, the market is not, and must not become, the place where the strong subdue the weak .... The great challenge before us, accentuated by the problems of development in this global era and made even more urgent by the economic and financial crisis, is to demonstrate, in thinking and behavior, not only that traditional principles of social ethics like transparency, honesty and responsibility cannot be ignored or attenuated, but also that in *commercial relationships* the *principle of gratuitousness* and the logic of gift as an expression of fraternity can and must *find their place within normal economic activity*. This is a human demand at the present time, but it is also demanded by economic logic. It is a demand both of charity and of truth.

(36)

Comment. Although the passage above is broader than marketing, it notes the distinct possibility of social and economic problems that can arise without a commitment to the common good. The fact that economic and marketing activities occur in a global world means that the importance of concepts central to CST like the common good and preference for the poor and vulnerable are essential. In fact, several "virtues" are mentioned specifically – transparency, honesty, and responsibility – that will enhance marketing and business activities. Both business firms and governments must then be key players in fostering the common good, not only for citizens of a country or region, but also for individuals living throughout the world.

On justice and economic/business/marketing activity

The Church's social doctrine has always maintained that *justice must be applied to every phase of economic activity*, because this is always concerned with man and his needs. Locating resources, financing, production, consumption, and all the other phases in the economic cycle inevitably have moral implications. *Thus every economic decision has a moral consequence.* The social sciences and the directions exhibited in the contemporary economy point to the same conclusion. Space also needs to be created within the market for economic activity carried out by subjects who freely choose to act according to principles other than those of pure profit, without sacrificing the production of economic value in the process.

(37)

Comment. The fact that justice should be an underpinning of all economic activity is a central theme of the entire *CiV* document. The statement above that every economic decision has a moral consequence is a strong one and could be argued to be an overstatement. But the fundamental point is that too many business and marketing decisions are made without identifying the potential moral consequences that extend beyond the immediate advertising target, or that affect the workings of a suppliers located far from both consumers and retailers who sell the item. This quote also instructs firms to pay closer attention to social impacts beyond those that can be measured merely by short term financial results. The quote above is closely allied with the CST principle of solidarity (see discussion of it in Box 7.1).

On the importance of stakeholders

[F]rom the perspective of the Church's social doctrine, there is . . . a growing conviction that *business management cannot concern itself only with the interests of the proprietors, but must also assume responsibility for all the other stakeholders who contribute to the life of the business*: the workers, the clients, the suppliers of various elements of production, the community of reference. In recent years, a new cosmopolitan class of managers has emerged, who are often answerable only to the shareholders . . . which . . . determine their remuneration. By contrast, though, many far-sighted managers today are becoming increasingly aware of the profound links between their enterprise and the territory or territories in which it operates . . . .

(40)

Comment. In these remarks, the letter endorses both the *stakeholder model* of business leadership and the investment approach that looks to long-term gains, avoiding both undue speculation and short-term financial perspectives. As argued by Laczniak and Murphy (2006: 167), "The adoption of a stakeholder orientation is essential to the maintenance and advancement of ethical decision making in all marketing operations." They contend that a basic normative approach to ethical marketing should emphasize the *stakeholder concept* and deconstruct the more prevalent "shareholder primacy" model. Indeed, the "stakeholder orientation" should be the new "marketing concept" because it makes both good economic *and ethical* sense. Recently, Laczniak and Murphy (2012) have argued that the stakeholder model should be viewed from a societal, rather than a firm-centric, perspective. The passage and commentary both emphasize stakeholder thinking rests on a perspective that draws on the CST principle of the "common good."

On duties and rights

> Many people today would claim that they owe nothing to anyone, except to themselves . . . . The link consists in this: individual rights, when detached from a framework of duties which grants them their full meaning, can run wild, leading to an escalation of demands which is effectively unlimited and indiscriminate. An overemphasis on rights leads to a disregard for duties. Duties set a limit on rights because they point to the anthropological and ethical framework of which rights are a part, in this way ensuring that they do not become license. Duties thereby reinforce rights and call for their defense and promotion as a task to be undertaken in the service of the common good . . . . *The sharing of reciprocal duties is a more powerful incentive to action than the mere assertion of rights.*
>
> *(43)*

Comment. This paragraph notes that in the twenty-first century too many individuals have become egoistic and do not see the correspondence of duties with responsibilities. Like others, we view duties and responsibilities as two sides of the same coin – one is inextricably linked to the other. If both the market and marketing-related activities are to operate in a fair manner, the notion of "dutiless rights" (Selborne 1994) must be surmounted by ethical managers. This ideal follows from the notion of *normative* marketing discussed above, where companies accept the fact that they have duties to customers and other parties in order to make the market system work fairly to all stakeholders. Companies and managers who do not respect the inherent rights of all individuals would be in violation of the CST principle of human dignity.

On business ethics

> *The economy needs ethics to function correctly* – not any ethics whatsoever, but an ethics which is people-centered . . . . Much in fact depends on the underlying system of morality. On this subject . . . social doctrine can make a specific contribution, since it is based on . . . the inviolable dignity of the human person and the transcendent value of natural moral norms. When business ethics prescinds [is detached] from these two pillars, it inevitably risks losing its distinctive nature and it falls prey to forms of exploitation; more specifically, it risks becoming subservient to existing economic and financial systems rather than correcting their dysfunctional aspects. Among other things, it risks being used to justify the financing of projects that are in reality unethical.
>
> *(45)*

Comment. For macromarketing, this would seem to be a very significant passage underscoring the importance of placing ethical concerns at the center of decision-making during the formulation and implementation of marketing campaigns. In addition, without referring to it directly, this statement argues for a Kantian framework for marketing conduct, one where persons should never be used as a means *merely* to achieve an economic end. Economic consequences ought to advance human welfare beyond the narrow interests of the individual business organization. The primacy of "putting people first" in marketing (Murphy *et al.* 2012) has its roots both in the secular marketing concept and the CST principle of human dignity.

On the collective responsibility to developing markets

> In *development programs*, the principle of the *centrality of human person*, as the subject primarily responsible for development, must be preserved . . . . Development programs, if they are to be adapted to individual situations, need to be flexible; and the people who benefit from them ought to be directly involved in their planning and implementation. The criteria to be applied should aspire towards incremental development in a context of solidarity – with careful monitoring of results – inasmuch as there are no universally valid solutions. Much depends on the way programs are managed in practice. "The peoples themselves have the prime responsibility to work for their own development. But they will not bring this about in isolation."
>
> *(47)*

Comment. With respect to market development efforts, the principle of human dignity leads to the application of two corollary CST principles: *solidarity* implies the extension of market development efforts to marginalized populations, not merely those that are already linked to the economic system, and *subsidiarity* implies that those affected populations should directly participate in planning and implementing those efforts. (For a further discussion of them, see Box 7.1.) Since the 1970s, academic marketers have charted the special obstacles faced by disadvantaged consumers (Andreasen 1975). Santos and Laczniak (2009b) categorize distinct streams of research involving vulnerable consumers of various types including the poor, the homeless, the illiterate, and the physically disabled. In another article, Santos and Laczniak (2009a) specifically derive the characteristics of a "just" market when sellers engage impoverished consumers from developing economies using the principles of CST as a foundation. Based on that analysis, they define and discuss the importance of concepts such as "authentic and non-exploitive intent," "cocreation of value," "interest representation," and "investment in future consumption" as necessary conditions of justice when marketing to the poor. As globalization continues its rapid growth in the coming decades, new ethical perspectives for the construction of fair and just markets would appear to be a seminal concern in marketing.

On the responsibility of stewardship

This responsibility is a global one, for it is concerned not just with energy but with the whole of creation, which must not be bequeathed to future generations depleted of its resources. Human beings legitimately exercise a *responsible stewardship over nature*, in order to protect it, to enjoy its fruits and to cultivate it in new ways, with the assistance of advanced technologies, so that it can worthily accommodate and feed the world's population . . . . Let us hope that the international community and individual governments will succeed in countering harmful ways of treating the environment. It is likewise incumbent upon the competent authorities to make every effort to ensure that the economic and social costs of using up shared environmental resources are recognized with transparency and fully borne by those who incur them, not by other peoples or future generations: the protection of the environment, of resources and of the climate obliges all international leaders to act jointly and to show a readiness to work in good faith . . . . One of the greatest challenges facing the economy is to achieve the most efficient use – not abuse – of natural resources, based on a realization that the notion of "efficiency" is not value-free.

(50)

Comment. One of the biggest challenges facing the world in general and marketers in particular is the stewardship of natural resources. As the first sentence above points out, future generations are at risk if a more responsible approach to environmental stewardship is not undertaken by societies moving forward. Although ecological problems have been identified for some time, the inclusion of this paragraph in *CiV* underscores the Catholic view that this is now a significant ethical issue facing worldwide development. The term "sustainable marketing" is often used to denote such stewardship by companies (Murphy 2005). A major effort has been launched by consumer products marketers to offer more environmentally friendly versions of their products including light bulbs, cleaning products, automobiles, detergents, and many others. The question can be posed whether these are good faith efforts or just attempts at "greenwashing" (over-stating environmental benefits) by some firms. Stewardship is also listed as one of the seven major CST principles in Box 7.1.

On the ethical responsibilities of consumers

Hence *the consumer has a specific social responsibility*, which goes hand-in-hand with the social responsibility of the enterprise. Consumers should be continually educated . . . with respect for moral principles without diminishing the intrinsic economic rationality of the act of purchasing. In the retail industry, particularly at times like the present when purchasing power has diminished and people must live more frugally, it is necessary to explore other paths: for example, forms of cooperative purchasing like the consumer cooperatives .... In addition, it can be helpful to promote new ways of marketing products from deprived areas of the world, so as to guarantee their producers a decent return. However, certain conditions need to be met: the market should be genuinely transparent; the producers, as well as increasing their profit margins, should also receive improved formation in professional skills and technology; and finally, trade of this kind must not become hostage to partisan ideologies.

(66)

Comment. This passage addresses the prospect of a consumer ethic that corresponds to the responsibilities of businesses concerning the impact of purchasing, usage, and disposal decisions on the environment and upon those less fortunate. In short, this appears to be clarion call for more responsible consumption including "fair trade" marketing initiatives. This also appears to be a call for "institution building" in the form of consumer cooperatives, in which the Church historically, has played a major role (Mittelstaedt *et al.* 1998). The CST principle that is most closely allied with this excerpt is solidarity.

Implications for marketing and the common good

These nine passages focus on the most relevant areas of *CiV* for marketing and business. Taken with the seven principles of CST shown in Box 7.1, they provide a framework for ethical and socially responsible marketing. While the specific application of many of these concepts may not be readily apparent in marketing practice, we see several positive trends occurring in business indicating that some of them are being lived in twenty-first century business.

First, the majority of large corporations in the United States and throughout the developed world are publishing annual or biennial corporate responsibility reports. These reports suggest that companies are following the thematics of paragraphs 36 and 43 on duties and responsibilities. Second, some firms like General Electric and Nike are engaging in regular "stakeholder dialogues" where the companies hear from their critics and representatives of NGOs, following the advice of paragraph 40. Third, a much greater general emphasis is being placed on sustainability in marketing with the growth of high-mileage automobiles, more environmentally benign versions of many consumer products, and increased levels of advertising for "green" products. Thus, the stewardship principle from both paragraph 50 and Box 7.1 are being followed much more seriously. Fourth, greater attention is being paid to the plight of the poor and vulnerable in developing and base of the pyramid markets (paragraph 47 and Box 7.1). Not only are pharmaceutical firms donating millions of dollars worth of drugs to these markets but also a serious attempt is being made to sell less expensive versions of durables as well as smaller package of consumer goods to meet the needs of these markets. Fifth, the global financial crisis and the public outcry for a more ethical and moral marketplace indicates that financial services and Wall Street firms are still lagging in adhering to the importance of trust and ethics advocated for in paragraphs 35 and 45. Sixth, the notion of worker rights from Box 7.1 has taken on an expanded meaning as major marketers such as Apple and Walmart have been criticized for the working conditions present at subcontractor production plants. Although these workers in far-flung places are not employees in the technical sense, the most powerful companies are expected to take more responsibility regarding the basic human rights of these individuals. Some progress has been made, but much more needs to be done.

Tom's of Maine is an illustration of how many of these principles might be applied to a particular company. This firm makes and markets natural personal care products such as toothpaste, mouthwash, deodorant, dental floss, and soap. In 2006 they were partially acquired by Colgate Palmolive but still seem to be operating much the same as they were before the merger. The company's website features what Tom's calls "Good Business: Beyond the Bottom Line" (Tom's of Maine n.d.). Under this moniker, the firm features several practices that might be seen as consistent with CST and *CiV*.

The first is the firm's "Reason for Being":

> To serve our customers' health needs with imaginative science from plants and minerals;
>
> To inspire all those we serve with a mission of responsibility and goodness;
>
> To empower others by sharing our knowledge, time, talents, and profits; and
>
> To help create a better world by exchanging our faith, experience, and hope.
>
> *(Ibid.)*

The second aspect emphasizes the "Stewardship Model" the company follows by including standards for "natural," "sustainable," and "responsible" products (bullet points provided for each). Finally, a commitment to the common good is demonstrated through the firm's employee community involvement and giving $150,000 to nonprofit organizations throughout the United States.

Evaluation of *CiV* and conclusion

These passages and comments address only a sampling of the economic commentary contained in *CiV*. We have emphasized those remarks that have marketing and ethical implications. The vision supported by *CiV* may be interpreted as radical by some observers because it certainly opposes the shareholder primacy and profit maximization models that many managers in the business world subscribe to. Yet the document, taken as a whole, contains a broad range of reflections and the moral principles that have broad applicability for marketing.

If the world economy is going to bounce back to its 2007 level of output and marketplace trust, the comments made in paragraph 35 concerning the importance of trust and distributive justice to fair markets must become more apparent. The pervasiveness of justice and ethics outlined in paragraph 37 challenges business and marketing executives to take a broader view of the marketplace such that the notion of the common good as discussed in paragraph 36 can be applied. We are not so naïve to think that businesses will always take a "common good" first perspective, but the Papal letter's focus on stakeholders (paragraph 40) is a very good starting point for expressing a higher level of societal concern that corporations need to embrace. While business firms and marketers often are notorious in their obedience to financial utilitarianism, the focus on ethics, duties, and responsibilities challenges the business community to aspire to a higher set of operating principles based on arguments advanced in paragraphs 43, 45, and 47. This new and expanded view of corporate responsibilities makes the concern for the natural environment and stewardship (paragraph 50) a logical extension of such thinking.

In conclusion, the message of *CiV* gives great insight into how marketing practices that further the common good might operate as we move forward in the twenty-first century. It is our position that there is much merit in examining the impact of these highlighted selections from *CiV* on the overall marketing system because they capture and underscore much of what has been advocated in the business ethics literature for creating socially responsible organizations.

Note

1 This chapter is based partially on, and draws from, Laczniak and Klein (2010).

References

Andreasen, A.R. (1975) *The Disadvantaged Consumer*, New York: The Free Press.

Klein, T.A. and Laczniak, G.R. (2009) "Applying Catholic social teachings to ethical issues in marketing," *Journal of Macromarketing*, 29: 233–43.

Laczniak, G.R. and Klein, T.A. (2010) "Caritas in Veritate: Updating Catholic social teaching for macromarketing and business strategy," *Journal of Macromarketing*, 30 (3): 293–96.

—— and Murphy, P.E. (2006) "Normative perspectives for ethical and socially responsible marketing," *Journal of Macromarketing*, 26 (2): 154–77.

—— and Murphy, P.E. (2008) "Distributive justice: pressing questions, emerging directions and the promise of Rawlsian analysis," *Journal of Macromarketing*, 28: 5–11.

—— and Murphy, P.E. (2012). "Stakeholder theory and marketing: moving from a firm-centric to a societal perspective," *Journal of Public Policy & Marketing*, 31 (2): 284–92.

Mittelstaedt, J., Klein, T.A., and Mittelstaedt, R. (1998) "Economies in transition: evidence of religious effects on models of economic development." Presentation to the Macromarketing Seminar, University of Rhode Island, August. Abstracted in *Journal of Macromarketing*, 18: 184.

Murphy, P.E. (2005) "Sustainable marketing," *Business and Professional Ethics Journal*, 24 (1 and 2): 171–98.

——, Laczniak, G.R., and Prothero, A. (2012) *Ethics in Marketing: International Cases and Perspectives*, New York: Routledge.

Pope Benedict XVI (2009) *Caritas in Veritate* [Charity in truth]. Vatican City, Libreria Editrice Vaticana, online: www.vatican.va/holy_father/benedict_xvi/

encyclicals/documents/hf¬¬_ben-xvi_enc_20090629_caritas-in-veritate_en.html (accessed September 26, 2009).

Santos, J.C.N. and Laczniak, G.R. (2009a) "Just markets from the perspective of Catholic social teaching," *Journal of Business Ethics*, 89: 29–38.

—— (2009b) "Marketing to the poor: an integrative justice model for engaging impoverished segments, *Journal of Public Policy & Marketing*, 28: 3–15.

Selbourne, D. (1994) *The Principle of Duty: An Essay on the Foundations of Civic Order*, London: Sinclair-Stevenson.

Tom's of Maine (n.d.) "Good business: Beyond the bottom line," online: www.tomsofmaine. com/business-practices (accessed June 15, 2012).

8

A COMMENTARY ON CATHOLIC SOCIAL TEACHING AND "WANTING THE RIGHT THINGS"

Timothy J. Gilbride

Laczniak, Klein, and Murphy (Chapter 7, this volume) introduce us to *Caritas in Veritate* (*CiV*) (Pope Benedict XVI 2009) and connect it to the broader exposition on Catholic Social Teaching (CST) in Klein and Laczniak (2009). The authors' intention is to promulgate CST as a normative ethical theory that can be studied, understood, and accepted outside the confines of Catholicism to address issues in marketing and business. I will comment on whether or not *CiV* or CST offers a prima facie case for or against marketing; the role of the individual as an ethical consumer, manager, or investor; and challenges to the greater study or acceptance of CST as a normative ethical theory.

CiV and marketing

Modern academic thought in marketing has sought to move enterprises away from a "production oriented" view of the firm to a "consumer oriented" view. In the production orientation, a good or service is produced and then potential customers are identified and/or consumers are persuaded to purchase the firm's offering. A consumer orientation starts with the wants and needs of customers and the firm tailors its offering to those wants and needs. In his seminal article, Smith (1956) referred to the first strategy as "the bending of demand to the will of supply" while the second "represents a rational and more precise adjustment of product and marketing effort to consumer or user requirements." Although any number of examples from industry or even academic articles could be cited as deviations from this norm, the primacy of the consumer is sacrosanct to the modern conception of marketing.

A reading of CST, and *CiV* in particular, might lead one to accept modern marketing (or at least its ideal form) as being consistent, or at minimum, not in direct opposition to the Church's teachings. When discussing economy and finance *CiV* states:

> Economy and finance, as instruments, can be used badly when those at the helm are motivated by purely selfish ends. Instruments that are good in themselves can thereby be transformed into harmful ones. But it is man's darkened reason that produces these consequences, not the instrument *per se*. Therefore it is not the instrument that must be called to account, but individuals, their moral conscience and their personal and social responsibility.
>
> *(36)*[1]

CiV (42) makes a similar case for globalization and makes clear that these "instruments," or processes, are not *a priori* bad. Couldn't the same also be said of marketing? As cited in Laczniak *et al.* (this volume), *CiV* (66) states that "it [marketing] can be helpful to promote new ways of marketing products from deprived areas of the world, so as to guarantee their producers a decent return." When combined with the notion of subsidiarity, a consumer centric approach to business appears to be consistent, or again, not directly opposed to CST. As explained in Klein and Laczniak (2009), the principle of subsidiarity pushes both decision-making authority and ethical responsibility down to the lowest level in society as is practical. While this is usually interpreted as involving larger units in the social hierarchy (e.g., indigenous peoples having input into their economic development as opposed to it being dictated by businesses, governments, or non-government organizations), it seems reasonable that families and/or individuals should be trusted to choose the goods and services that best meet their needs. Thus, there does not seem to be a prima facie case against marketing as a discipline or legitimate function of business.

Individuals and ethical consuming, managing, and investing

Nonetheless, modern marketing thought is not a disembodied instrument but is yielded by actual people, making actual decisions, in actual markets. As noted by Laurent (2010), *CiV* repeatedly invokes the role of individual responsibility in ensuring that economic relations are just and fair. While certainly not eschewing the role of regulations, governments, and collective action, one is struck with the "bottom-up" approach of *CiV* to creating an ethical society. Given this backdrop, it seems completely congruent for Laczniak *et al.* (this volume) to highlight paragraph (66) and the personal responsibility of consumption: "It is good for people to realize that purchasing is always a moral – and not simply economic – act." *CiV* is not indifferent to the choices made in modern economies and laments a proneness to "hedonism and consumerism" (51) and a form of "superdevelopment" in poorer countries, which results in waste and consumerism that forms an "unacceptable contrast" with other sectors of society (22).

It seems to me that any ethical system that begins with axiomatic principles of human dignity, autonomy, and self-determination but criticizes the outcomes of free choices essentially puts itself in the position of declaring "Consumers want the wrong things." When commentators give specific examples of the "wrong" or "right" things that consumers want, I believe that these are determined from the vantage point of the speaker: "Consumers should want organic food," "consumers should want to reduce their carbon footprint," "consumers should want to give more money to support the arts," etc. Pejorative comments on "consumerism" seem to stem from the observation that other people are spending their money on things which the speaker does not value. Even a society that agrees to arrange social systems and institutions to promote the "common good" must decide on what elements must be included. As noted by Andre and Velasquez (1992), in a pluralistic society, obtaining consensus on the "right" goals may be problematic. A systematic approach to ethics must therefore inform consumers on what are the "right" choices.

As an instrument, modern marketing thought is indifferent to what are the "right" wants and needs of consumers. Theoretically, if there is demand for organic food, low-carbon-footprint products, etc. then firms will step forward to supply those needs. Obviously sunk costs lead marketing practitioners to "bend demand to the will of supply," and differences in market development and market failures result in disparities between the supply and demand for goods. However, "third party," "top down," or authoritarian calls for firms to adopt specific issues such as "green marketing" or "anti-consumption" as the focus of marketing campaigns are more closely aligned with a production orientation than a consumer orientation, and are in contrast to modern marketing thought.

In certain sections, *CiV* seems to objectify business managers and shareholders as a separate ethical species:

> Without doubt, one of the greatest risks for businesses is that they are almost exclusively answerable to their investors, thereby limiting their social value. ... In recent years a new cosmopolitan class of *managers* has emerged, who are often answerable only to shareholders ...
>
> *(40)*

An antidote to this suggested in *CiV* (40), by Laczniak *et al.* (this volume), and others are for business managers to adopt a stakeholder orientation. However, to the extent that managers appropriate the resources of their shareholders to advance their own interests (even if they are aligned with other stakeholders), then this violates both property rights and the fiduciary responsibilities of the managers to the shareholders. For example, Tim Cook, when he was named the new CEO of Apple, Inc., announced the formation of a charitable foundation that will match employee's contributions to not-for-profits up to $10,000 per year. This is a stark contrast from the former CEO Steve Jobs' opposition to "giving money away" (Vascellaro 2011). Hypothetically, should Mr. Cook on his own accord pledge all of Apple's (then) $82 billion of on-hand cash for charitable contributions and good works; what about only half, $41 billion? This would still have left Apple with one of the largest cash hoards in the technology sector (Wilhelm 2011). It is hard to imagine how such benevolence on the part of Mr. Cook would be ethical without the consent of Apple's shareholders. Managers must act in concert with the shareholders, perhaps by persuading them of the wisdom of their proposed initiatives, or abdicate their positions.

However, the objectification of managers and investors, and the apparent conflict between the "shareholder" and "stakeholder" view of the firm, rests on two assumptions. First, shareholders and business managers check the ethical dimension of their personhood at the door once they enter the marketplace. And second, the "rules of the game" in business and marketing necessitate this outcome (cf. Miller 2009). However, *CiV* rejects both these assumptions: "Above all, the intention to do good must not be considered incompatible with the effective capacity to produce goods" (65) and,

> When we consider the issues involved in the *relationship between business and ethics*, as well as the evolution currently taking place in methods of production, it would appear that the traditionally valid distinction between profit-based companies and non-profit organizations can no longer do full justice to reality, or offer practical direction for the future. In recent decades a broad intermediate area has emerged between the two types of enterprise. It is made up of traditional companies which nonetheless subscribe to social aid agreements in support of underdeveloped countries, charitable foundations, ... This is not merely a matter of a 'third sector,' but of a broad new composite reality embracing the private and public sphere, one which does not exclude profit, but instead considers it a means for achieving human and social ends.
>
> *(46)*

We are brought back to *CiV*'s emphasis on personal responsibility and investors (i.e., shareholders) and managers' ability to form and manage business enterprises in a more socially desirable way, even within the current institutional structure. Thus, the interests of shareholders and stakeholders are not necessarily at odds with each other. Economics, finance, marketing, and business are not problematic if managers and investors "want the right thing." Once again, how does an ethical system inform managers' and investors' choices?

Greater consideration of CST as an ethical norm

For CST and *CiV* there are not separate answers for consumers, managers, and investors. In fact *CiV* rejects the notion of a separate "economic ethics" that exists independent of non-marketplace concerns: "*[A]uthentic human development concerns the whole of the person in every single dimension*" (11). It also sounds a cautionary note about "ethics" becoming a generic term and that when business ethics strays from "the dignity of the human person and … natural moral norms" it can become part of the problem, and not the solution (45). In *CiV*, authentic human development occurs when humans embrace truth, charity, and solidarity with their fellow man. This then permeates all decisions and becomes the standard for deciding which "wants" (consumer or managerial) are ethical. "What is needed is an effective shift in mentality which can lead to the adoption of *new lifestyles* in which the quest for truth, beauty, goodness, and communion with others for the sake of common growth are the factors which determine consumer choices, savings, and investments" (51). For Catholics, the ambiguity of these terms is resolved through a relationship with God:

> Only through an encounter with God are we able to see in the other something more than just another creature, to recognize the divine image in the other, thus truly coming to discover him or her to mature in a love that 'becomes concern and care for the other.'
>
> *(11)*

CiV then seems to call for greater personal fidelity to an ethical system whose axiomatic foundation includes "the inviolable dignity of the human person" and discernment based on reason, truth, and charity informed by a "transcendent vision of the person" (i.e., God).

The intellectual instrument of marketing stands ready to meet the wants and needs of consumers who adopt this "new lifestyle." The more relevant challenge is whether we as consumers, managers, and investors "want the right things." Are we willing to pay a little more, delay career advancement, and/or settle for a lower return on our investment in order to foster a more integral form of human development? Foregoing personal gain or agreeing to bear an unequal burden is also fundamental to fostering the "common good" (Andre and Velasquez 1992). As such, *CiV* and CST require us to reflect critically on our individual and, by extension, our collective choices.

In their conclusion, Klein and Laczniak (2009) note that CST has different philosophical "roots" even though it arrives at similar practical prescriptions as many other religious or secular ethical systems. In their chapter on *CiV*, Laczniak *et al.* (this volume) highlight issues on the role of markets, sustainability, business ethics, developing markets, and consumer responsibilities among others where CST provides by and large, a non-controversial perspective. I think the pragmatic approach of these authors is appropriate.

However, as most readers of this volume can attest, many critics of marketing doubt the legitimacy of the discipline altogether or castigate its corrosive effect on culture (see, e.g., adbusters.org). Often this results from an overly naïve or layman's view of marketing. Clearly the discipline can do a better job of informing the public of the many facets and broader purpose of marketing. When documents such as *CiV* attest to the good that marketing *can* do (e.g., (66)), this buttresses the legitimate role of marketing in society. Some critics of marketing reject the notion that firms react to the wants and needs of consumers and as a result take a more institutional approach. They argue that the market economy is "rigged" against individuals and/or the existing power relations are so entrenched that the notion of consumer sovereignty is a quaint, but nonexistent entity in today's world. These critics will reject the *CiV*'s emphasis of individual responsibility as a means of reforming the economy to be more fair and just. Even those who find themselves aligned with the overall message of *CiV* may advocate a more governmental, institutional, or "top-down" approach to marketing ethics, such as making it illegal to include toys in restaurant meals targeted to children. However, "forcing" firms to offer more virtuous products to an unreceptive market, again, is at odds with modern marketing thought.

A final, and perhaps more difficult objection to CST and *CiV*, is the reliance on a relationship with God as the final arbiter of making ethical decisions or of "wanting the right things." Many will reject or not consider CST at all due to its religious source; this denies CST a critical reading and analysis that will strengthen its intellectual foundation. This is unfortunate for the skeptic as well since it denies him/her the opportunity to examine the axiomatic underpinnings of his/her own ethical system. I think that efforts by scholars such as Laczniak, Klein, and Murphy that demonstrate the practical usefulness of CST will prompt a thoughtful assessment of the full range of Catholic Social Teachings.

Note

1   Throughout this comment I will use parentheses (XX) to refer to the numbered paragraphs in CiV. This section was not explicitly discussed in Laczniak *et al.*'s treatment of paragraph (36).

References

Andre, C. and Velasquez, M. (1992) "The common good," *Issues in Ethics*, V5, N1 (Spring). Online: www.scu.edu/ethics/publications/iie/v5n1/common.html (accessed April 10, 2012).

Klein, T.A. and Laczniak, G.R. (2009) "Applying Catholic social teachings to ethical issues in marketing," *Journal of Macromarketing*, 29: 233–43.

Laurent, B. (2010) "*Caritas in Veritate* as a social encyclical: a modest challenge to economic, social, and political institutions," *Theological Studies*, 71: 515–44.

Miller, V.J. (2009) *Consuming Religion: Christian Faith and Practice in a Consumer Culture*, New York: The Continuum International Publishing Group.

Pope Benedict XVI (2009) *Caritas in Veritate* (Charity in truth). Vatican City, Libreria Editrice Vaticana, Boston, MA: Pauline Books & Media.

Smith, W.R. (1956) "Product differentiation and market segmentation as alternative marketing strategies," *Journal of Marketing*, 21 (1): 3–8.

Vascellaro, J.E. (2011) "Apple in his own image," *The Wall Street Journal*, November 1. Online: http://online.wsj.com/article/SB10001424052970204394804577012161036609728.html (accessed November 2, 2011).

Wilhelm, A. (2011) "Big money: The companies with the biggest cash piles in tech," *The Next Web*, August 22. Online: http://thenextweb.com/insider/2011/08/22/big-money-the-companies-with-the-biggest-cash-piles-in-tech/ (accessed November 2, 2011).

PART IV

Sustainability issues in marketing

9

CONSUMPTION IN THE UN-COMMONS

The economic case for reclaiming the *commons* as unique *markets*

F. Byron (Ron) Nahser

[T]he ideas of economists and political philosophers, both when they are right and when they are wrong, are more powerful than is commonly understood. Indeed the world is ruled by little else.

(Keynes 1964: 383)

Why have we made so little progress in addressing the environmental crisis – everything from global warming to decline of virtually every ecosystem, including the alarming decline of biodiversity? Why can't we seem to connect the dots between our consumption habits and the overshooting of the earth's resources used to support our way of life? It certainly can't be for the lack of scientific evidence with an estimated 97 percent of the world's scientists verifying and testifying to the facts of global warming and anthropogenic carbon generation as a major cause of it (Anderegg *et al.* 2010). If it isn't lack of scientific information holding us back from taking dramatic steps, could it be the narrow focus of our deeply held economic ideas which Keynes referred to, and the language used to communicate them?

Just what are these ideas Keynes thought were so powerful? Who are these economists and philosophers? How and why do their ideas rule us? Many of them, such as the free-market model, have helped inspire citizens in overthrowing governments (e.g., Russia and Arab Spring) and in the creation of thriving emerging economies (e.g., China and India), lifting millions in societies all over the world out of poverty to better standards of living. But in the process, we are consuming beyond the material and environmental limits of the planet's resources. If Keynes is right about the power of ideas, resurrecting old time-honored concepts such as the commons could greatly help guide better economic strategies and financial invest-ment decisions to serve the common good. However, this task requires a winding but selective journey following the development of a handful of crucial economic ideas, looking for the language, narratives, and logic to make the case for a sustainable and just world. It will mean reclaiming original definitions about marketing – and especially its parent discipline, economics – to help us better understand how ideas about markets, deeply embedded in our minds, influence our thinking and actions. While not a trivial or simple task, these ideas, words, and concepts just might hold the key to helping us all construct better logic and language leading to making investment decisions which help serve the common good and foster a just, compassionate, and sustainable world.

Background

> There's no business to be done on a dead planet.
>
> *(David Brower, Founder of the Sierra Club)*

Since this volume focuses on *Marketing and the Common Good*, we need to examine the role marketing plays in creating society's demand-led consumption which ultimately is causing many of our pressing environmental crises. Overarching this is the Catholic Social Teaching (CST) on the Common Good, described as "the sum total of social conditions which allow people, either as groups or as individuals, to reach their fulfillment more fully and more easily" (Catechism of the Catholic Church, 2013, Sec. 1906).

The purpose of this chapter is to further develop another CST pillar, that of *Subsidiarity*, which simply states that the social order should be built from the ground up, not top down. This more organic view offers a countervailing force to the overwhelming trend of globalization of economies spreading across the world (Friedman 2008). Specifically, how might the perspective of the commons – places where we dwell and share together – impact our understanding of the purpose of marketing, simply defined as a "human activity directed at satisfying needs and wants through an exchange process?" (Kotler 1976). Economics, marketing's parent discipline, deals with both supply and demand and, not surprisingly, shares the same end: "All production is for the purpose of ultimately satisfying a consumer" (Keynes 1964).

The activities of satisfying needs and wants – supply and demand – can also be broadly portrayed as making up much of the activity of society, hence the central need to reclaim marketing and economics for the common good. Wouldn't it be ironic if one of the ideas to help us with this sought-for heightened awareness of the collective impact of consumption turned out to be thinking of the commons as markets, and that each commons or market is unique – uncommon – based on its history, geography, and ethical customs – its way of doing business.

"Commons as markets?" I can picture the business folks warming to this introduction … and hear the gasps and shouts from our NGO friends.[1] Talk about trading with the devil. After all, aren't marketing and advertising practices blamed for guiding and motivating our habits of consumption that got us into this unsustainable global economy in the first place? What about all the blatant efforts to put a price tag or intrusive advertising message on everything and privatize our shared resources? (Sandel 2012). Aren't "markets" what financial people make and trade in, whether in their physical "open outcry" trading pits and exchange trading floors, or now in the cyberspace, often seen as nothing more than global gambling casinos?

But stop and consider this obvious possibility: nature is an economy of supply and demand too. It shops locally, manufactures at ambient temperatures and there is no waste in its closed-loop systems (Lovins 2008; Benyus 1997). Debits and credits always eventually must balance for there are no externalities since "nature is a strict accountant" (Spencer 1861). Or, in street terms, there is no free lunch.

Specifically, to reclaim marketing as a discipline to serve the common good, we will have to take a long journey through economics as the foundation discipline from which marketing developed. Indeed, we must go back to the very roots of modern economics as a moral philosophy, articulated by Adam Smith. With this firm foundation, we will move through examining the commons as viable economic units, commons as cities and regions, then as markets which can be "branded." The development of these pictures, words, and logic, as Keynes suggested, leads and directs much of our daily activities of making, selling, and buying which collectively add up to the activities of our society. And they all occur in markets.

Historically, these each developed their unique cluster – cathedrals and churches, town halls, tribunals, guildhalls, and, yes, markets with their stalls, push carts, and entertainment – where people for millennia have come together to trade merchandise, ideas, culture, and gossip (Zamagni 2010). These activities, many say, gave birth to our democracies through the practices of the so-called "bourgeois virtues" (McCloskey, 2006) These economies developed, not just through technological advances, but because of the respect and dignity for the transactions conducted through trusting commercial relationships.[2]

And just maybe this so-called "deep re-framing" (Lakoff 2006) of the commons as economic markets might put the overwhelming scientific evidence of the environmental crisis into a more easily understood context by all sides of the issue. Continuing to berate the public on the dire consequences seems to have the opposite effect intended: doubt and denial, often using the evidence of the few skeptics among the scientific and meteorological communities (Boykoff 2011). Wouldn't you think meteorologists on the evening news would be the loudest champions of addressing the challenges of climate change? The more aesthetic proponents of the visual, audio, and tactile beauty of nature are quickly dismissed as "romantics" or are told that we have enough public parks and land. We might remind the frustrated environmentally concerned scientists and citizenry, who decry the narrow focus of many in the business community, of an old advertising admonition, which is to always remember to answer the underlying question in the customer's mind that every selling pitch has to address "what's in it for me?" Sell the benefit, not the feature. (It is so pervasive in sales circles that its acronym *WIIFM*, pronounced *wif-em*, has been made into a mantra.) Answer: *It's about developing and preserving markets*, as David Brower often reminded us.

To make that case we will turn to the task of examining several evolving narratives about marketing, economics and then the commons as markets, and the tangible locus where investment decisions affecting sustainable development are made, positively and negatively. Simply, with the important exception of internet sales, these investments materialize at some physical point-of-sale/exchange relationship. This paper will conclude by broadening these points-of-sale to the larger scale of markets seen as part of a naturally defined bioregion or watershed.

With this background, we now turn to examining the importance of language and the meaning of the three key words in this chapter: *commons*, *markets*, and *economics*.

The importance of language

> Words ought to be a little wild for they are the assault of thoughts upon the unthinking.
>
> *(Keynes 1933: 86)*

Consider the power of descriptive words and metaphorical images[3] used in the ecological conversations used to make the abstract and often-unseen crisis visible, understandable and actionable. First, there are descriptive sets of words such as global warming and climate change. Global warming is occurring, but since there is such a deliberate controversy about it, the more acceptable phrase now is "climate change." Then there are the analogies or metaphors to capture more elusive concepts such as "carbon footprint," "greenhouse gases," and the equally provocative "cradle-to-cradle," "bio-mimicry," and "economic ecosystems" all designed to stretch and spark the imaginations of designers and strategists. Drawing parallels from geological sciences, phrases like the "Anthropocene (human) Age" and the Ecozoic (ecological) Age have entered our vocabulary. And of course we have the *market*, which I am suggesting might be a worthy, memorable and actionable metaphor for the *commons*.

But are we simply playing with words to get people's attention and aid in their understanding? Adam Smith, whose work we shall engage in much more detail later, certainly didn't think so. He went so far as to say that, in his study of the sciences, "the analogy ... became the great hinge upon which everything turned" (Smith 1795). You have to admit that the word and concept of *markets* is a big hinge, a little "wild," and has a bite to it. Can we put it to good use?

What follows may seem like trivial rhetorical games, and simple harmless "reframing." But we recognize the power of rhetoric from millennia of results up to our post-modern era of neural linguistic analysis and economic rhetoric and behavior, the subject of recent Nobel Prizes (Tversky and Kahneman 1992). (For an example of the power of language from the current sustainability debate, the late Ray Anderson's conversion story is one to remember – Anderson 2009). Beneath all of these stories run deep economic currents of ideas which have immense impact on the investment decisions we make to meet demand. So, with the importance of language clearly in mind, we turn to get to the root meaning of several of our central words, starting with *commons*, *markets*, and *economics*.

Commons

Consider what the meaning of community or commons is made of. We might think that it's from the Latin words cum and unus "one with." It is *cum* – "with," but *munus* – which

> has an interesting cluster of meanings denoting first a *duty*, or *service* … second a *gift* … and finally a *sacrifice* with this implication both of giving something up and giving something back … *munus* is derived from the root *mei*, which denotes "exchange" and even more generally "change."
>
> *(Jordan 2003).*

This notion of sacrifice, duty, and service is what leads to fostering the common good, the exact opposite of the usual direction of thinking about exchange. And exchange takes place in markets.

Markets

I am not suggesting that we consider commons as markets in the conventional sense of shopping malls and industrial districts, but in the metaphorical or analogical meaning; a geographic area not only as place such as a bio-region or watershed with defined physical boundaries, but also as a place where environmental, cultural, political and consumer and business goods and services are exchanged to serve the needs of society.

We may take a clue from the Chinese ideograms for market or *shi chang*: 市场, *shi* meaning a place with leashes for animals and a place with mud walls, and *chang* meaning either a place not for farming but to honor gods, or when the sun is highest right above the land – the strongest time of positive energy. Together it is considered a place where people come together to conduct trade and barter in an organized and honorable way. This definition, particularly of *shi*, recalls one of the early definitions of ethics from *ethos* – originally meaning "stable or the habitat of horses" (Homer 1952). And don't forget that many of Socrates' dialogues took place in the Agora (marketplace) just below the Parthenon in Athens. From this understanding of habit or custom (an idea that will become central later) came our understanding of ethics as character, or what today we call "virtue ethics" explained by Aristotle in the Nicomachean Ethics (MacIntyre 1981).

Economics

If we believe in the power of language to help form mental models leading to action, then consider what perspective we in the West have lost by the narrowing of economics to "allocation of scarce resources which have alternative uses." That's a long way from our foundational definition of the word: Greek: *economica* – meaning *"stewardship of the household."*

Consider an equally stunning narrowing in the East. The word for economics is new in Eastern thought, so in modern Chinese characters *jing ji* (经) translates immediately as "economics" to anyone who reads Chinese. But this drains the original meaning of *jing ji* when it was coined to explain this new Western term of economics. The root *"jing"* 經 means "weave" and *ji* 濟 means "benefit/save/rescue." Our modern minds ask: weaving *what...*for the benefit of *whom*? The full classical symbols 經世濟民 make it clear: *"weaving the social fabric* and *benefitting people."* While "economics" has been practiced for at least forty centuries in China, by embracing Western economic concepts they are losing the original expansion and depth of meaning just as we are.

We need to reclaim economics as the process of making investment decisions as being good stewards (managing) our "households" and "weaving the social fabric for the benefit of people," i.e., the common good. Before we make the case for economics as a practice of moral philosophy we need to tell how marketing as a discipline has gone through an astonishing evolution of understanding its role in society ... from a simple distribution function in the economy to be a major driver of building demand.

A "new and improved" marketing concept

My unlikely approach to linking the commons to the economy through marketing is best summarized by our leading marketing educator, Philip Kotler, who was trained as an economist at University of Chicago and MIT, studying with Paul Samuelson and Milton Friedman, from whom we will hear much more later. Kotler defined the discipline as follows: *"Marketing serves as the link between society's needs and its patterns of industrial response ... It must be put at the heart of strategy"* (Kotler and Witzel 2003). His role in moving marketing from the distribution fringes of business activity to the central strategic role earned him fourth place in a recent *Financial Times* survey/poll of 1,000 global executives surveyed to determine leading business writers/thinkers (Kotler and Witzel 2003). My attempt in this chapter to further move marketing language by calling the commons as markets is just another step in a long process of development of the marketing discipline which is worth a much closer look.

In sustainability discussions, the focus often starts and ends on the supply side/ chain – how things are made, where and with what kinds of materials and how they are distributed. Overlooked too often is the blazingly obvious statement about the purpose of economics: "All production is for the purpose of ultimately satisfying a consumer." It took Keynes until Chapter 5 of *The General Theory of Employment, Interest and Money* to state that, however (Keynes 1964).

As a discipline, marketing has come a long way from its humble beginnings in the 1920s as consisting *"of those efforts which effect transfers in the ownership of goods, and care for their physical distribution"* (Clark 1923). Since then, scholars in marketing, and especially its parent discipline of economics, have attempted for decades to establish a quantitative science similar to the physical sciences, especially physics, for predicting and optimizing consumer behavior by manipulating everything from price points to advertising copy. However, there were other sources of inspiration. We are going to follow the thinking of several scholars in the development of marketing as a discipline of relationship, with Phil Kotler as a prophetic voice (Murphy 2012).

As we have already noted, Kotler initially defined marketing as a "human activity directed at satisfying needs and wants through an exchange process" (Kotler 1976). But as the years went on, and the editions of the ground-breaking *Marketing Management* textbook rolled all over the world, Kotler marked the evolution:

> Marketing started out as an analysis of how commodities are produced and distributed through an economic system. Subsequently we became interested in the distribution channels themselves and in the functions that markets performed. At a point, of course, all these things got combined. But, each time the field's focus shifted. What I think we are witnessing is a moving away from a focus on exchange and a narrow sense of transaction, and toward a focus on building value laden relationships, and marketing networks.
>
> *(Kotler 1991)*

Other leading scholars have weighed in with such insights as Theodore Levitt's landmark 1960 article on "Marketing Myopia" which moved *selling* from a product focus to *marketing* with a consumer focus, e.g., "You aren't in the railroad business, but in the transportation business" (Levitt 1960). Peter Drucker, who often weighed in on the side of marketing, stated: "There is only one valid definition of business purpose: *to create a customer*" (1954: 61, italics in the original). He goes on to say: "any business enterprise has two – and only these two – basic functions: marketing and innovation." He insisted that marketing was a function unique to business and that no other human organization undertook marketing of their product or service (Drucker 1954). Leading marketing scholars came to challenge that widely held idea as too limiting and it is key to our story.

Scholars such as Kotler, with distinguished Kellogg colleagues such as Sidney Levy, and later John Sherry, have done much to further the understanding of marketing as a deeply social as well as a business discipline. For example, Kotler and Levy in an article appropriately entitled: "Broadening the Concept of Marketing" (1969) helped the discipline take another giant step by stating:

> The authors see a great opportunity for marketing people to expand their thinking and to apply their skills to increasingly interesting range of social activity. The challenge depends on the attention given to it; marketing will either take on a broader social meaning or remain a narrowly defined business activity.
>
> *(p. 10)*

Of course, the answer, which we will explore more fully when talking about the marketing of cities/commons/markets, is that all kinds of organizations – some NGOs very reluctantly – now see themselves as "marketers." Further, Kotler and Levy (1971) wrote an article called "Demarketing, Yes, Demarketing" where manufacturers were actually encouraged to entertain the idea of selling less of their product, an unheard-of concept in many marketing circles where both increased sales and increased market share are the only measures of success. This article was partially in response to the environmental movement of the late 1960s and early 1970s where marketing was criticized for stimulating "over-consumption" of certain products.

Sustainable marketing concept

Here is a next step as Kotler has moved from the exchange model to the relationship model. He describes what he calls the *societal marketing concept*: "[T]he organization's task is to determine the needs, wants and interests of the target markets and to achieve the desired results more effectively and efficiently than competitors, in a way that preserves or enhances the consumer's or society's well-being" (Kotler and Keller 2009).

Entering the domain of the common good, Kotler (2011) dramatically launched his latest broadening of the marketing concept by attacking the largely unexamined assumptions marketers hold as eternal truths in his, what some might say, landmark article in the 75th Anniversary Issue of the *Journal of Marketing* entitled "Reinventing Marketing to Manage the Environmental Imperative." In his opening sentence he stated that "Marketers in the past have based their strategies on the assumption of infinite resources and zero environmental impact." He then outlines the "largely unexamined assumptions of marketers in the past":

- Wants are natural and infinite, and encouraging unlimited consumption is good.
- The planet's resources are infinite.
- The Earth's carrying capacity for waste and pollution is infinite.
- Quality of life and personal happiness increase with increased consumption and want satisfaction.

In contrast, the new assumptions necessary to deal with the environmental crisis are:

- Wants are culturally influenced and strongly shaped by marketing and other forces.
- The Earth's resources are finite and fragile.
- The Earth's carrying capacity for waste and pollution is very limited.
- Quality of life and personal happiness do not always increase with more consumption and want satisfaction.

This certainly takes us 180 degrees from marketing and advertising's long history, decried since the beginning of time, reaching decibel levels since the Industrial Revolution with the rise of opulence toward the end of the nineteenth century. These acerbic critics range from Mark Twain and *The Gilded Age* (Twain and

Warner 1873) to Thorsten Veblen's *The Theory of the Leisure Class* (Veblen 1899), and update to Vance Packard's *The Hidden Persuaders* (Packard 1957) followed by the continuing avalanche of books to today with Naomi Klein's influential book: *No Logo* (Klein 2000).

These issues are even more important today since we continually hear that the immediate way out of our Great Recession is to create jobs by stimulating consumption – get money in the hands of consumers. While the Chinese authorities worry that their economy isn't moving quickly enough to a consumer economy, American world observers worry what it means if 400 million Chinese do become avid consumers, as they move into the cities springing up all over China – buying everything from cars to air conditioners, and building the energy infrastructure to power them. What about mass transportation, health, culture, and education as other types of demand? Voices like Kotler are showing how concerned citizens can look to marketing to help them solve the seemingly intractable problems of awakening and engaging the public to develop more sustainable patterns of consumption.

Now that we have broadened the understanding of marketing as "the process through which economy is integrated into society to serve human needs" (Drucker 1958), we can turn to examine the narratives driving the underlying structure of marketing: economics. The stakes are higher and the path is longer with more twists and turns, because we will be challenging several of the "powerful ideas" Keynes thought ruled the world. I advocate that these ideas are central to reclaiming the commons as markets.

Reclaiming economics as moral philosophy

> Economics is not an exact science; it is in fact, or ought to be, something much greater: a branch of wisdom.
>
> *(Schumacher 1973: 254)*

Moving beyond consumption, the story of how we got to our present ecological (and financial) crisis, too often inspired and guided by a limited understanding of economics, is a long and complicated one. In many ways, however, it is an old and familiar story: greed, overspending, risk to the point of gambling, extending more credit than needed or deserved.

All these are vices as old as humankind, decisions about the purpose of human activity, which have been asked since the beginning of time in all cultures. And as noted above, the purpose of the enterprise revolves around providing what we need, which raises the fundamental questions driving moral philosophical inquiry which I have come to see and interpret as *marketing* questions, stimulating individual and organizational strategies:

What is the "good" or "flourishing" life?

What is it we, as individuals and as a society, need?

How do we get it?

What do we value – what is worthwhile?

What is our purpose?

What are our goals?

How do we achieve them – what work are we to do?

What if these are also seen as fundamental *economic* questions?

(Nahser 2009)

As we continue through our global economic and environmental crises, what if we are becoming aware that we must ultimately – again – face and address questions about the purpose of human activity, which have been asked since the beginning of time in all cultures? These perennial *philosophical* questions can be seen now as fundamentally *economic* questions as they bring to life the basic model of supply and demand. As each of us in cultures around the world plays a role in the unfolding story of the meaning of wants versus needs, we are impacting our economies and their resources: natural, social, human/individual, financial, and built (e.g., infrastructure and products).

How might the present economic discipline be broadened and connected to the common good, as we saw how marketing can be broadened? What if economics came to be seen as a framework of moral reasoning to develop "narratives" of purpose, values and goals to answer the questions posed above? (Daly and Cobbs 1994). But to accomplish this we must challenge the capitalist economic model sweeping the globe which states with its beguiling simple goal that the purpose of business is to optimize return to shareholders and investors. To reinforce the aim of this chapter: can we rescue marketing – and its parent, economics – from their century-long attempt to be a natural science to determine the laws of scarce resource allocation? Instead we should put these disciplines to their original use as the practice of moral philosophy to better decision-making that thoughtfully considers the full implication of those decisions.

This essential next step involves working our way back to economics' roots in moral philosophy; a critical analysis if we are to enlist the power of the analogy of markets to be a "great hinge" (Smith 1795) to further our understanding of places where we all endeavor to serve the common good. We start by re-examining and challenging the underlying purpose and goal of economics as it is practiced today.

What is the goal of economics?

In criticism of his old teacher Alfred Marshall, the father of modern economics and models of economic systems, Keynes, often stated that while mathematical models were useful to stimulate thought, ultimately economics is "a branch of logic, a way of thinking . . . . a moral science and not a natural science. That is to say, it employs introspection and judgments of value" (Keynes 1938).

We haven't been listening to him in the United States, particularly at the "Chicago school," the home of the most dominant school driving the capitalist logic which holds business practitioners and business schools in its grip:"maximize return to shareholders." Since this is such a core idea often attributed to an influential article by Michael Jensen (Jensen and Meckling 1987) we need to take the time to follow its development, if we are to rescue the common good from this investor-only perspective.

The Chicago School

Milton Friedman (Nobel award in 1976) and George Stigler (Nobel award in 1982) are leaders of the so-called Chicago School of economics which has done so much to develop, and at the same time give the concepts biting and memorable rhetoric which has helped polarize the society into the two camps:"profits vs. social purpose;" expressed in political philosophy terms as "capitalism/free markets vs. socialism." These dualisms can be seen as a major cause and source of confusion inhibiting the progress of corporations, organizations and government working together toward sustainable development and serving the common good. As stated above, the assumption driving the Chicago School's thinking and analysis is that the all economic agents are rational self-optimizers, and therefore the purpose of business is solely to "maximizing return to shareholders."

What we are working against in the Chicago School is best exemplified by Milton Friedman's famous and often-quoted cornerstone remark summarizing the role of capitalism in society:

> [T]here is one and only one social responsibility of business to use its resources and engage in activities designed to increase its profits so long as *it stays within the rules of the game*, which is to say, engages in open and free competition, without deception or fraud.
>
> *(Friedman 1962: 133, emphasis added)*

He goes on to say that other drives for social responsibility in business are "pure and unadulterated socialism." So much for the common good. But there is hope. Eight years later in a newspaper article intended to gain broad public exposure, he began with the now-familiar statement that the responsibility of executives is "to conduct the business in accordance with their desires, which generally will be to make as much money as possible while conforming to the basic rules of the society," but then he goes on to say something for our purposes radically new for him: "[B]oth those embodied in the law and those embodied in *ethical custom*" (Friedman 1970: 33, emphasis added).

Ethical custom is quite a journey away from "open and free competition without deception and fraud." How important is this? Well, David Hume, Adam Smith's great friend and student of experience said "It is not reason which is the guide of life, but custom." Custom or habit, stated earlier, is a key thought in the field of virtue ethics.

Friedman, perhaps unwittingly, has given us one key – a Smithian "great hinge" (Smith 1795) to connecting economics back to moral philosophy. Friedman's close friend and colleague at the Chicago School, George Stigler, led us to another.

Stigler has stated repeatedly the central importance of Adam Smith, father of modern economics, and his monumental "granite foundation" construct of the "self-interest-seeking individual within a competitive environment" (Stigler 1982: 147). Stigler, of course, has in mind Smith's insight into the self-interest of the rational individual in *Wealth of Nations* (*WN*). You know the familiar refrain: "It is not from the benevolence of the butcher, the brewer, or the baker, that we expect our dinner, but from their regard to their own interest" (Smith 1776/1979: 26-27).

But what great work of Smith's came before *WN*, and what was its seldom read or remembered opening sentence?

The Theory of Moral Sentiments

The next step in loosening this "profit-maximization," "free market," "self-interest seeking" grip on the discipline and to reconnect and reground micro- and macro-economics in the commons takes us back to economics' original focus as a *moral philosophy*, articulated by Adam Smith, but breathtakingly narrowed by Stigler. Smith began his book *Theory of Moral Sentiments* with this observation:

> How selfish soever man may be supposed, there are evidently some principles in his nature which interest him in the fortunes of others, and render their happiness necessary to him, though he derives nothing from it except the pleasure of seeing it.
>
> *(Smith 1759/1976: 9)*

So, there are other motives/sentiments beyond the singular focus on individual self-interest. This focus on happiness, by the way, is the understanding Thomas Jefferson drew from the Scottish Enlightenment when he wrote as one of our inalienable rights "the pursuit of happiness" (Wills 2002). Concern for others and common concerns we all share – including our impact on the environment – present a platform for us to "render" service to others. And *where* do we render those services? Smith was adamant that we needed to engage our "fellow-creatures ... to perfect and improve a certain beautiful and orderly system," which would ignite "the love of the order and beauty of a system which promote the public welfare" (Smith 1759/1976: 185). He pointed out that particular examples of systems, not general principles, were needed[4] which brings us to the next step on our journey of linking the commons with markets.

Rethinking the commons

I now present evidence for linking commons and markets to the economy with the announcement of the 2009 Nobel Prizes in Economic Sciences to Elinor

Ostrom and Oliver Williamson. (Dr. Williamson's work focused on cost-saving efficiencies within internal organization boundaries and the importance of trust, as does Dr. Ostrom's work). The headline for Ostrom's award was: "The Nobel Committee Announcement of the Dr. Elinor Ostrom Award: 'For her analysis of economic governance, especially the commons'." It is further stated that:

> Whereas economic theory has comprehensively illuminated the virtues and limitations of markets, it has traditionally paid less attention to other institutional arrangements. Economic transactions take place not only in markets, but also within firms, associations, households, and agencies.

> Over the last three decades these seminal contributions have advanced economic governance research from the fringe to the forefront of scientific attention.

> … The research of Elinor Ostrom and Oliver Williamson demonstrates that economic analysis can shed light on most forms of social organization.
>
> *(Nobel 2009)*

To put Ostrom's remarkable achievement in historical context, we need to show how her work begins to reclaim our key word that has had a troubled past: "The Commons" (Walljasper 2010).

The story begins with the "Tragedy of the Commons" which can be seen as the background assumption Ostrom was working against. It is more remarkable, or maybe more understandable, in that Ostrom is a social scientist, not an economist. This prompted one social activist friend to immediately see that it took an outsider to be a "whistle blower," difficult for someone classically trained within the economic field.

Tragedy of the Commons

Do you remember when you first encountered Garrett Hardin's (1968) monumentally challenging and depressing "Tragedy of the Commons?" (Some of us over a certain age remember its immediate impact when it was first published in *Science* magazine over 40 years ago.)

Hardin's brilliantly simple premise, originally inspired by the Cold War nuclear standoff, was that, since it is in the best interests of individuals to take as much from a common resource – such as a shared pasture or body of water – the result will be the eventual destruction of that common resource. Here is the sentence that went right at the heart of the dilemma of our vaunted capitalist free market economy: "[W]e are locked into a system of 'fouling our own nest,' so long as we behave only as independent, rational, free enterprisers" (Hardin 1968: 1245).

From this conclusion came Hardin's gloomy choice – a sort of "prisoner's dilemma" application of game theory – between either regulating the resource/ system or privatizing it. These are more examples of the contentious dualisms of

"Capitalism vs. Socialism," or "Free Markets vs. Government, especially "Big" Government." But there is hope for middle ground.

Answer to the tragedy of the Commons – Ostrom's Nobel Prize

The title of Dr. Ostrom's Nobel Prize lecture says it all: "Beyond Markets and States: Polycentric Governance of Complex Economic Systems" (Nobel 2009). Here's why and how this perspective will help to understand economics' potential to contribute to the field of ecological and sustainable practice, based on markets.

Ostrom's work empirically showed that other arrangements of rule-making agreed upon by participants could be worked out – not easily, of course – precluding the need for either privatization or regulation. Her decades-long research, and reporting on the work of dozens of other researchers, tells fascinating stories – scientifically documented – about examples such as farmer-managed irrigation systems, communal forests, inshore fisheries, and grazing and hunting territories managed cooperatively[5] (Ostrom 1990; Poteete *et al.* 2010). For example, in one series of studies, teams studied water distribution in Nepal. They found that large elaborate government-funded programs with top engineering guidance were less effective than simple arrangements run by local people.

Throughout her research, and the research of dozens of teams of collaborators all over the world, she continually found that neither individuals working in their own self-interest nor government or state-imposed rules and structures were uniformly successful. Sometimes they were and sometimes they were not. It took years of work searching for "principles" of governance before she came to the key insight that successful governance was dependent on other variables: clear boundaries, fair rules, consistent rewards and punishments. And the bedrock, – the "granite" – was trust, not some foreordained principle of either free-market or organized government intervention. She called these key elements of governance *polycentric systems* (Ostrom 2010). This will later serve our argument that a commons is a series of polycentric *market* systems – serving the needs and wants of society. They provide another step toward reclaiming commons as markets, providing for the common good.

An opportunity to rebuild our communities

To help us better understand the connection between markets and commons, Table 9.1 shows a key matrix from Ostrom's Nobel address. While she constructed this 2 × 2 chart to make a point of different goods and services provided to the commons, and highlight the problem areas of "free riders," it serves a larger purpose since she brings together in just one simple chart the range of public and private goods which a commons needs. Or, to use marketing language, it contains the products, services, and resources to satisfy human wants and needs. And from a supply standpoint, these involve all forms of capital – human, natural, social, and physical.

TABLE 9.1 Four types of goods

Difficulty of excluding potential beneficiaries	Subtractability of use	
	High	Low
High	Common-pool resources: groundwater basins, lakes, irrigation systems, fisheries, forests, etc.	Public goods: peace and security of a community, national defense, knowledge, fire protection, weather forecasts, etc.
Low	Private goods: food, clothing, automobiles, etc.	Toll goods: theaters, private clubs, daycare centers

Source: Adapted from Ostrom (2005:24).

She uses the table to show the various "free rider" problems so persuasively presented by Hardin. She divides goods by ones we share in common and those we own individually. And in consuming the goods, she divides them by whether our use decreases the ability of others to use them. In lower left quadrant of "private goods," where most traditionally understood marketing activity takes place, there is no problem of fairness (e.g., if I buy a car, no other "potential beneficiary" can buy it and there is one less car on the market – 100 percent subtractability). However, the upper left quadrant shows those environmental services which are usually identified as susceptible to the "free rider" problem: Hardin's tragedy. As an example, ground water and forests are common pool resources which have high accessibility and everyone has access to them. "I take more and then there is less for you." That's a problem.

Now think about the impact this has on the places where the product or service is created and manufactured. When you look at all those products and services, they can be delivered by private, public, nonprofit, or even the emerging so-called "Fourth Sector" or "Social Enterprise" organizations – those which combine the mission of NGOs and the discipline of business. In fact, this growing segment of organizational type focused on creating shared value is getting growing attention from business schools[6] (Porter 2011a,b).

Investment strategy and competition

This leads to our main point in considering the commons of both supply and demand as a market. Think about the possibilities for unique mixes of supply and demand that give every area, place, location its unique un-common ethical customs and character captured in a "brand," as we will explain later. It is obvious as you look at any list of cities – Detroit, or Silicon Valley, or Shanghai, or your hometown/ commons – and draw a list of Ostrom's "Four Types of Goods." These all require investments which help the cities run better, but also give them their unique histories, culture, competencies, and spirit (Boff 2011). It helps define them and informs their strategies in competition with other cities, a big area where marketing can help (Kotler *et al.* 1993, 1997; Porter 1990).

We further build on Smith's insights, with a reverent and deep bow to his best known work: *An Inquiry into the Nature and Causes of the Wealth of Nations* (Smith 1979).

An inquiry into the nature and causes of the wealth of markets

> I have long believed that talent attracts capital far more effectively and consistently than capital attracts talent. The most creative individuals want to live in places that protect personal freedoms, prize diversity and offer an abundance of cultural opportunities. A city that wants to attract creators must offer a fertile breeding ground for new ideas and innovations.
>
> *(Bloomberg 2012)*

In stating that talent is the cause of the wealth of cities, Bloomberg is updating the analog in Smith's opening paragraph on the division of labor in manufacturing pins, which he saw as a case source of the wealth of nations. Of course, there are many reasons that people are attracted to make choices of where to live, not the least of which are vibrant downtowns and neighborhoods with social, cultural and night life for the so-called "Cultural Creatives" (Florida 2002). Our case will be Chicago, telling just two stories of thousands which help shed light on the building of the unique culture of cities. The first is about educational institutions and the second is a neighborhood story.

What is the role of educational institutions as learning regions (Florida 2002) in developing the talent of a market? Many say it was the presence of Stanford University and its particular approach to entrepreneurial technology that made the difference in the growth of Silicon Valley. Consider the numbers in Chicago: there are approximately 100,000 college students in the metropolitan area of Chicago, with 65,000 of them concentrated in the Loop/downtown area of Chicago.[7] Certainly this means a great deal in terms of revenue to the city. But beyond that, what does this mean to the thriving, changing, innovative, entrepreneurial economy of Chicago?

And further, what is higher education institutions' role in developing their communities through their operations? We also need to know that these institutions are "walking the talk." While educational institutions all over the world are embracing the challenge of modifying existing curricula, or starting a brand-new programs, degrees, or even colleges to meet the environmental and social challenges, the question in students' minds invariably comes up whether the college is being managed by sound environmental and social principles as are being taught.

DePaul University in Chicago offers an exemplary lesson. With the explosion of returning veterans after World War II, DePaul found itself, as many universities in America did, in the enviable situation of having to dramatically expand to meet the demand. On the North Side of Chicago, its Lincoln Park campus had deteriorated from the Depression through the 1950s. Rather than consolidate in their downtown Loop campus, they engaged in the long and messy process of working with various stakeholders in the neighborhood. The result of this decades-long, and continuing, process has been a dramatic revitalization of the neighborhood.

This process of engagement stands in stark contrast to the University of Chicago's strategy, secretly buying property to provide barriers or buffers to separate the university from their poor, African-American neighbors. Another strategy of engagement was undertaken by the late Mayor Richard J. Daley who summarily leveled vast areas on the west side of Chicago to make way for the dramatic University of Illinois-Chicago campus. (O'Brien 2013) DePaul officials were, in effect, living their mission and values, as exemplified by the work of St. Vincent DePaul in seventeenth-century Paris, known as a superb manager and often quoted as saying: "It is not enough to do good, it must be done well."

Planning for the Chicago commons as a market

Today, Chicago is made up of 77 communities, each with its own unique character. This variety might explain the dramatic shifts in population from after World War II to today. Using census data, we can see the move to urban sprawl after the war, and then, in the last 20 years, the movement back to the city (Bennett 2010). This mass movement was accomplished without one single, dramatic dictate by statute, policy, or law; rather it reflects the many thousands of decisions like the DePaul and Andersonville case we will cover later, building step-by-step places where people wanted to live and connect.

These examples are part of a long history of Chicago planning, beginning with vision of natural abundance stated in the motto adopted at the city's incorporation in 1837: *Urbs in Horto* – "City in a Garden." But the real beginning took place with the 1893 Columbian exposition. The great success of the Exposition and its dazzling "Great White City" showed the city leaders that such planning could be effective and should be applied to solving the overwhelming congestion and health and poverty conditions in the city. That led to the famous Burnham and Bennett *Plan of Chicago*, "the first real comprehensive plan in the United States" (Ely Chapter 2009) and the accompanying *Wacker's Manual* (Moody 1915) a required educational textbook for all Chicago eighth-grade students.

Much of the *Plan of Chicago* was enacted – think of the beautiful Chicago lakefront, boulevards, and parks. And with the election of Richard M. Daley (Richard J. Daley's son) as mayor in 1989, with the help of his enlightened wife Maggie, he led the way for further beautification with everything from the first municipal rooftop garden on City Hall, to flower containers on Michigan Avenue median strips and the wildly popular projects like Navy Pier and Millennium Park aimed at fostering "urban tourism" (Bennett 2010). These efforts, often criticized as aesthetics only and deriding Daley as the "Martha Stewart of Mayors," went deeper to the very life of the city. In November 2006, he formed the Chicago

Climate Task Force, which published its findings and recommendations in the influential "Chicago Climate Action Plan" in 2008 (Chicago Climate Task Force 2008) with a follow-up "Lessons Learned: Creating the Chicago Climate Action Plan" (Parzen 2009) a year later. He proclaimed that he would make Chicago America's Greenest City driven by the belief that "environmental initiatives should not just be out on the West Coast, Alaska, or by the oceans, but in cities … otherwise no one will want to live here" (Chamberlain 2004) echoing similar sentiments from the *Plan of Chicago* nearly 100 years earlier.

Chicago region

> The economy is a wholly owned subsidiary of the environment, not the other way around.
>
> *Senator Gaylord Nelson (D: WI), founder of Earth Day*

However, little was accomplished at the macro-regional levels of planning. Despite recent efforts such as the innovative *Chicago Metropolis 2020* plan for a *five-county* area, which took direct aim at the problems of excessive private motor vehicle transportation (Johnson 1999), progress ground to a halt as local authorities and political groups protested the limits that might be placed on their jurisdictional authority, and on individual freedom and responsibility. This battle to gain public acceptance and will to embrace the change necessary to better use our resources continues, with the stakes ever higher (Schwieterman and Mammoser 2009; Bennett 2010). Most recently, in the midst of the "Great Recession" in 2008, the Chicago mayor succeeding Mayor Richard M. Daley, Rahm Emanuel, has focused more on economic planning for the Chicago Metropolitan Statistical Area as outlined in the 2012 draft of "A Plan for Economic Growth and Jobs: World Business Chicago" for cities, suburbs and neighborhood of *fourteen* counties, linking their economic fates together to build the "next economy" (Anderson *et al.* 2012). Economics and "economic ideas" reassert themselves within regions.

But speaking of economic fates linking together, what about being linked together by our ecosystems? Our human territorial boundaries are often drawn with no consideration for the bioregions they cover, governed by nature not legislatures, fundamentally defined by topography which configures weather, watersheds, soil, and drainages. We always need to consider and work within the constraints of this larger natural region on which we ultimately draw our necessary resources. As former Senator Nelson reminds us, nature is ultimately the economy on which we all depend and dictates our limits, because "nature to be commanded must be obeyed" (Bacon 1984).

In Chicago's case that means in addition to our soil, trees, rivers, etc. it means most importantly, Lake Michigan and the Great Lakes. In mid-November 2010, groups of environmental activists on both sides of the border declared the Great Lakes as a "Common Endowment" which was determined to be in danger of running virtually dry by 2090, citing the draining of 90 percent of the Aral Sea in Central Asia, once the fourth largest fresh-water body in the world.

FIGURE 9.1 Michigan's Great Lakes.

Source: Courtesy of Michigan Department of Natural Resources and Environment. Reprinted with permission.

The key graphic on their website shows the Great Lakes as a drainage, rightfully to be protected (Figure 9.1).

In the Fall of 2012, the Mendoza School of Business at Notre Dame sponsored a conference on the "Great Lakes Commons," building on the work of the "Great Lakes and St. Lawrence Cities Initiative" and Notre Dame's own "Global Commons Initiative."

While this striking image of the Great Lakes Bio-region as a watershed gives pause to consider just how interconnected we are, they might go further and think of this irreplaceable, invaluable natural resource as outlining and grounding a series of cities as *markets* – with interconnected systems of civil, social, economic *and* environmental resources.

The opportunity now is to have people think about places with uniquely different landscapes, consumption patterns and supply skills, some built up over generations or centuries in the case of leading global cities like Paris, London, Tokyo, Shanghai, Rio, and Mumbai. The challenge is to understand these regions and brand them so that people would identify with it as much as they do with their neighborhood, alma maters and local sports team – sources of local pride. This has the benefit of establishing an area with its own unique identity because of its geographic and cultural uniqueness. That's another advantage of considering the commons as a market, then harnessing the power of branding.

The market as a brand narrative – the un-commons

> Brands and branding are the most significant gifts that commerce has ever made to popular culture.
>
> *(Wally Olins, Said School, University of Oxford)*

There are many ways to tell the story of a city, its urban life and its development and prospects. The attention paid to the subject is vast (e.g., Cronon 1991; Bennett 2010). Just consider the fields of urban economics, economic anthropology, economic ecosystems, and technology clusters, urban development, urban design, urban architecture, community development, and urban ecology. And the seemingly endless list of commissions, councils, chambers, and groups on community development, all doing important work (e.g., Ely Chapter 2009).

We have long decried the fact that cities increasingly all look the same, especially when you get to the franchise fast food row and identical shopping malls with their anchor stores. ("Wait a minute … am I in Boston's Copley Place or Hong Kong's Grand Century Place?") Worse, many local stores have been either driven out of business or bought out by the larger retail consolidation, such as Macy's taking over Chicago's legendary Marshall Field's Department Store, eliminating such unique traditions as Uncle Mistletoe and Aunt Holly at Christmas which was long a source of local pride and identity. Sometimes there is hopeful news as in the case when design-conscious Target took over Carson Pirie Scott & Co.'s landmark State Street store designed by Louis Sullivan (Kamin 2011). But other times the takeover wake can be potentially brutal. Chicago, along with many other cities, has wrestled with the issue of what to do when Walmart wants to come to town. The case is a simple one in terms of the jobs and tax revenue – not to mention lower prices – which the big box will bring. Usually there is talk about displacing local merchants when the bargaining goes on, and most times Walmart wins.

However, a study in a North Side neighborhood conducted by the Civic Economics in Austin, Texas, and Chicago in cooperation with the Andersonville Chamber of Commerce and the Andersonville Development Corporation (Andersonville 2004) showed quite simply that the overall benefit to the neighborhood would be greater without Walmart than with Walmart. In a lengthy and carefully constructed argument, the key economic case came down to this stark and simple comparison:

- For every $100 in consumer spending with a local firm, $68 remains in the Chicago economy.
- For every $100 in consumer spending with the chain, $43 remains in the Chicago economy.

Business case made!

Notable for our purposes are those groups working to build fertile partnerships among the social, private, and public sectors. These groups, such as the Business

Alliance of Local Living Economies (BALLE), the so-called emergence of the "Fourth Sector Movement," and the fields of cultural and social entrepreneurship are actively building the kinds of commons to practice the common good economics we have in mind.

The only attempt here is to highlight all this work moving toward the development and functioning of *markets* from the point of view of what is required – demand – and production – sources of supply. Marketing offers a proven efficient and persuasive way to structure the narrative of a place as a market: what it means to live and work there, and what it might mean to visit there. It's what Friedman might even call each city's "ethical customs" (Friedman 1970). To speak poetically (Sherry and Schouten 2002), can we as marketers say that the city/market is where dreams are pursued and made; offering the promise of opportunity and adventure. And that, at heart, meets the simple definition of a brand: a promise of some experience, value, and benefit (Olins 2003). But it is not easy to do, as the Discovery Channel story to build a "Planet Green" channel tells. The company had to rebrand the channel as Destination America recently with an emphasis on patriotic programs focused on travel and food rather than an exclusively "eco-entertainment" programming (Stelter 2012).

Hopefully, by this point you are ready to respond more receptively and creatively to the question: "What can the discipline of marketing offer to this conversation concerning the common good?" Marketing thinking can serve as the bridge between the public, social and business communities. Each region has a unique environment, geography, skills, culture – "sustainable competitive advantages," as we refer to them in strategy terms. This unique "brand" is what I mean by each city being "un-common" (Cronon 1996).

In referring to cities as markets, unlikely as it might first seem, can help in making the economic case for longer-term, group decision-making with ecological economic systems as the bridge. The reason is that it would position the individual decisions of the free market within its rightful context, bringing the supply and demand of all four groups of goods and services in Ostrom's Table 1 together to serve a community (Ostrom 1990).

Then we might make the case that people would care about their city. Urban planners, mayors, city councils, civic boosters, chambers of commerce, and policymakers have been working on this for decades. As you think about ways to further your practice and consider the often contentious conversation especially between our political parties (e.g., "liberty" vs. "common good") remember how long and intractable these conversations have been. The commons as economic markets might be one way to bridge the gaps. A further advantage to this view leads to the education of managers since the concept of sustainable development and management opens a unique way to attempt to bridge the gap that exists between the business community and its social and physical environment. It moves the environment to the center of strategy, beyond corporate social responsibility, just as marketing has moved to the heart of strategy. Both share the same focus: concern for the commons and the common good (Nahser 2009).

Conclusion: un-commons, markets, and gardens

> Rootedness is perhaps the most important and least recognized need of the human soul.
>
> *Simone Weil (2005)*

This chapter has attempted to sketch a logic revealing the potential unifying power of presenting *markets* as the frame, image and language for understanding and building sustainable systems ... and help citizens expand their identity, affection, pride, and loyalty to embrace a larger region. It is presented in the belief that commons, seen as markets, can further foster the elusive common good in which we all can benefit. The goal of articulating how we are to live and serve the common good is not new, having been preached and practiced every day by thoughtful leaders and thinkers for millennia. Just as Adam Smith saw the ingenuity of the populace, harnessed by the division of labor as the Wealth of Nations, so today we can see our natural resources, technology, and culture – our "ethical customs" (Friedman 1970) – leading the way, with each community, region, bioregion, and watershed combining its assets in unique, sustainable, attractive ways to enliven their citizens and to serve society's needs. Every un-common market must be about building relationships based in trust and the promise of an experience – a brand, as in Chicago's motto *Urbs in Horto* cited above – which undergirds the marketing discipline.

Earlier, I noted Kotler's observation of the movement in marketing thinking from an exchange model to one based on relationships. One evening over dinner, I asked him just how far one can go in the movement of a close relationship with the customer. After some deepening of the conversation about relationship, Kotler responded by asking if I was thinking at the "I/Thou" relationship level of the great Hasidic mystic, Martin Buber. Quietly, I said yes. Kotler observed, with a wry smile, "it might be possible, but not much research has been done at that level." Obviously, Kotler himself in his studies of marketing has been driving to that deeper level since, in Buber's words: "All actual life is encounter" (1970: 62).[8] And in these encounters, Smith would add: "all the members of human society stand in need of each other's assistance" (Smith 1759/1976: 85). That sounds like a market to me.

Which brings us to a final marketing question concerning place: "Where do you dwell" – or "Where are you" as it is usually translated – is God's first question of us in the Bible: Genesis 3:9. We all dwell in a garden, a commons, which gives us roots; but there is nothing common about them. Each is a unique, un-common place we might call by name as a *market*. Here each unique/un-common individual shares and exchanges our natural and human resources – tangible and intangible – we have all been given to develop as we encounter and creatively serve one another in need. As every great moral tradition – even economics when practiced as moral philosophy – tells us: this is the true path to happiness.

Notes

1   I have to thank Daniel Carroll, Managing Editor of *Environmental Practice: The Journal of the National Association of Environmental Professionals* for this crisp summary of the possible range of response to my initial idea. This essay builds on my "Ethics and Economics" article for the September 2012 issue of *EPJ*.

2   A leading voice, and inspiration on this vital issue is Deirdre McCloskey. She has a long history of having shown the way to rethink economics as "rhetoric," which is why I share her belief in the effort to reclaim the language of marketing. See this remarkable scholar's extensive website as a place to start: www.deirdremccloskey.com.

3   There is a rich history of philosophy and semiotics in the issue of types of words. Charles S. Peirce referred to "signs, symbols and indexes" (Buchler 1955). Richard Dawkins recently introduced the idea of "memes" as units of meaning which enter a culture and act as genes to the transmission of knowledge. I have chosen to simplify and distinguish between literal and analogical or metaphorical attempts at meanings (Dawkins 1989). We also have in mind the remarkable work of Kenneth Boulding on images (Boulding 1961).

4   Smith had much more to say on "systems," which I take to mean the workings of a market. If anyone doubts the claim that Smith was a moral philosopher, they should at least read Part VII of *The Theory of Moral Sentiments* (1759/1976): "Of Systems of Moral Philosophy."

5   Obviously, they don't give out Nobels for a study or two, so the range of Ostrom's reports is vast. However, a good place to begin is with this clear overview of her work: the issues, the methodology and the results. Also see her Nobel lecture, referenced below.

6   The writings on this are growing exponentially, e.g., www.ft.com/intl/cms/s/2/b2eefd14-87e6-11e1-b1ea-00144feab49a.html#axzz1stJFvAJV. And consider the effort led by leading business schools such as HBS, Stanford, Wharton: www.fourthsector.net.

7   This draft summary of the aggregate data collected from twenty-four institutions that compose the Chicago Higher Education Civic Engagement Roundtable is also derived from the US Department of Education Integrated Post Secondary Education System (IPEDS). IPEDS is the most credible, comprehensive and independently verifiable source for information regarding your respective institutions of higher education. The data year reported encompasses the calendar year 2010-11.

8   Such an encounter in Buber's terms requires a complete fusion (probably a little beyond what is called for in marketing relationships).

References

Anderegg, W.R.L., Prall, J.W., Harold, J., and Schneider, S.H. (2010) "Expert credibility in climate change," online: www.pnas.org/content/107/27/12107.

Anderson, R. (2009) *Confessions of a Radical Industrialist*, New York: St. Martin's Press. See also videos online: www.youtube.com/watch?v=OUG4JXE6K4A (accessed May 27, 2013).

Anderson, T., Sacks, M., and Tilton, G. (2012) "A plan for economic growth and jobs: World Business Chicago," online: www.worldbusinesschicago.com/growthplan (accessed May 27, 2013).

Andersonville (2004) The Andersonville Study of Retail Economics, online: www.andersonvillestudy.com (accessed May 27, 2013).

Bacon, F. (1984) *Novum Oraganum*, Chicago: Encyclopedia Britannica.

Bennett, L. 2010 *The Third City*, Chicago: University of Chicago Press.

Benyus, J.M. (1997) *Biomimicry: Innovation Inspired by Nature*, New York: William Morrow.

Bloomberg, M. (2012) *Financial Times*, online: www.ft.com/intl/cms/s/0/c09235b6-72ac-11e1-ae73-00144feab49a.html#axzz1uQsdSTmK (accessed May 27, 2013).

Boff, L. (2011) *Virtues*, Eugene, OR: Cascade Press.

Boulding, K.E. (1961) *The Image: Knowledge in Life and Society*, Ann Arbor, MI: Ann Arbor Press.

Boykoff, M. (2011) *Who Speaks for the Climate?* Cambridge: Cambridge University Press.

Buber, M. (1970) *I and Thou*, New York: A Touchstone Book.

Buchler, J. (1955) *Philosophical Writings of Peirce*, New York: Dover Publications.

Catechism of the Catholic Church (2013) Online: www.vatican.va/archive/ENG0015/__ P6K.HTM (accessed March 19).

Chamberlain, L., "Mayor Daley's green crusade," online: www.metropolismag.com/ story/20040701/mayor-daleys-green-crusade (accessed May 27, 2013).

Chicago Climate Task Force "Chicago climate action plan: Our city, our future," online: www.chicagoclimateaction.org/pages/research___reports/8.php (accessed May 27, 2013).

Chicago Higher Education Civic Engagement Roundtable (2012) Preliminary draft, March.

Clark, F.C. (1923) *Principles of Marketing*, New York: The MacMillan Company.

Cronon, W. (1991) *Nature's Metropolis: Chicago and the Great West*, New York: W.W. Norton & Co.

—— (ed.) (1996) *Uncommon Ground*, New York: W.W. Norton & Company.

Daly, H.E. and Cobb, J.B., Jr. (1994) *For the Common Good*, Boston, MA: Beacon Press.

Dawkins, R. (1989) *The Selfish Gene*, Oxford: Oxford University Press.

Drucker, P. (1954) *The Practice of Management*, New York: Harper & Row.

—— (1958) "Marketing and economic development," *Journal of Marketing*, 22 (January): 252–59.

Ely Chapter (2009) *The Plan of Chicago @ 100*, Chicago: Ely Chapter, Lambda Alpha International.

Florida, R. (2002) *The Rise of the Creative Class*, New York: Basic Books.

Friedman, M. (1962) *Capitalism and Freedom*, Chicago: University of Chicago Press.

—— (1970) "The social responsibility of business is to increase its profits," *New York Times Magazine*, September 30.

Friedman, T. (2008) *Hot, Flat, and Crowded*, New York: Farrar, Straus and Giroux.

Hardin, G. (1968) "Tragedy of the commons," *Science*, 162 (3859): 1243–48.

Homer (1952) *The Illiad*, Chicago: Encyclopedia Britannica.

Jensen, M.C. and Meckling, W.H. (1987) "Theory of the firm: Managerial behavior, agency costs and ownership structure," *Journal of Financial Economics*, 3(4): 305–60.

Johnson, E. (1999) *Chicago Metropolis 2020*, online: www.amacad.org/publications/cm2020. pdf (accessed May 27, 2013).

Jordan, W.R. III (2003) *The Sunflower Forest*, Berkeley: University of California Press.

Kamin, C. (2011) Online: featuresblogs.chicagotribune.com/theskyline/2011/02/target-on-state-street-good-news-but-god-or-the-devil-will-be-in-the-details-.html (accessed May 27, 2013).

Keynes, J.M. (1933) "National self-sufficiency," *An Irish Quarterly Review*, 22 (86): June: 177–93.

—— (1938) Letter from J. M. Keynes to R.F. Harrod, July 4. Online: http://economia. unipv.it/harrod/edition/editionstuff/rfh.346.htm#23502 (accessed May 27, 2013).

—— (1964) *The General Theory of Employment, Interest and Money*, San Diego, CA: A Harvest Book, Harcourt.

Klein, N. (2000) *No Logo*, New York: Picardo.

Kotler, P. (1976) *Marketing Management*, 3rd edn, Englewood Cliffs, NJ: Prentice-Hall.

—— (1991) *Marketing Science Institute Review*, Cambridge, MA: Spring.

—— (2011) "Reinventing marketing to manage the environmental imperative," *Journal of Marketing*, 75 (4): 132–35.

—— and Keller, K.L. (2009) *Marketing Management*, 13th edn, Upper Saddle River, NJ: Pearson Prentice Hall.

—— and Levy, S. (1969) "Broadening the concept of marketing," *Journal of Marketing*, 33 (1): 10–15.

—— and Levy, S. (1971) "Demarketing, yes, demarketing," *Harvard Business Review*, 49(6): 74–80.

—— and Witzel, M. (2003) "Guru guide Phil Kotler: First among marketers," *Financial Times*, August 6.

—— Haider, D., and Rein, I. (1993) *Marketing Places*, New York: The Free Press.

—— Jatusripitak, S., and Maesincee, S. (1997) *The Marketing of Nations: A Strategic Approach to Building National Wealth*, New York: The Free Press.

Lakoff, G. (2006) *Thinking Points*, New York: Farrar, Straus and Giroux.

Levitt, T. (1960) "Marketing myopia," *Harvard Business Review*, July–August: 24–47.

Lovins, L.H (2008) In public talks.

McCloskey, D. (2006) *The Bourgeois Virtues, Ethics for an Age of Commerce*, Chicago: University of Chicago Press.

MacIntyre, A. (1981) *After Virtue: A Study in Moral Theory*, Notre Dame, IN: University of Notre Dame Press.

Moody, W.D. (1915) *Wacker's Manual of the Plan of Chicago: Municipal Economy*, Chicago: The Henneberry Company.

Murphy, P.E. (2012) "The contributions of Philip Kotler to CSR and marketing ethics," in *The Social and Ethical Side of Marketing*, Los Angeles: Sage.

Nahser, F.B. (2009) *Journeys to Oxford*, New York: Global Scholarly Publications.

Nobel (2009) The Sveriges Riksbank Prize in Economic Sciences in Memory of Alfred Nobel 2009. Online: www.nobelprize.org/nobel_prizes/economics/laureates/2009/ (accessed May 27, 2013).

O'Brien, S. (2013) "DePaul University's role in the redevelopment of Lincoln Park," unpublished honors thesis, June.

Olins, W. (2003) *On Brands*, London: Thames & Hudson.

Ostrom, E. (1990) *Governing the Commons*, Cambridge: Cambridge University Press.

—— (2010) "Beyond markets and states: Polycentric governance of complex economics systems," *American Economic Review*, June: 641–72.

Packard, V. (1957) *The Hidden Persuaders*, New York: D. McKay Co.

Parzen, J. (2009) "Lessons learned: Creating the Chicago Climate Action Plan," online: www.chicagoclimateaction.org/filebin/pdf/LessonsLearned.pdf (accessed May 27, 2013).

Porter, M. (1990) *The Competitive Advantage of Nations*, New York: The Free Press.

—— (2011a) "What is strategy? The five competitive forces that shape strategy," in *On Strategy*, Boston, MA: Harvard Business Review Press.

—— (2011b) "Creating shared value," *Harvard Business Review*, January–February.

Poteete, A.R., Janssen, M.A. and Ostrom, E. (2010) *Working Together*, Princeton, NJ: Princeton University Press.

Sandel, M.(2012) Online: www.theatlantic.com/magazine/archive/2012/04/what-isn-8217-t-for-sale/8902/ (accessed June 20, 2013).

Schumacher, E.F. (1973) *Small Is Beautiful: Economics As If People Mattered*, New York: Harper and Row.

Schwieterman, J.P. and Mammoser, A.P. (2009) *Beyond Burnham: An Illustrated History of Planning for the Chicago Region*, Lake Forest, IL: Lake Forest College Press.

Sherry, J. and Schouten, J.W. (2002) "A role for poetry in consumer research," *Journal of Consumer Research*, 29 (2), 218–34.

Smith, A. (1795) *Essays on Philosophical Subjects*, London: Printed for T. Cadell, Jun. and W. Davies in the Strand.

—— (1759/1976) *The Theory of Moral Sentiments*, London: Oxford University Press.

—— (1776/1979) *An Inquiry Into the Nature and Causes of the* Wealth of Nations, Indianapolis: Liberty Fund.

Spencer, H. (1861) *Physical Education*, online: http://oll.libertyfund.org/index.php?option=com_staticxt&staticfile=show.php&title=2249&search=%22accountant%22&chapter=212794&layout=html#a_3435693) (accessed May 27, 2013).

Stelter, B. (2012) "Discovery to remake Planet Green Channel," *New York Times*, online: http://mediadecoder.blogs.nytimes.com/2012/04/04/discovery-to-remake-planet-green-channel/ (accessed May 27, 2013).

Stigler, G.J. (1982) *The Economist as Preacher*, Chicago: University of Chicago Press.

Tversky, A. and Kahneman, D. (1992) "Advances in prospect theory," *Journal of Risk and Uncertainty*, 5: 297–323.

Twain, M. and Warner, C.D. (1873) *The Gilded Age: A Tale of Today*, Hartford, CT: American Publishing Co.

Veblen, T. (1899) *The Theory of the Leisure Class*, New York: Macmillan, pp. 64–70.

Walljasper, J. (2010) *All That We Share*, New York: The New Press.

Weil, S. (2005) *The Need for Roots*, London: Taylor & Francis Group.

Wills, G. (2002) *Inventing America*, New York: Houghton Mifflin Company.

Zamagni, S. (2010) "Catholic social thought, civil economy and the spirit of capitalism," in D.K. Finn (ed.) *The True Wealth of Nations*, Oxford: Oxford University Press.

Further reading

Bennis, W.G. and O'Toole, J. (2005) "How business schools lost their way," *Harvard Business Review*, 83 (5): 96–104.

Crooks, E., "Global warming manageable, says Exxon Chief," online: www.ft.com/intl/cms/s/0/1ff711c8-c066-11e1-982d-00144feabdc0.html#axzz1zgaOdGOL (accessed June 27, 2012).

Curran, C.E. (2002) *Catholic Social Teaching: 1981–Present*, Washington, DC: Georgetown University Press.

Daly, H.E. and Farley, J. (2004) *Ecological Economics*, Washington, DC: Island Press.

Datar, S., Garvin, D.A., and Cullen, P.G. (2010) *Rethinking the MBA: Business Education at a Crossroads*, Boston, MA: Harvard Business Press.

Fatemi, A.M., Fooladi, I., and Wheeler, D. (2009) "The relative valuation of socially responsible firms: An exploratory study," In H.-C. de Bettignies and F. Lépineux (eds) *Finance for a Better World: The Shift toward Sustainability*, New York: Palgrave Macmillan, pp. 140–67.

Frank, T. (n.d.) The *Baffler* No. 2 "Twentieth Century Lite," online: www.thebaffler.com/past/twentieth_century_life (accessed October 20, 2012).

Harkavy, I. and Puckett, J.L. (1994) "Lessons from hull house for contemporary urban university," *Social Service Review*, 68(3): 299–321.

Hawken, P. (1993) *The Ecology of Commerce*, New York: Harper Business.

——, Lovins, A., and Lovins, L.H. (1999) *Natural Capitalism*, Boston, MA: Little, Brown and Co.

Johnson, B. (n.d.) Online: http://thinkprogress.org/politics/2010/02/09/81411/inhofe-family-gore-mockery/?mobile=nc (accessed May 27, 2013).

Khurana, R. (2007) *From Higher Aims to Hired Hands*, Princeton, NJ: Princeton University Press.

Lehman, N. (2000) "The word lab," *The New Yorker*, October 16: 100.

Lovins, L.H. and Cohen, B. (2011) *Climate Capitalism*, New York: Hill & Wang.

McCloskey, D. (1985) *The Rhetoric of Economics*, Madison, WI: University of Wisconsin Press.

Mintzberg, H. (2004) *Managers, not MBAs*, San Francisco: Berrett-Koehler Publishers.

Nahser, F.B. (1997) *Learning to Read the Signs*, Boston, MA: Butterworth-Heinemann.

Ostrom, E. and Walker, J. (eds) (2003) *Trust and Reciprocity*, New York: Russell Sage Foundation.

Pollan, M. (2008) *In Defense of Food*, New York: The Penguin Group.

Walljasper, J. (2011–12) "A world that works for everyone," *Notre Dame Magazine*, online: http://magazine.nd.edu/news/27932-a-world-that-works-for-everyone/ (accessed May 27, 2013).

Werhane, P. (1999) *Moral Imagination and Management Decision Making*, New York: Oxford University Press.

10

MARKETING'S CONTRIBUTIONS TO A SUSTAINABLE SOCIETY

Jenny Mish and Alexandria Miller

This chapter offers an overview of the relationship between marketing and sustainability. We frame our discussion using three theoretical foundations: (1) The Natural Step scientific framework for sustainability, (2) the aggregate marketing system described by Wilkie and Moore (1999) in an influential *Journal of Marketing* article (abstracted in Chapter 2), and (3) the marketing mix (or Four Ps) model.

After introducing the first two of these concepts and providing a brief summary of the history of marketing for sustainability, we offer a definition of a *Sustainable* Aggregate Marketing System (SAMS), and a simple proposition to adapt Wilkie and Moore's (1999) groundbreaking analysis of the aggregate marketing system to the context of sustainability. We then illustrate the application of these insights in each of the four marketing-mix elements. The chapter concludes by highlighting the key role of standards and certifications and by discussing the potential for achieving sustainable levels of growth, which we identify as a requirement of a sustainable aggregate marketing system that contributes to the common good.

Sustainability and the aggregate marketing system

In 1983 the United Nations established the Brundtland Commission to explore the need for what came to be called sustainable development. The Commission recognized that the current pace and processes of social and economic development had become harmful to the surrounding natural environment (United Nations 1987). In order to address concerns like dwindling natural resources and increased health hazards, the Commission called for a change in the way nations approach economic and social growth. The Brundtland Commission defined sustainable development as "development that meets the needs of the present without compromising the ability of future generations to meet their own needs" (ibid.: Chap. 2, para. 1). Although many alternative definitions are also in use, the United Nations' concept of sustainable development has become the most widely adopted view of sustainability.

In practical terms, sustainability amounts to living within the carrying capacity of the earth's renewable resources. An "ecological footprint" measures human demand for the earth's ecological resources, or the relationship between aggregate levels of consumption and the earth's carrying capacity (Rees 1992; Wackernagel 1994). Using United Nations' data, the earth's carrying capacity was exceeded for the first time in 1980 (www.footprintnetwork.org). It is projected that the natural resource equivalent of two earths will be needed each year by 2030, using modest growth assumptions (World Wildlife Foundation 2010), unless human behaviors change significantly.

A scan of major trends influencing marketing threats and opportunities reveals a diminishing supply of natural resources to support increasing rates of consumption in many of the world's economies. Many indicators are available to support this conclusion. For example, in 2008, 1.4 billion people lived without access to adequate fresh water (Gardner 2010). The depletion of ecosystem supplies (such as seafood, minerals, and fresh water), and services (such as climate regulation, waste processing, and pollination) is of great concern to global business leaders, who are increasingly compelled to take responsive action. A comprehensive scan would include dozens of critical social and environmental concerns. As but one example, 53 percent of Latin American CEOs, 34 percent of Asia-Pacific CEOs, and 18 percent of Western European CEOs expressed concern about business growth impacts of biodiversity loss (PricewaterhouseCoopers 2010). A website for PricewaterhouseCoopers asserts that, "The private sector is an important part of tackling this challenge. Although biodiversity was once thought to be precious only to romantics and idealists, economists have more recently placed a hard value on it – currently $33 trillion" (www.pwc.com/gx/en/sustainability/hot-topics/biodiversity.jhtml).

To examine the relationship between marketing and sustainability, we use a conceptual framework known as The Natural Step (Holmberg and Robèrt 2000; Nattrass and Altomare 1999). Under the direction of Swedish oncologist Dr. Karl-Henrik Robèrt, an international body of over 50 scientists representing a broad cross-section of disciplines responded to the Brundtland Commission report by identifying the boundary conditions within which human activity could remain within the earth's carrying capacity. After 21 drafts, this group of scientists identified four parsimonious "system conditions," or global constraints, which must be met for a sustainable human future (see Figure 10.1). They agreed that nature must not be subject to systematically increasing (1) concentrations of substances extracted from the earth's crust (e.g., carbon), (2) concentrations of substances produced by society (e.g., plastics), or (3) degradation by physical means (e.g., deforestation). Finally, they agreed that in society, (4) people must not be subject to conditions that systematically undermine their capacity to meet their needs. The Natural Step framework comprises a set of sustainability planning tools based on these four system

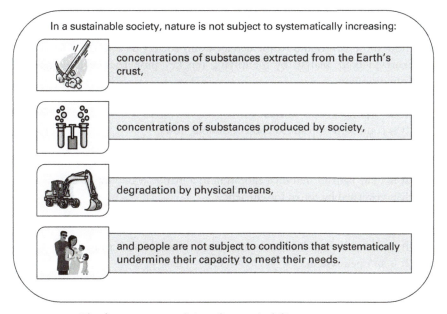

In a sustainable society, nature is not subject to systematically increasing:

concentrations of substances extracted from the Earth's crust,

concentrations of substances produced by society,

degradation by physical means,

and people are not subject to conditions that systematically undermine their capacity to meet their needs.

FIGURE 10.1 The four system conditions for sustainability.

Source: Adapted from The Natural Step 2009.

conditions, and it is used as a foundational framework for Martin and Schouten's (2012) textbook, *Sustainable Marketing*.

Marketing is often implicated as a force that encourages increasing levels of consumption, and thus may be seen as implicitly encouraging the violation of these four systems conditions for a sustainable human future. While continual innovations in the marketplace are signs of our creative and inventive culture, they may also produce unintended consequences. For example, planned product obsolescence and the cultivation of increasing consumer desires for material consumption have become powerful cultural phenomena with potentially catastrophic ultimate outcomes. As one of the main drivers in our current growth-driven market paradigm, marketing is seen as a contributor to the environmental and social problems that have resulted.

However, in contrast to this view, we believe that marketing can also *positively* contribute to a *sustainable* society. We see the potential of the marketing system to inspire and reward more sustainable consumption behavior as a power that can be harnessed for the benefit of society and the planet. We begin our exposition of this view by considering the comprehensive picture of the aggregate marketing system explicated in Wilkie and Moore's "Marketing's Contributions to Society," originally printed in the *Journal of Marketing* (1999).

Wilkie and Moore (hereafter W&M 1999) detailed the multitude of actors, events, and influences involved in the extensive web of marketing. They showed the diffuse nature of this web of relationships, permeating great swaths of human activity. They also discussed the benefits, criticisms, and problems of this system and how those contribute to (or detract from) society as a whole. The authors summarized their analysis by identifying ten key properties of the aggregate marketing system:

1   It incorporates many activities.
2   It is composed of planned and continuous flows.
3   It is extensive, in several respects.
4   It is sophisticated structurally.
5   It is a key basis for resource allocation in a market economy.
6   It is governed by forces for efficiency.
7   It is constrained by social forces.
8   It relies on coordinated processes.
9   It operates through human interactions, experience, and trust.
10 It is an open system.

In their concluding remarks, W&M (1999) acknowledged the importance of the marketing system's role in society: "That society has granted marketers substantial freedoms, and that these serve to allocate much of the nation's resources, is a key statement about a societal purpose of the aggregate marketing system" (p. 216). We find this insight to be indicative of the untapped potential for marketing to make even greater and more positive contributions to a sustainable society. In this chapter we explore that potential and suggest avenues through which marketing can be further leveraged for the benefit of society.

Characteristics of a sustainable aggregate marketing system

Applying W&M's (1999) analysis to the demands of a sustainable economy, we find that a *sustainable* aggregate marketing system has several unique identifiable characteristics. We define a Sustainable Aggregate Marketing System (hereafter SAMS) as *a global marketing system that is capable of allocating resources in such a way that the four Natural Step systems conditions are met.* This definition combines the powerful conceptual work of the scientists producing The Natural Step framework with W&M's (1999) comprehensively robust analysis of marketing as a global system.

Using W&M's (1999) ten propositions as our foundational framework, we find that a SAMS shares these same ten properties. However, we propose an extension to Proposition 7, which states that the aggregate marketing system is constrained by social forces. According to W&M, these forces primarily consist of the legal and political structures that govern markets and the society in which they operate, as well as government's interest in protecting the welfare of consumers. We admire the foresight of W&M (1999) in recognizing the inherent social limits of an aggregate marketing system. In addition, we assert that Proposition 7 must be expanded to acknowledge the limits of the earth's carrying capacity. A SAMS would also necessarily be constrained by *natural resource limits*. Thus, we propose that Proposition 7 be reformulated as:

7   The aggregate marketing system is constrained by social forces and natural resource limits.

This statement implicitly integrates the four system conditions from The Natural Step. It specifies that in addition to social constraints, marketing activities are ultimately constrained by (1) the supply of production inputs available from the earth's crust, (2) by the earth's capacity to absorb or accommodate humanly produced substances that are toxic to the planet's ecosystems, (3) by the earth's ability to recover from human activities that degrade ecosystems, and (4) by systemic conditions that undermine people's capacity to meet their basic needs. For example, the marketing of consumer electronics depends on production processes that may easily violate these thresholds. Such processes require rare metals from the earth's crust and chemical compounds that are not found in nature, as well as electricity and other inputs derived through physical degradation of the earth's ecosystems. Manufacturing facilities may undermine human capacity to meet basic needs by forcing relocation, reducing access to water, emitting toxins, or by employing workers in unsafe conditions or at wages that are too low to meet basic human needs.

How can a SAMS meet the four system conditions of The Natural Step Framework? In the remainder of this chapter, we briefly review the history of marketing for sustainability, and then examine how the marketing toolbox might best be leveraged to meet these four system conditions. To do this, we discuss the potential of each of the marketing mix elements for contributing to a SAMS, and explore the power of marketing to influence societal factors beyond the marketing mix.

History of marketing for sustainability

Marketing for sustainability began as "green marketing." In the 1960s and 1970s, various clashes between corporations and the natural environment resulted in increased legal challenges and widespread media attention (Bansal and Hoffman 2012). Consumers and advocacy organizations criticized business practices that damaged the environment. Although many firms chafed at the resulting environmental legislation, it created over a million new jobs by 1976 (Quarles 1976 in Murphy and Laczniak 1977). Some firms took steps to develop positive environmental reputations, for example by encouraging consumers to reuse the empty "egg" packages in which Legg's pantyhose were sold. However, as public relations departments attempted to promote ecological company images, critics pointed to misleading claims and partial truths, dubbing these efforts "ecopornography" (Murphy and Laczniak 1977).

In the 1980s and 1990s, market researchers discovered an untapped market in consumers who reported that they were concerned about the effects of their purchases on the environment and were even willing to pay a higher price for more environmentally friendly product packaging (Roper 1990; Mintel 1991). In response, marketers popularized product claims such as "natural," "environmentally friendly," "green," "recyclable," and "biodegradable."

However, academic and media reports found that such claims were often exaggerations or partial truths, thus creating confusion and distrust among overwhelmed consumers in the unregulated "green" marketplace (Simon 1992; Scammon and Mayer 1995). To alleviate these problems, in 1992 the Federal Trade Commission issued the "Green Guides," a set of regulatory guidelines for the appropriate use of environmental claims (US Code of Federal Regulations 1992). In addition, the 1980s and 1990s saw the development of numerous eco-labels around the world, such as Agriculture Biologique (France), EcoLogo (Canada), Ekologicky setrny vyrobek (Czech Republic), EnergySTAR (US), Environmental Choice (New Zealand), Forest Stewardship Council (Germany), Marine Stewardship Council (UK), and Rugmark (India), helping to increase the credibility of green claims through independent certifications (Mayer *et al.* 2001; Sahota *et al.* 2009). Despite these developments, unfounded promotional claims, or "greenwashing," continued to be widespread, and consumers continued to perceive corporate efforts as insincere, due in part to higher prices for green products that only narrowly considered environmental impact (Cotte and Trudell 2009; Gershoff and Irwin 2012; Peattie 2001; Peattie and Crane 2005). The resulting stagnation in consumer demand discouraged firms from pursuing more cost-effective green product innovations.

From the perspective of the firm, environmental concern gradually began to shift from legal compliance into economic opportunity (Porter and van der Linde 1995). By the late 1990s, cost reduction and competitive advantage had become prime motivators behind increasingly environmentally friendly business practices. For example, many firms decreased their pollution burden, adopted basic recycling practices, and reduced extraneous energy consumption, at least in part as cost-saving measures. However, easy opportunities to cut costs without radical changes in corporate strategy and culture were limited, and many firms found themselves facing a "Green Wall" at the end of the twentieth century (Peattie 2001).

As the new century dawned, the center of gravity had shifted from "green marketing" to the more robust concept of "environmental sustainability" (Scammon and Mish 2012). Rather than focusing on one or two individual environmental issues, sustainability-oriented marketing adopts an all-inclusive long-term perspective of global interdependence, and thus encompasses a broad range of stakeholders, concerns, and a timeline that includes the Brundtland Commission's reference to future generations. As firms and investors began to more seriously consider the future competitive landscape, it became apparent to an increasing number of managers that viability in the marketplace is inextricably connected to both the broader society and the ecological environment. The concept of a "triple-bottom-line," coined by Elkington (1998), became widely recognized as the "three-legged stool" of sustainability under various monikers, such as "people, planet, and profits." Environmentally responsive products began to gain market traction, especially in organizational markets, and in markets where eco-labels have been widely recognized by consumers.

Walmart offers a particularly dramatic and catalytic example of a business model shifting comprehensively toward a long-term resource stewardship perspective. Then-CEO Lee Scott announced in October 2005 that the mammoth retailer would pursue three radical goals: producing zero waste, using 100 percent renewable energy, and selling only sustainable products. By August 2006 when *Fortune* published a cover story on Walmart's shift toward sustainability (Gunther 2006), it was clear that these stretch goals aimed to break through the Green Wall, not only for Walmart but for the retailer's business partners as well. The initiative's first steps included tying internal management performance evaluations to contributions to the company's sustainability efforts, and requiring environmental impact reporting, initially from 60,000 top suppliers and eventually from over 200,000 providers (http://walmartstores.com/sustainability). Each of these business partners has in turn placed increased reporting demands on their suppliers, creating a ripple effect of business-to-business demand for environmentally sustainable products and services.

Many dozens of firms and institutions, such as hospitals, universities, and government agencies at municipal, state, and federal levels, have similarly adopted green purchasing policies, spurring a thriving business-to-business marketplace for products and services that aim for reduced impact on the earth's carrying capacity. Criteria used in these procurement policies commonly address triple-bottom-line concerns such as CO_2 emissions, energy efficiency, recyclability, toxicity, working conditions, and country or locality of origin. Reputable eco-labels are often specified as acceptable means of assuring compliance. Examples of business-to-business standards/certifications that have facilitated growth in organizational markets include the Voluntary Carbon Standard (for carbon credits; http://v-c-s.org), LEED (Leadership in Energy and Environmental Design, for buildings; www.usgbc.org), Greenguard (for indoor air quality; www.greenguard.org), Green Globes (for property management; www.greenglobes.com), Processed Chlorine Free (for manufacturing processes; www.chlorinefreeproducts.org), bluesign (for textiles; www.bluesign.com), and STARS (for colleges and universities; http://stars.aashe.org).

In several industries, the adoption and promotion of eco-labels facilitated public awareness beyond these organizational markets, resulting in strong and growing niche consumer markets. For example, the USDA Organic standard was launched in 2003 to designate food items grown without the use of synthetic chemicals (e.g., pesticides, herbicides, and fungicides) (www.ams.usda.gov/AMSv1.0), fueling double-digit consumer demand that has penetrated the early majority (www.ota.com). Certification for Fairtrade coffee (and since, other foodstuffs) was introduced in 1988 to differentiate coffee beans grown by farmers who were paid fair wages for their labor and products. According to Fairtrade International, global sales of Fairtrade-certified products have tripled in the last four years, and represent 20-50 percent of market share in some products and countries (www.fairtrade.net). Developments in social and environmental standards such as these have been important steps toward a cohesive and credible consumer market for sustainable goods.

In the new century, marketing scholars (e.g., Ginsberg and Bloom 2004) and consultants (e.g., Ottman 2004) advised firms to slowly and methodically phase green initiatives into their company cultures and product offerings allowing both employees' and consumers' perceptions of the company to gradually change alongside the evolution of the brand. As both consumer and business-to-business demand continued to grow, companies developed new marketing strategies for sustainable products, even through the Great Recession of 2008. The green retail market as a whole saw a 41 percent increase in growth from 2004 to 2009 despite heightened financial concerns for both consumers and firms (Mintel 2010). Techniques were developed to protect brand equity from activist criticism and integrate sustainability into a company's value system while moving toward greater social and environmental responsibility (Conroy 2007; Palazzo and Basu 2007).

The marketing mix in a sustainable aggregate marketing system

To examine marketing's potential contributions to a sustainable society, we adapted a classic lens from the field, perhaps the most widely applied theory in marketing – the marketing mix. This framework, articulated by then Notre Dame marketing professor E. Jerome McCarthy in 1960, identifies the "Four Ps" – product, price, place, and promotion – as the factors under control of marketing managers, amidst the various uncontrollable factors of the society in which the system is embedded (see Figure 10.2).

McCarthy was prescient in emphasizing both the customer as the central focus of managerial marketing decisions (via the "controllable factors"), and also the fact that every marketing activity is embedded within a broader ("uncontrollable") context. The demands of sustainability accentuate the key role of marketing managers in bridging these dimensions. Managers must simultaneously provide competitive value propositions to consumers who may not appreciate the systemic constraints of their consumption behaviors, while also helping to reduce the negative systemic impacts that may arise in production and distribution.

To better understand how a SAMS can meet The Natural Step system conditions needed for sustainability, we analyzed how each of the four marketing-mix factors might contribute to a sustainable marketing system. This allowed us to see not only where conventional and sustainable aggregate marketing systems align with and deviate from one another, but also what aspects of these identifiable properties may be controllable by marketing managers. We next discuss each of the four Ps in relation to sustainability and the four systems conditions.

Product

W&M (1999) recognized that the aggregate marketing system is governed by forces for efficiency; we find this to be evident in the product domain of a sustainable system. Echoing the ripple effect produced by Walmart, many major corporations

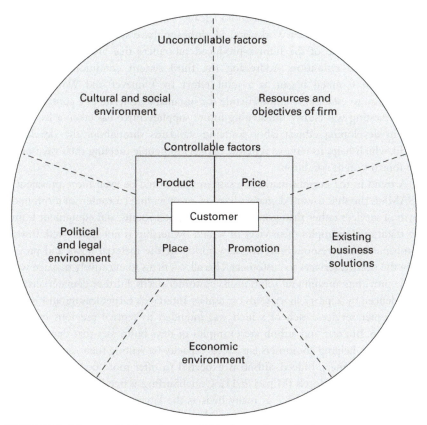

FIGURE 10.2 Uncontrollable and controllable factors in marketing.

Source: Adapted from McCarthy 1960; Perreault and McCarthy 1999.

are actively examining their product development and production processes to be able to reduce wastes, greenhouse gasses, water and energy requirements, and negative social impacts. A number of tools have been developed to facilitate measurement and management of systemic level impacts, such as the ISO 14000 Environmental Management Standards (www.iso.org/iso/iso_14000_essentials), industry-specific measures such as the Cool Farm Tool (www.coolfarmtool.org), and in-house systems such as Nike's Considered Design (www.nike.com/nikeos/p/gamechangers/en_US/considered) or P&G's Future Friendly program (www.futurefriendly.com).

Companies are actively working to develop products and production processes that meet the four system conditions identified by The Natural Step's group of international scientists. For example, managers in nearly every industry have become acutely aware of the need to reduce petroleum dependency, which reflects progress toward the first system condition (recall Figure 10.1). Mining companies and industries dependent on substances from the earth's crust (e.g., electronics and automotives) are seeking ways to reduce their dependencies through reuse, improved technologies, and increased efficiencies. Household cleaner manufacturers, such as Seventh Generation, Clorox GreenWorks, and SC Johnson, have systematically reduced or eliminated the use of the human-produced substances that are the focus of the second system condition. Addressing the third system condition, the Marine Stewardship Council began as a joint effort by Unilever and World Wildlife Foundation to establish an infrastructure for sustainable fisheries in a context where overharvesting was clearly threatening future supplies. Nike has taken a leadership role in developing ethical labor sourcing standards throughout the developing world, which helps to remove systemic barriers to people meeting their own needs, the fourth system condition.

A trend in the current marketing system that would be even more prevalent in a SAMS is the shift toward dematerialization, or providing customer solutions in the form of services rather than goods. Car rentals, hotel rooms, and equipment leasing are traditional examples of services in which ownership is not transferred. Instead, companies retain responsibility for stewardship of the material flows and provide only the needed services to customers. This allows firms to effectively manage waste while providing meaningful solutions to customer needs. Further dematerialization is evidenced by Zipcar's short-term car rentals, Interface's carpet leasing, and Xerox's photocopier services, each of which was intended to replace previous customer ownership. Buzzcar and airbnb are examples of new businesses that dematerialize even further, helping consumers tap excess capacity by renting their cars and homes to other consumers. Indeed, airbnb is expected to offer more beds worldwide in 2012 than Hilton Hotels (Mintel 2011). CouchSurfing, a free bed-exchange social network, offers almost twice as many beds as the largest global hotel chain, IHG (Chase 2012). Firms that fail to recognize the power of dematerialization risk losing market share and missing innovation opportunities.

While the marketing system currently provides consumers with numerous social and psychological benefits, as enumerated by Wilkie and Moore, marketing activities can also be directed toward innovations that offer experiential rewards. Csikszentmihalyi (2000) describes experiential rewards as those which address "the void that pervades consciousness when there is nothing else to do" (2000: 270). He asserts that although "shopping and surrounding ourselves with possessions is a relatively easy way to forestall the dread of nonbeing," active involvement in challenging tasks produces greater happiness while requiring lower environmental energy input. Research on quality of life has shown that, beyond a minimal threshold, quality of life is not enhanced by increased income or material consumption (e.g., Ryan and Deci 2001; Malhotra 2006; Kahneman et al. 2004). A SAMS would allocate more resources to market offerings that increase happiness rather than merely increasing possessions. Such an approach would be consistent with the proposals of Sheth et al. (2011), who present a business case for sustainability via "mindful consumption."

New products and especially services can help consumers improve their health, deepen family and other social relationships, and alleviate stressors such as time, information, and possession overload. Indeed, W&M (1999) identified a "central role for innovation in improving a society's quality of life" (p. 216). According to an article in the *Harvard Business Review*, sustainability has become "the new driver of innovation" (Nidumolu *et al.* 2009). Innovative product and service offerings that improve the quality of life of individuals and societies can address the fourth system condition by ameliorating circumstances that systematically undermine the capacity of people to meet their needs. This may be especially critical at the "bottom of the pyramid," where subsistence lifestyles are increasingly commodified (Viswanathan *et al.*, 2009).

However, marketers must also remember that market demand is not stimulated by adding environmentally friendly features to products that already exist – rather, consumer demand for more sustainable products is essentially the desire for *fundamentally better* products (Gershoff and Irwin 2012). Social and environmental advantages offer *secondary* benefits, increasing the overall benefit package, but they are not primary purchase drivers (Cotte and Trudell 2009).

Price

The aggregate marketing system is a key basis for resource allocation in a market economy (W&M 1999). We propose that this is also a characteristic of a SAMS, but with a key distinction. The value of a good or service is traditionally conceived of as the benefits that the customer perceives divided by the total incurred costs to the customer of purchasing the product. In a sustainable marketing system, this cost component must include not only economic costs and personal costs to the consumer, but also the social and environmental costs involved in the production, distribution, use, and disposal of the product.

For example, the costs involved in producing a cup of coffee (as illustrated by W&M in Figure 2.1 this volume, p. 17), would include costs paid for shipping, processing, packaging, storing, and so on, along the supply chain from the original grower of the beans to the distributor or retailer. However, these costs would not completely reflect the coffee's impact on The Natural Step's four system conditions for a sustainable planet. These might include increasing the concentration of atmospheric carbon extracted from the earth's crust during shipping; increasing concentrations of synthetic chemicals used in growing, processing, and packaging; ecosystem degradation from deforestation used to clear land for coffee growing; decreased health and welfare of the farmer, and so on. These added expenses, which are not adequately reflected in today's coffee prices, make that cup of coffee a more expensive product to produce.

This more complete account of value includes social and environmental costs that are currently unaccounted using a purely economic calculation. Making these triple-bottom-line value propositions successful in the marketplace challenges marketers to correspondingly increase the perceived benefits to the customer. However, the price tag must be determined with caution – while consumer demand for eco-positive products exists, the percentage of consumers actually willing to pay more for such products remains modest (Cotte and Trudell 2009).

Whole Foods provides a powerful example of skillfully managing this challenge. Using a motto of "Whole Foods, Whole People, Whole Planet," this grocery chain grew rapidly through a "more for more" positioning strategy, helping to demonstrate that mainstream consumers consider social and environmental impacts as part of the value equation. When the recession of 2008 created a belt-tightening consumer environment, Whole Foods stock initially plunged before rebounding to strong profitability by systematically educating shoppers and emphasizing the higher value proposition offered (Kotler and Armstrong 2011: 305-06). In this way, Whole Foods leveraged the price component of the marketing mix to incrementally shift the aggregate marketing system toward sustainability.

Thus, at least some of the value propositions offered in the marketplace are beginning to reflect social and environmental costs and benefits. When this is the case, the overall net resource efficiency of the marketplace is increased. In the context of the growing green building sector, the challenge of offering value propositions that reflect full-cost pricing is met when architects present the long-term costs of building operation along with initial investment costs of new construction. Buildings that are LEED certified by the US Green Building Council (www.usgbc.org) take advantage of natural light, heat, and cooling, use efficient materials, and provide healthier environments for their occupants. When operational costs are considered as part of the initial investment decision, significant cost-efficiencies become apparent.

Thus, in a SAMS, a value proposition includes the costs required to meet each of the systems conditions, which are otherwise borne by society as a whole. Whether through eco-labels or other skillful marketing (such as Whole Foods), in a SAMS the price component of the marketing mix must reflect a larger picture of the costs than conventional price tags.

Place

Several characteristics of the aggregate marketing system relate to the channel component of the marketing mix. W&M (1999) describe the distribution channel by identifying the marketing system as one that is extensive, sophisticated structurally, relies on coordinated processes, and is composed of planned and continuous flows. We find these same characteristics in a SAMS, to an even greater extent. The channel in a sustainable system is often broader than that of a traditional marketing system and can be thought of as a web connecting both traditional and non-traditional channel partners like NGOs, certification organizations, fair trade groups and government agencies. For example, Better World Books is an online retailer and social enterprise that uses its revenue to fund literacy programs around the world; this firm's channel involves a number of "non-traditional" channel partners. A sustainable system requires advanced development of aspects of the channel that measure and respond to social and environmental impact, such as sources of materials, labor practices employed, and water, carbon, and energy footprints.

A sustainable channel is not only far-reaching, but in the image of the natural environment that it seeks to mimic, is never-ending. McDonough and Braungart

(2002) introduced an influential design idea, that "all waste is food," meaning that all production outputs, including byproducts, will eventually serve as inputs to another production process. This shift transforms the traditional linear value chain into a value circle (e.g., Martin and Schouten 2012) that continues in a sort of spiral fashion. To verify and certify products that follow this principle, McDonough and his partners developed a "cradle-to-cradle" label, which differentiates these products from those that are designed "cradle-to-grave," or destined to end up in landfills. For example, all of the express envelopes used by the US Postal Service are cradle-to-cradle certified, confirming that they are designed for material reutilization and are made from components that are safe for human health and the environment across their life cycles, using renewable energy and efficient use of water (www.mbdc.com).

Material reutilization is the key to achieving a goal of "zero waste," or sending nothing to landfills. The Building Innovations division of DuPont accomplished this objective within three years, diverting 81 million pounds of waste annually (Koch 2012). Many organizations with similar goals have found it particularly challenging to find uses for the final 15-20 percent of hard-to-recycle materials. This in turn spurs innovation. For example, TerraCycle's business model is to create marketable products from previously hard-to-recycle waste, such as juice pouches, chip bags, and billboard vinyl (www.terracycle.net). TerraCycle uses "brigades" of school children and other volunteers to collect waste, and the company also receives "sponsored" waste from firms that want to dispose of "unusable" product wrappers and manufacturing wastes.

A channel in which material flows move in the direction opposite (or backward) of the usual forward motion of a supply or value chain is called a reverse channel (Fuller 1999). An example of an innovation in reverse logistics is the Super Sandwich Bale developed by Rocky Mountain Recycling (Martin and Schouten 2012: 101). Since 2006, Walmart has used this method to layer all of the loose plastic in its stores, such as shrink wrap, hangers, and shopping bags, along with cans, bottles, and office paper, between cardboard in its trash compactors to compress the plastic. This compacted "sandwich" allows Walmart to reduce waste volume and thus ship more efficiently (upstream) to recycling centers.

These examples illustrate the channel collaboration needed to meet the four system conditions of The Natural Step. As partnerships in sustainability proliferate, channel members are recognizing that "a joint effort by the many organizations and customers making up the product system life cycle is necessary to accomplish environmental progress" (Fuller 1999: 222). This coordination is critical to ensuring that the channel system addresses the needs of everyone from the firm to the natural environment.

As Murphy (2005: 190) advocates, marketing managers must plan with the after-sale in mind – that is, their responsibility extends beyond the transaction and throughout the entire lifecycle of the product. This approach requires firms to be more mindful of potential impacts during the use and disposal phases of the product's life, as these are times when the customer is largely in control of decision-making. Products can be designed and delivered so that it becomes easy and convenient for end users to minimize these impacts. A channel in which diverse stakeholders communicate and collaborate with one another facilitates the co-creation of additional forms of value. Convenient recycling, third-party eco-labels, ethical working conditions, and the opportunity for a customer to donate to a non-profit organization through his or her purchase are all channel-based forms of added customer value.

Promotion

Wilkie and Moore (1999) recognize that the aggregate marketing system operates through human interactions, experience, and trust, and that these factors pertain to promotion. However, as Murphy notes, "There is much misinformation in the marketplace [and] consumers have difficulty sorting out the benefits of sustainable products" (2005: 186). According to a 2010 TerraChoice study, all but one of 1,018 consumer products at several category-leading mass merchandisers made false claims about their environmental-friendliness (TerraChoice 2010).

Practices like greenwashing undermine credibility in the marketplace for all market players, reducing consumer confidence to an unhealthy level. The dearth of accurate, trustworthy public information about company impacts on The Natural Step's four system conditions has created a need for more transparent disclosures. Attempting to address this issue, the Federal Trade Commission updated Green Guides on environmental marketing claims in 2012 (http://www.ftc.gov/bcp/edu/microsites/energy/about_guides.shtml). However, despite a few legal actions taken by the agency, enforcement remains largely voluntary.

Investors, too, need credible information about company practices in order to make informed decisions. They want to know that firms are planning wisely and prudently in the face of climate change, dwindling aggregate supplies of petroleum, and the inevitable needs of future generations. Channel partners also require open, honest information to assess risks, plan initiatives, and collaborate meaningfully to solve persistent challenges and meet brand promises. Corporate sustainability or social responsibility reports have become more plentiful, but they are often carefully worded to avoid revealing potentially vulnerable information, and many rely on voluntary rather than third-party verified compliance with standards (Waddock 2008; www.corporateregister.com).

In a SAMS, marketing promotion would comprehensively educate and inform customers about the four system conditions identified by The Natural Step scientists. Because satisfaction of these conditions is directly tied to human actions, consumers essentially must "learn" the behaviors necessary to fulfill their part, and they are looking to business for that education (Murphy 2005: 183). Commonly used terms, such as "natural," need to be clearly defined. Eco-labels that certify compliance with third-party verified standards can be effective vehicles for this communication. The requirements behind these labels need to be clear and accessible so that consumers may accurately evaluate the information communicated by such claims. This process is not simply an added burden on the shoulders of managers, but an opportunity for promoting real customer value.

When companies incorporate The Natural Step's four system conditions throughout their operations, they can successfully add a sustainable or socially responsible component to their brand image. This can provide a competitive advantage, and incentive to cultivate relationships with customers, suppliers, and investors based on honesty and trust. Brand stories that illustrate a company's dedication and action toward sustainable business practices can be powerful marketing tools. For example, outdoor clothing company Patagonia has long been known for its dedication to protecting the natural environment, and it also has taken extensive steps to share this passion with its customers. One innovation that has now been widely imitated is the "Footprint Chronicles" feature on the Patagonia website, where the company allows consumers to track the environmental impact of each product, with details about the positives and negatives of each production step, including concerns related to each of the four system conditions which must be met to operate within the earth's carrying capacity. This illustrates promotion that uses the company's investments in a sustainable channel as a source of customer value. Open disclosure increases awareness and knowledge of sustainable issues and builds customer trust.

Effective brand-building and storytelling based on genuine commitments to sustainability promote consumer identification with the principles of sustainability. A hiking enthusiast who purchases her outdoor clothing and gear from Patagonia might feel that by doing so, she is making the choice that best preserves the natural world that she so enjoys. Providing consumers with such personally meaningful options can increase brand loyalty and overall consumer satisfaction. This function of marketing, the building of brands which influence individual identity and collective behavior, can be seen as a process of culture-creation.

Given examples such as bottled water, fast food, disposable paper products, and the pet industry, it is clear that the aggregate marketing system is capable of decisively influencing, or even creating consumer culture (Assadourian 2010a). Online social media provide dramatically expanded avenues for marketers to do this by creating and advertising dematerialized value propositions that meet non-material needs. In many arenas, consumers (citizens) are leading the way, creating online communities that meet social and status needs, as well as providing product and shopping information that is needed and desired but not provided by marketers. The opportunity to use the powerful promotional tools of marketing to foster a culture of trust, rather than one of mistrust, is largely untapped. This requires respectful and honest disclosure of two-way communication in relationships with all stakeholders.

Leveraging the "uncontrollable" factors

We have seen how the four "controllable" factors of the marketing mix – product, price, place, and promotion – are avenues through which marketing tools can be further leveraged to develop a SAMS, or a marketing system which does not exceed the earth's carrying capacity. Our analysis echoes that of Belz and Peattie (2009), who proposed an alternative marketing mix specifically for marketing for sustainability, the "four Cs." Replacing product, these authors emphasize the *Customer solutions* offered by a value proposition, which may or may not be a physical product. Rather than price, they focus on the total *Customer cost*, a more inclusive and contextualized concept that more fully reflects the customer's perspective by including use and post-use costs as well as purchase costs and price. Similarly, they offer *Convenience* instead of place, highlighting the customer value created by sustainable distribution networks. Finally, Belz and Peattie (2009) suggest reframing the promotion component of the marketing mix in terms of *Communication*, emphasizing the role of trust and dialogue in exchange relationships.

This positive portrayal of the potential of marketing to contribute to a SAMS expands the scope of the marketing mix, and harkens back to Wilkie and Moore's recognition of marketing's many positive contributions to society (1999). Some of these contributions are direct results of marketing-mix activities, while others are applications of marketing tools in the realms that Perreault and McCarthy (1999) called "uncontrollable" factors.

As shown in Figure 10.2 above, Perreault and McCarthy identified the following five factors as being beyond the purview of marketing managers: (1) Resources and Objectives of Firm, (2) Existing Business Situation, (3) Economic Environment, (4) Political and Legal Environment, and (5) Cultural and Social Environment. However, management of these "uncontrollable" forces has become a critical part of the job description for executives in companies across industries, including marketing executives. Marketing managers are responsible in part for informing and developing the sustainability-related resources and objectives of their firms. Existing business conditions, such as stages of industry development and competitive conditions are influenced by nearly every large marketing program, inclusive of ecological and societal impacts. Holiday promotions and consumer credit availability have dramatic influence on macro-economic trends, as well as on sustainable consumer behaviors. Public relations and reputation management activities routinely influence the public policy arena through publicity, lobbying, funded research and other activities, frequently addressing issues that pertain to the four Natural Step system conditions for sustainability. As discussed above, marketers have created entirely new product categories, such as fast food, and routinely catalyzed new cultural and social behaviors.

Fortunately, the marketing toolbox can also be effectively applied to influence each of these "uncontrollable" factors in ways that promote fulfillment of the four system conditions needed for a sustainable future. Category-leading firms (such as Toyota, P&G, and Dow) across industries are those that have adopted aggressive sustainability objectives and made systematic commitments to increasing resources needed to meet the four system conditions. Companies with foresight (such as IDEO, Best Buy, and Nike) see future competitive advantage stemming from the ability to reduce ecosystem degradation and concentrations of synthetic substances and those extracted from the earth's crust. These companies understand that people need to be able to meet basic needs in order to be consumers and workers. Global companies that use labor from developing countries or aim to serve the needs of "bottom-of-the-pyramid" consumers are acutely aware of their influence on the macro-economic conditions affecting these communities.

We suggest that the only forces which are completely "uncontrollable" by marketing managers are the four systems conditions of The Natural Step. These four conditions technically specify the social and natural resource constraints of a SAMS, which are out of the control of marketers. In addition to the four elements of the marketing mix, all other aspects of the marketing context, surrounding the Four Ps and the Customer in McCarthy's diagram, are at least partially controllable by marketers.

This clarification may help to address some of the criticisms of the marketing mix concept that have been advanced over time. For example, some scholars consider the Four Ps to be simplistic, exaggerating the seller's viewpoint, and over-emphasizing the product, compared with the fundamentally dynamic and relational nature of value (Belz and Peattie 2009; Constantinides 2006; Gronroos 2007). The marketing mix is only overly simplistic when one fails to recognize that marketers can and do also influence the "uncontrollable" factors. Earlier we have shown how the context of sustainability requires a broadening of the product concept to more fully embrace the service provided, and the relational nature of value exchange. Thus, each of these major criticisms of the marketing mix is addressed by shifting the frame of reference from an aggregate marketing system to a *sustainable* aggregate marketing system.

Conclusion

In this final section, we highlight two perspectives that we consider critical for marketers contemplating their role in ensuring a sustainable future. First, we identify standards and certifications as one of the most promising tools available to facilitate marketing's contributions to a sustainable society. Second, we discuss sustainable overall levels of consumption as one of the most daunting challenges for developing a truly sustainable aggregate marketing system.

Sustainability standards and certifications

W&M (1999) identify standardization as one of the 80-plus marketing activities in the aggregate marketing system. As we have seen, certifications and standards play a fundamental and pivotal role in a sustainable system, serving to identify and assess market activities that operate within (or exceed) The Natural Step's four system conditions. In W&M's coffee example discussed above, if fair wages paid to the farmer had been included in the pricing mechanism (and thus, the farmer belonged to a certified cooperative), then the finished product may be stamped with a Fairtrade label, signaling information to the consumer about the product's social and environmental responsibility. Independent third-party certification ensures the purchaser that he or she can have confidence in key components of the value proposition.

Earlier we discussed the function of eco-labels in ensuring that each of the marketing mix elements fits with a sustainable system: (1) delivery of systemically efficient value propositions; (2) verification of negative externality reductions included in prices; (3) facilitation of channel coordination needed to deliver sustainable value; and (4) promotional tactics that build trust, communicate social and environmental benefits, and support sustainable consumer cultures. For example, the Forest Stewardship Council (FSC) certification augments the value proposition for paper, lumber, and other forest products by verifying that sourcing has been done in compliance with detailed social and environmental standards. The FSC label confirms the internalization of negative externalities, such as loss of forest habitat and encroachment on traditional indigenous homelands. The FSC Chain of Custody certification specifically assures that all channel intermediaries have upheld FSC standards, and the label itself provides a powerful promotional tool for building trust with consumers and organizational customers.

In order for a customer to understand and believe that he or she is receiving social and environmental benefits, the value proposition must be communicated and rendered credible. Perhaps the most successful method for achieving this objective is the use of standards and certifications.

Sustainable levels of consumption

According to Martin and Schouten (2012), sustainable marketing is environmentally and socially benign, preserving or enhancing both natural and human capital. This means conducting marketing activities in a benign fashion, and it also implies proactively marketing the concept, cultural value, and set of practices that are needed for a sustainable society. "In other words, sustainable marketing's function is to help bring about a society in which striving for sustainability is the norm" (p. 11).

Since the earth's carrying capacity has already been exceeded, total levels of consumption must not just stabilize but decline. Assadourian (2010b) suggests that "cultural pioneers" may seize this innovation opportunity and catalyze a transition from societies focused on consumption to cultures and lifestyles that foster sustainability. Some cultural trends support this, such as increasing consumer demand for distributed small-scale food production, and direct consumer-to-consumer exchanges, sharing, and reuse, facilitated by online social networks.

The definition of sustainability suggests that this transition is inevitable, and if that is so, it may be driven in part by competitive pressures. For example, in September 2011, Patagonia launched a partnership with eBay to promote the resale of used Patagonia clothing rather than focusing entirely on sales of new goods (Nudd 2011). In lieu of typical Black Friday and Cyber Monday promotions, Patagonia ran ads detailing the environmental impacts of one of their jackets, and telling consumers, "Don't buy this jacket." Instead, the ad encouraged readers to sign a pledge not to buy unneeded items. Such actions are strategic marketing decisions which influence consumer expectations and raise the bar for competitors, if only incrementally.

As we have seen, marketing can contribute to this transition by helping to redefine quality of life in non-material terms. By offering value propositions that reflect a fuller range of human needs, marketers can help to produce consumers whose lifestyles meet the four system conditions for human activity to remain within the earth's carrying capacity, much as they produced "consumers" from a population that previously did not self-identify as such.

Marketing and sustainability are not inherently contradictory. Instead, we have argued that, in addition to the many contributions that Wilkie and Moore enumerated, marketing can significantly contribute to a *sustainable* society. Just as companies have applied concepts from psychology to cater to "wants" rather than merely to "needs," marketers can apply concepts from sustainability to cater to untapped wants and needs that fulfill the four system conditions of The Natural Step.

Marketing managers may find it challenging to shift away from conventional mindsets, but many pioneering companies have begun the process of reducing overall levels of consumption, often with dramatic reductions in waste and increases in inefficiencies. Companies that have persisted through numerous stages in the sustainability journey have consistently found greater opportunities for innovation as well as competitive advantages that were not apparent when they began the journey (Nidumolo *et al.* 2009).

Marketing's contributions to a sustainable society

Grounded in three theoretical foundations – The Natural Step, Wilkie and Moore's aggregate marketing system, and the marketing mix – we suggest a way of thinking about how marketing activities can and do contribute to a socially and ecologically sustainable marketplace. Specifically, we offer a definition of a Sustainable Aggregate Marketing System (SAMS), and a simple refinement to adapt W&M's (1999) groundbreaking analysis of the aggregate marketing system to the context of sustainability. We have demonstrated how marketers influence the "uncontrollable" environmental factors, and can leverage the marketing toolbox to help restore a viable balance between human activity and the earth's carrying capacity.

As we collectively move toward a sustainable future, marketers have the opportunity to recognize their unique position as the functional interface between society and the firm. This role may be conceived in a variety of ways, ranging from a strictly profit-seeking perspective to Kotler's inclusive societal marketing concept (1972), or the delivery of triple-bottom-line value.

The moral principle of the common good provides an ethical framework for approaching the relationship between marketing and sustainability. This concept can be found in many faiths, and is a foundational principle of Catholic Social Teaching. According to this principle, a SAMS must both affirm the right of private property and assure that the goods of the earth may be available for the benefit of all. Thus, this approach can fulfill the promise of the Brundtland Commission's definition of sustainable development, as that which meets today's needs without compromising future generations (United Nations 1987).

However it is conceived, the common good is increasingly an unavoidable imperative for market viability, and this is acknowledged by even the most profit-oriented business leaders (e.g., Karnani 2010). To operate within the earth's carrying capacity, marketers have no choice but to consider the long-term sustainability of society and the planet as requirements for firm success.

References

Assadourian, E. (2010a) "The rise and fall of consumer cultures," in *State of the World: Transforming Cultures From Consumerism to Sustainability*, Worldwatch Institute Report, New York: WW Norton and Company.

—— (2010b) "Transforming cultures: From consumerism to sustainability," *Journal of Macromarketing*, 30 (6): 186–91.

Bansal, P. and Hoffman, A.J. (eds) (2012) *Oxford Handbook of Business and the Natural Environment*, Oxford University Press.

Belz, F. -M. and Peattie, K. (2009) *Sustainability Marketing*, Chichester: Wiley.

Chase, R. (2012) "How technology enables the shared economy," May 3, accessed from: www.greenbiz.com (April 12, 2012).

Conroy, M.E. (2007) *Branded: How the "Certification Revolution" is Transforming Global Corporations*, Gabriola Island, BC: New Society Publishers.

Constantinides, E. (2006) "The marketing mix revisited: Towards the 21st century marketing," *Journal of Marketing Management*, 22 (4): 407–38.

Cotte, J. and Trudell, R. (2009) "Socially conscious consumerism: A systematic review of the body of knowledge," accessed from: www.nbs.net on 4/12/12.

Csikszentmihalyi, M. (2000) "The costs and benefits of consuming," *Journal of Consumer Research*, 27 (9): 267–72.

Elkington, J. (1998) *Cannibals with Forks: The Triple Bottom Line of 21st Century Business*, Gabriola Island, BC: Capstone.

Fuller, D.A. (1999) *Sustainable Marketing*, Thousand Oaks, CA: Sage Publications.

Gardner, G. (2010) "Vital signs," *World Watch*, 23 (3): 21.

Gershoff, A.D. and Irwin, J.R. (2012) "Why not choose green? Consumer decision making for environmentally friendly products," in P. Bansal and A.J. Hoffman (eds) *Oxford Handbook of Business and the Natural Environment*, Oxford University Press, pp. 366–83.

Ginsberg, J.M. and Bloom, P. (2004) "Choosing the right green marketing strategy," *MIT Sloan Management Review*, 79–84.

Gronroos, C. (2007) *In Search of a New Logic for Marketing*, New York: John Wiley & Sons.

Gunther, M. (2006) "The green machine," *Fortune*, 154 (3): 42–57.

Holmberg, J. and Robert, K-H. (2000) "Backcasting from non-overlapping sustainability principles – a framework for strategic planning," *International Journal of Sustainable Development and World Ecology*, 7: 291–308.

Kahneman, D., Krueger, A.B., Schkade, D., Schwarz, N., and Stone, A. (2004) "Toward national well-being accounts," *The American Economic Review*, 94 (May): 429–34.

Karnani, A. (2010) "The case against corporate social responsibility," *The Wall Street Journal*, August 22. Accessed from: http://online.wsj.com/article_email/SB10001424052748703338004575230112664504890-lMyQjAxMTAwMDEwOTExNDkyWj.html on 4/12/12.

Koch, W. (2012) "Companies aim for zero success in waste recycling," *USA Today*, January 30.

Kotler, P. (1972) "What consumerism means for marketers," *Harvard Business Review*, 50 (May): 48–57.

—— and Armstrong, G. (2011) *Principles of Marketing*, 14th edn, Boston, MA: Pearson.

McCarthy, E.J. (1960) *Basic Marketing: A Managerial Approach*, Homewood, IL: Irwin.

McDonough, W. and Braungart, M. (2002) *Cradle-to-Cradle: Remaking the Way We Make Things*, New York: North Point.

Malhotra, N.K. (2006) "Consumer well-being and quality of life: An assessment and directions for future research," *Journal of Macromarketing*, 26 (6): 77–80.

Martin, D.M. and Schouten, J. (2012) *Sustainable Marketing*, Upper Saddle River, NJ: Prentice Hall.

Mayer, R.N., Lewis, L.A., and Scammon, D.L. (2001) "The effectiveness of environmental marketing claims," in P. Bloom and G. Gundlach (eds) *Handbook of Marketing & Society*, Thousand Oaks, CA: Sage Publications.

Mintel (1991) *The Green Consumer Report*, London: Mintel.

—— (2010) *Green Living – US*, London: Mintel.

—— (2011) *Hotel Accommodations – US*, London: Mintel.

Murphy, P.E. and Laczniak, G.R. (1977) "Marketing and ecology: retrospect and prospect," *Business and Society*, 18 (1): 26–34.

—— and Laczniak, G.R. (2005) "Sustainable marketing," *Business & Professional Ethics Journal*, 24 (1): 171–98.

Nattrass, B. and Altomare, M. (1999) *The Natural Step for Business: Wealth, Ecology and the Evolutionary Corporation*, Gabriola Island, BC: New Society Publishers.

Natural Step, The (2009) *United States Sustainability Primer: Step By Natural Step*. Accessed from: www.naturalstepusa.org/storage/case-studies/Primer_USEdition_print_072009.pdf on 4/12/12.

Nidumolu, R., Prahalad, C.K., and Rangaswami, M.R. (2009) "Why sustainability is now the key driver of innovation," *Harvard Business Review*, September: 57–64.

Nudd, T. (2011) "Ad of the day: Patagonia; the brand declares war on consumerism gone berserk, and admits its own environmental failings," *Adweek*, November 28. Accessed from: www.adweek.com/news/advertising-branding/ad-day-patagonia-136745 on 4/12/12.

Ottman, J. (2004) *Green Marketing: Opportunity for Innovation*, 2nd edn, New York: BookSurge.

Palazzo, G. and Basu, K. (2007) "The ethical backlash of corporate branding," *Journal of Business Ethics*, 73 (15): 333–46.

Peattie, K. (2001) "Towards sustainability: the third age of green marketing," *Marketing Review*, 2 (Winter): 129.

—— and Crane, A. (2005) "Green marketing: legend, myth, farce or prophesy?" *Qualitative Market Research: An International Journal*, 8 (4): 357–70.

Perreault, W.D. and McCarthy, J. (1999) *Basic Marketing: A Global-Managerial Approach*, Boston, MA: Irwin/McGraw-Hill.

Porter, M.E. and van der Linde, C. (1995) "Toward a new conception of the environment-competitiveness relationship," *Journal of Economic Perspectives*, 9 (Fall): 97–118.

PricewaterhouseCoopers (2010) "PricewaterhouseCoopers 13th Annual Global CEO Survey 2010," in TEEB, *The Economics of Ecosystems and Biodiversity Report for Business*, Executive Summary. Accessed from: www.pwc.co.uk/eng/publications/teeb_for_business _summary.html on 1/28/12.

Rees, W.E. (1992) "Ecological footprints and appropriated carrying capacity: what urban economics leaves out," *Environment and Urbanization* 4 (2): 121–30.

Roper Organization (1990) *The Environment: Public Attitudes and Individual Behavior*, New York: Roper Organization and SC Johnson and Son.

Ryan, R.M. and Deci, E.L. (2001) "On happiness and human potentials: a review of research on hedonic and eudaimonic well-being," *Annual Review of Psychology*, 52 (141,66): 141.

Sahota, A., Haumann, B., Givens, H., and Baldwin, C. (2009) "Ecolabeling and consumer interest in sustainable products," in C.J. Baldwin (ed.) *Sustainability in the Food Industry*, Ames, IA: Wiley-Blackwell.

Scammon, D.L. and Mayer, R.N. (1995) "Agency review of environmental marketing claims: case-by-case decomposition of the issues," *Journal of Advertising*, 24 (2): 33–44.

—— and Mish, J. (2012) "From green marketing to marketing for environmental sustainability," in P. Bansal and A.J. Hoffman (eds) *Oxford Handbook of Business and the Natural Environment*, Oxford University Press, pp. 347–65.

Sheth, J.N., Sethia, N.K., and Srinivas, S. (2011) "Mindful consumption: A customer-centric approach to sustainability," *Journal of the Academy of Marketing Science*, 39 (1): 21–39.

Simon, F.L. (1992) "Marketing green products in the triad," *Columbia Journal of World Business*, 27 (Fall): 268–85.

TerraChoice (2010) "The sins of greenwashing: Home and family edition," UL Environment. Accessed from: http://sinsofgreenwashing.org on 6/2/12.

United Nations (1987) *Our Common Future*, World Commission on Environment and Development A/42/427 (June), Geneva, Switzerland. Accessed from: www.un-documents. net/ocf-02.htm on 4/12/12.

US Code of Federal Regulations (1992) "Green guides," 57 FR 36363, 61 FR 53311, 63 FR 24240.

Viswanathan, M., Seth, A., Gau, R., and Chaturvedi, A. (2009) "Ingraining product-relevant social good into business processes in subsistence marketplaces: the sustainable market orientation," *Journal of Macromarketing*, 29 (4): 406–25.

Wackernagel, M. (1994) *Ecological Footprint and Appropriated Carrying Capacity: A Tool for Planning Toward Sustainability* (PhD thesis). Vancouver, Canada: School of Community and Regional Planning, The University of British Columbia.

Waddock, S. (2008) "Building a new institutional infrastructure for corporate responsibility," *Academy of Management Perspectives*, 22 (3): 87–108.

Wilkie, W.L. and Moore, E.S. (1999) "Marketing's contributions to society," *Journal of Marketing*, 63 (10/02): 198–218.

World Wildlife Foundation (2010) "Living planet report 2010: Biodiversity, biocapacity, and human development," October. Available at: wwf.panda.org (accessed 10/9/11).

11

CREATIVE DESTRUCTION AND DESTRUCTIVE CREATIONS

Environmental ethics and planned obsolescence

Joseph P. Guiltinan

When I first started teaching marketing, Vance Packard's (1960) criticisms of planned obsolescence were widely discussed by students and faculty. The prevailing view was that it was unethical to design products that would wear out "prematurely" (i.e., have useful lives that were well below customer expectations), particularly if they were costly to replace. Today, the mounting numbers of functioning durable goods ending up in landfills have led to renewed criticism of product obsolescence. Sources indicate that in North America over 100 million cell phones and 300 million personal computers are discarded each year, and only 20,000 televisions are refurbished each year while 20 million are sold, resulting in tremendous environmental damage from lead, mercury, and toxic glass (cf. Boland 2001; Slade 2006). Additionally, when electronics are recycled, 50-80 percent are shipped to third-world nations where workers use dangerous, primitive processes for extracting recyclable materials, often exposing themselves to toxic gases in the process (Associated Press 2007). So, while advances in technology and increasingly skillful industrial design have enabled firms to develop innovative products in virtually every durable goods category, the nature of the materials that are often required and the rapid pace of product upgrading have resulted in negative environmental consequences for consumers and society (cf. Calcott and Walls 2005).

Per Figure 11.1, two aspects of new product development strategy drive these environmental problems. First, frequent introductions of replacement products increase the opportunities and motivation to replace functioning durables. Mindful of Schumpeter's theory that established firms are often replaced by innovators (through a "creative destruction" process), today's strategists focus on rapid new product development to defend their competitive space. Industrial designers and engineers also drive replacement frequency by incorporating desirable benefits or styles into new products (abetted by marketers who promote the incremental value

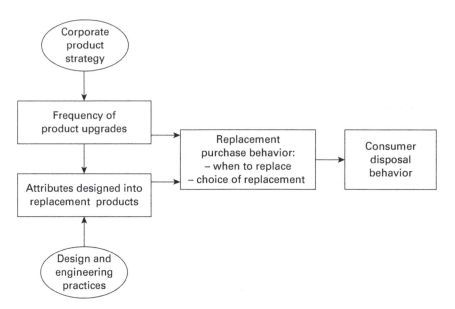

FIGURE 11.1 Product obsolescence and the environment: decisions and influences.

of these upgrades). Second, the recyclability of new products is influenced by choices of components or materials made by designers and engineers. Thus, environmental problems are exacerbated to the extent that corporate strategies emphasizing continuous improvement and those actually involved in creating and marketing new products are insensitive to the need for sustainable innovation, and promote excessive consumerism.[1]

In this chapter, I specify the set of product development practices that are included under the umbrella of planned obsolescence, and I explain why planned obsolescence is so ubiquitous among durable goods manufacturers. I then examine the ecological responsibilities and responses of technical and managerial product development professionals. I show that design practices (prodded by regulatory initiatives) can be developed for assuring that "creations for consumers" will be less destructive to the environment in the future, but that cultural changes at the product design level are likely to be somewhat constrained by corporate and marketing realities and perceptions. I conclude that the lack of understanding of consumer behavior with respect to replacement and disposal of durable goods is an impediment to marketers and public policy makers seeking this goal, creating an important opportunity for scholars in the field of marketing.

Planned obsolescence practices

The objective of planned obsolescence is to stimulate replacement buying by consumers. The most direct way to speed replacement demand is to shorten the usable life of a product through one or more of the following physical obsolescence mechanisms:

- *Limited functional life design (or "death dating")*. In a recent book, Slade (2006) notes that in the 1950s and 1960s death dating was standard practice for many appliances. (At one point portable radios were designed to last for only 3 years).
- *Design for limited repair*. Disposable single-use cameras were designed to be non-repairable, although a small recycling industry emerged for a time until Fuji and Kodak took these firms to court for copyright violations (Adolphson 2004). McCollough (2007) suggests that the price of repair for consumer electronics encourages disposal, and household income correlates positively with the propensity to dispose of and replace appliances rather than repair them.
- *Design aesthetics that lead to reduced satisfaction*. Cooper (2005) shows how aesthetic characteristics can influence premature disposal. One example is the design of "faultless forms and surfaces" on products like small appliances which leave a pristine and polished appearance which, with everyday use quickly becomes damaged, engendering user dissatisfaction and premature disposal.

Faster replacement can also be achieved through new product replacement strategies designed to foster *technological* obsolescence. Packard (1960) termed this form of obsolescence "voluntary" because there was no reason that consumers could not continue to be satisfied with their existing products.

- *Design for fashion*. Although comic detective Dick Tracy kept his two-way wrist radio from 1946 until he retired in 1977, today fashion influences many durables replacement decisions. Increasingly designers have applied fashion thinking to watches, mp3 players, cell phones, and even laptop computers. Slade (2006) suggests that the rise of General Motors and its displacement of industry leader Ford was the first victory of fashion positioning over durability positioning among "hard" goods.
- *Design for functional enhancement through adding or upgrading product features*. Technological development frequently allows firms to expand the number of uses or benefits of a product (e.g., adding a camera feature to a cell phone) or to improve the level of performance on existing benefits (as when a laptop maker increases memory and speed or reduces weight). Note that if there are clearly stratified benefit segments in a market, the early generation product may not have a high-demand cross-elasticity with the new one because the new level of performance may not be (at least initially) desired or needed by all customers. In such cases older platforms may be retained as long as there is significant demand for them (cf. Saunders and Jobber 1994) and the obsolescence effect will be minimal. The obsolescence effect is stronger when many consumers perceive the old products to be "unfashionable" (cf. Mason 1985) or when the incremental features of the new products are universally perceived as beneficial and desirable.

Drivers of obsolescence and fast replacement

Durable goods producers face a specific challenge in maintaining a high rate of sales growth. This "durables problem" – the core driving force behind planned obsolescence in any market structure (from monopoly to intensive competition) – occurs when successful sellers quickly saturate their markets. The more reliable and long-lasting the product, the longer the repeat purchase cycle and the slower the rate of sales growth. If a firm chooses to rent its goods, it would receive a consistent flow of revenue for several years, but once a firm sells its durable goods output it no longer has a vested interest in the value of those goods. Instead its interests lie in the next generation of goods. (To economists this is known as the "time inconsistency" problem.) The existence of a market for used versions of the durable further complicates the problem, because the more durable the product is the greater is the competition between new and used versions and the lower is the price of replacement products (Bulow 1986). Thus, durability becomes a drag on replacement sales volume and, when a used market exists, on the prices of replacement goods. To mitigate competition from the used market, firms increase the frequency of the revision (upgrade) cycle (Iizuka 2007). Thus, increasing the rate of replacement through obsolescence will enable firms to: (1) stimulate revenues through faster replacement; (2) reduce competition from any used good markets; (3) by virtue of making used or owned goods less competitive, increase prices for the replacement product.

Competitive pressure for technological obsolescence

While the "durables problem" exists even in monopoly settings, as Sonntag (2000) notes, competitive considerations create additional pressures for obsolescence. Pointing out that a consensus has emerged that cost, quality, time-to-market, and performance based on distinctive product features are hallmarks of competitive businesses today (see also Hua and Wemmerlov 2006), Sonntag argues that advances in manufacturing practice that yield faster product cycles are now a defining force in business strategy. Through the use of flexible, modular, and faster design software and production equipment, concurrent product development processes, and information technology, firms have reduced both the length of the production process and the time required to adapt production to demand and competitive actions. The result is rapid execution of orders and delivery, faster implementation of new product concepts, and reduced capital, inventory, and unit costs. Perversely, such systems demand growth in output because the technologies amplify economies of scale and scope which can only be realized through faster product replacement and increasing consumption of products designed for particular needs. The competitive success of such technologies and processes has led to emulation by other firms. Thus, the incentives for obsolescence in the traditional "durables problem" are compounded in industries in which rapid new product development is embedded in the competitive environment.

Gillette's strategy of regularly replacing its market-leading razors is often cited as an exemplar of the competitive necessity of a self-cannibalizing product replacement strategy. That firm saw the wisdom of this strategy after its experience in 1962 when a small British cutlery and garden tool-maker, Wilkinson Sword, created a stainless-steel blade that lasted three times as long as Gillette's offering and took away 20 percent of Gillette's share. Gillette had resisted introducing a stainless-steel blade itself due to concern for cannibalization of its existing market leading brands and because of the negative demand impact of the longer-lasting feature of the blades (Tellis and Golder 2001). Thus, the managerial dilemma regarding "willingness to cannibalize" is that if a firm will not cannibalize its own product's sales, its competitors will.

Additionally, an idea that has gained currency among marketing managers and strategic planners is that brand loyalty is a route to high profitability because of the higher "lifetime value" of customers who can be retained for multiple repeat purchases. Firms want to facilitate migration of their customers to their own version of the next technological advance rather than risk losing them to competitors because it is generally much less expensive to retain customers than to acquire new ones. Notably, durable goods upgrades may provide avenues to customer retention even in non-durable industries. Witness the cellular phone service competition in which free phone upgrades are offered every 2 years as incentives to consumers to renew cellular service contracts.

Thus, the existence of a highly competitive environment, combined with the fundamental economic motives for obsolescence discussed earlier have created a sort of path-dependence for product development strategies geared toward faster replacement of durables.

The impact of consumer decision-making processes

The success and consequences of technological obsolescence ultimately depend on consumer behavior in the marketplace. Consumers decide whether and when to replace functioning durables with new versions. In at least some cases, consumers also have choices among replacement products that differ in their durability or in their environmental benefits and liabilities.

In general, little is known about consumers' durable goods replacement decision-making processes. However, technical product obsolescence is clearly a more significant driver of replacement timing than physical obsolescence. Grewal *et al.* (2004) compared "unforced" replacement decisions driven by technological (including fashion) obsolescence with replacement decisions that were "forced" by poor product performance. They found that durable product replacement intervals were shorter for unforced decisions, explaining the result with the argument that, in the case of voluntary replacement, consumers are more excited about and interested in the decision to replace and thus more motivated to act. (The major exception to the finding that technological obsolescence is more of a driver of replacement purchasing than physical obsolescence is that unexciting, out-of-view durable – the washing machine (Box 1983).) The Grewal *et al.* study also identified various attitudinal functions served by durable goods, including social approval, utilitarian, and "value-expressive" functions. It is difficult to speculate on the relative impact of fashion changes versus functional enhancements in replacement buying. However, if "fashion" is defined to include industrial design aesthetics, then it is likely to be a factor in the purchase of luxury utilitarian goods and value-expressive goods, as well as goods where replacement is motivated by the desire for social approval.

Interestingly, rates of technological obsolescence influence the value that consumers attach to upgrades. Rapid product improvements can increase the household discount rate (or the "impatience" rate) so that consumers value purchases made in the near term more than the savings from delayed purchase (Winer 1997). Moreover, even when improvements are not obvious, an empirical study by Boone *et al.* (2001) indicated that more frequent introductions of upgrades may be interpreted by consumers as cues to higher rates of intergenerational improvement, so a policy of "continuous upgrading" creates a heightened sense among consumers that their existing durable is outmoded. Thus, more rapid introductions appear to motivate faster replacement regardless of the actual level of quality enhancement. In sum, based on what we do know from the limited studies available, replacement buying behaviors are complex, heterogeneous, and perhaps based more on heuristics and extrinsic cues than on a calculative cost–benefit tradeoff process.

With respect to the process of choosing among alternative replacement durables, there is little evidence that durability is a key consumer buying motive. Economic theory generally assumes that warranties signal higher quality, and that firms that build in quality and signal it through warranties are rewarded with higher prices (cf. Utaka 2006). But a study in the UK (Cooper 2004) indicates that consumers who buy premium appliances do not do so because they view high prices as signals of higher durability. Moreover, a recent retail study of TV purchasing concluded that warranty information trailed behind picture quality, brand name, price, and picture size in rated importance (Cervini 2005). There is also substantial evidence that consumers ignore information on features that reflect product durability (cf. the discussion of the furniture industry consumer in George 2000). Indeed Cooper's aforementioned study concluded that: consumers are equally divided on whether appliance life spans are adequate; often do not consider durability to be a critical attribute; and see product life span as a quality issue – not an environmental issue (Cooper 2004).

Similarly, environmental attributes play a modest role at best in durable goods decision-making with green purchasing restricted to a small segment of the population; any expectation that consumers will suddenly become dramatically pro-environment in their purchasing behavior seems excessively optimistic. A Finnish study by Niva and Timonen (2001) on product purchasing points out why this is the case: (1) consumers lack knowledge about the environmental implications of their purchases – even in product categories where such impacts are widely discussed in the media; (2) consumers believe it is the responsibility of manufacturers to produce environmentally benign products and for distributors to screen for such qualities, and that consumers have little impact on those activities. Of course environment-related attributes will only influence purchase choices when there is some variance among the alternatives offered on the environmental dimension. If competitors do not create or promote such attributes one cannot expect "green" purchasing by consumers.

Ethical responsibilities and responses

While innovation and technological progress are good (*ceteris paribus*), the gains from some new products may not always be worth the consumer or societal cost. To the extent consumers and society at large incur the economic and environmental costs associated with disposal of durable goods, the more frequent the replacement and the less recyclable the durable, the greater the problem.

The responsibility for the negative consequences of planned obsolescence is a shared one. First, when technical professionals (engineers and industrial designers) involved in new product development design durables to foster premature physical obsolescence they create corporate (and possible personal) gains at the expense of consumer welfare and the environment. Second, managers responsible for product replacement strategies act in ethically questionable ways if they "psychologically condition" consumers to believe that the utility of a product is diminished simply because a new version becomes available. By extension, offering frequent product "upgrades" while touting minor or illusory benefit improvements might be considered a wasteful and potentially misleading practice (cf. Giaretta 2005). Third, from the perspective of utilitarian theory, consumers may also act unethically when they add to the public burden with what some might consider frivolous, self-serving replacement behavior as well as when they knowingly use or dispose of products in ways that are environmentally harmful in order to save time or money. Even when new products yield significant increases in consumer benefits, mass replacement of the existing stock can still be a negative if improper disposal is a result. For example, one can anticipate mass replacement of analog television sets as high-definition TV-set ownership diffuses through the market.

What are the options available to firms for addressing the environmental concerns about planned obsolescence? This is a question that must be answered at two levels: (1) the designers and engineers responsible for choosing specific components, materials, architectures, and interfaces, and (2) marketing and business strategists.

Environmental ethics: Responses from industrial design and engineering

With respect to product development practice, one could argue that significant progress is being made in building a sustainable design culture among industrial designers and engineers involved in new product development. Design trade groups have placed sustainable and ethical design practices high on their educational agendas, and many firms that employ designers and design firms are buying in to such practices (Cooper 2005). Design is one way of attempting to increase replacement intervals. For example, classic designs (such as the one used for years by Volvo) or local, cultural designs that communicate a community identity are sources of "timeless" designs that make a product's appeal long lasting (cf. Zafarmand *et al.* 2003). Typologies of strategies for sustainable design are available from several sources (cf. Charter and Tischner 2001).

Similar kinds of strategies are being developed in engineering. For example, Sonntag (2000) suggests that firms could adapt the current technologies of lean and flexible manufacturing for producing value-added products that will be more intensively used by consumers (such as multifunction products). One option for coping with changing needs driven by culture, fashion, or function is "design for adaptability" (cf. Kasarda *et al.* 2007) – the development of new products that are amenable to adaptation by replacing subsystems or modules as an alternative to full product replacement.

Many new processes and technologies have also been developed for the cross-functional communication process in firms where sustainable new product development is a priority. These include important tools like "design for environment," "life cycle assessment," and "environmental effect analysis" (cf. Tingstrom and Karlsson 2006). Pujari (2006) argues that the leading firms in developing eco-innovations are those that have fully integrated such tools into their new product development planning so that they think in a positive sustainability mode rather than a reactive mode of just eliminating environmentally problematic features. For example, King and Burgess (2005), recognizing the strength of the culture of fashion obsolescence, argue for applying platform strategy thinking in which key components and subassemblies can be remanufactured and integrated into new products.

These developments would seem to bode well for the evolution of environmentally friendly product development or, at least, for increased attention on creating products that consumers will keep longer. However, design decisions at the individual product level will have to be consistent with the firm's strategic priorities on positioning and growth objectives. (Per Figure 11.1, the specific attributes designed into new products will usually, in part, reflect strategic decisions regarding the frequency of product change.)

Corporate responsibility and marketing/business strategy

As noted earlier, relentless product change has become the centerpiece of new product development strategy in many durable goods industries. But to some observers (cf. Giaretta 2005) relentless product change is a one-sided strategy because it focuses on the needs of the firm at the risk of detriment to the environment and to consumer welfare. She argues that a firm should seek a market positioning that distinguishes it on the basis of true customer satisfaction, environmental friendliness, and reliable long-term usefulness of its products. Adolphson (2004) offers an insight on what is entailed in redefining a firm's agenda to implement such repositioning. Following Werhane's (2002) concept of "moral imagination" he argues that firms need to revise their mental schemas for new product development to include a "biophysical" perspective which places the economic system in the larger context of an ecological system. In this perspective, value cannot always be captured in monetary terms. For example, nature performs work that is valuable without any exchange of money. This occurs when farmers reuse seeds from produce to plant future crops. On the other hand, the single-use camera forces premature disposal and thus wastes energy resources. This constitutes a waste of "natural capital" that would normally be ignored in estimates of the consequences of a given decision.

Such thinking would mean that managers should consider the costs of product disposal to be real costs that someone must bear rather than as "externalities," so that the decision-making "script" (i.e., the protocol by which new product proposals move through the development process from concept to launch) for each new product development business case includes an ecological dimension. A Swedish example of revising the script is reported by Byggeth *et al.* (2007). They developed a specific set of "sustainability product assessment modules" for evaluating proposals that could be easily adapted to a variety of established protocols to pro-actively identify opportunities for improved sustainability (such as energy savings, use of recyclable materials, and disposability). A similar initiative being applied in Ireland is reported in Maxwell and van de Horst (2003).

These perspectives are consistent with the "stakeholder" model of corporate responsibility which would acknowledge the possibility that a responsible product replacement strategy may compromise profitability (cf. Godfrey and Hatch, 2006). They are also consistent with the American Marketing Association's statement of Norms and Values. That statement calls on marketing professionals to support specific ethical values including "Responsibility – to accept the consequences of our marketing decisions" and "Citizenship – to fulfill the economic, legal, philanthropic, and societal responsibilities that serve stakeholders in a strategic manner." However, Sonntag (2000) indicates that the World Business Council for Sustainable Development (a CEO-led global association of 200 companies) purposely does not include extending product durability on their list of eco-efficient practices because of the belief that fast repeat purchase is healthy for their bottom lines as well as for the public goal of higher levels of employment. The latter point raises a challenging issue for public policy: when two public goals – employment and the environment in this case – are in potential conflict, how does one resolve this dilemma. It also reflects the reality that individual firms operate in a complex environment that includes investor norms and expectations.

Public policy initiatives

To corporate strategists, asking firms for voluntary reductions in the rate at which new product improvements are brought to market would be akin to a request for unilateral competitive disarmament. Moreover, absent a matching response from other firms, the net effect on the total volume of durables sold may not change – just the distribution of market shares. So, it would take industry agreements (anti-trust issues notwithstanding) to reduce such cycles or to assure that all sellers deliver to the market durables which are equally environmentally benign (at the likely cost of reducing some consumer benefits). Because this will lead to the return of the "durables problem", industry-wide economic sacrifices are the price of sustainability. Thus, we have a social dilemma.

Such dilemmas also exist at the consumer level. The cost and effort of recycling, trading off lower price or some other desirable benefit to buy a more environmentally friendly product, and denying oneself (or delaying) the benefits of a prospective upgrade are examples of perceived sacrifice that impedes more "green" consumer behavior.

One solution for a social dilemma is public policy action. Many of the strides being made in sustainable design were initially motivated by public policy directives. For example, the European Union is stipulating minimum reuse and recovery rates for end-of-life automotive vehicles (cf. Ferrao and Amaral 2006), and another EU directive on waste electrical and electronic equipment makes manufacturers and importers responsible for the treatment and disposal of products discarded by consumers in those categories. Product "take-back" laws are "on the books" in many parts of Europe and East Asia, and efforts to enact such legislation have occurred in nearly all of the 50 American States (Toffel 2004).[2] These efforts are based on the belief that such laws provide incentives to firms to implement design changes that will reduce the environmental burden created by future new products while shifting the cost from local government.

Because product take-back laws increase the unit cost of new products (when disposal costs are factored in), they are an "upstream solution" – one that is intended to motivate the design and marketing of green products. Current environmental policy wisdom favors "upstream" solutions over "downstream" solutions (those that focus on recycling incentives and taxes) (cf. Thorgerson 2000). As Calcott and Walls (2000) argue, downstream solutions such as disposal fees only influence upstream behavior when there is a fully functioning recycling market in which recyclers pay each household for each recycled item and the price varies with the value of recyclable components of the product. Because such systems appear infeasible, they argue that the next best approach is a deposit-refund system (producers pay a tax and recyclers receive the refund).

Thus, public policy initiatives have the potential to motivate business and marketing strategists to support environmentally friendly designs emerging from new product designers and engineers. But as Malcolm (2005) notes, the effectiveness of upstream solutions ultimately depend on whether "greener" products will be competitive in the mind of the consumer with "less green" alternatives once the costs and benefits of green alternatives are weighed against the cost (tax included) and benefits of less green options. Additionally, the effectiveness of take-back laws presumes compliance on the part of the consumer who must still bear the transaction costs of returning durables to manufacturers' recycling drop-off sites.

Conclusion

The World Business Council on Sustainable Development includes the following as a major action point: "Encourage consumers to prefer eco-efficient, more sustainable products and services" (WBCSD 2000). As noted, such products could include goods that pose fewer toxic threats that are more readily recyclable, or that consumers will keep longer. Prospects for achieving this goal are enhanced by the fact that sustainable product development is now a motivating force for many product development engineers and designers. Additionally, this action point is consistent with public policy initiatives focused on "upstream" solutions. However, two impediments exist: (1) the competitive pressure for and consumer expectations of frequent upgrades for durable goods; (2) the lack of consumer concern for environmental consequences when contemplating upgrades of durable goods. Thus, achieving the WBCSD's goal requires not only green design but also effective green marketing by firms and public policy initiatives that offer the right mix of consumer and manufacturer incentives.

Iyer (1999) makes the pessimistic argument that a sustainability paradigm based on encouraging "green" consumer behavior is inadequate. He notes that this "anthropocentric view" presumes that more pressure by green consumers will result in products that do not reduce human quality of life, yet there is little evidence that consumers exercise their market votes in a way that will achieve this outcome. It is not clear that we know why this is the case. However, as Moisander (2007) notes, a consumer's motivation to act partly depends on his/her perception of the degree of behavioral control they have in a given situation. Ecologically responsible purchase/consumption/disposal often requires practical skills and knowledge that are not readily available to consumers, so for consumers to have behavioral control they need meaningful choices and complete and relevant information about those choices. Managers and public policy-makers need to know what constitutes a choice that is "meaningful" to consumers and how information about these choices can best be communicated. Specific questions of interest would include:

- What information content, framing, timing, and sources will be effective in educating and motivating consumers to consider and choose "greener" options or to make more "rational" or cost-effective evaluations of when to purchase upgrades?
- What would the consumer response be to new products that were more resistant to technological obsolescence (e.g., adaptable products per the discussion of sustainable design strategies from above) or to leasing of durables that might be modified or refurbished/remanufactured for next generation production? (Recall that rental of durables reduces the reliance of the manufacturer on repeat purchase demand for future revenue. It also assures that consumers will return the good to the manufacturer or its agent.)
- What incentives (tax credits, rebates, trade-in discounts) or disincentives (deposits, taxes) will influence upgrade purchasing patterns or choices?
- What kind of information about disposal options or costs (personal and societal) of durables will be evaluated and used in the consumer's decision-making process?

Unfortunately, as noted earlier, the marketing literature offers very little insight on the drivers of upgrade behavior or on the decision-making processes involved. Our current theoretical understanding about how consumers perceive, understand, and use environmentally related goods product information has limited managerial utility because of the complexity and variety of the decision situations that might be studied (Leire and Thidell 2005). Moreover, what we do know about why people are motivated to perform certain green behaviors (e.g., energy-saving practices) is not readily translated to other contexts such as durable purchasing behaviors (Cleveland *et al.* 2005). Thus, marketing scholars would seem to have a great opportunity to contribute to the understanding of how consumers interpret and respond to green marketing overtures and to government incentives for green behavior.

Notes

1   Replacement products also may offer positive environmental benefits if they are more energy efficient, made from more eco-friendly materials, or create fewer undesirable side-effects. Van Nes and Cramer (2006) offer an approach to assessing the lifecycle impact (production, distribution, usage, and disposal) of a product on the environment that includes the calculation of both positive and negative benefits.
2   That the European Union is more advanced than the United States on take-back laws can be attributed in part to the political strength of Green Parties (notable in Germany which pioneered such laws), in part to the division of regulatory powers between the states and the federal government in the USA, and perhaps to a more communitarian political ethos in the EU.

References

Adolphson, D. (2004) "A new perspective on ethics, ecology and economics," *Journal of Business Ethics*, 54: 203–16.
Associated Press (2007) "Destination of recycled electronics may surprise you," online: www.computertakeback.com/news_and_resources/destination.cfm (accessed November 11, 2007).
Boland, M. (2001) "Water and the environment," *Forbes*, 168 (6): 60–62.
Boone, D., Lemon, K., and Staelin, R. (2001) "The impact of firm introductory strategies on consumers' perceptions of future product introductions and purchase decisions," *Journal of Product Innovation Management*, 18: 96–109.
Box, J. (1983) "Extending product lifetime: prospects and opportunities," *European Journal of Marketing*, 17: 34–49.
Bulow, J. (1986) "An economic theory of planned obsolescence," *The Quarterly Journal of Economics*, 101: 729–49.
Byggeth, S., Broman, G., and Robert, K. (2007) "A method for sustainable product development based on a modular system of guiding questions," *Journal of Cleaner Production*, 15: 1–11.
Calcott, P. and Walls, M. (2000) "Can downstream waste disposal policies encourage upstream design for environment?" *American Economic Review*, 90: 233–37.
—— (2005) "Waste, recycling and design for environment: roles for markets and policy instruments," *Resource and Energy Economics*, 27: 287–305.

Cervini, L. (2005) "TV: Shoppers choose quality over size," *TWICE*, June 20: 22.

Charter, M. and Tischner, U. (2001) *Sustainable Solutions: Developing Products and Services for the Future*, Sheffield, UK: Greenleaf.

Cleveland, M., Kalamas, M., and Laroche, M. (2005) "Shades of green: linking environmental locus of control and pro-environmental behaviors," *Journal of Consumer Marketing*, 22: 198–212.

Cooper, R. (2005) "Ethics and altruism: what constitutes socially responsible design?" *Design Management Review*, 16, 10–18.

Cooper, T. (2004) "Inadequate life? Evidence of consumer attitudes to product obsolescence," *Journal of Consumer Policy*, 27: 421–49.

Ferrao, P. and Amaral, J. (2006) "Design for recycling in the automobile industry: new approaches and new tools," *Journal of Engineering Design*, 17: 447–62.

George, R. (2000) "Your lifetime guarantee won't guarantee sales," *Upholstery Design & Management*, 13: 24–27.

Giaretta, E. (2005) "Ethical product innovation: in praise of slowness," *The TQM Magazine*, 17: 161–181.

Godfrey, P. and Hatch, N. (2006) "Researching corporate social responsibility: an agenda for the 21st century," *Journal of Business Ethics*, 70: 87–98.

Grewal, R., Mehta, R., and Kardes, F. (2004) "The timing of repeat purchase of consumer durable goods: the role of functional bases of consumer attitudes," *Journal of Marketing Research*, 41: 101–15.

Gunther, M. (2007) "Sony champions free recycling," *Fortune*, August 22.

Hua, S. and Wemmerlov, U. (2006) "Product change intensity product advantage and market performance: an empirical investigation into the PC industry," *Journal of Product Innovation Management*, 23: 316–29.

Iizuka, T. (2007) "An empirical analysis of planned obsolescence," *Journal of Economics & Management Strategy*, 16: 191–226.

Iyer, G. (1999) "Business, consumers and sustainable living in an interconnected world: a multilateral ecocentric approach," *Journal of Business Ethics*, 20: 273–88.

Kasarda, M., Terpenny, J.P., and Inman, D. (2007) "Design for adaptability – a new concept for achieving sustainable design," *Robotics & Computer-Integrated Manufacturing*, 23: 727–734.

King, A. and Burgess, S. (2005) "The development of a remanufacturing platform design: a strategic response to the directive on waste electrical and electronic equipment," *Journal of Engineering Manufacture*, 219 (Part B): 623–31.

Leire, C. and Thidell, A. (2005) "Product-related environmental information to guide consumer purchases – research on perceptions understanding and use among Nordic consumers," *Journal of Cleaner Production*, 13: 1061–70.

McCollough, J. (2007) "The effect of income growth on the mix of purchases between disposable goods and reusable goods," *International Journal of Consumer Studies*, 31: 213–19.

Malcolm, R. (2005) "Integrated product policy – a new regulatory paradigm for a consumer society?" *European Environmental Law Review*, 14: 134–44.

Mason, R. (1985) "Ethics and the supply of status goods," *Journal of Business Ethics*, 4: 457–64.

Maxwell, D. and van de Horst, R. (2003) "Developing sustainable products and services," *Journal of Cleaner Production*, 11: 883–95.

Moisander, J. (2007) "Motivational complexity of green consumption," *International Journal of Consumer Studies*, 31: 404–09.

Niva, M. and Timonen, P. (2001) "The role of consumers in product-oriented environmental policy: Can the consumer be the driving force for environmental improvements?" *International Journal of Consumer Studies*, 25: 331–38.

Packard, V. (1960) *The Waste Makers*, New York: David McKay.

Pujari, D. (2006) "Eco-innovation and new product development: Understanding the influences on market performance," *Technovation*, 26: 76–85.

Saunders, J. and Jobber, D. (1994) "Product replacement: Strategies for simultaneous product deletion and launch," *Journal of Product Innovation Management*, 11 (5): 433–50.

Slade, G. (2006) *Made to Break: Technology and Obsolescence in America*, Boston, MA: Harvard University Press.

Sonntag, V. (2000) "Sustainability – in light of competitiveness," *Ecological Economics*, 34: 101–13.

Tellis, G. and Golder, P. (2001) *Will & Vision*, New York: McGraw-Hill.

Thorgerson, J. (2000) "Psychological determinants of paying attention to eco-label in purchase decisions: model development and multinational validation," *Journal of Consumer Policy*, 23: 285–313.

Tingstrom, J. and Karlsson, R. (2006) "The relationship between environmental analyses and the dialogue process in new product development," *Journal of Cleaner Production*, 14: 1409–19.

Toffel, M. (2004) "Strategic management of product recovery," *California Management Review*, 46: 120–41.

Utaka, A. (2006) "Durable-goods warranties and social welfare," *The Journal of Law, Economics and Organization*, 22: 508–22.

van Nes, N. and Cramer, J. (2006) "Product lifetime optimization: A challenging strategy towards more sustainable consumption patterns," *Journal of Cleaner Production*, 14: 1307–18.

WBCSD (2000) *Eco-Efficiency: Creating More Value with Less Impact*, Geneva: World Business Council for Sustainable Development.

Werhane, P. (2002) "Moral imagination and systems thinking," *Journal of Business Ethics*, 38: 33–42.

Winer, R. (1997) "Discounting and its impact on durables buying decisions," *Marketing Science*, 8: 109–18.

Zafarmand, S., Suguyama, K., and Watanabe, M. (2003) "Aesthetics and sustainability: the aesthetic attributes promoting sustainability," *Journal of Sustainable Product Design*, 3: 173–86.

PART V

Public policy issues in marketing

12

SHOULD MARKETERS BE PERSUADING OUR CHILDREN?

A controversial question

Elizabeth S. Moore

Introduction

Marketing is ever-present in the daily lives of American children. Recent estimates suggest that children and teens spend over seven-and-a-half hours a day on average watching television, using computers, playing video games, listening to music, and watching movies (Rideout *et al.* 2010). This represents a vast increase in children's media use over time, much of it fueled by the ready availability of online and mobile media. Thus, marketers are contacting our children to an extent unprecedented in history.

Concern about children's ability to comprehend and evaluate marketing messages has stimulated a national debate since the early 1970s. Embedded in this discussion is the contention that marketing to children is inherently "unfair." Critics assert that it is unfair because children lack the cognitive skills and life experiences needed to resist persuasive claims. Supporters, on the other hand, suggest that children's vulnerabilities are often overstated, and that by providing product information, marketing messages help both parents and children to make more informed decisions. This debate has gained renewed fervor in recent years due to the rapid increase in childhood obesity and concerns about the role that marketing might be playing as a contributor to this critical public health problem.

This chapter examines some of the key issues that have defined the debate about marketing to children in the past, and points to several developments that might influence public policy as we look to the future. Particular emphasis is placed on the dramatic changes that have occurred in how products are being marketed to children and teens.

The youth market

Marketers have long recognized the economic potential of the youth market. American children (ages 3–11) account for approximately $22 billion in direct spending each year, and parents purchase an additional $138 billion in food, clothing, and personal items for them (Packaged Facts 2008). This picture is incomplete however as children are estimated to influence as much as 47 percent of all household spending (Economist 2006). Youth are also considered a future market, and thus often the target of campaigns aimed at building brand loyalties at a young age (Moore and Wilkie 2005; Moore *et al.* 2002).

A vast array of marketing stimuli stands ready to help shape children's product preferences. Each year children ages 2-11 see over 25,000 advertisements on television alone (Holt *et al.* 2007). For adolescents (ages 12-17) annual exposure tops 31,000 ads. Ad exposure occurs not only during programming targeted at youth but also during shows aimed at a more general audience. Close to one-third of the ads children see appear during prime-time shows (after 8:00 p.m.), which means that children are exposed to many more ads than those explicitly targeted at them.

Marketing messages appearing in "unmeasured" media such as company-owned websites, product placements in movies and television, advergames, in-store displays, promotions, and smart phones have been more difficult to quantify. However, nontraditional communication tools are an increasingly important feature of the marketing mix. This is due in part to the rapid escalation in digital media use among children and teens. In 2011, 20 million children (ages 11 and younger) were internet users. This is expected to rise to 25.7 million by 2015 or 49 percent of all children in this age group (emarketer 2011a). Within the teen population (12-17), 96 percent are already users (emarketer 2011b). The rise in mobile media access is equally dramatic. As many as 37 percent of 4-5 year olds are already using mobile devices such as smart phones and tablet computers (Troianovski 2012). Somewhat unexpectedly, digital media consumption has not diminished TV viewing, but rather led to an increase in "media multi-tasking" (Rideout *et al.* 2010). Children and teens now manage to pack a total of 10 hours and 45 minutes of content into the seven-and-a-half hours they spend with media each day because of simultaneous usage (e.g., surfing the Web while watching TV). Although there are almost limitless opportunities for marketers to reach children, it is also the case that children are considered to be a "vulnerable group." As a result, marketers must operate under certain constraints when targeting this audience.

Children as a vulnerable audience

At the center of the debate about marketing is the question of children's unique vulnerabilities. Concerns about children range from their inability to understand and evaluate advertising claims, to fears that without benefit of mature critical thinking skills they may learn to be unduly materialistic and impulsive (Linn 2004). Industry specific issues such as the marketing of violent video games and music to children (Federal Trade Commission 2009), the impacts of the fashion and beauty industry on the body image of children, especially girls (e.g., Quart 2004), and poor dietary choices that may result from heavy exposure to the marketing of sugar-laden and high-fat foods have also been a source of concern (e.g., McGinnis *et al.* 2006).

Developmental considerations

Drawing on developmental theories from psychology, and inspired by the work of Swiss psychologist, Jean Piaget, consumer researchers have studied what children understand in commercial messages, under what conditions they are persuaded, and how their responses change as they mature (see, e.g., John 1999; Moses and Baldwin 2005). Among the most basic tenets of this research is that younger and older children differ substantially both in terms of their understanding of advertising's purpose as well as in how they deploy this knowledge when responding to specific appeals. Younger children (ages 3-7) are generally thought to be especially vulnerable. They are less likely to understand advertising's basic purpose, tend to believe message claims, and have more positive attitudes about advertising. To critically evaluate advertising, children must acquire at least two key information-processing skills that, as adults, we commonly employ. First, they need to be able to distinguish between commercial and non-commercial content. Second, they should be able to recognize advertising's persuasive intent and actively draw on this understanding to effectively deal with the selling messages they encounter.

By about age five, most children can make a perceptual distinction between commercials and television programs (John 1999). Young children can articulate that commercials are "shorter" or "funnier" than television programs. However, perceptual differentiation does not necessarily mean that children have a conceptual understanding that the content of an advertisement is independent of the entertainment that surrounds it. Children at this age have not yet fully developed the "executive functioning" skills needed to monitor and control their thoughts and actions (McAlister and Cornwell 2009; Moses and Baldwin 2005). So, they may be drawn to appealing but irrelevant inputs and have difficulty shifting their attention to more pertinent information such as product quality or disclaimers when needed.

Children aged 7-11 are more multidimensional in their thinking than younger children and are able to recognize multiple perspectives, including that of an advertiser (John 1999). By about eight years of age, most children have an understanding that advertising's purpose is to sell products, and a rudimentary understanding of the biased nature of the information provided. This is viewed as a developmental milestone by many researchers and policy-makers. It has traditionally been assumed that once children have an understanding of persuasive intent that they will become more skeptical of advertising and thus capable of resisting its appeal. And, it is true that older children (aged 10-12), when asked, readily acknowledge that advertising does not always "tell the truth" and are more likely to express cynical views of advertising (e.g., Boush et al.1994). However, performance deficits still persist among older children, and a general understanding of advertising and a skeptical attitude may not be sufficient. Although children in this age group are more flexible and analytic thinkers, they tend not to invoke their knowledge of persuasion and influence when exposed to a television commercial, unless explicitly reminded (Brucks et al. 1988; Moore and Lutz 2000). Thus, possessing the requisite "cognitive and attitudinal defenses" is not the same as actually using them.

This difference has turned out to be a crucial one for this age group, and is likely more of a factor when the distinction between advertising and entertainment is less apparent, such as in branded online games and promotions.

Among adolescents, other developmental issues come to the forefront. Although teens have the cognitive skills to understand how advertising works, this age group is more impulsive and self-conscious than adults. This impulsivity may impact their decision making leaving them less likely to consider the consequences of excessive consumption particularly of high-risk products, such as high-fat foods, tobacco, and alcohol (Pechmann *et al.* 2005).

The nature of children's vulnerabilities is an important issue in considering what kinds of protections may be needed in the marketplace, and for what age groups. In the United States, policy-makers and industry leaders have historically focused their attention on children under age 12.

The development of marketplace protections

Although corporations enjoy considerable freedoms in the United States to promote their products to children, important steps have been taken over the years both by government regulators and industry leaders to implement needed safeguards. In the early 1970s a consumer advocacy group known as Action for Children's Television (ACT) petitioned the Federal Communications Commission (FCC) to develop policies to protect young children. The eventual outcome of this petition was that the Commission adopted, for the first time, federal policies restricting advertising to children.[1] The FCC now limits the amount of television advertising allowed during children's programming (10.5 minutes per hour on weekends and 12 minutes per hour on weekdays) (FCC 2011). It also requires that a clear distinction be maintained between programs and commercials. To do so, content providers must insert separators (e.g., "We'll be right back after these messages") between television programs and commercials. It also prohibits "host-selling" (i.e., branded character endorsements) during or adjacent to television shows which feature that character, because it may be difficult for children to discriminate between the program and the ad that follows. The FCC also restricts the display of website addresses during a children's program if the primary intent is to advertise or promote e-commerce. The Federal Trade Commission (FTC) shares responsibility with the FCC for regulating advertising, though each agency has a separate mandate. The FTC currently has the authority to regulate marketing and advertising that is judged to be "unfair" or "deceptive" in any medium.

In 1978, the FTC's Bureau of Consumer Protection staff produced a controversial report which recommended a series of remedies that included the following: (1) a ban of all TV advertising to children (under 8 years of age), (2) a ban of all TV advertising for sugared food products directed to older children (ages 8-12), and (3) a requirement that all other TV advertising for sugared products seen by significant proportions of older children to be balanced by health messages also paid for by the advertiser (FTC 1978). The Bureau staff argued that advertising to children too young to understand its selling intent is "inherently unfair and deceptive," under Section 5 of the FTC Act. Much of the concern at that time centered on the health risks of dental caries, reminiscent in some sense of the current debate about marketing's impacts on childhood obesity.

In response to the staff's recommendation, the FTC invited public comment on the advisability and implementation of such a trade regulation rule. Opposition to the proposed rule was swift and powerful. Representatives from the manufacturing, broadcasting, and advertising industries engaged in extensive lobbying, citing First Amendment ("freedom of speech") considerations, the potential loss of children's programming, and the inconclusive or conflicting nature of some research reports. Congress criticized the proposed rule as grossly overreaching and the Washington Post asserted that it would turn the FTC into a "national nanny" (Beales 2004). The FTC subsequently terminated the rulemaking proceeding, and Congress stripped the Commission of its power to adopt any rules concerning children's advertising (Mello 2010).

Beyond this episode, the FTC has had significant impact, particularly in the domain of children's online privacy. In 1998, Congress passed the Children's Online Privacy Protection Act (COPPA) requiring the FTC to issue and enforce a rule governing marketers' online data collection practices. The primary goal is to place parents in control over what information is gathered from their children. Effective in 2000, this rule prohibits unfair or deceptive practices in the collection, use or disclosure of personally identifiable information from children (under age 13) on the Internet. The rule requires that commercial websites post their privacy policies, obtain verifiable consent from a parent or guardian before they collect personal information from children, and protect the confidentiality and security of any information obtained (Federal Register 1999). The specific provisions of the rule are currently under review by the FTC to ensure that it keeps pace with technological advances in advertising networks and consumer usage patterns (Federal Register 2012).[2]

The early activities of the FCC and the FTC raised the public profile of the children's advertising issue. In response to public criticism and the potentials for government intervention in the 1970s, significant self-regulatory steps were also taken. The Children's Advertising Review Unit (CARU) of the Council of Better Business Bureaus was created in 1974; it continues to play a primary role in promoting responsible advertising targeted at children today. At its inception, it vowed to ensure "truthful, non-deceptive advertising to children under 12" and to respond to public complaints about potentially misleading advertisements. CARU publishes detailed "Self-Regulatory Guidelines" for advertisers. These guidelines focus on issues such as safety concerns, product presentation, the use of endorsements, disclaimers, sales pressure, contests, and online sales and have been updated several times over the years to adapt to changing marketplace conditions (CARU 2009). CARU also does extensive monitoring and evaluation of child-directed ads. When an ad is found to be misleading or inaccurate, CARU seeks the voluntary cooperation of the advertiser to resolve the problem. This self-regulatory body serves a critically important role in protecting children from misleading ads in whatever medium they appear. There are vocal critics of CARU, however, who assert that it is not providing adequate protections given the rapid advance of new marketing techniques and the unhealthy diet promoted to children via food marketing (e.g., Center for Science in the Public Interest 2006; Sharma *et al.* 2010).

Refueling the debate: Food marketing in a new age

After the termination of the "kidvid" rulemaking process in 1980, attention to advertising's impacts on children waned considerably both among academic researchers and policy-makers. This was quite consistent with the Reagan administration's broader deregulatory policy, which was affecting many federal agencies at the time (Wilkie 1994). As noted above, significant steps were taken to regulate children's online privacy in the late 1990s but little else happened on the policy front. A principal result of this diminished interest was that fundamental questions about children's capacity to understand, and defend themselves, against marketing were never fully resolved. Such an occurrence is not unique to the children's advertising debate, as other consumer protection questions have also been "left behind" (and left unresolved) as researchers turn their attention to other frontiers of concern (Andreasen 1997).

Almost 25 years went by before major questions surrounding marketing to children resurfaced in the public sphere. This resurgence was driven by two key factors – the dramatic rise in childhood obesity (with associated questions about marketing's contributory role), and the rapid advance of technologically sophisticated marketing tools that are being used to target children. The specific significance of these issues is discussed below.

The rise of childhood obesity

In its reports, the World Health Organization (WHO) now refers to childhood obesity as a global epidemic. Approximately 110 million children are overweight worldwide (Cali and Caprio 2008). In the United States, obesity rates have tripled since 1980. National surveys indicate that 26.7 percent of 2-5 year olds, 32.6 percent of 6-11 year olds, and 33.6 percent of 12-19 year olds are either overweight or obese (Ogden *et al.* 2012).[3] These averages don't tell the full story, however, as levels among some ethnic minorities are even higher. Obesity in children has a range of adverse health effects including elevated risks of hypertension, atherosclerosis, obstructive sleep apnea, chronic inflammation, and metabolic disorders such as diabetes (e.g., Daniels 2006; Friedemann *et al.* 2012). Psychosocial consequences include risks of low self-esteem, social isolation, and poor school performance (Caprio *et al.* 2008; Kipping *et al.* 2008). Obese children are also more likely to become overweight adults, with all the attendant health risks.

There is no question that a number of influences shape children's food preferences and eating behavior. Multiple factors – from the individual (e.g., genetics, taste predispositions) to the family (e.g., parent food intake, household food availability, family meals, socio-economic status), the community (e.g., schools, food retail outlets), and macro-system forces (e.g., culture, food production and distribution systems, advertising, governmental regulations) influence children's food consumption (McGinnis *et al.* 2006). In attempting to disentangle potential contributors to obesity, particular attention in the public sector is being focused on the impacts of food marketing.

Food and beverage marketing represents a significant proportion of the promotional resources directed at children and teens. Proprietary data provided by major marketers in response to a recent Federal Trade Commission (FTC) compulsory process order shows that the 44 leading food marketers in the United States spend approximately $1.6 billion to promote food and beverages directly to children and adolescents (FTC 2008). Breakfast cereals, fast foods, carbonated beverages, and snacks are among the most heavily promoted product categories to this audience.[4] The predominant themes used to promote these foods are fantasy, fun, novelty, and taste (e.g., Gantz *et al.* 2007).[5]

In the last decade, three comprehensive reviews of research investigating the impacts of food and beverage marketing on children have been published, one by the Food Standards Agency in the UK (Hastings *et al.* 2003), a second in response to a US Congressional directive by the Institute of Medicine (IOM) (McGinnis *et al.* 2006), and the third by the World Health Organization (Cairns *et al.* 2009). In its analysis, the IOM concluded that television advertising influences key dietary precursors including children's (ages 2-11) food and beverage preferences, purchase requests and product choices. Correlational evidence further linked TV advertising exposure to adiposity (body fatness) in both children and adolescents, a finding also reported by the World Health Organization. One of the key conclusions of the IOM report was that "food and beverage marketing practices geared to children and youth are out of balance with healthful diets and contribute to an environment that puts their health at risk" (p. 10). The review by the WHO further confirms that in both developed and developing countries children are exposed to extensive marketing, and that the advertised diet is largely inconsistent with the public health community's recommendations (Cairns *et al.* 2009).

An evolving marketing landscape

Much of the evidence on which current policy conclusions are based is derived from research investigating the effects of television advertising on children. To this point, only a relatively small number of studies have examined the impacts of new media. Although television remains a major medium used to reach a young audience (approximately 46 percent of all food marketing expenditures), most marketing programs aimed at this group have become much more diversified in recent years, with digital and other new media assuming an increasing share of the promotional budget (FTC 2008). Interactive promotional platforms are being used in conjunction with traditional "measured media" (television, radio, print) to create appealing integrated marketing campaigns. Themes in television commercials, for example, are reinforced on websites for children that contain branded advergames, characters, and promotions (Moore and Rideout 2007). These same themes are emphasized in colorful packaging, displays in stores or restaurants, movie tie-ins and contests delivered via mobile media (see e.g., Montgomery 2007). From a marketer's perspective, this is an effective strategy. Research shows that brand messages which appear in multiple media or via integrated marketing communications (IMC) campaigns are both more easily remembered and more persuasive (Naik and Raman 2003).

The food and beverage industries have been quick to embrace digital technologies, particularly the Internet, in the development of their IMC campaigns aimed at children and teens. One of the strengths of the Internet is its capacity to engender high levels of interest and engagement. It is distinctive as an advertising medium in that it combines the audiovisual aspects of TV, the text-based elements of print and the two-way capacity of a phone. Surfing a website is an inherently active process as it requires a continuous stream of decisions and actions. It is this feature that distinguishes the Internet from a more passive medium like television. Rather than capturing children's attention for thirty seconds, the advertiser may now engage them for several minutes. The emergence of mobile devices such as smart phones and tablets has extended the reach of these communications still further. Even young children can readily master the intuitive touch screens on these devices, often well before they can read (Troianovski 2012).

One of the key characteristics of the new media landscape is the blurring of the lines between advertising and entertainment (Moore 2004). This is particularly true on the Internet where commercially created "branded environments" featuring activities such as interactive games, video, promotions, viral marketing, movie tie-ins and celebrity endorsements are centered on a food or beverage brand. Explicitly created for children or teens, these websites are designed to be involving and fun, with "brand immersion" as a key objective (Ferrazzi and Benezra 2001). Advertising may also be embedded in video games, in games on mobile devices or on social networking sites, venues that are particularly likely to appeal to youth (e.g., Khan 2010). The potential impact is vast given that gaming is second only to social media in terms of how Americans spend their time online (Nielsenwire 2010). In-game advertising is growing rapidly (outpacing gains in other media) with revenues of $1 billion forecasted by 2014 (Durrani 2009). The integration of a branded message in a game or other content may mask the persuasive intent of the marketer, thus making it more difficult for young children to recognize it as an advertisement (Moore 2004). Even if children do recognize it as a marketing message, however, placing ads in an entertainment vehicle can be a very effective way to reduce children's skepticism, and thus create more openness to a brand message (Lindstrom and Seybold 2003). As the distinctive properties of digital media as a platform for integrated marketing campaigns have become more well-known, concerns about young children's vulnerability have been rekindled, and new apprehensions about potential risks to adolescents have surfaced (see e.g., Montgomery 2007).

Escalating challenges: Findings of the Notre Dame "advergaming" study

Such concerns have prompted calls by the public health community for more research on digital marketing practices (e.g., McGinnis *et al.* 2006). One communications tool that has been widely adopted by major food marketers are branded websites that are either explicitly designed for, or contain content that is likely to appeal to children under age 12 (Moore 2006). With the goal of informing policy-makers, the Kaiser Family Foundation was the first to sponsor a comprehensive study of these websites, a study that was undertaken at the University of Notre Dame (ND) by this author and a team of student research assistants (Moore 2006; Moore and Rideout 2007).[6]

A total of 77 websites including over 4,000 pages of content were analyzed in the ND study.[7] The results showed that among food brands that were heavily advertised to children on television at that time, 85 percent were also promoted to them on food marketers' websites (Moore 2006). According to Nielsen Net Ratings, these websites receive approximately 49 million visits by children ages 2-11 on an annual basis, and once there, children spend anywhere from a few seconds to well over an hour. Some of these sites are simple, containing only a few activities, and others are more elaborate, incorporating not only a large number of branded games but also promotions, viral marketing, membership opportunities and media tie-ins. Although some study sites focused on only a single brand, others contained upwards of 40 brands (some more prominently displayed than others). Brand marks, including logos, brand characters, packages, food items, and corporate logos were prominently placed throughout the sites' content. So, for children visiting these websites, it was rare to find content that did not provide some brand reinforcement.

On the basis of this study, an analysis of website features of particular interest to marketers and policy-makers concerned about deleterious youth impacts was conducted (Moore and Rideout 2007). Eleven online marketing practices of potential consequence were identified, only a subset of which are discussed here.

One of the most prominent features on the websites was advergaming (with 546 games appearing on 77 websites). These are Internet games that are created by a company with the explicit purpose of promoting a brand or company in an engaging way.[8] They are similar to arcade and other video games, with vivid animation, music and sound effects. Sites containing such games have been likened to "virtual amusement parks" (Goetzl 2006). As noted earlier, one of the long-standing concerns about children centers on their ability first to understand a marketer's persuasive intent and then to draw on this knowledge when they see an advertisement. When food brands are embedded in an online game, and the lines between advertising and entertainment are not distinct, children may be less motivated and cognitively ready to defend themselves against the marketing message. The game itself is the center of attention, so the brand logo, package or character may be processed only peripherally. To younger children (ages 3-7) it may not even be obvious that these sites are explicitly designed to promote a brand. Yet, their preferences (as well as those of older children) may be shaped by "mere exposure" to a brand element in a game. Even among adults, there is evidence showing that incidental ad exposure can lead to more positive beliefs and attitudes about a brand even if they don't process a marketing message very deeply (e.g., Janiszewski 1993; Nordhielm 2002). Thus favorable brand attitudes can be formed as a result of ad exposure even though consumers may have little insight as to why.

Subsequent research has borne out these predictions. For example, in an experimental study, Mallinckrodt and Mizerski (2007) found that 8-year-olds who played an advergame for the Froot Loops cereal brand reported significantly greater preference for the brand compared both with other cereals and with other types of foods. Only a small proportion of the children identified Kellogg as the game's source, suggesting that they may have found it more difficult to recognize advertising when it appeared in this medium. More recently, Harris *et al.* (2012) found that exposure to brands via advergames also influences children's choices and the amount of food they consume. In a study with 7-12-year-olds, these authors showed that exposure to healthy foods via an advergame led to a greater intake of nutritious snack foods. However, after playing games with less nutritious foods embedded in them, children tended to consume more unhealthy snacks, and fewer fruits and vegetables. These effects were most pronounced among children who had played advergames on previous occasions, and were not limited to the specific foods advertised. For example, children who played a game that promoted Pop Tarts and Oreos were more likely to choose to snack on potato chips and cookies than children who had played games advertising healthier options. Together, these studies show that children are influenced in significant albeit yet not fully under-stood ways when exposed to food brands in advergames. Recent evidence suggests that these games are rapidly expanding onto new platforms including smart phones and tablets, thus increasing their accessibility, and raising new questions with regard to their impacts on children (Troianovski 2012).

A second issue of potential interest that surfaced in the ND study was the use of viral marketing on the majority (64 percent) of websites examined. Children were encouraged to send email to their friends containing brand-related greetings (e-cards) or invitations to the site. This approach turns email into an endorsement because the messages are very brand focused, typically containing the brand name, logo, and often a brand character. In some cases, the sender is given the opportunity to personalize the message by choosing the layout, colors, or text. Young children who are still learning how advertising works may not realize that by sending these messages they are advancing the cause of a corporation. If so, is it appropriate to encourage children to use their social networks to promote a brand?

A coalition of consumer advocacy groups has recently filed a complaint with the Federal Trade Commission (FTC) arguing against the use of such approaches. Organizations including the Consumer Federation of America, the Center for Science in the Public Interest, and the Center for Digital Democracy have joined forces to ask the FTC to update its privacy rule in order to better protect children from marketers' data gathering and behavioral targeting practices, including the collection of email addresses, photos, and use of cookies. Coalition members assert that by encouraging children to provide friends' email addresses without parental consent, food marketers are in violation of the Children's Online Privacy Protection Act (COPPA) (Morrison 2012). Food marketers, on the other hand, have stressed that the complaint mischaracterizes the rule's provisions. Debate on this issue is likely to continue at least until the FTC determines what changes should be made to the COPPA rule.

A third policy relevant issue that arose in the ND study was the question of limits to children's advertising exposure. Unlike television, there are no policy-driven restrictions on the extent of children's exposure to marketing messages on the Internet. Children are free to visit commercially sponsored websites, spend unlimited time there and return for subsequent visits. If public policy dictates that limited exposure to television advertising is in the best interest of children, then it seems reasonable to ask whether restrictions in other media might also be needed. As the lines between media blur (enabled by new technologies) and children's media choices shift, it will become increasingly important to consider such questions. For example, television commercials or "webisodes" frequently appeared on websites (53 percent of the sites in this study). There were no limits to the number of times a commercial could be viewed, and in some cases children were given added incentives to watch the ads while visiting the site. For example, children might be given access to special games if they viewed commercials on the site. Some marketers also used their websites to encourage children to rate the appeal of different TV commercials. In such cases, children may be providing the firm with market research data without fully comprehending what they are doing.

Food marketers used a variety of other creative approaches to generate children's interest on the study websites such as child-oriented sales promotions (e.g., premiums, sweepstakes) – evident on 65 percent of the sites, movie or television tie-ins (47 percent), downloadable items such as branded screensavers, desktop icons or wallpaper (76 percent), membership opportunities (25 percent) and even direct inducements to purchase (39 percent). In this case, children were offered special rewards on a website such as access to "secret" site locations, the chance to play advanced games or to obtain brand-related merchandise, in exchange for a purchase or series of purchases (as evidenced by codes obtained in the brand's package).

Given the lack of limits on online ad exposures and the array of sophisticated techniques being used to appeal to children, it is appropriate to ask whether there are mechanisms in place to remind children that the content on these websites is advertising. Again, television policy may be instructive. As noted above, the FCC requires that advertisers insert separators during children's television programs (FCC 2011). These short segments shown before and after commercial breaks are designed to remind children that they are watching ads, and to encourage them to be more vigilant. The boundaries between advertising and other content may be harder to distinguish on the Internet, because unlike on television, there are no natural breaks. Online activities such as advergames and viral marketing (e.g., send a friend an invitation to a branded website) provide a kind of camouflage for selling intent that may make it difficult for young children to discern. Yet, only a small number of advertisers (18 percent of those in the ND study) provided "ad break" reminders. The costs of providing "ad breaks" are not substantial, but the potential benefits to children are significant. If designed well, they may cue children's advertising defenses, at least among older children who have the requisite ad knowledge but may not activate it unless reminded.

The ND study illustrates that the landscape of marketing to children has moved a long way from the days when industry leaders and policy-makers first recognized the unique vulnerabilities of children. Much needs to be learned about what kinds of marketing efforts are appropriate, which are not and how this varies as a function of the communication medium and a child's maturity level. Studies of adolescent behavior suggest that the emphasis on children under age 12 may be incomplete (e.g., Pechmann *et al.* 2005). Research interest in the broad topic of marketing's impacts on children, and to the influence of new media in particular, has gained considerable momentum of late. This corresponds to a renewed emphasis on public policy options, particularly with respect to food marketing and childhood obesity, the topic of the closing section.

Key developments in the public policy sector

The problem of childhood obesity has attracted the attention of public policymakers, consumer interest groups, health professionals, academics, industry leaders and the public. Pressures to develop workable solutions are coming from all sectors and prominent campaigns such as First Lady Michelle Obama's "Let's Move" campaign (White House Task Force on Childhood Obesity 2010) have heightened the profile of this issue further.

As might be expected, perspectives vary considerably with regard to the most effective course of action for addressing marketing's role in reducing childhood obesity. Stakeholders such as the American Psychological Association (Kunkel *et al.* 2004), the Campaign for a Commercial Free Childhood (Linn and Golan 2011), the American Academy of Pediatrics (AAP 2006), and the International Obesity Task Force (2008) have called for some government restrictions on marketing to children. This would not be without precedent. In the UK for example, the Office of Communications (national media regulatory agency) approved new rules in 2007 banning ads for high fat, salt, and sugar foods in and around television programs that are either designed for, or that appeal to children under age 16 (OfCom 2007). In the United States, however, pursuit of self-regulatory solutions has been the primary focus of attention in recent years.

Multiple workshops on children's health, marketing and self-regulation have been held by the Federal Trade Commission to solicit inputs from industry leaders, academics, public health officials and consumer advocates (in 2005, 2007, 2009, 2011).

At the first one, then FTC Chairman Deborah Majoras articulated the Commission's position:

> We are well aware that some already are calling on government to regulate rather than facilitate. We believe that government has an important role to play in this important national health issue. From the FTC's perspective based on years of experience with advertising, we believe that a government ban on children's food advertising is neither wise nor viable. It would be, however, equally unwise for industry to maintain the status quo. Not only is downplaying the concerns of consumers bad business but if industry fails to demonstrate a good faith commitment to this issue and take positive steps, others may step in and act in its stead.
>
> *(FTC 2005, p. 16)*

Industry reactions

Heeding this advice, the Council of Better Business Bureaus (CBBB) initiated two major changes to the self-regulatory system. First, significant revisions were made to CARU's self-regulatory guidelines. CARU now takes action not only on advertising judged to be deceptive to children but also on advertising that is "unfair" (as these terms are applied under the FTC Act) thus significantly expanding its scope of protection. The revised guidelines also strengthen CARU's charge to advertisers regarding depictions of serving size, balanced nutrition, and healthy lifestyles (CARU 2009).

The CBBB also announced the creation of the Children's Food and Beverage Advertising Initiative (CFBAI), a voluntary self-regulatory program with major food and beverage manufacturers as participants. Under the terms of this program, which were revised effective January 2010, participating companies pledge that 100 percent of their advertising primarily directed to children under 12 will be for healthier dietary choices or better-for-you products (CBBB 2009). This applies to child targeted placements in a range of media including television, radio, print, company-owned websites, video or computer games, DVDs, movies, and cell phones. Each participating company prepares its own pledge, which describes its commitment and implementation schedule.[9] Firms also currently set their own nutrition criteria, but they must be consistent with established scientific and/or government standards (e.g., US Department of Agriculture's dietary guidelines, Food and Drug Administration's (FDA) standards for health claims). By December 2013, these firm-specific nutrition criteria will be replaced by uniform product category standards (CBBB 2011b). At its inception in late 2006, there were 10 participants in the CFBAI. Currently, there are 16 participating companies which together represent approximately 75 percent of the advertising appearing during children's programming (CBBB 2010). Since the announcement of the CFBAI in the United States, other nations including Canada, Australia, the European Union, Russia, India, Brazil, Thailand, Mexico, Switzerland, and South Africa have introduced similar self-regulatory programs.[10]

The controversy rages on

The response to these self-regulatory developments has been decidedly mixed. Public health researchers and consumer advocates, while acknowledging that progress has been made, have argued that the provisions of the CFBAI are weak and its impact on reducing children's exposure to food marketing inadequate (e.g., CSPI 2010; Harris *et al.* 2009, 2010; Kunkel *et al.* 2009). Industry representatives, on the other hand, point to their "excellent compliance record," the evolution of program provisions since its inception, and the improving nutritional profile of foods being advertised to children (CBBB 2009, 2010, 2011a).[11] Supporters also contend that advances in the self-regulatory arena have led to many product reformulations and the introduction of healthy alternatives (CBBB 2011a).[12]

A number of issues underpin these divergent points of view (Ralston Aoki and Moore 2012). First, the Initiative focuses exclusively on *child-targeted* advertising, not the entire set of ads that children routinely see. Since a substantial proportion of children's TV ad exposure occurs during programming aimed at a general audience, children are still seeing many ads for products that don't meet the nutrition criteria in the company pledges. Further, the public health researchers argue that the nutrition criteria themselves are weak. So, food that they deem to be nutritionally inadequate may still be promoted to children. There are also potentially powerful marketing tools that are implicitly or explicitly excluded from the program such as product packages, company-owned characters (e.g., Toucan Sam), sponsorships, point-of-purchase displays, and sales promotions. Finally, consumer advocates argue that marketing aimed at adolescents (ages 12-17) should be subject to the Initiative and that the program should cover all food manufacturers, retailers and media firms, not just those who volunteer to participate.

The government proposal: Is it déjà vu all over again?

Amidst these uncertainties, and in an effort to promote children's health, Congress directed four federal agencies – the Federal Trade Commission, the Food and Drug Administration, the Centers for Disease Control and Prevention, and the US Department of Agriculture to create an interagency working group to develop a set of recommendations for food marketing to children and adolescents aged 2-17. In the spring of 2011, the working group released a set of preliminary principles that would guide industry self-regulatory efforts and invited public comment. The voluntary principles addressed the nutritional quality of foods that are most heavily marketed to youth and also include proposed definitions of advertising, and other marketing activities to which the nutrition principles would apply.[13]

By the time the comment period closed in July 2011, over 600 detailed commentaries had been received from groups ranging from the American Cancer Society and the American Academy of Pediatrics to the American Grocery Manufacturers Association and the American Beverage Association (FTC 2011). Over 100 US Senators and Representatives from both sides of the political aisle also weighed in with their assessments.[14]

Perspectives varied considerably as to the usefulness of the principles, with strong arguments levied both supportive and critical. The public health community and consumer advocates reacted quite favorably to the proposed guidelines, believing that their impact on reducing the marketing of unhealthy foods and beverages to youth would be substantial, and a clear improvement over existing self-regulatory efforts (e.g., Roschke and Campbell 2011). They also argued that the standards would incent manufacturers to develop healthier options and applauded the inclusion of adolescents within the proposal.

At the same time, more than 150 industry trade groups registered their opposition, citing issues such as feasibility, cost, overreach, and First Amendment considerations (Greene 2011). The nutritional guidelines were judged to be too stringent by many in the industry, raising concerns that an unintended consequence would actually be to reduce manufacturers' incentives to develop healthier options. This is a key consideration given that many existing products produced by CFBAI participants have either been altered or new ones created to meet science-based nutrition standards since the Initiative was announced (CBBB 2011a). Based on a commissioned research study, critics also claimed that if implemented the proposal would result in significant job losses and reduced advertising revenues. The Association of National Advertisers further argued that the proposal was not really voluntary but would instead reflect "backdoor regulation" by powerful government agencies (Jaffe and Scarborough 2011), an accusation that the FTC patently rejected (Vladek 2011).

Somewhat reminiscent of the events in the 1970s, powerful lobbying efforts and opposition to government intervention have prevailed. In response to mounting political pressures, Congress required that the FTC and its sister agencies provide a cost–benefit analysis of the impact of the voluntary standards in reducing obesity levels before issuing its final report. The agencies said such a study was unprecedented for a voluntary guideline and would be far too expensive (Wilson and Roberts 2012). Also at issue were the complexities of providing scientific evidence that would isolate food marketing's causal role in the obesity epidemic, given the simultaneous contribution of many other personal and environmental factors. As a result, in early 2012, FTC Chairman Leibowitz said that it was "time to move on," and that the effort to write voluntary standards would no longer be an agency priority (Leibowitz 2012).

Into the future

The goal of this chapter was to explore the reasons why marketing to children is such a controversial and challenging area. It should now be clear why this is the case. In terms of public policy, the events of late are reminiscent of the 1970s, in part, because many of the issues raised at that time were never really resolved. The difference is that the world of marketing to children today is much more technologically complex, and a constant of daily life. Children are being exposed to an appealing and sophisticated set of marketing activities in both traditional and new media. As children spend more and more of their day interacting with media, their total exposure to marketing messages is also increasing. Although the issue of advertising to children has resurfaced in the public consciousness, it is not obvious what, if any, additional policy developments may be forthcoming with regard to food marketing in the near term. The market system in the United States grants marketers substantial freedoms relative to many other countries (Wilkie and Moore 1999).[15] As a nation, we have chosen to place our trust in that system to market products to young children in a responsible manner, one that takes into account the knowledge and maturity of this audience. With the increase in childhood obesity, the stakes have risen even higher. Altering the social, political, and marketplace conditions that contribute to obesity in children is an extraordinarily challenging task. Success will require the constructive efforts of diverse stakeholders whose interests may not always align and who operate under different sets of constraints and opportunities. With its vast creative talent, financial resources, and powers of persuasion, marketing can be a powerful force for promoting healthy diets and lifestyles in children. As we think about marketing and the common good, this should be our long-term societal goal.

Acknowledgment

The author wishes to thank the Notre Dame Deloitte Center for Ethical Leadership for its generous support.

Notes

1 The Federal Communications Commission regulates interstate and international communications in the United States (and US territories) by radio, television, wire, satellite, and cable. Its primary goal is to ensure that content providers operate in the public interest (FCC 2011). These policies were relaxed significantly in 1984 amid the general trend toward deregulation that occurred during the Reagan administration. With the passage of the Children's Television Act in 1990, Congress reinstated restrictions as a statutory requirement for broadcasters.
2 In 2011, the FTC issued a "Notice of Proposed Rulemaking" outlining some possible changes to the COPPA rule. These proposed modifications are intended to clarify the scope of the rule and strengthen its protections of children's personal information (Federal Register 2012). Among its provisions, the revised rule would hold both site operators and third-party service operators (e.g., ad networks) responsible for third-party data collection on a site. The FTC is also considering an expanded set of parental verification methods, tighter exceptions to parental consent requirements, a revised definition of "web site or online service directed to children," and a broadened definition of personal information (e.g., to include items such as photos). Changes to the existing rule are needed to keep pace with technological advances and shifts in consumer usage patterns in recent years. For example, Consumer Reports (2012) found that over 5.6 million children under age 13 have Facebook accounts despite restrictions limiting access to the site for children in this age group.
3 The terms overweight and obesity are often used interchangeably when referring to children. However, the CDC defines obesity as a BMI at or above the 95th percentile for children of the same age and sex based on the 2000 CDC Growth Charts for the United States. Overweight is defined as ≥ 85th percentile and < 95th percentile for a child's age and gender (www.cdc.gov/obesity/childhood/basics.html).
4 An additional $8 billion was also spent by these marketers to reach a more general audience, a significant proportion of which also reaches the youth market (FTC 2008).
5 In contrast, nutrition and health themes tend to be emphasized in parent-targeted communications of the same child-oriented food products (Cairns et al. 2009).

6 Those interested may wish to view a video on the project that the University of Notre Dame produced and ran on the NBC football broadcast of ND vs. Stanford in 2007 (http://video.nd.edu/131-internet-marketing).

7 See Moore (2006) or Moore and Rideout (2007) for a detailed description of how the brands and websites were selected for study. Information about the coding process and data analysis can also be found there.

8 The term advergame is sometimes also used to refer to a regular video game (online, console) which may include advertisements that have been paid for by a sponsoring company. For example, during game play you might see a billboard promoting a particular brand or a racecar with a brand logo on it.

9 Individual company pledges for CFBAI participants can be accessed at: www.bbb.org/us/children-food-beverage-advertising-initiative/.

10 Specifics of international programs are available at: www.yaleruddcenter.org/marketing-pledges/search.aspx.

11 CFBAI program requirements have been expanded since its introduction. The original requirement stated that participants would commit 50 percent of their child-directed advertising in covered media to better for you products or healthy lifestyle messages. The provision for healthy lifestyle messages has been removed and 100 percent of advertising must be for better-for-you products. The list of media covered has also been expanded to include DVDs (G-rated movies), cell phones, and video and computer games (CBBB 2010).

12 For example, beginning in 2012, McDonalds' Happy Meals include apple slices and a new smaller serving of french fries (or two packages of apples in lieu of fries) as the default side option. This represents a 20 percent caloric reduction in its most popular children's meals (Morrison 2011).

13 In developing these nutrition principles, the agencies were guided by dietary recommendations established by the DHHS and USDA in the 2010 Dietary Guidelines for Americans, and also by regulations set forth by the FDA following the Nutrition Labeling and Education Act of 1990, and by the USDA, governing nutrient content and health claims in food labeling (IWG 2011).

14 All public comments on the Interagency Working Group's Proposed Nutrition Principles can be found at: www.ftc.gov/os/comments/foodmarketedchildren/.

15 In a survey of 73 countries, the World Health Organization found that 85 percent (62 countries) regulate children's television advertising in some fashion (Hawkes 2004). At that time, 46 countries had statutory requirements and 51 had self-regulatory guidelines. In approximately half of the countries surveyed, government regulation and self-regulation coexist. There are also some statutory or voluntary regulations for other types of media and marketing activities. See Hawkes (2007) for additional developments and a country-by-country analysis.

References

American Academy of Pediatrics (2006) "Policy statement – children, adolescents, and advertising," Committee on Communications, *Pediatrics*, 118 (December): 2563–69.

Andreasen, A.R. (1997) "From ghetto marketing to social marketing: bringing social relevance to mainstream marketing," *Journal of Public Policy & Marketing*, 16 (Spring): 129–31.

Beales, J.H., III (2004) "Advertising to kids and the FTC: a regulatory retrospective that advises the present," *George Mason Law Review*, 12: 873–94.

Boush, D.M., Friestad, M., and Rose, G.M. (1994) "Adolescent skepticism toward TV advertising and knowledge of advertiser tactics," *Journal of Consumer Research*, 21 (June): 165–75.

Brucks, M., Armstrong, G.M., and Goldberg, M.E. (1988) "Children's use of cognitive defenses against television advertising: a cognitive response approach," *Journal of Consumer Research*, 14 (March): 471–82.

Cairns, G., Angus, K., and Hastings, G. (2009) *The Extent, Nature and Effects of Food Promotion to Children: A Review of the Evidence to December 2008*, Geneva, Switzerland, World Health Organization.

Cali, A.M. and Caprio, S. (2008) "Obesity in children and adolescents," *Journal of Clinical Endocrinology & Metabolism*, 93 (11): S31–6.

Caprio, S., Daniels, S.R., Drewnowski, A., Kaufman, F.R., Palinkas, L.A., Rosenbloom, A.L., and Schwimmer, J.B. (2008) "Influence of race, ethnicity, and culture on childhood obesity: implications for prevention and treatment," *Diabetes Care*, 31(11): 2211–21.

Center for Science in the Public Interest (2006) *Guidelines for Responsible Food Marketing to Children*, Washington, DC.

—— (2010) *Report Card on Food-Marketing Policies*, Washington, DC.

Children's Advertising Review Unit (2009) *Self-Regulatory Program for Children's Advertising*, 9th edn, New York: Council of Better Business Bureaus.

Children's Online Privacy Protection Rule (1999) Final Rule November 13, *Federal Register*, 64 (212), 59888–915.

Consumer Reports (2012) *Facebook & Your Privacy*, Consumers' Union, June, 24–31.

Council of Better Business Bureaus (2009) *The Children's Food & Beverage Advertising Initiative in Action – A Report on Compliance and Implementation During 2008*, Arlington, VA: Council of Better Business Bureaus, Inc.

—— (2010) *The Children's Food & Beverage Advertising Initiative in Action – A Report on Compliance and Implementation During 2009*, Arlington, VA: Council of Better Business Bureaus, Inc.

—— (2011a), *The Children's Food & Beverage Advertising Initiative in Action – A Report on Compliance and Implementation During 2010 and A Five Year Retrospective: 2006–2011*, Arlington, VA: Council of Better Business Bureaus, Inc.

—— (2011b), *The Children's Food & Beverage Advertising Initiative, White Paper on CFBAI's Uniform Nutrition Criteria*, Arlington, VA: Council of Better Business Bureaus, Inc.

Daniels, S.R. (2006) "The consequences of childhood overweight and obesity," *The Future of Children*, 16 (1), 47–67.

Durrani, A. (2009) "Screen digest forecasts $1 bn boom for in-game advertising," *Brand Republic*, May 26. Available at: www.brandrepublic.com/News/908125/Screen-Digest-forecasts-1bn-boom-in-game-advertising/, accessed 8/26/11.

Economist, The (2006) "Trillion-dollar kids," December 2, 381 (8506), 66.

emarketer (2011a) U.S. Child Internet Users, 2010–2015. Available at: www.emarketer.com/Reports/All/Emarketer_2000736.aspx, accessed 9/14/11.

—— (2011b) U.S. Teen vs. Total Internet User Penetration, 2010–2015. Available at: www.emarketer.com/Reports/All/Emarketer_2000760.aspx, accessed 9/14/11.

Federal Communications Commission (2011). Available at: www.fcc.gov/guides/childrens-educational-television, accessed 8/22/11.

Federal Register (1999) Children's Online Privacy Protection Rule, Final Rule, 16 CFR Part 312, Federal Trade Commission, November 3, 64 (212), 59888–915.

—— (2012) Children's Online Privacy Protection Rule, 16 CFR Part 312, Federal Trade Commission, 77 (151), 46643–653.

Federal Trade Commission (1978) *FTC Staff Report on Television Advertising to Children*, Washington, DC: U.S. Government Printing Office.

—— (2005) Remarks of Chairman Deborah Platt Majoras at the Marketing, Self-Regulation, and Childhood Obesity Workshop, transcript, Washington, DC: Federal Trade Commission, 16.

—— (2008) *Marketing Food to Children and Adolescents – A Review of Industry Expenditures, Activities and Self-Regulation*, A Report to Congress, Washington, DC.

—— (2009) *Marketing Violent Entertainment to Children: A Sixth Follow-up Review of Industry Practices in the Motion Picture, Music Recording & Electronic Game Industries,* A Report to Congress, Washington, DC.

—— (2011) #378; Interagency Working Group on Food Marketed to Children To Hold Forum for Comment on Proposed Voluntary Principles on May 24 FTC File No. P094513. Available at: www.ftc.gov/os/comments/foodmarketedchildren/, accessed 9/1/11.

Ferrazzi, K. and Benezra, K. (2001) "Journey to the top," *Brandweek,* April 16, 28–36.

Friedemann, C., Heneghan, C., Mahtani, K., Thompson, M., Perera, R., and Ward, A.M. (2012) "Cardiovascular disease risk in healthy children and its association with body mass index: systematic review and meta-analysis," *BMJ,* 345, e4759.

Gantz, W., Schwartz, N., Angelini, J.R., and Rideout, V. (2007) *Food for Thought – Television Food Advertising to Children in the United States,* Henry J. Kaiser Family Foundation Report, Menlo Park, CA.

Goetzl, D. (2006) "Television has competition in pursuit of kids," *Television Week,* February 20, 8 (10).

Greene, J. (2011) "Cereal killers," *The National Law Journal,* August 29. Available at: www.law.com/jsp/tx/PubArticleTX.jsp?id=1202512857224, accessed 8/31/11.

Harris, J.L., Schwartz, M.B., Brownell, K.D., and Sarda, V., Weinberg, M.E., Speers, S., Thompson, J., Ustjanauskas, A., Cheyne, A., Bukofzer, E., Dorfman, L., Byrnes-Enoch, H. (2009) *Cereal Facts: Evaluating the Nutrition Quality and Marketing of Children's Cereals,* Rudd Center for Food Policy and Obesity, October, New Haven, CT: Yale University.

——, Schwartz, M.B., Brownell, K.D., and Sarda, V. (2010) *Fast Food Facts: Evaluating Fast Food Nutrition and Marketing to Youth,* Rudd Center for Food Policy and Obesity, October, New Haven, CT: Yale University.

——, Speers, S.E., Schwartz, M.B., and Brownell, K.D. (2012) "U.S. food company branded advergames on the internet: children's exposure and effects on snack consumption," *Journal of Children and Media,* 6 (1): 51–68.

Hastings, G., Stead, M., McDermott, L., Forsyth, A., MacKintosh, A.M., Rayner, M., Godfrey, C., Caraher, M., and Angus, K. (2003) *Review of Research on the Effects of Food Promotion to Children, Report to the Food Standards Agency,* Glasgow, UK: Center for Social Marketing, University of Strathclyde.

Hawkes, C. (2004) *Marketing Food to Children: The Global Regulatory Environment,* Geneva, Switzerland: World Health Organization.

—— (2007) *Marketing Food to Children: Changes in the Global Regulatory Environment 2004–2006,* Geneva, Switzerland: World Health Organization.

Holt, D.J., Ippolito, P.M., Desrochers, D.M., and Kelley, C.R. (2007) *Children's Exposure to TV Advertising in 1977 and 2004: Information for the Obesity Debate,* Bureau of Economics Staff Report, Washington, DC: Federal Trade Commission.

Interagency Working Group [IWG] (2011) Interagency Working Group on Food Marketed to Children – Preliminary Proposed Nutrition Principles to Guide Self-regulatory Efforts, Request for Comments. Available at: www.ftc.gov/os/2011/04/110428foodmar ketproposedguide.pdf, accessed 10/31/11.

International Obesity Task Force (2008) Recommendations for an International Code on Marketing of Foods and Non-alcoholic Beverages to Children, London. Available at: www.cspinet.org/nutritionpolicy/CI%20CODE%20OFFICIAL%20ENGLISH.pdf, accessed 6/1/11.

Jaffe, D.L. and Scarborough, K.A. (2011) Re: Interagency Working Group on Food Marketed to Children: General Comments and Proposed Marketing Definitions: FTC Project no.

P094513, letter to Donald S. Clark, Secretary Federal Trade Commission, July 13, Washington, DC: Association of National Advertisers.

Janiszewski, C. (1993) "Preattentive mere exposure effects," *Journal of Consumer Research*, 20 (December): 376–92.

John, D.R. (1999) "Consumer socialization of children: a retrospective look at twenty-five years of research," *Journal of Consumer Research*, 26 (December): 183–213.

Khan, A. (2010) "A brief look at in-game advertising," *Social Times*, May 26, Available at: http://socialtimes.com/a-brief-look-at-in-game-advertising_b13631, accessed 9/14/11.

Kipping, R.R., Jago, R., and Lawlor, D.A. (2008) "Obesity in children. Part 1: Epidemiology, measurement, risk factors, and screening," *British Medical Journal*, 337 (7675): 922–27.

Kunkel, D., Wilcox, B.L., Cantor, J., Palmer, E., Linn, S., and Dowrick, P. (2004) *Report of the Task Force on Advertising and Children*, Washington, DC: American Psychological Association.

—— McKinley, C., and Wright, P. (2009) *The Impact of Self-Regulation on the Nutritional Quality of Foods Advertised on Television*, Oakland, CA: Children Now.

Leibowitz, J. (2012) Testimony before the House Subcommittee on Financial Services, March 27, Washington, DC.

Lindstrom, M. and P.B. Seybold (2003) *Brand Child*, London: Kogan Page.

Linn, S. (2004) *Consuming Kids - The Hostile Takeover of Childhood*, New York: New Press.

—— and Golan, J. (2011) Comments submitted to the Interagency Working Group on Marketing to Children, Federal Trade Commission, July 14.

McAlister, A.R. and Cornwell, T.B. (2009) "Preschool children's persuasion knowledge: the contribution of theory of mind," *Journal of Public Policy & Marketing*, 28 (Fall): 175–85.

McGinnis, J.M., Gootman, J., and Kraak, V.I. (2006) *Food Marketing to Children and Youth: Threat or Opportunity?* Institute of Medicine, Washington, DC: The National Academies Press.

Mallinckrodt, V. and Mizerski, D. (2007) "The effects of playing an advergame on young children's perceptions, preferences and requests," *Journal of Advertising*, 36 (2): 87–100.

Mello, M.M. (2010) "Federal Trade Commission regulation of food advertising to children: possibilities for a reinvigorated role," *Journal of Health Politics, Policy and Law*, 35 (April): 227-76.

Montgomery, K.C. (2007) *Generation Digital*, Cambridge MA: MIT Press.

Moore, E.S. (2004) "Children and the changing world of advertising," *Journal of Business Ethics*, 52 (June): 161–67.

—— (2006) *It's Child's Play: Advergaming and the Online Marketing of Food to Children*, Menlo Park, CA: Henry J. Kaiser Family Foundation.

—— and Lutz, R.J. (2000) "Children, advertising, and product experiences: a multimethod inquiry," *Journal of Consumer Research*, 27 (June): 31–48.

—— and Lutz, R.J. (2002) "Passing the torch: intergenerational influences as a source of brand equity," *Journal of Marketing*, 66 (April): 17–37.

—— and Rideout, V.J. (2007) "The online marketing of food to children: is it just fun and games?" *Journal of Public Policy & Marketing*, 26 (Fall): 202–20.

—— and Wilkie, W.L. (2005) "We are who we were: intergenerational influences in consumer behavior," in S. Ratneshwar and D.G. Mick (eds) *Inside Consumption: Frontiers of Research on Consumer Motives, Goals and Desires*, London: Routledge, pp. 208–32.

Morrison, M. (2012) FTC complaints accuse McDonald's, General Mills and others of collecting kids' data," August 22. Available at: http://adage.com/article/digital/ftc-complaints-accuse-marketers-collecting-kids-data/236813/, accessed 9/18/12.

—— (2011) "McDonald's bows to pressure with more healthful Happy Meal," *Advertising Age*, July 26, Available at: http://adage.com/article/news/mcdonald-s-bows-pressure-healthful-happy-meal/228939/, accessed 8/17/11.

Moses, L.J. and Baldwin, D.A. (2005) "What can the study of cognitive development reveal about children's ability to appreciate and cope with advertising?" *Journal of Public Policy & Marketing*, 24 (Fall): 186–201.

Naik, P.A. and Raman, K. (2003) "Understanding the impact of synergy in multimedia communications," *Journal of Marketing Research*, 40 (November): 375–88.

Nielsenwire (2010) "What Americans do online: social media and games dominate activity." Available at: http://blog.nielsen.com/nielsenwire/online_mobile/what-americans-do-online-social-media-and-games-dominate-activity/, accessed 8/30/11.

Nordhielm, C. (2002) "The influence of level of processing on advertising repetition effects," *Journal of Consumer Research*, 29 (December): 371–82.

Office of Communications (2007) *Television Advertising of Food and Beverage Products to Children, Final Statement.* Available at: www.ofcom.org.uk/consult/condocs/foodads_new/statement/, accessed 9/9/11.

Ogden, C.L., Carroll, M.D., Kit, B.K., and Flegal, K.M. (2012) "Prevalence of obesity and trends in body mass index among US children and adolescents, 1999-2010," *Journal of the American Medical Association*, 307 (5): 483–90.

Packaged Facts (2008) *The Kids and Tweens Market in the U.S.*, 9th edition, Rockville, MD: Packaged Facts.

Pechmann, C., Levine, L., Loughlin, S., and Leslie, F. (2005) "Impulsive and self-conscious: adolescents' vulnerability to advertising and promotion," *Journal of Public Policy & Marketing*, 24 (Fall): 202–21.

Ralston Aoki, J. and Moore, E.S. (2012) "Self-regulation as a tool for promoting healthier children's diets: Can CARU and the CFBAI do more?" In J.D. Williams, K.E. Pasch, and C. Collins (eds) *Advances in Communication Research to Reduce Childhood Obesity*, New York: Spring.

Quart, A. (2004) *Branded: The Buying and Selling of Teenagers*, Cambridge, MA: Perseus.

Rideout, V.J., Foehr, U.G., and Roberts, D.F. (2010) *Generation M² Media in the Lives of 8 to 18 Year-Olds*, Menlo Park, CA: Henry J. Kaiser Family Foundation.

Roschke, G. and Campbell, A. (2011) General Comments on Interagency Working Group's Proposed Nutrition Principles on Food Marketed to Children, Washington, DC: Institute for Public Representation, Georgetown University Law Center.

Sharma, L.L., Teret, S.P., and Brownell, K.D. (2010) "The food industry and self-regulation: standards to promote success and to avoid public health failures," *American Journal of Public Health*, 100 (2): 240–46.

Troianovski, A. (2012) "Child's play: food makers hook kids on mobile games," *The Wall Street Journal*, September 18: A1.

Vladek, D. (2011) *What's On the Table.* Available at: http://business.ftc.gov/print/1861, accessed 7/14/11.

White House Task Force on Childhood Obesity (2010) *Solving the Problem of Childhood Obesity within a Generation*, A Report to the President.

Wilkie, W.L. (1994) *Consumer Behavior*, 3rd edn, New York: Wiley.

—— and Moore, E.S. (1999) "Marketing's contributions to society," *Journal of Marketing*, 63 (Special Millennium Issue): 198–218.

Wilson, D. and Roberts, J. (2012) "How Washington went soft on childhood obesity," Reuters Special Report, April 27. Available at: www.reuters.com/article/2012/04/27/us-usa-foodlobby-idUSBRE83Q0ED20120427, accessed 10/3/12.

13

FIREARMS AND THE COMMON GOOD

A meaningful discussion about solutions

Kevin D. Bradford

Firearms in the United States

The politics associated with the laws, restrictions, and accessibility of firearms is one of the most divisive and hotly contested subjects in US society. It is more than a political debate, it is a social debate that has been among the most contentious and intractable issues in American politics (Chemerinsky 2004). The politics are clear and the problems in society from the use of firearms are becoming clearer.

It is unquestioned that firearm-related violence is a major societal threat to human life and health in the United States today. Firearm injuries in the United States have averaged 32,300 deaths annually between 1980 and 2006 (about 88 per day). It is the second leading cause of death from injury after motor vehicle crashes (Firearms and Injury Center at Penn 2009). Approximately 100,000 people are treated annually in US hospital emergency rooms for firearm injuries (274 people per day, or two every ten minutes). Further, firearms are associated with 70 percent of homicides and over 50 percent of suicides (Firearms and Injury Center at Penn 2009).

Compared with other industrialized countries, violence and firearm death rates in the United States are disproportionately high. Of the approximately 50 upper- and middle-income countries with available data, an estimated 115,000 firearm deaths occur annually and the United States contributes about 30,000, or 26 percent (Firearms and Injury Center at Penn 2009). Gun-related homicide rates are over 19 times higher in the United States than at least 23 other "high income" countries (Richardson and Hemenway 2011) and children under 15 in the United States die of gunshot wounds at a rate 12 times greater than that of children from the 25 other industrialized countries (Krug *et al.*1998).

In 2005, 477,040 persons (about 1,306 persons per day) were victims of a crime committed with a firearm (Department of Justice 2006). The aforementioned nearly half-million crimes do not include firearms that are simply used to intimidate, or the indirect effects of firearms on society. For example, 7 percent of students have avoided school or certain places at school because they were afraid of being harmed in some way (Self Esteem Health 2009). Every day in the United States, approximately eight young Americans aged 19 and under are killed in gun homicides, suicides, and unintentional shootings (Children's Defense Fund 2012). In 2008 and 2009, six times as many children and teens – 34,387 – suffered nonfatal gun injuries as gun deaths. This is equal to one child or teen every 31 minutes, 47 every day, and 331 children and teens every week who are injured by guns (Children's Defense Fund 2012).

The extended costs of firearm violence are estimated to exceed $100 billion in the United States over a decade ago (Cook and Ludwig 2001). Indirect costs to society such as more security, loss of business due to fear, property damages, loss of productivity due to sick days, and health care insurance costs are a burden to society that has to be absorbed, and these costs can affect all of society not just specific businesses. The other real and psychological costs such as intimidation, loss of foot traffic affecting property values, pain, sorrow, and the secondary costs of anger often go unspecified, but affect society deeply (Cook and Ludwig 2001).

The gun debate emanates from the second amendment which grants citizens of the United States the right to bear arms. This right attracts much scrutiny but those that embrace it believe that the right to bear arms is an absolute right. They regard firearms laws that limit the ability of people to purchase, possess, or carry firearms as unnecessary (Utter and True 2000). Though the literal translation of the second amendment can be debated, the amendment's impact on the possession of guns in the United States is unquestioned. It is estimated that the number of guns in the United States is 270 million and approximately 100 million of these are handguns (Karp 2007). The rate of private gun ownership in the United States is 88.8 firearms per 100 people. Americans continue to purchase guns at a high rate. In fact, 2011 was another record-breaking year for gun sales, with Americans purchasing some 10.8 million firearms (a 14 percent increase over the previous year and up over 50 percent from 10 years ago) (Children's Defense Fund 2012; National Shooting Sports Foundation 2012).

Distribution of guns in the United States

The distribution of firearms consists of a primary and a secondary market. In the primary market there are basically two types of firearms distribution: business to business and business to consumer. A general rule governing the distribution of firearms is that firearms manufacturers can only sell a gun to a federally licensed entity. A federally licensed entity can be a retailer, a wholesaler, or an individual. Consequently, there is a very small "business to consumer" legal distribution channel in the firearms industry. Fundamentally, the majority of firearms are distributed through the business to business channel. Most commonly, the general public and potential consumers purchase firearms from retailers (i.e., gun shops and general retail stores). Retailers buy the firearms directly from firearms manufacturers or through a wholesaler who has purchased the products from a firearms manufacturer.

The primary market consists of approximately 65,000 federally licensed dealers (ATF 2012). (For comparison purposes, in the United States, there are 36,569 grocery stores (Food Marketing Institute 2011), and 14,098 McDonalds restaurants (McDonalds 2012: 9).)

The "secondary" market involves the distribution (retail selling) of firearms by unlicensed persons. It is estimated that 2–3 million firearms were sold in the unregulated secondary markets (Cook and Ludwig 1997). There is a legal market to support this secondary market and it most commonly occurs at gun shows. The primary and secondary firearms markets are closely linked because almost all firearms in the secondary market have their origins in the primary market (Gundlach *et al.* 2010).

There are approximately 5,400 licensed firearms manufacturers and 950 licensed importers in the United States who distribute over 2.4 million handguns and more than 3 million rifles and shotguns into commerce per year (ATF 2011). These manufacturers, wholesalers and importers mostly sell their products to retailers. Retailers are the dominant mode of firearms acquisition by consumers. There are numerous retailer types: gun stores, big box stores, major department stores, sporting goods stores, gun shows, and many others such as individual independent dealers.

The central societal and marketing issue: Diversion

A societal issue that affects the distribution of firearms is diversion. Firearm diversion is defined as "any movement of firearms from the legal to the illegal marketplace through an illegal method or for an illegal purpose" (Gundlach, *et al.* 2010). See Table 13.1 for the description of the illegal market for firearms (Bradford *et al.* 2005). The societal problem is that diversion is prevalent in primary markets. Figure 13.1 depicts the distribution channel for firearms in the United States and the areas in the distribution channel where diversion occurs. It was found that 10 percent of handguns and 25 percent of junk guns[1] distributed to the primary market in 1996 were used in violent crimes by 2000 (Gundlach *et al.* 2010). Thus, firearms dealers are known to play an important function in the diversion of firearms from the primary market (Brady Center 2007). A study in Los Angeles found that 59 percent of criminals that used guns in crime acquired their guns through a retail store (*NAACP* v. *Accusport et al.* 2003).

Diversion occurs with retailers and dealers in a number of ways. Bradford *et al.* (2005) integrated findings from reports by the Bureau of Alcohol, Tobacco, Firearms and Explosives (known as ATF) and extant marketing literature to categorize the channels for diversion for firearms in retail channels. Their findings are summarized as follows.

Unscrupulous/corrupt dealers

Corrupt and unscrupulous dealers are those licensed firearms dealers that directly align with criminals to engage in illegal sales and those that are willing to sell to

TABLE 13.1 The illegal market in the United States[a]

Determination of legality	Description of persons that constitute the illegal market
It is unlawful for any person to sell a firearm to any person having the following characteristics:	Is under indictment for, or has been convicted in any court of, a crime punishable by imprisonment for a term exceeding one year
	Is a fugitive from justice
	Is an unlawful user of or addicted to any controlled substance
	Has been adjudicated as a mental defective or has been committed to any mental institution
	Who, being an alien, is illegally or unlawfully in the United States
	Who has been discharged from the Armed Forces under dishonorable conditions
	Who, having been a citizen of the United States, has renounced his or her citizenship
	Is subject to a court order that restrains from harassing, stalking, or threatening an intimate partner or child of the intimate partner or person, or engaging in other conduct that would place an intimate partner in reasonable fear of bodily injury to the partner or child
It is unlawful for any licensed importer, licensed manufacturer, licensed dealer, or licensed collector to sell or deliver . . .[b]	. . . any firearm or ammunition to any individual who the licensee knows or has reasonable cause to believe is less than eighteen years of age
	. . . if the firearm, or ammunition is other than a shotgun or rifle, or ammunition for a shotgun or rifle, to any individual who the licensee knows or has reasonable cause to believe is less than twenty-one years of age
	. . . any firearm to any person in any State where the purchase or possession of a firearm would be in violation of any State law applicable at the place of sale, delivery or other disposition, unless the licensee knows or has reasonable cause to believe that the purchase or possession would not be in violation of State law
	. . . any firearm to any person who the licensee knows or has reasonable cause to believe does not reside in (or if the person is a corporation or other business entity, does not maintain a place of business in) the State in which the licensee's place of business is located

Source: Adapted from table in Bradford *et al.* (2005), p. 288.

Notes:
[a] Information in this table is from the Gun Control Act of 1968.
[b] Does not apply to transactions between licensed importers, licensed manufacturers, licensed dealers, and licensed collectors.

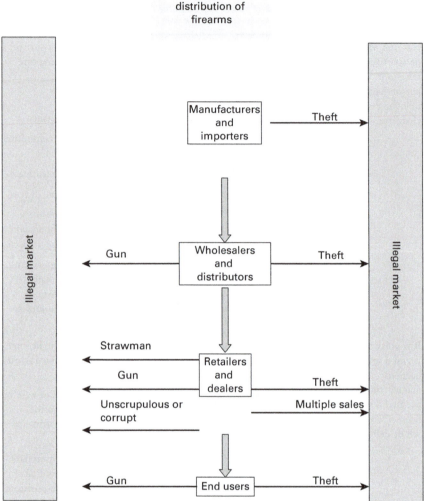

FIGURE 13.1 Representation of the primary market distribution and the major channels for diversion.

prohibited purchasers (e.g., Spiegler and Sweeney 1975). A small proportion of corrupt dealers are a major source of diverted firearms. For example, all of the firearms recovered by police throughout the nation and reported to ATF for investigative gun tracing during 1998 originated with just 14 percent of the nation's gun dealers (Koper 2007). Another report found that only 120 dealers nationwide were linked to nearly 55,000 crime guns recovered from 1996 to 2000 and these crime guns accounted for 15 percent of all recoveries reported to ATF during that time (Koper 2007). Thus, a small number of dealers has a significant negative impact on society.

Nonstore/nonstocking dealers

There are people that possess Federal Firearms Licenses but sell firearms from their private property (Gundlach *et al.* 2010). This category of firearms dealers also represents retail store venues that typically do not stock firearms (Wachtel 1998). These nonstore/nonstocking dealers are a major source of diverted firearms (US General Accounting Office 1996). Approximately 23 percent of firearms used in crime were purchased from nonstore/nonstocking dealers (ATF 2000a).

Gun shows

A gun show is an exhibition or gathering where guns, gun parts, ammunition, gun accessories, and literature are displayed, bought, sold, traded, and discussed (Gundlach *et al.* 2010). There are approximately 5,000 gun shows per year (about 100 gun shows per week) in the United States (Coalition to Stop Gun Violence & Educational Fund 2012). Interestingly, this source of guns is not regulated by federal statutes. All kinds of vendors of guns can participate in gun shows including licensed dealers (those with Federal Firearms Licenses or FFLs), unlicensed gun dealers who display the guns they want to sell in booths, and even individuals that attend the gun show and walk the aisles selling their guns (Gundlach *et al.* 2010).

Gun shows are generally open to the public and often run over a two-day period. The cost of entry to gun shows for vendors is low, with fees for participation ranging from $5 to $50 per table. The typical gun show has 50 to 2,000 tables and the guns are displayed on these tables. Unlicensed private sellers are not required to have a federal firearms license and 25–50 percent of firearm vendors at gun shows are unlicensed (Coalition to Stop Gun Violence & Educational Fund 2012). Though federal firearms laws apply to both FFLs and private sellers at gun shows, unlicensed private sellers are under no legal obligation to ask purchasers whether they are legally eligible to buy guns or to verify purchasers' legal status through background checks (Harlow 2001).

Unfortunately, gun shows have historically been shown to be a prominent channel for diversion of firearms (US Department of Justice 2001; Coalition to Stop Gun Violence & Educational Fund 2012). Thirty-one percent of diverted firearms are purchased at gun shows (ATF 2000b). In one analysis of just 1,530 firearms trafficking investigations during the period July 1996 through December 1998, gun shows were found to be associated with the diversion of approximately 26,000 firearms (Koper 2007).

Straw purchases

Straw purchases occur when a licensed and/or legal person buys a firearm for the purposes of providing the firearm to another person who is legally prohibited from purchasing a firearm (e.g., Gundlach *et al.* 2010). Straw purchases are one of the most common sources of diversion and the very act of selling the firearm to a legally forbidden person is a felony (Educational Fund to Stop Violence 2012; Gun

Control Act of 1968). Straw purchases are a felony violation for the straw purchaser (who can also be charged with lying on Federal Form 4473) and the ultimate possessor (the person who cannot legally possess a firearm). Persons who cannot legally own a gun include ex-criminals, minors, and drug addicts to name a few. The Gun Control Act of 1968, which forbids straw purchasing, is of societal importance because most gun crime in the United States is accounted for by people not legally allowed to possess guns (Cook *et al.* 2007). Straw purchasing is also of societal importance because it accounts for almost 31 percent of firearms diverted (ATF 2011).

Multiple sales

Diversion also occurs through transactions involving "multiple sales." Multiple sales are the purchase of two or more handguns by an unlicensed person within a 5-day period (Gundlach *et al.* 2010). To get an idea of their importance in understanding diversion and their prevalence, crime gun trace data from 2000 showed that 20 percent of all retail handguns recovered in crimes were purchased as part of a multiple sale (Law Center to Prevent Gun Violence 2012). Understanding and preventing multiple sales is complicated because one in four gun owners own more than one gun, so the idea that an unlicensed person may purchase multiple guns at one time does occur.

Theft

Theft is also a major source of diversion. FFL dealers submitted more than 7,500 theft/loss reports to ATF in the calendar years 2008, 2009, and 2010. These reports found that more than 74,000 firearms were lost or stolen during that time. This represents a significant improvement over a 10-year span (US Department of Justice *et al.* 2012).

A stolen firearm occurs when an FFL dealer is the victim of a burglary, larceny, or robbery (Gundlach *et al.* 2010). FFL dealers are a significant target of theft in that they accounted for more than 83 percent of the firearms lost or stolen and they filed more than 90 percent of the FFL firearms theft/loss reports in the years 2008 through 2010 (ATF 2012). The amount of theft/loss is staggering. For example, in 2007, after inspecting just 9.3 percent of FFLs nationwide, ATF reported that more than 30,000 guns in the dealers' inventories had been lost or stolen (Mayors Against Illegal Guns 2012). It should be noted that of the 74,000 firearms reported stolen in the years 2008 through 2010, 46 percent were handguns used in a crime (ATF 2012).

Theft is a significant source of diverted firearms. Eleven percent of diverted firearms were found to be obtained by theft (ATF 2000b). To complicate understanding and combating of diversion through theft, it is known that deliberate diversion may be reported as theft (Brill 1977). Thus, the reporting and inventorying of firearms theft is a troubling source of diversion for society. Further, theft is not idiosyncratic to store fronts. Guns can also be stolen and or lost from private homes or in transport from the manufacturer (almost 600,000 guns are stolen each year from private homes, according to poll data on gun-owning households) (Mayors Against Illegal Guns 2012).

Laws that affect the distribution of firearms

Though many efforts have been expended to limit the number and types of laws that can affect a person's right and ability to obtain and/or possess firearms, laws do influence distribution of firearms in the United States. An overview of some of the key laws affecting the distribution of firearms follows. The Federal Firearms Act (1938) generally requires firearms manufacturers, distributors, dealers, and importers to obtain licenses, and it also restricts the sale and possession of guns to those not eligible to possess them (e.g., felons). The Gun Control Act (1968) imposed more restrictions on the sale and possession of firearms and focuses on regulating interstate commerce in firearms by prohibiting interstate transfers of firearms except among licensed manufacturers, dealers and importers. This act also banned mail-order sales of firearms. The 1988 Armed Career Criminal Act made the penalties for possession of firearms by those not eligible to have them (e.g., felons and others) more severe. The Crime Control Act of 1990 is the first to address and limit the importation and manufacture of semiautomatic weapons ("assault weapons"). The Crime Control Act (1990) also established "gun-free school zones." The Brady Handgun Violence Prevention Act of 1993 is the impetus for waiting periods for possession of guns and background checks for the sale of guns to unlicensed people. The 1994 Violent Crime and Law Enforcement Act severely limits the sales and use of automatic weapons and prohibits youth from possessing or selling handguns. The Youth Handgun Safety Act of 1994 prohibits anyone under 18 from possessing a gun. (For a summary of federal firearms legislation, see Bradford *et al.* 2005, 286.)

Complications with the enforcement of laws for the distribution of firearms

The enforcement of these laws falls under the jurisdiction of ATF, now part of the Department of Justice (Homeland Security). ATF is a federal law enforcement organization and it is responsible for the investigation and prevention of federal offenses involving the unlawful use, manufacture, and possession of firearms. Firearms crime investigation and prevention falls squarely on the shoulders of this organization. However, ATF has historically had trouble in the prevention and prosecution of firearms distribution crimes. Further, a perception exists that legal restrictions preclude ATF from being as effective as it might be because it is unable to inspect FFLs thoroughly or frequently. For instance, in 1986 Congress passed the Firearm Owners' Protection Act. This law limits ATF to a single, unannounced inspection of a gun dealer in any 12-month period. Compounding this specific issue for ATF is its perception that it is understaffed to accomplish its mission (Curtis 2007).

Another issue for ATF is that it seems to continuously have difficulty in establishing the burden of proof in order to bring legal action against perceived violators of laws. To bring legal action, ATF must establish that gun dealers violated the law "willfully." Thus, in cases that are criminal, a prosecutor not only has to prove that the gun dealer engaged in illegal conduct, but that the dealer also acted with a bad purpose and with knowledge that conduct was harmful. This is very difficult to prove in a court of law because the dealer can easily deny knowledge of conduct that was unlawful or harmful. Thus, ATF typically has to show repeated violations of the law to meet this high burden of proof.

ATF is also burdened by not having remedies to violations of law by FFLs other than revocation or prosecution. Complicating this burden is the fact that federal law places severe restraints on ATF's ability to revoke licenses from gun dealers that violate federal law. As an example, in fiscal year 2003, ATF completed 1,812 dealer inspections that uncovered almost 150,000 violations of federal law with an average of more than 80 violations per dealer (US Department of Justice 2004). Despite this large number of dealers with multiple violations, ATF issued only 54 notices of license revocation that year. On average, ATF revokes about 110 FFLs per year (FFL Guard 2012). This small number is likely due to the overly burdensome requirement that ATF prove that a dealer "willfully" violated the law, requiring proof that the dealer not only broke the law but also knew that this conduct was unlawful.

Behind the laws: Gun control and gun rights

A major debate about firearms in the United States emanates from the perception that more laws should be enacted by the courts. As previously mentioned, on one side of the debate are efforts to preserve the individual's right to bear arms (pro-gun). This right is outlined in the Second Amendment of the United States Constitution and it is fiercely protected by many gun advocates. Gun rights leaders (such as Neal Knox, the former head of the National Rifle Association's (NRA) Institute for Legislative Action (ILA) and head of the Firearms Coalition (a more uncompromising group of NRA members)) contend that seeking or accepting a "reasonable compromise" serves to motivate gun control supporters to get more aggressive on the firearms industry (D'Alessandro 2012). Gun rights supporters believe that compromise on any front of firearms laws (even if one law passes) will cause a slippery slope that will ultimately lead to the abolition of guns, the second amendment, and, ultimately, society as we know it (Utter and True 2000). They fundamentally believe the second amendment guarantees the most critical among the freedoms specified in the Bill of Rights. In their view, the other rights gain greater significance because armed citizens can check a government which would otherwise be tempted to violate such freedoms (Utter and True 2000). Gun rights supporters simply do not believe that new firearms laws will have their desired effect.

The slippery slope argument is strongly embraced by the gun rights advocates. The slippery slope position states that a relatively small first step leads to a chain of related events culminating in some significant effect. Other metaphors describe the fears of the gun rights supporters that consider relenting on any one issue may ultimately lead to complete eradication of guns. For instance, "the camel's nose" is used because once a camel has managed to place its nose within a tent or room, the rest of the camel will inevitably follow. "The boiling frog" suggests that if a frog is placed in boiling water, it will jump out, but if it is placed in cold water that is slowly heated, it will not perceive the danger and will tolerate the heating of the water until it is cooked to death. These arguments have been advanced by the NRA and other gun rights proponents to underscore their slippery slope position.

The interpretation of the second amendment is an issue for some

The heart of the argument for gun rights advocates is their interpretation of the second amendment. Central to the second amendment is that a well-regulated militia is necessary for the security of a free state and that the right of the people to keep and bear arms shall not be infringed. Fundamental to this right is the interpretation of the "rights of individuals" versus the "collective right of state militias" to possess firearms and the extent to which that right may be limited. Clearly gun rights advocates champion an unqualified right and reject all laws that restrict in any way the ability of people to purchase, possess, or carry firearms. These individuals do not acknowledge the conditional phrase that the right to keep and bear arms is linked with the preservation of a "well-regulated militia."

Gun control forces in the United States interpret the second amendment quite differently. Gun control advocates argue that it is the responsibility of the government to prevent crime, maintain order, and protect the well-being of its citizens as it would a preventable and harmful disease (Bruce and Wilcox 1998). Accordingly, many physicians liken gun violence to a harmful and preventable disease. Generally, they argue that concerned citizens should imagine a preventable disease that kills 35,000 and injures another 100,000 each year in the United States. They ask citizens to suppose the costs associated with the disease surpass $100 billion annually and that the disease affects those that are 15-24 years old at an alarmingly high rate. Then, they propose imagining that the source of this disease is a consumer product that lacks comprehensive monitoring or regulation by any federal safety organization. The argument assumes that that general community and certainly the medical community would consider this threat a moral imperative to address and that doctors would not hesitate to intervene (i.e., Marchione 2012). The fatality rate of firearm violence is similar to HIV, which is recognized as an epidemic by the Centers for Disease Control and Prevention (CDC). This analogous reality suggests that the firearms industry is an under-scrutinized and large-scale social problem that, if it were not politically and socially contentious in nature, would be attended to with urgency. Gun control advocates and many concerned citizens contend that the control of guns should be a national obligation because of the associated social problems, death, intimidation, harm, and destruction.

The lobbies and interest groups associated with the debate

Professional lobbying groups influence legislation on behalf of a special interest which hires them. There are numerous groups making gun-related filings to lobby Congress. The largest of these lobbying groups is the NRA. It has 4.3 million members and has annual revenues of $205 million (National Rifle Association 2012). The NRA spends tens of millions of dollars to lobby against gun control. It organizes voters and campaign volunteers to focus citizen communications and interests when anti-gun rights legislation is under consideration at both the federal and state levels.

Initially, the NRA supported gun laws intended to prevent criminals from obtaining firearms but opposed any new restrictions that affected gun owners or potential gun owners who are law-abiding citizens. Many gun rights advocates considered the perspective of preventing anyone from obtaining guns amenable to the aforementioned slippery slope positions leading to more gun control. Consequently, the most conservative gun rights advocates began forming other gun rights groups such as the Gun Owners of America (GOA). The GOA has 300,000 members and spent $1,307,000 lobbying politicians in 2012 (Gun Owners of America 2011; Open Secrets 2012). The GOA rejects any gun-related laws that infringe on the rights of law-abiding citizens and at the outset put themselves at odds with the NRA on many dimensions (Pratt 1997). Other national gun rights groups took even stronger stances than the NRA. These groups include groups such as The Second Amendment Sisters who also believe any compromise leads to incrementally greater restrictions.

The major gun lobbies that support gun control are the Brady Campaign to Prevent Gun Violence and the Coalition to Stop Gun Violence. The Brady Campaign to Prevent Gun Violence was originally called Handgun Control Inc. (HCI) and was founded in 1974 by Mark Borinsky (Brady Campaign to Prevent Gun Violence 2012a). Important to the history of HCI is that it formed a partnership with the National Coalition to Ban Handguns (NCBH), also founded in 1974. NCBH was smaller than HCI but it was generally considered to be much tougher in its efforts to control firearms. NCBH and HCI split and in 1990 NCBH was renamed the Coalition to Stop Gun Violence (Bruce and Wilcox 1998).

HCI enjoyed a spike in support both from an interest perspective and certainly in fundraising as a result of the murder of John Lennon in 1980 (Garrett 2012). However, the incident that propelled HCI to its height of effectiveness and interest from the American public was the assassination attempt on President Reagan in

1981 (Garrett 2012). The assassination attempt on the President provided a significant call to action for gun control advocates. However, the injury to James Brady sparked the unrelenting interest of his wife, Sarah Brady. She joined the board of HCI in 1985 and in 2001 HCI was renamed the Brady Campaign to Prevent Gun Violence (Brady Campaign to Prevent Gun Violence 2012b).

Gun rights lobbyists are currently more active in their legal filings as evidenced by their total filings exceeding gun-control lobbying by the ratio of approximately 3:1. From a financial perspective, gun rights lobbyists also spend much more. In 2011, gun rights political spending on lobbying totaled $5,535,651 and gun control spending on lobbying was only $240,000 – a ratio of 23 to 1 (OpenSecrets.org 2012).

Marketing topics and issues in the courts

Firearms have received considerable attention in the courts and the marketing of firearms has a central role in many cases. Knowledge of marketing concepts and theory is increasingly becoming an asset for both gun rights and gun control advocates. The types of marketing issues in the courts are numerous but in the main can be classified into six areas of legal inquiry.

The first area is product liability claims against manufacturers for injuries caused by guns. Central to this argument is that product liability laws are designed to protect the public from the sale of dangerously defective products (Richard 1984). One theory that supports finding handgun dealers strictly liable for handgun-related injuries is that a product is defective not only if it fails to perform as safely as the ordinary consumer would expect, but also if the dangers posed by the product's design outweigh its social utility. Another theory holds that the seller's failure to prevent distribution of handguns to incompetent purchasers places the gun in a condition unreasonably dangerous to the public. In product liability claims against manufacturers of firearms, plaintiffs generally argue that the manufacture, distribution, and sale (the marketing) of firearms is an abnormally dangerous activity and that gun manufacturers, distributors, and retailer should be held liable for injuries related to gun violence (Richard 1984).

Negligent entrustment is another marketing issue in the courts. Negligent entrustment is a general theory in which the plaintiff alleges that the retailer is negligent by allowing someone to buy a gun when one is not capable of using it safely, or when the retailer knew or should have known that the person could injure a third party (Todd 1983). Thus, a manufacturer may be negligent by failing to take reasonable precautions that would prevent their guns from being acquired by individuals likely to use them for criminal purposes (i.e., diversion or leakage of guns into criminal markets). For example, precautions that could prevent gun from being acquired by individuals likely to use them for criminal purposes include voluntary marketing safeguards such as refusing to supply firearms to retail dealers who sell a disproportionate number of guns used in crimes (Bradford et al. 2005).

The actual design and fabrication of firearms can also be a marketing issue. Manufacturers of firearms have been blamed in court for injuries that have been caused by the misuse of a gun that could have been prevented by equipping the gun with a safety device (Lytton 2007). As a general rule, manufacturers can be held liable for harm and injuries caused by defects in the design of guns they manufacture even if the gun is used appropriately and accidently goes off. Plaintiffs argue that the failure of gun manufacturers to equip their firearms with safety features such as gun locks or personalization technology can be considered a design shortcoming or deficiency. A product design is defective when the "foreseeable risks of harm posed by the product could have been reduced or avoided by the adoption of a reasonable alternative design . . . and the omission of the alternative design renders the product not reasonably safe" (Lytton 2007: 7). Thus, plaintiffs argue that the lack of safety features for firearms amounts to a design defect. Another creative but practical example of a safety feature is a "chamber-loaded indicator" that would warn a person that the gun has a live round in the chamber.

Oversupply is a common marketing concept used by plaintiffs in the courts. For instance, in *Hamilton* v. *Beretta* (2001), the plaintiffs contended that gun manufacturers knowingly oversupplied handguns to dealers in states with weak gun controls (Lytton 2007). Consequently, this oversupply of guns is sold and resold to individuals in states with more strict gun controls and these guns are subsequently used in crimes. The key rationale behind this concept is that gun manufacturers oversupplied handguns to dealers in Florida with the knowledge that many of those guns would be transferred illegally to more strict states for use in crime (Hamilton and Beretta 2001). To support this argument, the plaintiffs produced federal law enforcement statistics showing that 40 percent of handguns used in crimes in New York City between 1989 and 1997 were originally sold in five southern states with weaker gun control laws (Lytton 2007). The plaintiffs also found that manufacturers were supplying guns to retail dealers in states with weaker gun control laws far beyond the reasonable demand for guns among residents in those areas (Hamilton and Beretta 2001).

An argument against the marketing of guns includes that criminal use of a gun can be avoided by more restrictive marketing and sales practices (Lytton 2007). Manufacturers are negligent in training and monitoring retail dealers to prevent illegal sales. It is argued that if manufacturers and distributors train dealers to comply with gun laws, to keep better track of store inventory, and to spot fraudulent buyers, it would reduce access to guns by criminals (Gundlach *et al.* 2010). It is believed to be within manufacturers' capability and responsibility to not supply dealers who have a history of illegal sales or to whom large numbers of crime guns are traced.

The sixth major marketing concept in the courts regarding firearms relates to public nuisance doctrine. The general definition of a public nuisance is an unreasonable interference with a right common to the general public (Lytton 2007). Plaintiffs argue that the widespread illegal secondary market in firearms represents a public nuisance for which the gun industry is responsible. For example, a lawsuit brought by the City of Chicago asserted that manufacturers design and advertise weapons in ways attractive to criminals and fail to discipline irresponsible dealers. Plaintiffs argue that oversupply, overpromotion, and the failure to supervise retail dealers are all unreasonable interferences with the public right of Chicago residents to be free from the human and financial costs of gun violence (Siebel 1999).

Researchers are providing an understanding of the gun market and the marketing of firearms and consequently are contributing to the gun debate (Adams 2004; Cook *et al.* 2007; Davidson 2003). This area of research is vibrant, and the potential to contribute to the national discourse on this societal issue is as high as it has ever been.

Firearms distribution and the common good

The distribution of firearms is a controversial and highly contested topic. The stakeholders, including the firearms industry, society in general, and the government, are responsible for the current state of affairs of the firearms debate in the United States. If the common good is valued by a society, measures should be taken to protect the safety of its citizens. The common good is clearly adversely affected by firearms and there are several implications for society.

The most severe common good implication is the death and injury that is caused by firearms. There were approximately 31,347 firearms deaths in the United States in 2011 (the approximate average for the last 30 years) (Centers for Disease Control and Prevention 2012; Firearms and Injury Center at Penn 2009). Firearms injury is so prevalent that it is the second leading cause of death from injury after motor vehicle crashes (Firearms and Injury Center at Penn 2009). Firearms injury represents a significant public health impact and effect on the common good, accounting for 6.6 percent of premature deaths in this country (Firearms and Injury Center at Penn 2009). Firearms minimize victims' ability to contribute to society.

The rates of death and injury are higher in the United States than other developed countries. Compared with other industrialized countries, violence and firearm death rates in the United States are disproportionately high (Firearms and Injury Center at Penn 2009). The US firearm-related death rate is more than twice that of the next highest country (Firearms and Injury Center at Penn 2009). The United States is a country of vast resources and a capable citizenry; however, it allows the common good to be more negatively affected by firearms than other affluent countries.

The protection of the second amendment motivates many to preserve the distribution of firearms as is. However, the distribution of firearms to criminals and for criminal activities surrounding the distribution of firearms is unlawful, unwelcome, and not in the best interests of the common good. The protection of the second amendment is a different argument than allowing crime. If the United States could more closely follow and enforce existing laws regarding the distribution of firearms and develop and embrace common sense measures to preclude criminals from possessing firearms, crime would decrease and society (the common good) would benefit (Gundlach *et al.* 2010).

The costs to society and the common good caused by firearms must be illuminated. Society pays for firearms violence and even those not directly affected pay. The associated costs not only include the devastating impact on families but many other direct and indirect personal and social costs (i.e., medical costs, fear and intimidation, depression, protective and medical services, building repairs, increased measures to secure our society). These costs are not easy to aggregate or quantify; thus, they are easily overlooked or minimized. The common good should account for the direct and indirect costs associated with firearms' negative effects on society.

Society has not attended to the negative effects of firearms as an informed public. Beyond not accounting for costs of the negative effects of firearms appropriately, a troubling pattern is that information dissemination, information gathering, and the information itself is often suppressed or hotly contested with the intention to minimize its potential to inform. Also, organizations that investigate and aggregate information regarding the negative effects of firearms are contested, underfunded, and minimized. For example, the CDC, which collects and monitors firearm injury data and funds related research as part of its mission, was forced by Congress (influenced by lobbyists) to dramatically reduce its firearm-related research and CDC-funded gunshot injury surveillance programs. This organization was working towards fact-based rationale so that society can attend to the problem of firearms injuries. The CDC is important because it applies the science of epidemiology and the principles of public health to injuries. The point is that many scientists and doctors believe firearm violence warrants epidemic consideration but even the traction for research of firearm violence in the United States is contested. People avoiding a deeper understanding of the impact of firearms (and to perhaps address it as a problem) is disturbing (Kistner 1997). An example of the problematic nature of firearms violence in the United States is the rate of firearms-related suicide; it was at one time 11 times higher than the combined rate for children in 25 other industrialized countries (Firearms and Injury Center at Penn 2009). Information gathering and dissemination about the distribution of firearms, firearms crime, firearms solutions, and societal costs must be a part of the national dialogue. This understanding will contribute a greater commitment to the common good of society.

Fundamental to the issue of firearms injury and its negative implications to the common good is that injury and death is preventable (Firearms and Injury Center at Penn 2009). Thus, if there are aspects of the distribution of firearms to criminal markets that are a problem, they are addressable. Firearms, especially handguns, are unfortunately very effective lethal weapons with the capability to escalate often-impulsive acts of interpersonal violence or suicidal thoughts into death (Firearms and Injury Center at Penn 2009). Simply addressing diversion by providing support to address existing laws and implementing common sense guidelines for the distribution of a potentially deadly force (that has historically been associated with a tremendous amount of death and injury in the United States) will contribute to the common good of society. At a minimum, society should embrace measures to provide a safer environment so that the pursuit of life and liberty can occur without fear and real threats to safety from the diversion of firearms to criminals.

Note

1   Junk guns are small handguns that are easily concealable and inexpensive, but often unreliable, inaccurate, and poorly made (Vernick *et al.*1999).

References

Adams, R.J. (2004) "Retailer-manufacturer responsibility in the marketing of firearms: exploring the concept of negligent distribution," *Journal of Retailing and Consumer Services*, 11 (3): 161–69.

ATF (2000a) "Following the gun: enforcing federal laws against firearms traffickers," US Department of the Treasury, Bureau of Alcohol, Tobacco, Firearms and Explosives.

—— (2000b) "Crime gun trace reports (1999) national report," Bureau of Alcohol, Tobacco, Firearms and Explosives. Available at: www.atf.gov/pub/fire/ycgii/1999/inex.htm. Accessed August 8, 2005.

—— (2011) "Firearms commerce in the United States," US Department of the Treasury, Bureau of Alcohol, Tobacco, Firearms and Explosives. Available at: www.atf.gov/publications/firearms/121611-firearms-commerce-2011.pdf. Accessed March 2012.

—— (2012) "Theft/loss reports; Calendar years 2008–2010," US Department of the Treasury, Office of Strategic Intelligence and Information Federal Firearms Licensee Statistics, Bureau of Alcohol, Tobacco, Firearms and Explosives. Available at: www.atf.gov/statistics/ffl-theft-loss-reports/FFL-theft-loss-statistics-01122012-update-ii.pdf. Accessed October 2012.

Bradford, K.D., Gundlach, G.T., and Wilkie, W.L. (2005) "Countermarketing in the courts: the case of marketing channels and firearm diversion," *Journal of Public Policy & Marketing*, 24 (Spring): 284–98.

Brady Campaign to Prevent Gun Violence (2012a) "Our history," available at: www.bradycampaign.org/about/history. Accessed October 2012.

—— (2012b) "Biographies: Sarah Brady," available at: www.bradycampaign.org/about/bio/sarah. Accessed November 2012.

Brady Center (2007) "Shady dealings: Illegal gun trafficking from licensed gun dealers," available at www.bradycenter.org/xshare/pdf/reports/ shady-dealings.pdf. Accessed July 2009.

Brill, S. (1977) *Firearm Abuse: A Research and Policy Report*, Washington, DC: The Police Foundation.

Bruce, J.M. and Wilcox, C. (1998) *The Changing Politics of Gun Control*, Oxford: Rowman and Littlefield Publishers.

Centers for Disease Control and Prevention (2012) "All injury," available at: http://www.cdc.gov/nchs/fastats/injury.htm. Accessed March 2012.

Chemerinsky, E. (2004) "Putting the gun control debate in social perspective," *Fordham Law Review*, 1: 1.

Children's Defense Fund (2012) "Protect children, not guns," available at: www.childrensdefense.org/child-research-data-publications/data/protect-children-not-guns-2012.pdf. Accessed October 2012.

Coalition to Stop Gun Violence and Educational Fund to Stop Gun Violence (2012) "America's gun shows: Open markets for criminals," available at: www.csgv.org/storage/documents/GUN20SHOW%20LOOPHOLE%20MEMO.pdf. Accessed October 2012.

Cook, P.J. and Ludwig, J. (1997) "Guns in America: National survey on private ownership and use of firearms," prepared for U.S. Department of Justice; Office of Justice Programs; National Institute of Justice.

—— (2001) "Toward smarter gun laws," *Christian Science Monitor*, 93 (February 6).

——, Ludwig, J., Venkatesh, S., and Braga, A.A. (2007) "Underground gun markets," *The Economic Journal*, 117 (November): F558–F588.

Curtis, H.P. (2007) "Secrecy law, lack of staff hurt ATF in battling guns," Orlando Sentinel. Available at: www.realpolice.net/forums/archive/t-66250.html. Accessed October 2012.

D'Alessandro, J. (2012) Review of book "The Gun Rights War," RealGuns.Com. Available at: www.realguns.com/books/review138.htm. Accessed October 2012.

Davidson, K. (2003) *Selling Sin: The Marketing of Socially Unacceptable Products*, 2nd edn, Westport, CT: Praeger.

Department of Justice; Federal Bureau of Investigation; Criminal Justice Information Services Division (2006) "Crime in the United States," available at: www2.fbi.gov/ucr/cius2006/offenses/violent_crime/index.html. Accessed October 2012.

Educational Fund to Stop Gun Violence (2012) "Utilizing the 'buying power' strategy to reform the gun industry," available at: www.csgv.org/storage/documents/csgv 20counter marketing%20report.pdf. Accessed October 2012.

FFL Guard (2012) "Gun dealers licenses denied and revoked," available at: http://fflguard.com/wp-content/uploads/2011/11/ATF-Revocations-and-Non-Renewals-00004321.pdf. Accessed 2012.

Firearms and Injury Center at Penn (2009) "Firearms injury in the U.S.," available at: www.uphs.upenn.edu/ficap/resourcebook/Final 20Resource %20Book%20Updated%20 2009%20Section%201.pdf. Accessed October 2012.

Food Marketing Institute (2011) "Super market facts," available at: www.fmi.org/research-resources/supermarket-facts. Accessed October 2012.

Garrett, B. (2012) "Political shootings and restricted gun rights: The effects of high-profile political shootings on new gun control laws," available at: http://civilliberty.about.com/od/guncontrol/a/Political-Shootings-Gun-Control.htm. Accessed October 2012.

Gun Owners of America (2011) "Larry Pratt, Executive Director, GOA," available at: http://gunowners.org/larry-pratt.htm. Accessed December 2012.

Gundlach, G.T., Bradford, K.D., and Wilkie, W.L. (2010) "Countermarketing and demarketing against product diversion: Forensic research in the firearms industry," *Journal of Public Policy and Marketing*, 29 (1) (Spring): 103–22.

Hamilton v. Beretta USA Corp., 750 NE2d 1055 (NY 2001).

Harlow, C.W. (2001) "Firearm use by offenders," Bureau of Justice Statistics, NCJ, Washington, DC: 189369.

Karp, A. (2007) "Completing the count: Civilian firearms," *Small Arms Survey 2007: Guns and the City*, Cambridge: Cambridge University Press.

Kistner, W. (1997) "Firearms injuries: The gun battle over science," Center for Investigative Reporting. Available at: http://www.pbs.org/wgbh/pages/frontline/shows/guns/pro-con/injuries.html. Accessed March 2012.

Koper, C.A. (2007) "Crime gun risk factors: Buyer, seller, firearms, and transaction characteristics associated with gun trafficking and criminal gun use," available at: www.ncjrs.gov/pdffiles1/nij/grants/221074.pdf. Accessed October 2012.

Krug E.G., Powell, K.E., and Dahlberg, L.L. (1998) "Firearm-related deaths in the United States and 35 other high and upper-middle-income countries," *International Journal of Epidemiology*, 27: 214–21.

Law Center to Prevent Gun Violence (2012) "Multiple purchases & sales of firearms policy summary," available at: http://smartgunlaws.org/multiple-purchases-sales-of-firearms-policy-summary. Accessed October 2012.

Lytton, T.D. (2007) *Suing the Gun Industry: A Battle at the Crossroads of Gun Control and Mass Torts*, Ann Arbor, MI: University of Michigan Press.

McDonalds (2012) *2011 Annual Report*, available at: www.aboutmcdonalds.com/content/dam/AboutMcDonalds/Investors/Investors%202012/2011%20Annual%20Report%20Final.pdf. Accessed October 2012.

Marchione, M. (2012) "Doctors target gun violence as a social disease," Associated Press, *USA Today*, Gannett Press. Available at: http://usatoday30.usatoday.com/news/health/story/2012-08-11/guns-public-health/56979706/1. Accessed October 2012.

Mayors Against Illegal Guns (2012) "Reporting lost and stolen guns," available at: www.mayorsagainstillegalguns.org/html/local/lost-stolen.shtml. Accessed 2012.

NAACP v. AccuSport, Inc. (2003) F. Supp. 2d 435 (Eastern District for New York).

National Institute of Justice (2012) "Gun violence: How prevalent is gun violence in America?" Available at: www.nij.gov/topics/crime/gun-violence/welcome.htm. Accessed November 2012.

National Rifle Association (2012) "National Rifle Association statistics," available at: www.statisticbrain.com/national-rifle-association-nra-statistics. Accessed December 2012.

National Shooting Sports Foundation (2012) "Don't lie for the other guy," available at: http://nssf.org/newsroom/releases/show.cfm?PR=011812.cfm&path=2012. Accessed July 2012.

OpenSecrets.Org: Center for Responsive Politics (2012) "Gun rights lobbying," available at: www.opensecrets.org/lobby/indusclient.php?id=q13&year=2011. Accessed October 2012.

Pratt, L. (1997) "A letter from Larry Pratt to the Directors of the NRA," available at: http://gunowners.org/ldp2nra.htm. Accessed October 2012.

Richard, L., III (1984) "Strict products liability: application to gun dealers who sell to incompetent purchasers," *Arizona Law Review*, Note 26: 889.

Richardson, E.G. and Hemenway, D. (2011) "Homicide, suicide, and unintentional firearm fatality: Comparing the United States with other high-income countries, 2003," *Journal of Trauma-Injury Infection & Critical Care*, 70 (1): 238–43.

Self Esteem Health (2009) "Bullying statistics," available at: www.self-esteem-health.com/bullying-statistics.html. Accessed October 2012.

Siebel, B.J. (1999) "City lawsuits against the gun industry: A roadmap for reforming another deadly industry," *St. Louis University Public Law Review*, 28: 247–90.

Spiegler, J. and Sweeney, J. (1975) "Gun abuse in Ohio," report published by Administration of Justice Comm., affiliate of Governmental Research Institute (June). Included in appendix to 1975 Congressional hearings Part 4 (Cleveland), 1510.

Todd, B.J. (1983) "Symposium on firearms legislation and litigation: Negligent entrustment of firearms," *Hamline Law Review*, 6 (2): 467.

US Department of Justice (2001) "Gun violence reduction: National integrated firearms violence reduction strategy," available at: www.usdoj.gov/archive/opd/gunviolence.htm. Accessed July 2009.

—— (2004) "Inspections of firearms dealers by the Bureau of Alcohol, Tobacco, Firearms and Explosives," Office of the Inspector General, Evaluation and Inspections Division.

———, Bureau of Alcohol, Tobacco, Firearms and Explosives, Office of Strategic Intelligence and Information (2012) "Federal firearms licensee statistics, theft/loss reports," available at: http://www.atf.gov/statistics/ffl-theft-loss-reports/FFL-theft-loss-statistics-01122012-update-ii.pdf. Accessed March 2012.

US General Accounting Office (1996) "Federal firearms licensees: Various factors have contributed to the decline in the number of dealers," available at: http://www.gao.gov/assets/230/222478.pdf (accessed November 25, 2012).

Utter, G. and True, J.L. (2000) "The evolving gun culture in America," *Journal of American & Comparative Cultures*, 23 (2): 67–79.

Vernick, J.S., Webster, D.W., and Hepburn, L.M. (1999) "Effects of Maryland's law banning Saturday night special handguns on crime guns," *Injury Prevention*, 5: 259–63.

Wachtel, J. (1998) "Sources of crime guns in Los Angeles, California," *Policing, an International Journal of Police Strategies and Management*, 21 (2): 220–39.

Legislation

Brady Handgun Violence Prevention Act (1993) Public Law 103-159, H.R.1025.

Federal Armed Career Criminal Act Public Law (1988) Public Law Number 92-05, 18 U.S.C. § 924(e).

Federal Firearms Act (1938) 18 United States Code, Chapter 44.

Firearm Owners' Protection Act 1986, Public Law 99-308.

Gun Control Act of 1968, Public Law 90-618, The National Firearms Act (1934), Title 26, United States Code, Chapter 53.

Violent Crime and Law Enforcement Act (1994) Public Law 103-322, H.R. 3355.

Youth Handgun Safety Act (1994) 18 U.S.C. § 922.

14

NOTRE DAME AND THE FEDERAL TRADE COMMISSION

Patrick E. Murphy and William L. Wilkie

Although the connection between the current Notre Dame Marketing faculty and the Federal Trade Commission (FTC) goes back 40 years, the seeds of this relationship were planted almost a century ago. President Woodrow Wilson established the FTC in 1914. His assessment of the first few years for the FTC was captured by this phrase during his acceptance speech at the 1916 Democratic Convention: "have relieved businessmen of unfounded fears and set them on the road of hopeful and confident enterprise" (Wilson 1916). This statement runs counter to the modern interpretation that the FTC's only role was to "regulate" business. One of the initial FTC commissioners was Edward Nash Hurley, a "self-made man, an elementary school dropout [sic, see below] who built successful businesses" (Winerman 2003). The link to Notre Dame in all of this is that Hurley gave the money to build the first business building on the ND campus in 1930.

Hurley's role at the FTC and Notre Dame

Edward N. Hurley was born in Galesburg, Illinois in 1864. His parents were Irish immigrants and devout Catholics. His education concluded with his graduation from high school. He was a self-made man who built several successful businesses. As is true today, he was an exception as a FTC commissioner in that he did not possess a law degree. His history with Wilson went back to 1910 when he served as an intermediary role in recruiting Wilson for the gubernatorial race in New Jersey. His business career was very successful in manufacturing (pneumatic tools, vacuum cleaners, and washing machines) and banking. He was a lifelong proponent of foreign trade. An accurate characterization of Hurley is: "Edward Hurley was a model beneficiary of the American free enterprise in an era when the country most valued the rags to riches saga" (Temple 1992: 10).

Hurley met Fr. John O'Hara, C.S.C. of Notre Dame when Hurley was dispatched to South America by Wilson to study the continent's business and economic conditions. After getting to know Hurley on this trip, Fr. O'Hara wrote to Notre Dame's President, Fr. John Cavanaugh, in June of 1918 that "a Chicagoan named Ed Hurley had accepted the deanship, although the college was still not established" (Temple 1992: 8-9). (The College of Foreign and Domestic Commerce was not instituted until 1921, with O'Hara, not Hurley, as Dean.) O'Hara continued to court Hurley by asking him to be the commencement speaker at Notre Dame.

After the FTC, Hurley held positions at the War Trade Board, Red Cross War Council and as Chairman of the US Shipping Board, where he was responsible for gathering a fleet of ships necessary to transport men and materials during World War I. O'Hara wrote to Hurley with a list of priority needs to start the new college. He was hoping that Hurley would be the major benefactor. In 1930, 12 years after O'Hara's initial plea, while serving on Notre Dame's Board of Trustees, Hurley did contribute $200,000 "for the erection of a new building to be known as the College of Foreign and Domestic Commerce" (Hurley, letter to President O'Donnell, Appendix A). This new building was called the Edward N. Hurley Building, the first time the university had ever named a structure after its major benefactor (Temple 1992: 28).

Hurley not only gave the money but had strong opinions about the new building's design and construction. He hired the Chicago architectural firm of Graham, Anderson, Probst and White, Inc. to supervise the building. This firm was involved in developing major Chicago landmarks such as the Museum of Natural History, the Shedd Aquarium, and the Wrigley Building. The details of Hurley's vision are outlined in the letter to Fr. O'Donnell (shown in Appendix A). The seventh paragraph ("In order that the students may visualize what modern transportation and communication have done . . .") describes the murals that would grace the atrium of the building. (For a description of the famous globe and mural in the Hurley building, see Appendix B, from Temple 1992: 30-31.)

Notre Dame faculty at the FTC

To date, five current and former Notre Dame faculty members have served at the FTC in a variety of positions. They are: Bill Wilkie, Pat Murphy, Neil Beckwith, Greg Gundlach, and Debra Desrochers. The first two are still faculty members at Notre Dame and the last two have left; Neil Beckwith is now deceased. In a survey of Marketing Academics at the FTC, Murphy (1990) found that no other university has had more than three of its marketing faculty members spend significant time advising the FTC. Before discussing Notre Dame's involvement, we would like to set the context for marketing faculty at the Commission.

In 1970, Commissioner Mary Gardiner Jones contacted Professor George Day, then at Stanford, about his willingness to serve as an in-house consultant to the FTC. Since the FTC is the major regulator of marketing and advertising, it is a bit surprising that it took almost 60 years since its founding to strike upon this idea.

Day was unavailable but recommended his former student, Murray Silverman (who currently serves on the faculty of San Francisco State), who took the initial position as one of only a few advisors to Commissioner Jones.

Due to the legal environment of the FTC as a law enforcement agency, the commissioners at points serve in judicial capacities when deciding on cases before them. This means that they (and their advisors) cannot interact with the staff of the FTC during the preparation of a case. Thus, Silverman found that he was unable to offer useful insights to much of the work going on at the time. He therefore asked his former Stanford classmate, William L. Wilkie, about his interest in serving in an advisory role for the staff of the FTC. It happened that at that time the Sears–Roebuck Foundation had agreed to fund a new initiative of the AACSB (American Assembly of Collegiate Schools of Business), the "Federal/Faculty Fellowship Program." This program was intended to familiarize business school faculty members with the purposes and operations of government (a year-long program serving the government was hosted by the Brookings Institution as part of the program), while also offering government agencies assistance in obtaining new advances in management practices from the business community. At the time, Wilkie was in his second year as an Assistant Professor on the faculty of Purdue University. The Purdue administration was enthusiastic about the faculty taking part in the program, and approved his leave of absence to participate.

William Wilkie

Wilkie joined the faculty program in Summer 1972, and was retained as an in-house consultant reporting to the Director of the Bureau of Consumer Protection at the FTC, Robert Pitofsky (the FTC has three major Bureaus – Competition, Consumer Protection and Economics).

At the time of his arrival the FTC, as a law enforcement agency, was staffed almost entirely by attorneys, with PhD economists offering academic insights on many issues. The agency was inexperienced in using expertise regarding the marketing and consumer research fields, and provided Professor Wilkie with an office, an assistant, and considerable flexibility across the organization. He reports on his experience as follows.

"It's useful to remember that I arrived at the very beginning of this type of work at the commission, so things were very flexible. Also, it's important in my case to look beyond my time spent there, as I continued my activities after returning to the university world. So I've divided my recollections into these two zones. Let's start with my time in residence at the FTC, which commenced in June of 1972 (I learned later that my wife and I were moving into our Alexandria, VA apartment the same night that the Watergate burglars were breaking into those offices!). The FTC was quite interested in what our field might contribute to its work, and I agreed to pursue four projects during my tenure there."

Projects while in-house at the FTC

Project 1. Corrective advertising

"This was a controversial new remedy being developed by the FTC. It was in response to recognizing that some consumers could be deceived by an advertising campaign, which itself would later be stopped by an FTC order, yet the deceived consumers might never be informed of the actual facts and might continue to rely on the earlier misinformation. This would be harming not only these consumers, but also honest competitive marketers who would otherwise have benefitted from their purchases. There were many complexities to be addressed here (the remedy eventually was upheld in the Federal courts in the famous *Listerine* case), and I worked on them generally as well as in the context of specific cases in which the remedy was applied. Among my contributions was the proposal of a new approach to the remedy, in which the FTC would take itself out of the business of creating the corrections themselves, allowing consumer research to be used to ensure that consumer were no longer misled – this proposal was employed in the *Hawaiian Punch* case, and was praised by both conservatives (an editorial in *The Wall Street Journal*), and liberals (reports from 'Nader's Raiders'). If anyone is interested, they can find much detail on this program in an article I later wrote, entitled 'Marketing's Scarlet Letter ...' (Wilkie *et al.* 1984)."

Project 2. Cigarette warning statements

"This was another very controversial area, as it had been less than ten years previously that the nation had firmly decided that cigarette smoking carried grave health dangers and that people should know this. Prior to my arrival, then, many steps had been proposed, and some implemented, including the required health warnings on every pack of cigarettes and in every ad. My role was to contribute to the continuing assessment of the FTC's possible role going forward, and this was a fascinating assignment. I brought more structured analysis to the issues through the use of formal communication models as well as theories of consumer behavior, but also learned a lot about the law, politics, government constraints, and public health from these discussions and meetings (which included private sessions with the Surgeon General of the U.S. and with the FTC Commissioners). As is the case with many of my activities there, this was confidential, and I have never written about this topic. For those readers who are interested, however, this is still a major area of dispute now 40 years later. The Food and Drug Administration has now been granted power over cigarette marketing (viewing them as akin to a drug), and its proposal for very strong, graphic consumer warnings has been in the courts for a number of years. There should be easily available accounts of this battle in the popular press."

Project 3. Service as the "Behavioral Science Expert" for the legal staff of the Bureau of Consumer Protection

[*"A quick aside on this: Bureau Director Robert Pitofsky (a brilliant man who later became Chairman of the FTC and Dean of Georgetown Law School) called me into his office to discuss this role, and asked me if his draft announcement introducing me to the hundreds of legal staff (the FTC has over 500 attorneys today, and there are seven divisions within the Bureau of Consumer Protection) would suffice. I noticed that he'd called me a 'Behavioral Science Expert,' and politely demurred, saying that I surely didn't deserve that title. He then patiently explained that in Washington, DC people only listened to two types of persons – those with power, and those with expertise – all others were simply ignored. Since it didn't appear that I possessed power… I thought it over quickly, then agreed to the draft announcement, and became an"Expert."*]

"The FTC staff was young, brilliant (mostly from Ivy League law schools), idealistic, and motivated to bring and win cases. I met with many attorneys, and at all stages of their cases, from background investigation to in-court cross-examinations (I was not allowed to speak to the court, but could sit beside the lead attorney and provide him or her with advice.). I didn't keep track of how many attorneys I dealt with (some only briefly and others for extended periods on a particular case), but it could well have been one hundred or more.

It was clear that the fields of marketing and consumer behavior were quite central to these issues, and while at times I didn't have much to offer, I do believe that I made significant contributions to many of the matters. Among these was a potential deceptive advertising case involving a major firm, on which there was staff disagreement – was this advertising actually deceptive or not? I proposed that we pay for an ad copy test to see how consumers were reacting. This was a budget item that I don't believe had ever been expended by the FTC previously, at least for case selection purposes … I had the test conducted by a nationally recognized market research firm. The results came back and were eagerly scrutinized by everyone involved. They indicated little likelihood of deception, and the potential case was dropped. This was an appropriate result, I think, and also proved to be a significant start for copy-testing at the FTC, a practice that has been much adopted since that time.

Another notable memory from this project was the case I worked on with Ben Stein, who has become a television and Hollywood star today (and Ferris Buehler's memorable teacher!). He was my age, a young attorney at the FTC, having graduated from Columbia, then Yale Law School. His father was the Chairman of the Council of Economic Advisors for President Nixon, so he was well-connected in Washington (I believe he became a presidential speechwriter shortly thereafter). I recall him as very bright: a pleasant colleague who was actually interested in some of the ideas coming from my field of work and willing to try them out. We worked together very well on the case at hand.

Again, all of my work with the staff was confidential, so I have never written directly about it. I did, however, give talks to my field about public policy issues at academic conferences, and wrote a journal article with David Gardner (who began serving at FTC's Office of Policy Planning as I was there) entitled, 'The Role of Marketing Research in Public Policy Decision Making.' This appeared in the *Journal of Marketing* and reached a broad market, who received it with much interest. It was sought out for reprinting in three readings books, and was later named as among the '50 most-cited marketing articles' written during the decade of the 1970s (Wilkie and Gardner 1974). I also wrote several teaching cases for text-books, posing the challenges faced by FTC decision-makers, and asking students to take on the decision-making processes in order to arrive at the best and fairest outcomes."

Project 4. Creating a continuing marketing and consumer research presence at the FTC

"Led by Commissioner Mary Gardiner Jones' advocacy for our area, the FTC was interested in how to best plan for a continuing presence of our field within their work. Hiring Murray Silverman was the first step, bringing me on board was the second, and shortly thereafter the new Office of Policy Planning reached out and brought a third marketing professor, David Gardner (University of Illinois) in as a consultant on their staff. Murray, Dave, and I continued discussions as we learned more about the policy setting and types of needs that needed attention. We were concerned that creation of a permanent staff or division might diminish the quality, and certainly the independence, of insights provided to the FTC. In contrast, we believed, that a number of fine researchers would be interested in working with the agency and contributing to resolving the problems being addressed. However, because our field's doctoral education typically avoids exposure to public policy issues, distant relationships might not work well either – the marketing professors likely would not truly understand the problem setting.

We therefore instituted a continuing "Marketing Academic Consultancy" at the FTC in 1972. Each year the FTC would bring two (prominent) marketing professors in-house, one in the Bureau of Consumer Protection and one in the Office of Policy Planning. These persons would be expected to continue the same sorts of tasks that Dave and I were undertaking within the FTC. In addition, we wanted them to serve as eternal liaisons to the marketing academic community (as we had been) by delivering conference talks and writing papers on public policy issues. Finally, they were to identify their replacements and keep the program rolling. I still remember how very pleased I was when Professor Harold Kassarjian from UCLA, a major figure in consumer behavior, agreed to take my place in BCP, and Neil Beckwith (then of Columbia, later Wharton and Notre Dame) agreed to replace Dave in OPP (and to take over the wonderful Alexandria apartment where Barbara and I had been living).

In my view this program was a smashing success, with almost 30 people serving as in-house FTC consultants over the next decade (see Murphy 1990 for an overview and report). This was not only a fabulous experience for them personally, but also clearly improved the work of the FTC. In addition, it led to the development of a vibrant field of inquiry on Marketing and Public Policy issues that continue on to the present time!"

Continued consultation with FTC afterwards

"The issues I was encountering while at FTC were big, important, and continuing in nature. Thus such consulting did not end when I returned to Purdue, then to Harvard and the Marketing Science Institute, then to the University of Florida, and finally back to Notre Dame – I worked for many years thereafter as an outside FTC consultant, sometimes paid, sometimes *pro bono*. Beyond specific cases, here are three interesting programs/projects with which I was involved:

- *FTC rulemaking:* In 1975 Congress passed the Magnuson–Moss Warranty Act, which directed the FTC to add rule-making activities to its previous legal case-by-case approach to marketing regulation. This was intended to add efficiency to the competitive marketplace – positive rules (say, for example, in the funeral industry's marketing activities) could guide all competitors in an industry as to appropriate actions, and consumers would benefit from both better information and fewer questionable marketing schemes in the marketplace. During the 1970s, rule-making processes were initiated on a range of topics, including product labeling, life insurance, used cars, funerals, advertising to children, and other areas in which evidence showed that consumers would sometimes encounter problems and/or that better information might improve purchases or save money. Together with Professor Joel Cohen, I did extensive research on possible rules (again all confidential, so no publications on these). Interestingly, our research contributed to stopping one of the initiatives and advancing another. As a set, however, the rule-making activities generated huge political controversy which reached Congress, and the rule-making processes were essentially ended by about 1980. (In fact, the FTC was shut down for one day in May, 1980 when Congress failed to extend appropriations, largely due to the rulemaking activities undertaken by the Commission.)
- *The FTC Consumer Information Task Force:* As the 1970s progressed, it was becoming increasingly clear that FTC remedies involving consumer information were to be preferred when possible. Not only does this comport with economic theory (in our competitive marketplace buyers are assumed to hold sufficient good information about their alternatives as to be capable of making good purchasing decisions for themselves, and these in the aggregate will guide allocations within our society), but it also tends to be a relatively less intrusive option for the government in its relations with the businesses it

regulates. Nonetheless, this is still a complex area since it involves consumers' processing issues, technical issues involving the precise measurement and characterization of product or service attributes, and myriad legal issues, such as freedoms accorded to a marketer in our economic market system (e.g., freedom of speech).

Accordingly, the Commission launched a blue-ribbon "Consumer Information Task Force" toward the end of the decade, charged to provide a comprehensive review of knowledge in this area, and a set of guidelines for the FTC follow in the future. As I recall, it comprised some FTC internal attorneys and economists, as well as a few leading academics from each of the fields of Law, Economics, Psychology, and Marketing. After leaving the FTC, I had done quite a bit of research on consumer information (e.g., Wilkie 1974a,b, 1975, 1978a,b, 1979; Wilkie and Greyser 1974; McNeill and Wilkie 1979; Hutton and Wilkie 1980) and was one of the three or four people from Marketing invited to serve on the Task Force. The discussions were stimulating, and I learned a lot (and contributed some as well) – everyone there was an expert in his or her area.

In addition to the formal FTC session reporting on the findings, a large volume entitled "Consumer Information Remedies" was issued (FTC 1979). I used that volume for many years in the PhD seminar on Marketing and Public Policy that I taught. The students responded to it with great favor, as it combined high levels of theory with real issues in the public policy, marketing, and consumer protection domain. (It was thick, and printed with a bright yellow cover. They called it 'The Yellowback,' and my personal supply dwindled across time as some of its PhD borrowers 'forgot' to get it back to me.) I did not personally write any direct follow-up articles on the Task Force in the academic journals, but others did, which led to considerable impact on research in our field during the 1980s.

- *The Affirmative Disclosure Project:* As I mentioned above, our field's work was clearly central to many of the FTC's activities, and this became increasingly recognized as the decade progressed. Following completion of the consumer information task force, the marketing academics in residence at FTC at the time (Michael Mazis and Kenneth Bernhardt) approached me to see if I was willing to take on a large evaluation research project on the topic of 'affirmative disclosure.' Affirmative information disclosures are a class of regulatory actions in which a marketer is required to inform consumers of certain facts about a product or service. They can take on a variety of forms, including provision of basic information about product characteristics, qualifications of product claims, warnings of risks with use of a product, how to reduce risk, and so forth (the corrective advertising program discussed earlier is thus a form of affirmative disclosure). I agreed, and set about to work under the terms of a formal contract. It turned out to be a massive undertaking – an investigation of some

225 case dockets, in all of which the FTC had ordered some form of affirmative disclosures to be made to consumers because there was reason to believe that they had been deceived by an earlier marketing effort. This took me a long time, as I needed to ensure that I understood the nature of the case, the product or service, the consumers involved, as well as examining the exact remedy that had been ordered. Some efficiency was available because of relationship among some cases (e.g., when a particular disclosure would be ordered for a set of firms in an industry, such as cigarettes or weight loss). Still, it was a massive undertaking, and I spent many weekends in Washington headquarters diving through the docket rooms. Fortunately, it was very interesting, and I again learned much. My final report was voluminous, and apparently quite helpful: I understand that it became assigned reading for FTC staff contemplating using these remedies for their cases.

Sometime after the report was finished, I received a phone call from Professor Thomas Kinnear (University of Michigan), who had recently started a new publication, the *Journal of Public Policy & Marketing*. He asked if I was planning to write a journal article on the project. I replied that I probably would not, as I didn't see any way to condense it down to the limited pages for a journal. He then offered the possibility of a series of articles (reflecting the chapters of my FTC report), as well as the assistance of his talented copy editor, if I would place the work into his new journal. We agreed that one article per year would work, and did so over the ensuing years. At the end, there were five articles, and these did have impact on researchers wishing to study consumer information issues. When *JPP&M* instituted its 'Outstanding Article Award' in 1992 or so, they went back to the 1985 Affirmative Disclosure article and named it the outstanding paper to have appeared in the first five years of the journal's publication (Wilkie 1982, 1983, 1985, 1986, 1987).

All in all, the initiative taken by Commissioner Mary Gardiner Jones served to clearly improve the operations of the FTC. Further, it happened to lead me into an unexpected, but very fruitful, series of experiences and research undertakings for my career, something I've always appreciated!"

Neil Beckwith

Neil Beckwith served as a Visiting Professor of Marketing at Notre Dame from 1995 to 1999. He had previously held impressive academic appointments at Columbia University and the Wharton School of Business at the University of Pennsylvania, and had also served as Vice-President of Marketing for both ARA Services (now Aramark) and Deluxe Check Corporation before joining Notre Dame. While at Columbia, Neil went on leave to replace David Gardner at the FTC's Office of Policy Planning and Evaluation. He was instrumental there in changing the regulatory environment regarding comparative advertising.

The use of comparative advertising (in which a rival company's brand name is actually used in an ad) was a measure to encourage more transparent quality and/or price competition among advertisers. When Neil joined the FTC in 1973, there was considerable controversy involving comparative advertising, as (voluntary) advertising industry codes of conduct were prohibiting the practice, and several major television networks were refusing to accept such commercials. He spent much of his time at the FTC writing up a long, thorough, document which went through the various issues and gave examples of trade association's policies and presumably argued that these were anti-competitive. For example, such a prohibition could be harmful to a competitor who might wish to introduce a new product that offers either superior performance or lower price to the consumer market (see Wilkie and Farris 1975 for discussion of these issues). There was, however, significant opposition at the time, evidently by some powerful opponents, as at some point he was visited by (presumably) federal investigators at his FTC office and they took away many boxes of his papers/records as evidence. His son offered this comment about Neil's work on comparative advertising:

> I know he felt that he played a large part in getting the ban on comparative advertising changed, as for many years afterward, when a TV commercial came on that relied upon comparison, such as the "Pepsi Challenge," he would often say "you're welcome" to the TV set.
>
> *(Beckwith 2012)*

Patrick E. Murphy

Patrick Murphy joined the FTC in the summer of 1980 while he was a faculty member at Marquette University. He took part in the Sears AACSB Fellowship Program and was placed in a new Office of Management Planning in the Bureau of Consumer Protection. The office was headed by Steven Kelman, on leave from the Kennedy School of Government, at Harvard. The other professional in the office was Dee Pridgen, an attorney, now at the University of Wyoming Law School. (As a side note, this was probably the first office within the FTC that actually had management in its title.)

"My role was summarized in an article that I published subsequent to my time at the FTC (Murphy 1984). The first of three major projects that I was involved in was a depth interview technique with twenty opinion leaders about the external trends affecting the FTC at that time. Thirteen of these experts were marketing professors who had worked or consulted with the Commission. The others were three law professors recommended by Commissioner Robert Pitofsky and four consumer group leaders. Among the consumer protection problems identified by the interviewees were: new technologies, energy, services, non-store marketing, deception in local advertising, the aging of the population and marketing to minorities and immigrants (pp. 60–62). It is uncanny how many of these issues remain ones of concern over 30 years after this initial report was written.

The second project was a study of changing consumer lifestyles and their implication for FTC activities. An attempt was made to identify significant long-term lifestyle changes that would have impact on consumer behavior and may result in deceptive marketing activities. A reference was made in the article on the 'current emphasis on healthy lifestyles' (p. 62). This too is a focal point of much marketing in the second decade of the twenty-first century. However, as Betsy Moore indicates (Chapter 12 this volume), the stress on healthy lifestyles did not become an actuality those years ago when one views the obesity problems of current day.

A third project involved a major survey of Montgomery County consumers concerning their experiences with heating and air conditioning firms. From the surveys, we were able to publish a list of 'recommended' heating and air conditioning firms in the area. The report was covered by the *Washington Post*. The purpose of this project was twofold: one was for a federal agency to work with a local office of consumer affairs and second, the study highlighted the importance of positive information in the market. One of the points of emphasis of the Office of Management Planning was to look for ways of accentuating positive information about companies rather than bringing cases against firms for their illegal activities.

I left the FTC during the Summer of 1981 to go on sabbatical. Soon after my departure, the new Chairman of the FTC, James Miller who was appointed by Ronald Reagan, disbanded the office. Kelman returned to Harvard and Dee Pridgen was reassigned within the Bureau of Consumer Protection. Although many might consider the office that lasted less than two years a failure, we were able to bring a more strategic attitude to the Bureau (see Murphy 1984 for detailed coverage of these efforts)."

Greg Gundlach

Greg Gundlach joined the Notre Dame faculty in 1987 as an Assistant Professor of Marketing from the University of Tennessee. Greg was unique in the fact that he held both a PhD in Marketing and a law degree from UT. As a part of his law program while at the University of Tennessee, Greg was a Research Assistant in the Office of Policy Planning in the Bureau of Competition at the FTC during the summer/fall of 1984. At the time, and as part of its policy planning role, the Office was examining competition policy surrounding distribution relationships and the merits of current policy regarding vertical distribution restraints. These restraints – which include resale price maintenance, territory restrictions, customer restrictions and related practices – are the subject of considerable interest to policymakers. They are seen as restricting intrabrand competition, but are justified as increasing interbrand competition. Economic thinking at the time concluded that these effects could result in procompetitive and anticompetitive effects depending on how they were practiced by marketers. Given this state of affairs, the Office felt that insights from research on marketing distribution relationships might help to further inform competition policy at the time. Accordingly, Greg was tasked with assembling relevant knowledge from marketing that might enhance extant thinking. The assignment provided him with the opportunity to interact with members across the Commission including both lawyers and economists.

Greg's assessment of his work at the FTC is as follows:

> Although it remains a question as to whether my work in the Office added value at the time, it was an important experience that yielded a firsthand look at the interface of marketing scholarship and public policy. The brief time and exposure at the Office subsequently led to my enrollment in the University of Tennessee Doctoral Program upon the completion of my MBA and while still in the JD program. The experience also motivated me to investigate distribution related questions in marketing with a particular interest on public policy questions relating to competition.
>
> To date my contributions to marketing have included a number of projects that address competition policy questions in distribution. These include academic projects examining resale price maintenance, category management, slotting fees, and marketing channel systems. They also involve forensic research on these topics as a part of my professional practice. In sum the Federal Trade Commission experience and subsequent engagement at the University of Notre Dame were important in shaping the areas of academic and professional contributions that have defined my career.
>
> *(Gundlach 2012)*

Greg left Notre Dame in the early 2000s to take a position at the University of North Florida. While he was a faculty member at Notre Dame, he was also active in Washington, DC, convening legal conferences and providing testimony to Congress as a Fellow of the American Antitrust Institute. He also collaborated with Bill Wilkie and other colleagues on a number of significant articles, including a major literature review of all marketing and public policy research undertaken from 1970 to 1988 (Gundlach and Wilkie 1990), a national survey on the hidden world of "slotting fees" (Wilkie *et al.* 2002), and the highly controversial topic of illegal diversion of firearms from legitimate marketing channels of distribution (Bradford *et al.* 2005; Gundlach *et al.* 2010).

Before turning our attention to the work of Debbie Desrochers at the FTC, we want to discuss another link between Notre Dame and the FTC. In 1989 Professors Murphy and Wilkie convened a major "invitation-only symposium" commemorating the seventy-fifth anniversary of the FTC. Held on the Notre Dame campus, the symposium brought together a select group of participants that included past and present commissioners and high level officials of the agency, leading attorneys and economists, members of the American Bar Association Task Force on the FTC, and some thirty professors academics who had participated in the marketing academic consultancy program at the FTC. The successful symposium examined a special American Bar Association report assessing deficiencies of the FTC during the 1980s, the significant events in the history of the FTC (including an historical perspective on the FTC's first 50 years – Zuckerman 1992), the contributions of marketing academics to the Commission over the years, and discussions over the future of the agency. Debate was high-level, informed, and civil but intense.

The event was a smashing success according to its participants, and our book covering its contents (Murphy and Wilkie 1990) has been named as one of "Six Superlative Sources" on the Federal Trade Commission by a Library of Congress specialist on this agency (Infography 2012). As one measure of the Symposium's impact, the FTC commissioners requested that we organize a day-long briefing session at FTC headquarters to probe the promise of our field for future efforts of the Commission. Following that session, and with the especially strong support of Commissioner Andrew Strenio, the FTC opted to renew its support for a rotating academic consulting position for marketing faculty members, commencing in the early 1990s.

The Notre Dame Symposium also galvanized the marketing academic participants, who agreed that future meetings of this type would be most valuable. Paul Bloom and Michael Mazis volunteered to arrange academic conferences each of the next two years in Washington, DC. These were well attended and included strong research presentations and excellent discussions, and became the annual "Marketing and Public Policy Conference." This conference is now in its twenty-third year, and is held under the auspices of the American Marketing Association. It serves the important function of regularly bringing together marketing academics, government leaders, and public policy officials to examine issues of importance both to the marketing academic community and larger policy-making world.

Debra Desrochers

Debra Desrochers joined the Notre Dame Marketing faculty in 1999 and stayed until 2008. She had multiple stints at the FTC. From January through June of 2004, she worked in the Bureau of Economics (BE), which supports both the Bureau of Competition and the Bureau of Consumer Protection. Since her research to that point had focused on trade promotion practices such as slotting allowances and category captain arrangements that were potentially anti-competitive, she expected to support the Bureau of Competition. However, upon her arrival BE was just starting a project on children's exposure to television advertising and Debbie was asked to participate in that effort. Over the next few years, she served at the FTC for two more extended periods to continue work on this project. The first subsequent stay was during the summer of 2005 and later during the fall semester of 2006. In her words: "It was a thrilling and rewarding experience that changed the direction of my research" (Desrochers 2012).

The television advertising study was conducted in response to a variety of calls for government action regarding the increasing prevalence of childhood obesity. As obesity rates were increasing, other notable changes were taking place in the areas of children's television, TV advertising, the number of food products developed for and marketed to children, and children's screen time. After an extensive review of academic studies of these coincident trends, the Institute of Medicine (IOM) concluded that there is strong evidence that exposure to television advertising is associated with obesity in children aged 2–11 years (IOM 2006: ES-7). Meanwhile, a study by the American Psychological Association suggested that advertising to children was unfair due to their undeveloped cognitive abilities and that the government should act to protect this vulnerable population (Wilcox *et al.* 2004).

In response to such assertions, Debra J. Holt, Pauline M. Ippolito, and Christopher R. Kelly, all from the FTC, and Professor Desrochers prepared a comprehensive review of children's advertising exposure on television. For this study, the FTC received television audience and advertising data from Nielsen that included local and national broadcast, cable, and syndicated programs for four weeks, one from each of the four sweeps periods from fall 2003 through summer 2004. The objective of this report was to document how much advertising children see, when they see it, on what programs, and for which products. The complete description of the state of the 2004 television advertising environment was used to identifying the possible implications of any policy changes regarding advertising on children's programming. In addition, the state of television advertising in 2004 was also compared to the state of television advertising in 1977 when the last, similar study was performed by the FTC. The comparison was used to address the assumed causal impact of television advertising on obesity.

The final FTC report (Holt *et al.* 2007) is titled, "Children's Exposure to TV Advertising in 1977 and 2004: Information for the Obesity Debate," and was released June 1, 2007. In the fall of 2007, Debra J. Holt and Debra Desrochers published a peer-reviewed version in the *Journal of Public Policy & Marketing* which is based on the FTC report (Desrochers and Holt 2007). In less than 18 months, this paper became the fifth most highly cited article from this journal since 2000 and was a 2009 finalist for the Thomas C. Kinnear/*Journal of Public Policy & Marketing* Award.

Conclusion and relationship with the common good

As this chapter indicates, the relationship between the University of Notre Dame and the Federal Trade Commission is a long and significant one. Little did Edward Hurley and Father O'Hara know that there would be Notre Dame faculty involved with the FTC for several decades in the late twentieth and early twenty-first centuries. The involvement of the faculty with the FTC has informed their research and teaching both at Notre Dame and other institutions. The "body of work" produced by these scholars is impressive on a number of dimensions.

The theme for this entire volume revolves around the "common good." Despite Wilson's early pronouncement about the FTC being an arm of business, most of its 100-year history has been devoted to promoting the common good by insuring a more competitive marketplace and guarding against false and deceptive advertising that violates this core principle. The FTC over its now 100 years has worked tirelessly to promote a "fair" marketplace for both consumers and companies through the work of the Bureaus of Consumer Protection and Competition. The work undertaken by Notre Dame faculty on affirmative disclosures, corrective advertising, cigarette warning statements, FTC rulemaking, positive information about service providers, comparative advertising, identification of trends that influence both the practice of marketing and the FTC actions, resale price maintenance, slotting fees and the link between advertising and obesity all have ramifications for society and the promotion of larger social goals that are laudatory. Both the FTC and Notre Dame's Department of Marketing have longstanding and deserved reputations as guardians of the "common good."

References

Beckwith, B. (2012) Personal communication with the authors.

Bradford, K.D., Gundlach, G.T., and Wilkie, W.L. (2005) "Countermarketing in the courts: The case of marketing channels and firearms diversion," *Journal of Public Policy & Marketing*, 24 (2): 284–98.

Desrochers, D.M. (2012) Personal communication with the authors.

—— and Holt, D.J. (2007) "Children's exposure to television advertising: Implications for childhood obesity," *Journal of Public Policy & Marketing*, 26 (2): 182–201.

Federal Trade Commission Task Force (1979) *Consumer Information Remedies*, Washington, DC: US Federal Trade Commission.

Gundlach, G.T. (2012) Personal communication with the authors.

—— and Wilkie, W.L. (1990) "The marketing literature in public policy: 1970–1988," in P. Murphy and W. Wilkie (eds) *The Future for Marketing and Advertising Regulation: The Federal Trade Commission in the 1990s*, Notre Dame, IN: University of Notre Dame Press, pp. 329–44.

—— Bradford, K.D., and Wilkie, W.L. (2010) "Countermarketing and demarketing against product diversion: Forensic research in the firearms industry," *Journal of Public Policy & Marketing*, 29 (1): 103–22.

Holt, D.J., Ippolito, P.M., Desrochers, D.M., and Kelley, C.R. (2007) "Children's exposure to TV advertising in 1977 and 2004: Information for the obesity debate," Federal Trade Commission, Bureau of Economics Staff Report, www.ftc.gov/os/2007/06/cabecolor. pdf, released June 1 (accessed February 18, 2012).

Hutton, R.B. and Wilkie, W.L. (1980) "Life cycle cost: A new form of consumer information," *Journal of Consumer Research* (March): 349–60.

Infography (2012) Available at: www.infography.com/content/977851617139.htm (accessed October 25, 2012).

Institute of Medicine (2006), *Food Marketing to Children and Youth: Threat or Opportunity?* Washington, DC: The National Academies Press.

McNeill, D.L. and Wilkie W.L. (1979) "Public policy and consumer information: impact of the new energy labels," *Journal of Consumer Research*, June: 1–11.

Murphy, P.E. (1984) "Strategic planning at the FTC," *Journal of Public Policy & Marketing*, 3: 56–66.

—— (1990) "Past FTC participation of marketing academics," in P.E. Murphy and W.L. Wilkie (eds) *Marketing and Advertising Regulation: The Federal Trade Commission in the 1990s*, Notre Dame, IN: University of Notre Dame Press, pp. 205–15.

—— and Wilkie, W. (eds) (1990) *Marketing and Advertising Regulation: The Federal Trade Commission in the 1990s*, Notre Dame, IN: University of Notre Dame Press.

Temple, K. (1992) *O'Hara's Heirs: Business Education at Notre Dame – 1921–1991*, College of Business Administration, University of Notre Dame.

Wilcox, B.L., Kunkel, D., Cantor, J., Dowrick, P., Linn, S., and Palmer, E. (2004) *Report of The APA Task Force on Advertising and Children*, Washington, DC: American Psychological Association, available at: www.apa.org/pi/families/resources/advertising-children.pdf (accessed May 30, 2012).

Wilkie, W.L. (1974a) "Analysis of effects of information load," *Journal of Marketing Research*, 11 (November): 462–66.

—— (1974b) "Consumer information processing research: Product labeling," Cambridge, MA: Marketing Science Institute, September.

—— (1975) "New perspectives for consumer information processing research," *Communication Research*, 2 (July): 216–31.

—— (1978a) "Consumer information processing and public policy research," in J. Cady (ed.) *Marketing and the Public Interest: Essays in Honor of Dean E. T. Grether*, Cambridge, MA: Marketing Science Institute, pp. 223–37.

—— (1978b) "Consumer information processing: Issues for public policymakers," in R. Lund (ed.) *Consumer Research for Consumer Policy*, Cambridge, MA: Center for Policy Alternatives, MIT, pp. 88–117.

—— (1979) "Professional advertising's impact on consumers," in R. Blair and S. Rubin (eds), *Regulating the Professions*, Lexington, MA: D.C. Heath, pp. 283–98.

—— (1982) "Affirmative disclosure: Perspectives on FTC orders," *Journal of Public Policy & Marketing*, 1: 95–110.

—— (1983) "Affirmative disclosure at the FTC: Theoretical framework and typology of case selection," *Journal of Public Policy & Marketing*, 2: 3–15.

—— (1985) "Affirmative disclosure at the FTC: Objectives for the remedy and outcomes of orders," *Journal of Public Policy & Marketing*, 4: 91–111.

—— (1986) "Affirmative disclosure at the FTC: Strategic dimensions," *Journal of Public Policy & Marketing*, 5: 123–45.

—— (1987) "Affirmative disclosure at the FTC: Communication decisions," *Journal of Public Policy & Marketing*, 6: 33–42.

—— and Farris, P.W. (1975) "Comparison advertising: Problems and potential," *Journal of Marketing*, 39 (October): 7–15.

—— and Gardner, D.M. (1974) "The role of marketing research in public policy decision making," *Journal of Marketing*, 38 (January): 38–47.

—— and Greyser, S.A. (1974) "Consumer research inputs to public policy and legal decisions," in S. Ward and P. Wright (eds) *Advances in Consumer Research: Vol. 1*, Association for Consumer Research, pp. 511–22.

——, McNeill, D.L., and Mazis, M.B. (1984) "Marketing's 'scarlet letter': the theory and practice of corrective advertising," *Journal of Marketing*, 48 (2): 11–31.

——, Desrochers, D.M., and Gundlach, G. (2002) "Marketing research and public policy: the case of slotting fees," *Journal of Public Policy & Marketing*, 21 (2): 275–88.

Wilson, W. (1916) Acceptance speech at the Democratic Convention, September 2.

Winerman, M. (2003) "The origins of the FTC: Concentration, cooperation, control and cooperation," *Antitrust Law Journal*, 71: 1–97.

Zuckerman, M.E. (1992) "The Federal Trade Commission in historical perspective: The first fifty years," in P.E. Murphy and W.L. Wilkie (eds) *Marketing and Advertising Regulation: The Federal Trade Commission in the 1990s*, Notre Dame, IN: University of Notre Dame Press.

Appendix A

E D W A R D   N . H U R L E Y

208 S O U T H   L A   S A L L E   S T .

C H I C A G O

November
Eight
1 9 3 0

The Reverend Charles L. O'Donnell, C.S.C.,
The President,
University of Notre Dame,
Notre Dame, Indiana
Dear Father O'Donnell:

The University of Notre Dame is rendering valuable service to American industry by educating young men in its School of Foreign and Domestic Commerce, particularly because the University features the great importance of foreign trade to the future industrial development of our country. In recognition of this service, I wish to contribute to the University the sum of two hundred thousand ($200,000.00) dollars for the erection of a new building to be known as the College of Foreign and Domestic Commerce.

As a member of the University's Board of Lay Trustees, I have been impressed with the educational advantages which you offer to the three thousand and more students of the University, and the remarkable progress you are making in equipping young men to go into the fields of foreign and domestic commerce, engineering, the professions, etc. Through the small tuition fee charged to regular students and through your employment plan by which you enable some 350 other students to help defray their expenses through college, at the liberal rate of compensation allowed, you really are subsidizing the education of many ambitious young men who could not otherwise afford to go to college. Thus from the close contact I have had with the University, and the insight which this has afforded me into its inner workings, I have come to understand why Notre Dame is justly regarded as one of the leading universities of America.

As an inspiration to the students in the now College of Foreign and Domestic Commerce building, may I suggest that each of the six principal study halls be named for distinguished American industrial leaders of international vision who have rendered special service to our country in their particular lines of endeavor and that an oil portrait of each sponsor be placed in his respective study hall to serve as a constant reminder – to the students – of his boyhood struggles, phenomenal success and subsequent leadership.

I should like very much to have the University name the following gentlemen: James A. Farrell, New York, President of the United States Steel Corporation, to represent Steel Manufacturing and Overseas Shipping; Ernest R. Graham, Chicago, senior member of the firm of Graham, Anderson, Probst and White – Architecture; Samuel Insull, Chicago, Chairman of the Commonwealth Edison Company – Electric Public Utilities; Charles E. Mitchell, New York, Chairman of the National City Bank – International Banking; John D. Ryan, Now York, Chairman of the Anaconda Copper Company – Copper Mining and Manufacturing; Gerard Swope, New York, President of the General Electric Company – Engineering and Electrical Manufacturing; all of whom would be highly honored to be identified with Notre Dame.

The young men graduating from the College of Foreign and Domestic Commerce will blaze the trail of modern and equitable business methods just as our forefathers blazed the trail for civilization and commercial progress by exchanging goods for furs with the Indians.

At our present stage of economic development, it is most important that we should recognize that those same sound business principles must apply to our foreign commerce and that the essence of trade is exchange. We are only a part of the world and no more important than any other country. We have to have orders from foreign countries to be successful, but foreign customers cannot buy our goods unless they sell their own. When all nations are in a healthy economic condition, the reaction is favorable to all and we must learn to recognize the absolute necessity of buying as well as selling. In this connection, I should like to suggest that Notre Dame exchange scholarships with universities of the principal industrial nations of the world where courses are taught similar to yours which lay special emphasis upon the importance of the unfettered movement of goods in the channels of world trade, and which are designed to train specialists in the theory and practice of international exchange of goods and services.

In order that the students may visualize what modern transportation and communication have done towards bringing the nations of the world into closer contact, the four walls of the main or memorial hall of the new College of Foreign and Domestic Commerce building are to have a mural painting in colors of a map of all the countries of the world, showing the seven seas and the trade routes featuring the seaports of the world, giving the nautical miles between the principal international ports and the shortest time it requires for the fastest passenger and cargo service between different countries, as well as cable and radio telephone communication systems to the countries covered by that service.

This map should impress the students with the importance and responsibility of the United States in the world of commerce. It will show the American flag flying from the mast of an American ship in every foreign port of the world which, for fifty years, has been the great ambition of the American people. And it should help the students to realize that the same economic problems we have are to be found in all countries and that the peoples of the world share our ambitions to make their respective countries better places in which to live.

It is my hope that my contribution may be helpful in furthering your expansion plan for the College of Foreign and Domestic Commerce in order that the graduates may enter business life with a more thorough knowledge not only of our own economic needs, but of all nations, particularly as they apply to the importance of imports and exports.

Sincerely yours,

Edward N. Hurley

Source: Edward N. Hurley to Rev. Charles O'Donnell, CSC, November 8, 1930. President Records: Rev. Charles O'Donnell, CSC (UPCO 4/85). University of Notre Dame Archives, reprinted with permission.

Appendix B: Description of Hurley Building

At the center of this two-story foyer was to be an eight-foot globe, depicting the world's historic trade routes, installed in a recessed pit. The revolving globe was fitted with a mechanism by which it could be raised and lowered. That mechanism, President O'Donnell insisted, must be foolproof, and immune to the vandalism and mischief of students prone to taking a device apart in order to see how it works.

A Lockport, Illinois, native, John Warner Norton, who had become well-known for painting murals in the Chicago area, was selected to paint the walls and globe – according to these specifications from Alfred Shaw, the project's construction superintendent: "I think the scheme will be extremely interesting; the globe is done in cool colors – grays, greens and browns, and stands in a room which is otherwise quite warm – terrazzo floor, plaster walls, decorative painting on the ceiling, and the colors of the seven maps would be in warmer tones."

While the lobby was the building's focal point and central gem, the two-story, E-shaped, Gothic edifice with its leaded glass windows and handsome brick and stonework provided a solid yet resplendent environment in which to study business. It was a showpiece building of which the whole University could be proud. And the college deserved it, Hurley explained, because "the young men graduating from the College of Commerce will blaze the trail of modern and equitable business methods just as our forefathers blazed the trail for civilization and commercial progress by exchanging goods for furs with the Indians."

On May 13, 1932, the building was dedicated. The University's board of trustees met in the lobby with the faculty dressed in full academic garb. Students, who had been excused from classes to attend, watched from the stairways and balconies. Much to the students' delight, the ceremony was brief; few people spoke – as had been awkwardly predicted in the student paper: "The program will not be long, but in keeping with the dignified tone of the arrangements will be brought to a short termination." Notre Dame, then, had not only a Hurley Building, but also a college called the Edward N. Hurley College of Foreign and Domestic Commerce, a name it bore more or less officially until 1961 when it became the College of Business Administration.

Source: Temple 1992: 30–31.

PART VI
Ethical issues in marketing

15

FROM TWINS TO STRANGERS

Considerations of paired kidney donation across gift and market economies

Tonya Williams Bradford

Advances in medical technology provide opportunities for society and its members to experience improved quality of life. One such advancement is organ and tissue transplantation. Where such procedures began with donations from deceased persons, continued advancements have made transplantation a possibility with organs from living donors (Fox and Swazey 2002). There are over 112,000[1] individuals on the official waiting list for an organ transplant, with approximately 85 percent of them seeking a kidney (United Network for Organ Sharing, www.UNOS.org). Each living person may donate one kidney, a portion of their liver, or a lobe of their lungs, though kidneys are in highest demand and most frequently donated. Taking into account the family, professional, and community networks of those awaiting an organ in the United States, the total number of lives impacted by organ transplantation is likely in the millions. While the waiting list provides hope, eighteen individuals on the waiting list lose their lives each day.

Living organ donation, once considered a novel medical procedure, has become accepted practice as medical technology and pharmaceutical innovations provide increased opportunities for sharing organs between unrelated individuals (Rothman *et al.* 2007). The first successful living organ donor kidney transplant in the United States occurred in 1954 between identical twins. Most individuals are born with two kidneys, yet can function effectively with one, making the kidney an ideal organ for gifting and transplantation. Theoretically, the possible number of available living donor kidneys exceeds demand, yet the conversion of possible to actual transplants due to living donation has not increased significantly in recent years.

The marketplace provides an opportunity for every individual in need of a kidney to receive one, yet it is the gift economy – living and deceased donors – upon which the market relies for supply. Two factors contribute to the supply gap. The first is that donations of cadaver organs remain stagnant. The second is that most living organ donation is directed, meaning that individuals volunteer to donate their organ to a known other. While both forms of donation are noble, in the current process neither provides a scalable nor systemic solution. One means of addressing the gap between supply and demand is a recent marketplace innovation: paired donation. Paired donation is a process where a series of gifted organs – both living and cadaver – are matched to recipients such that each donor's recipient receives a kidney. For example, Mary Beth may require a kidney and though her father, Joseph, is willing to donate, he is not deemed to be a medically suitable donor for her. Mary Beth and Joseph may choose to participate in paired kidney donation to obtain a suitable kidney for Mary Beth, where Joseph donates his kidney to someone, and in return Mary Beth receives a kidney.

The kidney paired donation experiences described in the media by medical personnel and beneficiaries provide a snapshot of how the gift and market economies work together to improve the quality of lives:

> "We finally beat the 'Grey's Anatomy' record for domino transplants," Robert Montgomery, chief transplant surgeon at Hopkins, joked at a news conference hours after the last [kidney paired donation] surgery was completed . . . . A chain of surgeries is arranged in which each donor is matched with a transplant candidate they don't know but who is compatible with the kidney being donated. Chain transplants typically also involve an altruistic donor, who is willing to donate a kidney to anyone ....
>
> *(Aratani 2009)*

> In what is the largest single-hospital kidney swap in California, five patients received new kidneys from five healthy donors in a marathon series of operations .... The procedure is known as "paired donation," a relatively new phenomenon in transplantation surgery .... None of the patients needing kidneys turned out to be compatible with his or her willing donor – a friend, spouse or adult child. But another donor was found through the paired donation process .... The 10 people from all over Northern California were required to remain anonymous to each other before the surgery, and are not permitted to contact one another until everyone agrees .... "You don't know who it is and it really doesn't make a difference .... It's a gift."
>
> *(Colliver 2011)*

Through donor chains, clinicians practice medicine as science and imitate art, and in turn, art imitates science. In parallel, those on waiting lists as well as those capable of gifting organs observe art which is likely to influence their perception of possibilities. Through art as discussed in the media, the market has the potential to influence the supply of organs gifted by donors.

In this chapter, I examine the interdependent and complex process of paired kidney donation that integrates gift and market economies to achieve organ transplantation. I describe the emergence of living organ donation, the rise of donor chains, and markets within living donation and transplantation. In closing, I discuss common good implications, and ethical considerations related to living organ donors and donor chains.

The emergence of living organ donation

The Uniform Anatomical Gift Act of 1968 regulates cadaver donations, the National Organ Transplantation Act of 1984 regulates living donor organs, and the Charlie M. Norwood Act of 2007 regulates paired donations. A characteristic shared by these regulations is that organs must be gifts and may not be sold. More specifically, these laws provide the marketplace with control over the transmission of gifted organs between individuals. These policies, critical to the development of an efficient organ donation and transplantation system, support organ gifting, yet they lag the pace of market innovation and subsequent possibilities in organ transplantation.

Cadaver donation was the first option considered in transplantation due to the availability of candidates and the lowered risk by having only one living patient (Sharp 2006). It is meant to allow for straightforward gifting: upon death, one's usable organs are gifted to allow other people to gain improved quality of life. With cadaver donors, it may be possible to gift as many as nine organs (Fox and Swazey 2002), making cadaver gifting an attractive option for the market. Given the number of deaths each day in the United States, cadaver donations theoretically could amply supply the growing demand for organs.

As direct a premise as cadaver donation appears to be, challenges are evident when loved ones are unaware of the deceased's intentions. The tragedy of a loved one dying may seem too great, and opting to donate what is perceived to be part of that individual may be viewed negatively (Sharp 2007). By giving an organ, a part of the donor literally lives on within the body of the recipient, while the recipient receives a second chance at life. The transplant occasion may provide a transformative experience for both the donor and recipient families (Sharp 1995). The attractiveness of transformation via organ donation provides motivation for some families of deceased individuals to participate in cadaver organ donation.

America's current system requires individuals to register in their state to become a cadaver donor of organs and tissue (http://organdonor.gov/become. asp), that is, individuals must choose to opt-in to participate. With an opt-out option, meaning all individuals upon death become cadaver donors, such as in Sweden, the need for organ donations could be met (Sharp 2007). In American society, it is unlikely that citizens will allow the government to control individuals' deceased bodies to support organ donation. However, it may be worth examining an opt-out versus opt-in approach to cadaver donations. Though the possibility exists, cadaver organs have yet to deliver the number of needed organs for those on waiting lists; thus the need for an alternative.

Transplanted cadaver kidneys have proven effective, yet organs transplanted from living donors show even better results (e.g., quality of organs, clinical matches, and better performance) in recipients, making them the preferred option. Market advances in clinical practice and pharmaceuticals created opportunities for living donors to supplement cadaver donors in giving life. Living donation was not a routine medical practice until the advent of medications to suppress body's natural function to attack "foreign" objects – including life-saving organs. With the development of a class of anti-rejection drugs, living organ donation became a more viable option. When living organ donors supplying organs for transplantation, there are two patients: the donor and the recipient (Murray 2004). For kidney donors, surgical innovations have progressed such that the donation is primarily laparoscopic, and thus less invasive, resulting in a shorter recuperation period (Rothman et al. 2007). For recipients, they experience improved quality of life often as soon as waking from anesthesia. A challenge with living donation is that individuals choose to direct their organ to another who may not be a match – in fact, only 25 percent of same parent siblings are clinical matches (Peters 2001).

Lives of individuals are impacted due to the gap between the supply of gifted organs and the demand for them. Where cadaver donors continue to be prevalent in the organ donation, an immediate solution is often desired, and may be sought through a living donor. The organ donation process is only viable when market and gift economies work together. Yet, this very interaction leads to questions about the inherent value of human life (Titmuss 1997). With loved ones of cadaver donors, the concern lies in how much care is given to save the life of their loved one, versus saving the life of a potential recipient (Goodwin 2006). Living donors come to the process in excellent health (or they would not have been accepted as a donor), make an undisputed choice to give, and simultaneously seek assurances that the gift of their organ will ensure enhanced quality of life for their loved one. The living donor may be an excellent candidate for organ donation, yet, they may not be an ideal donor for their chosen recipient. Thus, living donors and cadaver donors gift organs and rely upon medical practitioners (the market) to optimize the transplantation experience as good stewards of usable organs. This consumer need paved the way for a new market offering: donor chains.

Organ donor chains: Integrating gift and market economies

Organs, by law, must be gifted. The market, in turn, transplants such gifts into recipients – at times with no contact between the gift-giver and the recipient. A hallmark of gifting is that it nurtures relationships through sacrifice evident in the gift (Mauss 1967). Few gifts embody sacrifice more than gifting an organ. Gifts may be monadic (to the self) (Mick 1996; Sherry et al. 1995), dyadic (between two parties) (Belk 1996; Sherry 1983), systemic (among three or more parties) (Bradford 2009; Giesler 2006) or manifest in some combination of the three forms. Organ donation may be viewed as monadic gifting when the gift-giver does so to enhance self-esteem (Mick and DeMoss 1990). Organ donors, by definition, participate in dyadic gifting as they provide a desired object and receive gratitude

(Belk 1976; Sherry 1983). Further, individuals may participate in systemic gifting as they donate to a stranger in order to receive an organ for their loved one (Bradford 2009; Giesler 2006). Donor chains are a form of systemic gifting.

Creating a system of incompatible donor and recipient pairs is the newest way the market enables transplants. A donor chain uses a similar strategy to the paired kidney donations in that the process also requires healthy, willing, but incompatible, donors (see Figure 15.1). The chain typically is initiated by a non-directed altruistic donor. An altruistic donor is considered a donor who presents without a designated recipient but with the explicit wish to donate a kidney to someone in need of a kidney transplant. Kidneys from altruistic donors are used to initiate a cluster of kidney transplants, all for patients who have potential, but incompatible, donors. For

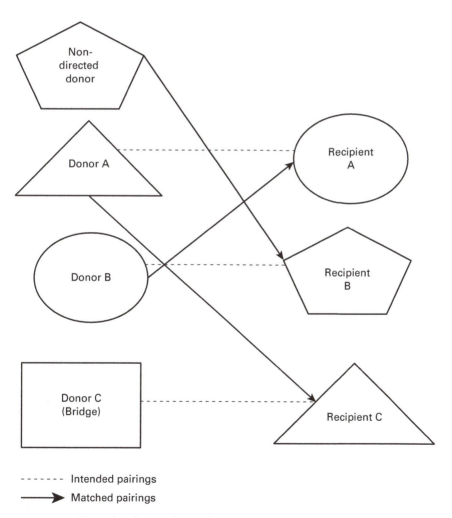

FIGURE 15.1 Example of organ donor chain.

each of these clusters, there is one potential donor who has not donated a kidney but whose partner has received a kidney. This "bridge donor" can be used to initiate another cluster of transplants. These chains can be terminated by donating a kidney to the deceased donor waiting list, or the chain can be continued by donation to another cluster of transplants. This is beneficial for the compatible donor–recipient pair if the recipient receives an immunologically better matched kidney, a younger kidney graft, or a better size-matched donor kidney. Hence, all recipients benefit by participating in such an exchange.

The market provides a mechanism for matching gifted organs with transplant recipients. The regionally networked national mechanism had been unchallenged prior to the increased availability of living donation and transplantation. While donors and their desired recipients employ the market to ascertain fit of the gift, armed with data confirming a non-fit, individuals may turn to the gift economy. Making the donation decision puts donors and recipients within the gift economy, and the market declaration that they are incompatible can lead to an exit or expansion of their participation in the gift economy. In an exit, the potential donor remains just that, with the potential unreleased, as does the potential recipient. In an expansion of participation in the gift economy, potential donors and recipients become active participants in gift networks to obtain the (near) perfect gift: a match. These individuals post their offered and sought gift specifications (e.g., blood type, tissue type) through social media sites in hopes of attracting a match for their recipient. Marketers initially used social media to educate individuals about living organ donation (e.g., Kidney.org); however, individuals have co-opted some of these forums and created an effort to accelerate the location of potential gift givers and recipients for donor chains. Social media provides individuals with more control over their consumption choices and market experiences through consumer interactions (Kozinets *et al.* in press), and increases the reach and effectiveness of gift offers and solicitations.

Potential donors participating in online donor forums are more likely committed to the living donation process, thus marketing the benefits of organ donation to them is redundant. Rather, attracting more individuals to become potential donors is necessary. Prior studies find that individuals may have difficulty in becoming an organ donor depending on how they view the parts of the self (Belk 1990; Sanner 2001; Sharp 1995). Further, some body parts may be perceived to be more of the self (Belk 1988) or representative of the self (Sanner 2001) than others. Spirituality may influence how individuals perceive gifting organs (Belk 1990; Lwin *et al.* 2002). Thus, differences in perception about the body, or spirit, may lead to different attitudes towards and outcomes for donating and receiving organs.

Signs of hope exist for increasing living donation. Most living donors, 95 percent, found the experience to be positive and claim they would donate again (Dew *et al.* 2007), given the heightened feelings of self-worth and purpose (Satel 2007). For loved ones of deceased donors, good is found through gifting to aid others in need. Is it possible that organ donation may simply need to overcome an information challenge, such as was once faced by blood banks (Waldby and Mitchell 2006)?

Markets in living organ donation and transplantation

Market exchanges represent an offering provided for an agreed price between two, often anonymous, entities. Organ transplantation is a complex and lucrative market exchange, the success of which hinges on the altruism of donors – family, friends, and now due to medical innovations, even strangers. The supply of organs is a gift that can never be repaid by recipients. This is in stark contrast to the various market participants who are (necessarily) involved to allow the gift to manifest, namely medical professionals and insurance companies. Money and prestige are likely motivators for attaining and maintaining the status of "transplant providers." And for the recipient, there can be no price placed on the improved quality of life. Thus, the two individuals at the heart of the gift exchange most likely experience the essence of gifting – the communication of care through sacrifice and gratitude in exchange. This sacred experience is bound within the market with the donor and recipient seeking means to maintain the sacred experience of life giving and life receiving, while the market is driven by technical competence for high reward.

Compensation would appear to drive the market actively to encourage transplantation, yet the alternative of dialysis, is also lucrative. One year of end stage renal disease treatment costs an average of $43,335 (Rubin 2009). With medical advances, the breakeven rate for transplants when compared with dialysis is less than two years (Schweitzer *et al.* 1998). Individuals can live out their life on dialysis, and many do, given the relatively low numbers of kidney transplants annually. Yet economic facts are insufficient to motivate gifting. A broader conceptualization of transplantation to motivate organ gifting is necessary. Such a conceptualization will likely influence policy changes as well as individual choice, with respect to organ donation.

Gifts are sacred objects used to communicate between gift-givers and recipients (Belk 1976; Sherry 1983). In modern society, these objects are often acquired in the market, yet transformed through the infusion of meaning and affect (Cheal 1988; Sherry 1983). With organ donation and transplantation, the organ is transformed, as donors make peace with parting with a piece of themselves to provide life to another. This symbolic transformation is within the realm of the sacred, though the physical transplant occurs squarely within the profane market.

Gifting, as a social process, occurs between individuals to support relationship and societal norms through the enactment of obligations to give, receive, and reciprocate (Belk 1976; Joy 2001; Mauss 1967; Sherry 1983). Organ gifting for transplantation is possible between family members, friends, and strangers. One challenge recipients hope to avoid is the *tyranny of the gift* – the emergence of a debtor–creditor relationship between recipients and donors (Scheper-Hughes 2007). Yet the rejection of a gift signals the rejection of the gift-giver (Bradford 2009; Sherry 1983; Vernale and Packard 1990). Another option is to accept gifts from strangers within our society – individuals acting as citizens working together (Allen 2004). Strangers – living or dead – may be ideal organ donors as their acts support the advancement of individuals within society, and the society itself, and reflect a citizenship obligation within society. This approach retains the gift economy as central to organ donation, yet transfers the indebtedness of gift-giving and receiving to the societal rather than interpersonal level.

Blood, like organs, must be donated. Similar to the current organ shortage, the early years of blood donation did not see high participation (Titmuss 1997). The source of the shortage was not due to technology, but rather individual perceptions of blood donation (Titmuss 1997). Changing these perceptions occurred through marketing communications such that blood donation is now perceived as a cultural norm in the United States. Though blood donation is not quite the commitment that organ donation represents, there may be an opportunity to leverage lessons to advance organ donation. More specifically, is it likely that being a blood donor is a (potential) first step to donating other types of life-giving tissues or organs? Could our understanding of marketing strategies (Lee *et al.* 1999; Murphy 1985) increase the conversion of blood donors to organ donors?

An alternative approach to a gift economy nestled within the market is to make organs available for purchase. Gifts of sperm and ova, provided for by compensated "donors" and purchased by recipients, is another form of life-giving that is gaining prevalence in the market (Hirschman 1991). These exchanges are carefully scripted to be perceived as gifts, offered to change lives and make dreams reality. Ironically, these particular donations are stored in "banks." Many believe that creating a legalized market for organs similar to the sperm and egg markets is a possible solution to the shortage of organs. Selling a part of oneself may be viewed as a defilement of the human body, though individuals participate in market exchanges for cash of cherished life-giving tissues.

The pressure to reproduce the gift by the recipient may be eliminated if a needed organ is purchased, yet other societal challenges may emerge, as those with abundant resources (e.g., health insurance, cash, social capital) will be most likely to obtain organ transplants (Scheper-Hughes 2007). Further, when behavior is motivated extrinsically (price) versus intrinsically (altruism), the system may become less effective (Rothman *et al.* 2007). An example may be found in Japan, where sales of blood from donors lead to an increase in health challenges within donor and recipient populations driven by profit motives (Titmuss 1997). Beyond access, the nature of transplantation may change. The purchase of organs may lead to donors and recipients requesting options such as warranties and performance metrics. For example, potential donors (recipients) may prefer to enter into sales contracts for their organ(s) with recipients (donors) who commit to adhere to specific patterns of behavior. Likewise, recipients' willingness to pay may be effected by donor behaviors (un)related to organ quality. Further, brokers may promote "good" organs to "good" recipients based on criteria other than clinical matches.

For some recipients, a viable alternative is to escape the gift economy (Marcoux 2009) and become a medical (transplant) tourist. These individuals work through brokers who organize all aspects of the transplant inclusive of sourcing the donor – often within the black market. The black market is fueled by economics, where (typically) poor donors sell a kidney as a means of providing for themselves and their families, a choice at times foisted upon a donor by family members (Goodwin 2006; Scheper-Hughes 2007). While recipients escape the gift economy through medical tourism, their actions merely shift rather than eliminate the societal and familial pressures of a gift economy (Scheper-Hughes 2007). To further compound the issue, donors selling their organ to help their family usually do not escape poverty and may endanger their abilities as wage earners, given employers' potential reluctance to hire them (Rothman *et al.* 2007). Finally, limiting transplants to those affluent recipients able to afford a kidney suggests that wealthy lives are the only ones worth saving.

The market and gift economies meet in organ donation

The first kidney transplant in the United States occurred between identical twins. A perfect clinical match, a willing donor seeking to save the life of his brother and best friend, and court approval were insufficient to quell the concerns of the physicians:

> Any form of medical treatment is a balance between intended good and potentially adverse effects. For the healthy donor, however, there is no physical benefit. For us surgeons who had been taught to make sick persons well, subjecting Ronald, a healthy human being, to an extensive surgical procedure required a basic qualitative shift in our thinking. To this extent, we were compromising the physicians' injunction to "do no harm." Therefore, we had to assume that the low risk to Ronald was justified by the expected benefits for Richard.
>
> *(Murray 2004: 76)*

Since this initial successful transplant, technological and legal advancements have progressed such that kidney donation and transplantation are possible options for individuals. These advances enable the realm of gift-givers to extend beyond family to include friends and more significantly strangers. Technological advances alone will not make transplantation a widely available practice. The nucleus of the transplantation is the sacrifices by individuals that are only transformed into gifts by market processes – namely matching, surgery, and insurance.

Typically, gifting is considered a social process between individuals as relationship nurturance (Belk 1976; Mauss 1967; Sherry 1983). In organ donation, a donor is legally obliged to offer their organ as a gift free of obligations and without compensation, through a market mediated process to a recipient. While donors may select a recipient upon which they seek to bestow their gift, it is market participants who ultimately decide. Where the initial conundrum was how to accept such a gift by (potentially) doing harm to a healthy individual, the current challenge is to maximize the utility of gifted organs across recipients, including the donor's desired recipient. Donor chains provide the potential to improve access to transplantation while simultaneously influencing the nature of gifting organs. Essentially, donor chains invite donors to participate in systemic gifting such that their participation ultimately benefits their recipient.

Donors, acting as members in gift economies, may choose to gift to their recipient for a variety of reasons. When a donor is found to be incompatible – essentially a rejection of the donor's gift – they may experience solace (or angst) when presented the option to participate as a member of a donor chain. Donor chains may introduce another form of the "tyranny of the gift," as the donor feels obliged to give to a stranger with the hopes that their target recipient receives their needed gift. What roles are appropriate for market participants as they attempt to transition from a dyadic to systemic gift system? When a donor decides to gift an organ to an individual, the transplantation process is straightforward and is more likely to allow the donor time to plan for the gifting process as well as healing – physically and emotionally. With donor chains, the process is more complex, as matches are orchestrated across several individuals with distinct circumstances, and may require a cadaver donor to complement the chain. While donor chains ultimately achieve the goal desired by donors (and their recipients), it is crucial that donors not feel they are held hostage while a donor chain is created. Thus, independent donor and recipient advocates to support and facilitate the process, and protect the interests of the different parties, are necessary.

The increased use of donor chains may influence how potential donors and recipients perceive their bodies. Two different views of the body are found in the literature – the body as self or as machine (Belk 1990; Sanner 2001). Modern medicine seems to advocate the view of the body as machine with interchangeable parts. Medical interventions are ubiquitous in American society as individuals desire to continue activities in spite of physical limitations due to birth defects, ailments, injury, or aging. Technological advances to save, grow, repair, or replace organs, tissues, and limbs are watched closely. These advances and their transformative powers have received media attention through factual news reports (e.g., the first face transplant, the anniversary of the first test tube baby, reports of possibilities due to tissue engineering) as well as in fictional television shows (e.g., *CSI*, *House*, *Numb3rs*, and *Grey's Anatomy*) (Morgan *et al.* 2009). Further, individuals are less likely to describe a person through their limitation (e.g., blind person) and more likely to depict the limitation as a type of possession (e.g., a person with blindness). Thus, it is worth considering the conditions under which individuals consider the body as self versus machine, and whether such a view influences donors differently than recipients in the transplantation process. Also, it is necessary to examine the experiences of loved ones of cadaver donors and their view of the body as machine or self. It is likely that the view of the body differs for living versus cadaver donors, a difference that may matter as the market solicits organ gifts.

Organ transplantation is reliant upon the generosity of individuals with their healthy organs. For the donor, the gift is not reciprocated in kind but rather through positive feelings that result from helping others. Recipients gain another chance at life. Through donor chains, these benefits are amplified across multiple families and social systems. In parallel to the gift economy, the market generates financial transactions to compensate the parties making the gift a reality. While transplantation is heralded as the best treatment option for kidney failure, many individuals remain on dialysis. The overall market supporting those with kidney failure must be examined. Though tremendous financial rewards are possible for entities supporting organ transplantation, not every hospital may be designated as a transplant facility. Thus, there is tension in the market due to competing financial incentives. Those market systems equipped and authorized to conduct transplants are likely to encourage waiting list registration for potential recipients, testing for potential organ donors, and ultimately transplantation. Those market systems where transplants are not permitted are incented to maintain individuals on dialysis to preserve a steady (and lucrative) revenue stream. More research is needed to understand the dynamics between compensation systems and market actions in support of organ donation and transplantation.

Non-profit organizations (e.g., Donate for Life, Kidney.org), state license bureaus, and the federal government (e.g., Health and Human Services) each employ market tools in attempts to increase organ donation for transplantation. While those efforts are slowly increasing awareness, many donors and recipients in the United States are turning to social media to control (Kozinets *et al.* in press) and transform the experience of organ donation and transplantation from unusual and market-driven, to normative and gift-focused. An orchestrated, market-enabled gift-centric approach to organ donation is most likely to increase the supply of organs in America, but the question of how to reach possible donors remains.

Marketing for the common good: Organ transplantation as a form of citizenry

Sharing blood, organs, or tissue to improve another's quality of life is a means of expressing belonging and citizenship (Waldby and Mitchell 2006). Blood donation has been characterized as a community service act, where one can imagine helping various unknown others in society (Waldby and Mitchell 2006). From the marriage of medical innovation and federal laws, organ donation has advanced significantly: from a court blessing allowing the gift of life between identical twin brothers, to federally regulated gifts of life between strangers brokered by gatekeepers. Organ transplantation is a particular, though generalizable, case of citizenry that represents a relationship between scientific advancements, media communications for public education, and expressions of concern for (un) known others through gifts of self.

With individuals exercising agency for their emotional and physical well-being, recipients (or their loved ones) may solicit citizens, as friends or even strangers, to participate as donors in gift systems. The potential to positively impact a larger number of lives through donor chains is one result. Donor chains introduce a new era in transplantation yet maintain prior notions of organs as gifts, and donation as citizenry. It is imperative to assess the societal benefits of transplantation within market systems, the sacrifices made by organ donors and their loved ones within gift systems, as well as the unintended consequences of the process.

One unintended consequence of the current transplantation process is that some individuals feel that lives are unequally valued such that some individuals may be left to die so that others may be saved (Scheper-Hughes 2007). Such opinions may only deepen with the increasing use of donor chains, where non-directed donors are invited and welcomed into the process. These strangers may join the process because they inherently value human life, or for other reasons unknown to those in the chain. More specifically, a donor may seek notoriety through potential recipients to amplify the donor's contribution to society by saving a life they value more highly than others, or participating in creating a new record for number of lives impacted. Where policy ensures this is not the case, public opinion prevails. Thus, an additional consideration is necessary: How should it be decided who may participate in organ transplantation? What roles for gift-givers, or market participants? Should motives be a factor to disqualify a potential donor, or market participant, even when other lives are at stake? The answers to these questions are complex, yet they point to an opportunity for marketing to be of better support to society.

Marketing, as a social process, has a role not only in touting victories but also educating citizens about opportunities to benefit society through transplantation. Marketing processes may be employed to increase the transparency of the transplantation process (i.e., the UNOS tracker of those on the transplant registry) such that as a society, we are aware more generally of the need, and specifically actions we can take to help. Individuals are increasingly using market resources (e.g., Facebook, Craigslist) to find an organ for transplant, and newspaper accounts celebrate the efficiency with which such pleas yield expedient and efficacious results. It is likely that market processes which emerge from, or coexist with policy could be improved upon by observing how citizenship is enacted through social networks and word of mouth. Such *ad hoc* approaches may provide a useful model for marketers generally, and transplant professionals specifically, to identify the necessary matches, motivate attitude change, and facilitate social benefit.

Organ transplantation is heralded as a medical miracle – one only possible through the union of technology, policy, marketing, and citizenship. As members of society, we benefit from offerings borne of this union in our everyday lives – the first American on the moon, the creation of cyberspace, and the first kidney transplant. Thus citizenship is not only about celebration, but more importantly, participation. All may not be capable of discovering innovations; however, we each have a role to play for society to attain the maximum benefit from the talents of each member, unencumbered by challenges we have the collective resources to address.

Note

1 The UNOS waiting list has 112,932 individuals (on February 8, 2012 at 4:03pm), yet the actual number of individuals is likely much larger due to the process for individuals to be put on the waiting list. Medical practitioners screen individuals based upon medical and psychosocial criteria to determine candidacy for a donor organ, and as a result of that screening, they determine whether the individual is suitable to be put on the waiting list. More specifically, individuals may meet the medical criteria and not have relevant support (e.g., financial, insurer, family) to allow them to be a viable candidate for the waiting list. Likewise, individuals may have the relevant support and a medical condition that will lead to the need for a transplant yet the individual may not have achieved the medical milestones allowing them to be considered for a transplant. These are critical issues however they are not addressed in this chapter.

References

Allen, D.S. (2004) *Talking to Strangers: Anxieties of Citizenship since Brown V. Board of Education*, Chicago: University of Chicago Press.

Aratani, L. (2009) "Dominoes align for key kidney transplant," *Washington Post*, July 8, 2009.

Belk, R.W. (1976) "It's the thought that counts: a signed digraph analysis of gift-giving," *Journal of Consumer Research*, 3 (3): 155–62.

—— (1988) "Possessions and the extended self," *Journal of Consumer Research*, 15 (2): 139–60.

—— (1990) "Me and thee versus mine and thine: How perceptions of the body influence organ donation and transplantation," in J. Shanteau and R.J. Harris (eds) *Organ Donation and Transplantation: Psychological and Behavioral Factors*, Washington DC: American Psychological Association, pp. 139–49.

—— (1996) "The Perfect Gift," in C. Otnes and R.F. Beltramini (eds) *Gift Giving: A Research Anthology*, Bowling Green: Bowling Green Popular Press, pp. 59–84.

Bradford, T. Williams (2009) "Intergenerationally gifted asset dispositions," *Journal of Consumer Research*, 36 (1): 93–111.

Cheal, D. (1988) *The Gift Economy*, Cambridge: University Press.

Colliver, V. (2011) "Hospital's 5-transplant kidney swap a state record," *The San Francisco Chronicle*, April 2.

Dew, M.A., Switzer, G.E., DiMartini, A.F., Myaskovsky, L., and Crowley-Matoka, M. (2007) "Psychosocial aspects of living donation," in H.P. Tan, A. Marcos, and R. Shapiro (eds) *Living Donor Transplantation*, New York: Informa Healthcare USA, Inc., pp. 7–26.

Fox, R.C. and Swazey, J.P. (2002) *The Courage to Fail: A Social View of Organ Transplants and Dialysis*, New Brunswick, NJ: Transaction Publishers.

Giesler, M. (2006) "Consumer gift systems," *Journal of Consumer Research*, 33 (September): 283–90.

Goodwin, M. (2006) *Black Markets: The Supply and Demand of Body Parts*, New York: Cambridge University Press.

Hirschman, E.C. (1991) "Babies for sale: market ethics and the new reproductive technologies," *Journal of Consumer Affairs*, 25 (2): 358–90.

Joy, A. (2001) "Gift giving in Hong Kong and the continuum of social ties," *Journal of Consumer Research*, 28 (2): 239–56.

Kozinets, R.V., Belz, F.M., and McDonagh, P. (2012) "Social media for social change: A TCR perspective," in D.G. Mick, S. Pettigrew, and C. Pechmann (eds) *Transformative Consumer Research to Benefit Global Welfare*, Taylor & Francis, pp. 205–23.

Lee, L., Piliavin, J.A., and Call, V.R.A. (1999) "Giving time, money, and blood: similarities and differences," *Social Psychology Quarterly*, 62 (3): 276–90.

Lwin, M.O., Williams, J.D., and Lan, L.L. (2002) "Social marketing initiatives: national kidney foundation's organ donation programs in Singapore," *Journal of Public Policy & Marketing*, 21 (1): 66–77.

Marcoux, J-S. (2009) "Escaping the gift economy," *Journal of Consumer Research*, 36 (4): 671–85.

Mauss, M. (1967) *The Gift*, New York: Norton.

Mick, D. (1996) "Self-gifts," in C. Otnes and R. Beltrami (eds) *Gift Giving: An Interdisciplinary Anthology*, Bowling Green, KY: Popular Press, pp. 99–120.

—— and DeMoss, M. (1990) "Self-gifts: phenomenological insights from four contexts," *Journal of Consumer Research*, 17 (3): 322–32.

Morgan, S., Movius, L., and Cody, M. (2009) "The power of narratives: the effect of entertainment television organ donation storylines on the attitudes, knowledge, and behaviors of donors and nondonors," *Journal of Communication*, 59 (1): 135.

Murphy, P.E. (1985) "Recruiting blood donors: a marketing and consumer behavior perspective," *Advances in Nonprofit Marketing*, 1: 207–45.

Murray, J.E. (2004) *Surgery of the Soul: Reflections on a Curious Career*, Sagamore Beach, MA: Science History Publications.

Peters, T. (2001) "Kidney transplant matching: What it means," online: www.aakp.org/aakp-library/kidney-transplant-matching/ (accessed February 7, 2012).

Rothman, S., Rozario, N., and Rothman, D. (2007) "What body parts do we owe each other?", *Society*, 44 (5): 24.

Rubin, R. (2009) "Dialysis treatment in USA: High costs, high death rates," *USA TODAY*, August 23.

Sanner, M.A. (2001) "Exchanging spare parts or becoming a new person? People's attitudes toward receiving and donating organs," *Social Science & Medicine*, 52: 1491–99.

Satel, S. (2007) "Desperately seeking a kidney: What you learn about people – and yourself – when you need them to donate an organ," *The New York Times Magazine*, December 17, 62–67.

Scheper-Hughes, N. (2007) "The tyranny of the gift: Sacrificial violence in living donor transplants," *American Journal of Transplantation*, 7: 507–11.

Schweitzer, E.J., Wiland, A., Evans, A.D., Novak, M., Connery, I., Norris, L., Colonna, J.O., Philosophe, B., Farney, A.C., Jarrell, B.E., and Bartlett, S.T. (1998) "The shrinking renal replacement therapy 'break-even' point," *Transplantation*, 66 (12): 1702–08.

Sharp, L.A. (1995) "Organ transplantation as a transformative experience: anthropological insights into the restructuring of the self," *Medical Anthropology Quarterly*, 9 (3): 357–89.

—— (2006) *Strange Harvest: Organ Transplants, Denatured Bodies, and the Transformed Self*, Berkeley and Los Angeles: University of California Press.

—— (2007) *Bodies, Commodities, & Biotechnologies: Death, Mourning & Scientific Desire in the Realm of Human Organ Transfer*, New York: Columbia University Press.

Sherry, J.F. (1983) "Gift giving in anthropological perspective," *Journal of Consumer Research*, 10 (2): 157–68.

——, McGrath, M.A., and Levy, S. (1995) "Monadic giving: Anatomy of gifts given to the self," in J.F. Sherry, Jr. (ed.) *Contemporary Marketing and Consumer Behavior: An Anthropological Sourcebook*, Thousand Oaks, CA: Sage, pp. 399–432.

Titmuss, R.M. (1997) *The Gift Relationship: From Human Blood to Social Policy*, New York: The New Press.

Vernale, C. and Packard, S.A. (1990) "Organ donation as gift exchange," *Journal of Nursing Scholarship*, 22 (4): 239–42.

Waldby, C. and Mitchell, R. (2006) *Tissue Economies: Blood, Organs, and Cell Lines in Late Capitalism*, Durham, NC: Duke University Press.

16

ETHICS IN SELLING

A case-oriented, stakeholder-focused approach

John A. Weber

This chapter explores research in educational psychology and learning theory in a search for insights to enhance corporate ethics training. Useful educational principles uncovered are then applied to the development of an ethics training initiative for sales professionals. A specific case example is included – suggesting in some detail how the educational principles discussed might be integrated into sales ethics and broader corporate ethics training initiatives.

Introduction

Research suggests that corporate ethics training can positively influence ethical behavior in the workplace (Ferrell *et al.* 2012; Murphy *et al.* 2005). Reflecting this, formal corporate ethics training, often mandatory, is now common in companies around the globe. Ethics training also occurs less formally through the publicizing of ethics policies and codes and the encouraging of all employees to carefully review ethics handbooks and related video. In large corporations, most of the current ethics training is conducted online, usually on an annual basis. Likewise, dedicated phone lines offer assistance to employees confronting an ethical dilemma and ethics newsletters have become common ethics training supplements. The rationale for greater emphasis on ethics training is that employees who are exposed to realistic scenarios and questions about company policies will be less likely to commit ethical transgressions in the future.

Goals of corporate ethics training

Kohlberg's theory of "cognitive moral development" provides useful perspectives for identifying appropriate goals for corporate ethics initiatives, including ethics training programs (Kohlberg 1969; Narvaez and Rest 1995; Ferrell *et al.* 2012; Murphy *et al.*

2005). The inference of Kohlberg's model for corporate ethics is that some managers are less sophisticated than others in terms of the considerations they bring to bear on business decisions with potential moral consequences. Managers at the low end of the cognitive moral development spectrum tend to make moral judgments as to what is "right" based primarily upon egoistic self-interest. Managers at higher levels of moral development take more factors into consideration in determining what is right – factors such as potential impact on others, both inside and outside of their immediate corporate environment. In a recent text on ethics in marketing, Kohlberg's theory suggests that values, ethical sophistication, and related ethical behavior of managers can advance over time with maturity, experience, and education. Ethics training can play an important role in that moral maturation process. For business researchers, as well as those charged with designing corporate ethics initiatives, the critical question becomes whether measures of individual cognitive moral development are good predictors of ethical behavior in a business organization.

Most experts agree that an individual's cognitive moral development does indeed play a role in how his or her values and actions are shaped in the workplace (Ferrell *et al.* 2012). We move forward making that assumption. Therefore, to the degree that one accepts Kohlberg's theory, a reasonable operational goal of corporate ethics training initiatives is to help individual managers move out on the cognitive moral development spectrum – taking more "other-oriented" factors into consideration in determining what is "right." That progression should, in turn, enhance the ethical business behavior of affected managers by stimulating them to go well beyond self-interest when making business decisions that have moral implications.

Marketing managers differ in moral imagination and development

Organizations seeking to instill improved ethical reasoning in their managers should recognize that managers differ in their ability to evaluate and resolve ethical issues. This is because, owing to different life experiences, individual core values, and human character, the quotients of moral sensitivity and capability differ from manager to manager. Murphy *et al.* (2012) offer a framework (based on Kohlberg 1969) for explaining this variance in moral sensitivity and capability among managers – recognizing four broad types of managers. These include:

- *egoist/relativist* managers – who use their own immediate interests or societal norms to determine what is right or wrong;
- *legalist* managers – who espouse the law as their guide to the moral propriety of any action;
- *moral striver* managers – who consider multiple stakeholders (i.e., empathy for others) when adjudicating what constitutes moral propriety;
- *principled* managers – who address ethical dilemma by applying both prevailing ethical norms and applicable laws to determine what is right or wrong (Murphy *et al.* 2012: 18–19; Kohlberg 1969).

Moral strivers and stakeholder analysis

Murphy *et al.* (2012) conclude that the majority of managers are of the *moral striver* type – i.e., who consider multiple stakeholders (i.e., empathy for others) when assessing the moral propriety of any given action. Utilizing a stakeholder analysis can help to clarify this situation for the moral strivers.

A stakeholder is any individual or group that can affect or be affected by a relevant decision. From a corporate point of view (that is, going beyond ethics *per se*), companies find it helpful to distinguish among more important and less important stakeholders in terms of their potential impact (positive or negative) on the company and its performance. Typical corporate stakeholders might include stockholders, managers, peers, other employees, suppliers, customers, family, friends, industry groups, host communities, and other parties. Because most stakeholder groups can potentially affect a company's business for better or worse, it is no accident that more and more companies are accepting the stakeholder concept and are developing pro-active strategies for important stakeholder groups (Carroll and Buchholtz 2003; Murphy *et al.* 2005). To implement this "stakeholder analysis" and related strategies, a company might take steps such as: identifying more important stakeholders and the company's responsibilities to each; identifying potential opportunities or conflicts with each stakeholder group; and developing and implementing creative, pro-active strategies for taking advantage of opportunities and eliminating potential conflicts with each stakeholder group.

One effective way to use stakeholder analysis in corporate ethics training is to pose specific corporate ethical dilemmas (e.g., in short case group discussions) and then ask participants to identify and discuss how alternative choices might potentially impact different stakeholder groups. (Carroll and Buchholtz 2003; Weber 2003, 2007) This approach offers an opportunity to stimulate participating managers to draw from their previous experience. In doing so, they can provide explicit examples of negative business, professional, or personal impacts that can result from ignoring certain stakeholder groups when making specific business choices. The over-riding lesson should be clear to discussants – not considering others can be bad for company business and can also negatively impact one's professional career and personal life.

Positive lessons to be drawn from stakeholder analysis are even more important. The discussions of stakeholder impacts should bring to the floor examples and general recognition of how considering other affected groups or individuals when making difficult moral choices can engender the trust and confidence of relevant stakeholder groups. That trust and confidence, in turn, can yield significant long-term dividends for one's business, career, and personal life.

In sum, stakeholder analysis discussions provide an opportunity for managers to realize that becoming more "other-oriented" in evaluating alternatives (i.e., moving further along the cognitive moral development continuum) makes good sense from both business and personal points of view.

Integrating stakeholder analysis into an ethics training initiative for sales professionals

Why ethics training for sales professionals?

Since the salesforce most directly connects the company and the customer, the relationship between the salesperson and the customer offers each firm an important potential opportunity to demonstrate a commitment to integrity. Unfortunately, however, this key relationship between company and customer has been compromised in many ways. The selling profession in general has long been plagued with rampant criticisms for mal-intention, manipulation, fraud, lying, and generally compromised behavior (Li and Murphy 2012). Whether or not justified, salespersons and professional selling in general have been heavily and regularly criticized by the public at large. The negative stereotyping of sales-persons has resulted from anecdotal stories of flagrant sales abuse in selected industries. Unethical selling behavior gains further exposure and credence from stories of alleged selling abuse regularly appearing in newspaper reports and evening news stories, from multiple horror stories of friends and colleagues and, perhaps above all, from one's own unsatisfactory personal experiences with sales-persons in everyday life.

Overall, the salesperson suffers from a general image as one who is too willing to compromise integrity for company or personal gain. This sullied reputation in the primary link between the company and the customer is hardly a formula for building any company's overall image of corporate integrity. The goal here is to design a training program that can help a company to enhance the morality of everyday selling decisions. This, in turn, can potentially help the company to wit-ness a culture of integrity. As summarized in Box 16.1, consider a few of the many ethical issues that can arise during the selling process. The table indicates that there are eight areas in the selling process with two to four specific situations where unethical behavior might arise.

The first set of scenarios pertains to the "opportunity identification" stage of the selling process where salespeople consider how to select and approach potential customers with a sales message. The third and fourth group of ethical issues focuses on "stimulating awareness" and the "first sales contact" stages where salespeople can take advantage of customers due to lack of experience, creating concerns where none existed and feigning interest in topics to build rapport. The latter stages of "negotiation and closing" as well as "sales management" present equally difficult ethical challenges in trying to induce the buyer to say "yes" and the use of quotas by sales managers as a way to place pressure on the salesperson. These short sce-narios cover both retail and business to business selling situations. Themes regarding unethical behavior that cut across the stages are bias, misrepresentation, exaggera-tion, downplaying negative aspects of the product, and unwarranted enthusiasm. (If the reader is interested in more details about any of the situations, the author is willing to provide them.)

BOX 16.1   EXAMPLES OF SOME SELLING ETHICS ISSUES

Identifying opportunities

- *Selling out-of-date product.* A retail sales person knowingly tries to sell an overstocked, soon to be out-of-date product at full price, specifically targeting an uninformed customer.
- *Inefficient use of selling time.* An industrial product sales person, who regularly exceeds her quota by far, uses a good portion of her workday pursuing a personal hobby (golf), with full knowledge that her sales manager expects that she is out selling.
- *Customer profiling and related prejudice.* A retail sales manager tells a retail sales associate not to "waste time" on a potential customers who are not well dressed and, who the sales manager projects, will purchase very little, if anything at all.
- *Variable offers.* A retail sales person purposefully fails to offer a customer a better price, simply because the customer is unaware of the special coupon available (under the counter) for anyone who asks.

Background research and pre-call planning

- *Presenting false or misleading information on the company's own products or services.* A salesperson presents the information on the company's market offer in the best possible light – in a manner that could easily lead a customer to think the product's price performance is better than it will prove to be, once purchased and used.
- *Vaporware.* In order to keep from losing a long-time customer to a competitor that is adding an important new capability, a salesperson suggests that her own firm will introduce its own similar upgrade in the near future (even though she has no idea of her own firm's plans in this area).

Stimulating awareness and interest

- *Taking a potential customer from latent pain to pain.* A sales person attempts to cause concern or stress for a potential buyer by bringing from unconsciousness to consciousness a pain that the buyer almost certainly does have (e.g., someone 100 lbs overweight considering a health spa membership).

(Continued)

- *Providing unproven, exaggerated, or false reference stories.* A sales associate exaggerates her own background and experience in order to qualify for a potential new position or promotion.
- *Using unauthorized, proprietary information to stimulate interest.* A salesperson uses unauthorized, proprietary information about a current customer in order to impress a potential new customer.
- *Tech talk – stimulating interest with purposefully incomprehensible jargon.* A salesperson takes advantage of the inexperience of a customer by using technical jargon to up-sell the customer to purchase much higher end product than truly needed by the customer.

First sales contact

- *Insincerity in rapport building.* In order to help build rapport, a salesperson feigns significant interest in a hobby of known interest to a prospective client.
- *Presenting your company only in its best light, while purposefully camouflaging the shortcomings of your company's market offer.* A salesperson purposefully fails to provide the full picture of her market offer to the prospective customer, hiding important post sale costs from the buyer.
- *Purposeful delay in divulging solution cost.* A salesperson purposefully delays telling the prospective customer the total cost of a solution – waiting until she has a chance to build a more complete vision of the total value of the solution offered.

Vision building

- *Misguiding the buyer.* A sales person tries to steer a prospective buyer toward purchasing her company's solution, knowing full well that a competitor has a more appropriate solution for a buyer.
- *Enhancing stress and anxiety as an integral part of the selling process.* A salesperson with a sincere goal of helping the prospective buyer, knowingly and purposefully goes to extremes in pain building and anxiety creation in order to get the sale.
- *Selling unproven solutions.* A salesperson, having successfully helped the prospective buyer arrive at a vision of a solution, suggests that her company can indeed provide the set of capabilities necessary to match the customer's new vision – when she really doesn't know at this point whether or not she can put together a package of such capabilities.

Finding and accessing power and proof management

- *Using biased references.* A salesperson focuses only on the strong points of the company's relevant market offer – in this case, by offering a biased sample of reference clients.
- *Purposefully overlooking or downplaying transition issues.* A salesperson makes a sale knowing full well that the buyer will have significant difficulty in implementing the solution successfully – not informing the buyer of that likely difficulty.

Negotiation and closing and following through on a sale

- *Trying to close a deal prematurely.* Salesperson uses "tech talk" and multiple (true) reference success stories to try to catch the customer off guard and close a substantial deal before the buyer has a chance to fully exercise responsible stewardship and consider all the details of a final proposal.
- *Using gratuities to influence a prospective customer.* The salesperson offers a substantial gratuity to the prospective buyer – intended as personal benefits for key decision makers in order to try to sway the buying decision to favor of the salesperson's market offer.
- *Providing incomplete solutions.* A salesperson knowingly sells the customer an incomplete solution, forcing the customer to come back for expensive add on options after the initial sale.

Managing the process – sales management

- *Sandbagging to reduce quota for next year.* In order to relieve pressures that can come from being asked to make a higher and higher quota each year, the sales person hides orders from sales management until start of next quarter or next year.
- *Setting artificially high quotas.* In order to improve the probability of achieving one's own assigned sales objectives, a sales manager artificially inflates the sales targets for each sales rep.
- *Going great! – the "sunshine pump."* For fear of incurring sales manager wrath or pressure, the salesperson knowingly lies about how well a particular sales effort is proceeding.
- *Favoritism by sales manager.* Sales manager offers prime potential accounts to a particular salesperson because of personal friendship.

A selling ethics training initiative using stakeholder analysis: A case study approach

Active small group discussions of selling ethics cases form the heart of the selling ethics training initiative outlined here. The design integrates stakeholder analysis, given its potential for helping to move individual salespersons along the moral continuum.

A short case such as the one appearing below is read by participants. The facilitator then introduces questions that provide clues to help participants identify the multiple potential moral ramifications that can be involved in what, at first, may seem to be straightforward selling decisions. In the case discussions, individual participant's initial views are both informed and enriched by the views of others within the group setting. Causal relationships, stimulated by the specific case questions, are discussed. Moral development begin to occur as views emerge regarding what criteria are felt (individually and by the overall group) to be the most important determinants of whether or not a specific selling practice crosses self-set or group-set "ethical boundaries."

Case example

The following case, on negotiation and closing, illustrates the different dimensions of gift-giving: intention, amount, and timing.

Golfing for dollars – H.C. Hunt

Heather Danner has just moved from Grand Rapids to Kalamazoo, Michigan to become the new National Accounts Sales Manager at H.C. Hunt, a brake parts manufacturer. Hunt sells brake pads and related parts to OEM brake manufacturers, directly to the new automobile makers, and in the aftermarket. Currently, Heather is trying to get distribution for Hunt brake pads in Dad's Parts, a national retail auto parts distributor serving the automobile aftermarket. This could be a huge step forward for Hunt. Heather's immediate boss, Hunt President Ron Blankenship, has instructed Heather to "pull out all the stops" to try to get this business.

On Monday morning, Heather meets with Jeff Snyder, VP of Procurement for Dad's Parts. Fifteen minutes into the meeting, it has become clear to Heather that Jeff is quite pleased with his two current brake pad suppliers and feels he does not need yet another one. During this brief introductory discussion, Heather sees several golf trophies as well as a putter and a practice cup along one side of Jeff's office. Heather is the reigning Lady's City Champion in Grand Rapids and really knows the game. She tries to build rapport with Jeff by talking about golf in general, revealing that she has a three handicap and asking him about local courses where she might play now that she has moved to Kalamazoo. After this cordial side discussion, Heather then enthusiastically launches into a short presentation showing the comparative durability of Hunt pads versus the competition. Swayed by their rapport as well as by the convincing statistics, Jeff agrees to tour the Hunt plant later this week (on Friday) and to continue the discussion with Hunt about possibly becoming a Pep Guy's supplier.

Upon her return to the office, Heather reports her tentative success to her boss, Ron Blankenship. Ron, himself also a golfer, suggests that Heather select an appropriate golfing-related gift to send to Jeff just prior to his upcoming visit to Hunt. The purpose is to soften Jeff up and make him more favorably disposed toward more serious consideration of and hopefully eventually approving Hunt as a new Dad's Parts supplier.

Case discussion

Lessons hopefully "self-discovered" by participants through the case discussion are drawn from the group and concisely summarized by the facilitator in a debriefing session (with the focus being on stakeholder analysis). Participants are expected to come to a conclusion regarding the three aspects of gift-giving outlined above – intention, amount, and timing.

Wide-ranging potential stakeholder impacts

The next potential lesson is self-discovery of the benefits of methodically considering how a single integrity compromise can potentially impact a very wide range of stakeholders. This outcome is intended as the primary lesson of this particular

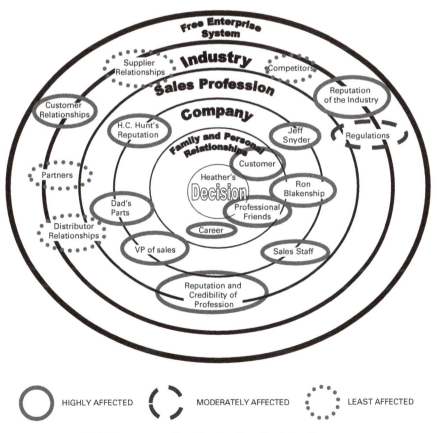

FIGURE 16.1   Stakeholder impact chain for "golfing for dollars" case.

sales training initiative. Building and discussing the "Stakeholder Impact Chain" for the case can enlighten participants by helping them to realize the wide range of stakeholders who can be negatively impacted by gift-giving. Figure 16.1 is used to stimulate the group discussion of stakeholder impacts.

Other learning points

Wide range of integrity issues

Another potential lesson learned is self-discovering the benefits of becoming more aware of the wide range of and ethical dilemma that can arise as a normal part of the selling process (recall Box 16.1 above). The minority who do not perceive an integrity issue in this case (even with the trip to the Masters) is likely surprised to learn that some colleagues feel an integrity issue is indeed involved – even if the gift is only a relatively inexpensive book or a dozen golf balls. Arguments likely to be advanced by those considering the acceptance of any gift to create a situation where the recipient is putting him/herself in a position of "owing" something to the gift-giver.

Identifying one's own integrity guidelines, standards, or principles

Self-discovery of the benefit of identifying what principles (if any) one uses to try to address moral selling dilemma (virtue/duty-based, golden rule, newspaper test, circumstantial, net positive result, etc. – see Murphy *et al.* 2005) serves as another potential lesson. Most participating in the session are likely to be surprised if even one of their colleagues holds to a value-/duty-based integrity standard that disallowed *any and all gift-giving* as a vehicle for trying to influence a sale. On the other end of the spectrum, some in the group typically hold a very loose integrity/ethical standard that allows them to feel comfortable doing pretty much whatever is necessary to get the business, as long as it does not violate the law. Most participants recognize that gift size and timing do affect whether or not a specific gift offer compromises integrity.

Benefits of creative search for alternative behaviors or approaches

The next potential lesson is self-discovery of how pausing and brainstorming for alternatives when facing difficult moral selling dilemma can generate innovative alternatives. For example, a facilitator can ask subsets of the overall group to each brain-storm for creative alternative selling tactics that would clearly not compromise integrity while still moving the selling process forward. Individual sub-groups come up with creative positive alternatives not thought of by other groups. This experience highlights the benefits of stopping, pausing, thinking, and talking with colleagues about alternatives before jumping at the easiest alternative when facing potential moral selling dilemma. (This process is described as "when in doubt, don't" in the ethics literature – see Murphy *et al.* 2012: 24.)

Benefits of a corporate code of (selling) conduct in domestic and foreign markets

Yet another potential lesson is self-discovery of the benefits of having a corporate code of selling conduct. Discussants from different companies are asked to assess their corporate codes of conduct – being encouraged to give positive testimony regarding the benefits of their companies' aggressive enforcement of detailed codes of selling conduct in particular. These professionals emphasize that the very existence of specific codes and standards not only makes their moral selling choices much easier with respect to gift-giving, but also *stimulates them to think of other, more positive ways to influence customers*. The group as a whole is typically impressed to hear specific stories about how the very existence of a company's code of selling conduct can actually help nurture more solid, longer term, productive relationships with specific domestic and international customers.

An alternative to creating a separate code of ethics for selling is to discuss the four areas shown in Box 16.2. This is a type of ethical audit for selling that could be used in sales meetings and regular staff discussions about the impact of selling activities. It extends the stakeholder analysis discussed above (although the second point focuses specifically on stakeholders) and encourages salespeople and sales managers to evaluate the full range of activities including intentions, means, and ends (#1), as well as both intended and unintended consequences of sales actions (#3 and #4).

BOX 16.2   A FRAMEWORK TO EVALUATE SALES ETHICS

The following points capture the highlights of this approach:

1 Actions with ethical ramifications have at least three components: (a) the intent behind the action, (b) the action itself (the means), and (c) the outcomes that flow from that action. In considering the ethical propriety of an action, one must consider all three components. Thus, scrutiny of what the sales rep *does* (the action) alone is too limited. One must also look at the intent preceding the action and any subsequent outcomes.

2 If the action results in a substantial negative outcome or any stakeholder, it is almost always unethical. For example, if a salesperson engages in bid-rigging (the means) with the outcome of driving competition from the marketplace, the action is unethical (a significant negative outcome), even though the by-product may be the provision of some product to customers at a currently lower price (a good outcome). Similarly, even if a sales rep has made full disclosure (an appropriate means), it would probably be

(Continued)

(Continued)

unethical to sell a buyer a product that had attributes that the buyer simply did not need (a negative outcome).

3 If there are unintended side-effects (outcomes) to an action taken by a salesperson and these side-effects cause a *major* negative outcome, the action is almost always unethical. Suppose the sales representative of a pharmaceutical firm has been providing experimental drugs to a research institute to be used in animal research. In the course of the sales process, the salesperson learns that the drugs are to be used on human subjects. In such an instance, it may be unethical to go ahead with the transaction, because the side-effects of the sale could produce significant negative consequences for other individuals (the unsuspecting human subjects). Major negative side-effects, even if unintended, must be avoided.

4 Almost any action can have unintended side-effects. He or she may take an action having side-effects if the foreseen consequences of that side-effect are *minor*. For example, in making a sale to a buying organization, a sales rep may learn that the sale will result in a competing salesperson losing a sales contest involving an overseas trip. Obviously, it would still be ethical for the salesperson to complete the transaction even though there would be a negative consequence for his or her counterpart. Minor negative side-effects, when not the purpose of the action, can be tolerated.

Source: Caywood and Laczniak (1986).

Summary and conclusions

In recent years, corporate scandals have created a negative view of large corporations and their leaders. As a response to this crisis, companies are renewing efforts to practice and publicize their integrity in their dealings with all constituencies. Companies have appointed ethics officers for the purpose of policing and promoting ethical behavior. Companies have also created rules or codes of ethical conduct and developed mandatory ethics training initiatives to help ensure that the commitment to integrity is taken seriously at all levels of the organization.

The chapter has suggested that the application of selected principles from learning theory and educational psychology can help in developing effective corporate ethics training initiatives. The specific training approach described uses an inductive, case-based discussion process focused on stakeholder analysis to help participants come to their own personal conclusions about what are "right" and "wrong" business decisions. An example of the proposed approach was provided, in the form of applying stakeholder analysis in an ethics training initiative designed specifically for sales professionals.

Evaluating the impact of selling actions on stakeholders relates closely to the theme of the book regarding the common good. If multiple stakeholders are delineated, examined, discussed, and ultimately engaged, this process should yield benefits not just to the company and its sales force but the members of the overall community as well. To the extent that sales organizations follow ethical procedures and are honest and transparent with their customers, this too promotes the common good because it leads to a more trustworthy social system. The role that ethics and sales training plays in this process should not be understated. As mentioned in the opening of this chapter, salespeople are too often associated with high-pressure, unethical and, some would say, unsavory, actions. To the extent that more ethical sales departments and companies become the rule than the exception going forward, the common good of society is advanced. This will be a challenge in the future as the move toward a global marketplace will place pressure on salespeople to act in unethical ways (Li and Murphy 2012).

Sales organizations that follow the Kohlberg approach to moving their members along the continuum toward more principled behavior with a sales training process like the one describe in this chapter contribute to the common good by making their employees less selfish. This process will have spillover effects on society where individuals who are encouraged to act in an ethical manner at work will probably do so in their personal lives as well. The Kohlberg approach is a secular version of the principles of Catholic Social Thought that were discussed in Part III of this book. As mentioned there, the common good is a guiding principle for ethical behavior. In sum, training sales employees to be broader thinkers by recognizing and responding to all relevant stakeholders contributes to both the organizational and societal common good.

Questions for discussion

1 *Intention of the gift.* Is the gift intended to make Jeff feel indebted – thus potentially affecting his buying choice?
2 *Size of the gift.* At what value does a gift prior to a sale become a bribe? Would it be an inappropriate gratuity and, therefore, compromise integrity if:

   * Heather sent Jeff a $15 book by Bob Rosburg on putting? Why or why not?
   * Heather sent Jeff a dozen Titliest Pro V golf balls (worth about $50)?
   * Heather and Ron invited Jeff and a friend for a round of golf at Heather's Boss Ron's exclusive golf club in Kalamazoo (worth about $280)?
   * Heather and Ron invited Jeff and a friend to the second round of the Masters golf tournament, all expenses paid (a $2,000 value).

3 *Timing of the gift.* Is gift-giving prior to a sale more ethically problematical than gift-giving after a sale?

References

Carroll, A.B. and Buchholtz, A.K. (2003) *Business and Society: Ethics and Stakeholder Management*, 5th edn, Cincinnati, OH: SouthWestern Publishing Co.

Caywood, C.L. and Laczniak, G.R. (1986) "Ethics and personal selling: '*Death of a Salesman*' as an ethical primer," *Journal of Personal Selling & Sales Management*, 6 (August): 81–88.

Ferrell, O.C., Fraedrich, J., and Ferrell, L. (2012) *Business Ethics: Ethical Decision-Making and Cases*, 9th edn, Boston, MA: South-Western College Publishing.

Kohlberg, L. (1969) "Stage and sequence: The cognitive developmental approach to socialization," in D.A. Goslin (ed.) *Handbook of Socialization Theory and Research*, Chicago: Rand McNally, pp. 347–480.

Li, N. and Murphy, W.H. (2012) "A three country study of unethical sales behavior," *Journal of Business Ethics*, 111 (2): 219–35.

Murphy, P.E., Laczniak, G.R., Bowie, N.E., and Klein, T.A. (2005) *Ethical Marketing*, Upper Saddle River, NJ: Pearson Prentice Hall.

——, ——, and Prothero, A. (2012) *Ethics in Marketing: International Cases and Perspectives*, New York: Routledge.

Narvaez, D. and Rest, I. (1995) "The four components of acting morally," in W.M. Kurtines and J.L. Gewirtz (eds) *Moral Development – An Introduction*, Boston, MA: Allyn and Bacon, pp. 385–99.

Weber, J.A. (2003) "Integrity in selling," paper presented at a special session, American Marketing Association Summer Educators' Conference, August 18.

—— (2007) "Business ethics training: insights from learning theory," *Journal of Business Ethics*, 70 (January): 61–85.

17

DISCERNING ETHICAL CHALLENGES FOR MARKETING IN CHINA

Georges Enderle and Qibin Niu[1]

Introduction

Over ten years ago, on November 10, 2001, China was formally approved to enter the World Trade Organization (WTO). Since then, China has experienced a rapid economic rise. "This growth surprised the world, and it has even gone beyond Chinese expectations," said Long Yongtu, the former minister of Foreign Trade and Economic Cooperation and one of the four heads of China's delegation to the WTO negotiations. China's GDP surged to 40 trillion yuan (6.29 trillion USD) in 2010, from 11 trillion yuan in 2001, making the nation the world's second largest economy (China Watch 2011: 2).

Along with this stunning growth, marketing has become a multi-billion (dollar) business.[2] It has brought about far-reaching changes in how customers and citizens in China perceive business activities and evaluate the reputation of enterprises. While the levels of information and access concerning products and services have significantly improved and marketing has become aesthetically better – compared with the beginnings of the economic reform and opening-up in the 1980s – one should also mention that the last ten years have brought about a plethora of marketing scandals increasingly reported in the media in China and abroad.

Scandals have broken in a wide range of industries and among Chinese and non-Chinese companies alike. Some concrete examples may illustrate the pervasive lack of ethics in marketing:

- the melamine-tainted milk scandal (Santoro 2009: 49 ff.);
- supplier fraud at Alibaba.com, which provides business-to-business services on the internet (sources of Alibaba case);
- Baidu selling links to unlicensed medical sites with unproven claims for their products (sources of Baidu case);

- Baxter International selling the blood thinner heparin with contaminated ingredients produced in China (Santoro 2009: 47 ff.);
- Carrefour using misleading price tags and fake discounts (sources of Carrefour case);
- Walmart labeling ordinary pork as organic (sources of Walmart case);
- Groupon China selling fake Tissot-branded watches (*Financial Times* 11/8/2011: 17);
- Da Vinci claiming fake production location (in Italy) and selling counterfeit products (sources of Da Vinci case);
- double standards in marketing practices of multinationals in China (Nestle, HP, and Toyota; Wu *et al.* 2011);
- Otis running unsafe escalators (sources of Otis case);
- fraudulent listing of Chinese stocks in the US capital market (Liu *et al.* 2011);
- Foxconn's exploitative working conditions with ten young workers killing themselves (sources of Foxconn/Apple case);
- Apple's supplier responsibility with Foxconn and Unitec (sources of Apple case);
- the Jilin chemical plant explosions and subsequent toxic pollution of the Songhua river (sources of Jilin case);
- ConocoPhilips's oil spills in the Bohai Bay (sources of ConocoPhillips case).

This is not a new problem as further examples from the 1990s can be found in Ryan *et al.* (2000: 73–84, 179–88) and Xu Dajian (in Lu and Enderle 2006: 144–50).

Despite this multitude of scandals, little attention has been paid, until now, to a more systematic approach to marketing ethics in China. The most recent survey on business ethics in research, teaching, and training in China shows that this topic area is addressed quite rarely (see Zhou *et al.* 2010). Marketing ethics is not mentioned at all in teaching and ranks 16th out of 17 positions as topics in training. As a theme in research, it ranks 23rd out of 48 positions before finance (33rd) and accounting (37th). And even if other topic areas related to marketing ethics (such as corporate social responsibility and business ethics) are included, study and training in marketing ethics are still in their infancy.

Therefore, the time appears to have come to more clearly perceive a need for marketing ethics in China and to deepen its understanding. This chapter attempts to discern several ethical challenges for marketing in China. It uses a framework for international marketing ethics developed elsewhere (Enderle 1998) and applies it to a selection of cases, some mentioned above. The sample includes both negative and positive cases from Chinese and non-Chinese companies operating in China. Although the framework was designed for international marketing, it is also relevant for the Chinese context, given China's close connections with international business through the WTO. The emphasis of the article is placed on discerning rather than meeting those challenges, on the assumption that identifying and understanding the problems are indispensable first steps before these problems can be solved. Of course, resolving ethical problems remains the ultimate purpose of marketing ethics.

The framework consists of four ethical guidelines, which capture the fundamental features particularly relevant to marketing activities. Each highlights a specific dimension with a certain value, which is interconnected with the other dimensions: communication, human development, cultural and religious embedment, and the natural environment. We do not claim that there exist no other important dimensions or that we could dispose of the key concepts of ethics such as "responsibility," "justice," "rights," and "avoiding harm." Rather, these concepts are, in one way or another, included in the guidelines and would need explicit consideration in other studies. They would also draw on the growing literature of marketing ethics in general and business ethics in China in particular.[3]

The four guidelines are:

1   practicing honest communication;
2   enhancing human capabilities;
3   fostering creative intercultural diversity;
4   promoting sustainable growth and eco-efficiency.

In the following, each guideline is briefly characterized and subsequently applied to a few cases. The article concludes by sharing a few research perspectives.

Practicing honest communication

Communication is the lifeblood of marketing. It flows through all types of activities and affects sellers and buyers alike. Communication is a two-way process in which each side collects, transforms, and provides information. Thus, it comes as no surprise that communication is subject to all kinds of uses and misuses. Some people argue that communication in itself be "value free," and only the use of it should be considered an "ethical issue." While not denying the instrumental value of communication, the very use of communication presupposes some "intrinsic value." Otherwise, communication cannot take place. Simply speaking, a liar can only lie if his statement pretends to be true in itself.

Sissela Bok, who has written extensively on lying and deceiving, states,

> the potential for deceit is present in all communication between human beings. The intentional effort to mislead people – whether labeled deceit, fraud, duplicity, or lying – constitutes the simplest and most tempting way of making people act against their will. In turn, it gives rise to the most common reason of distrust.
>
> *(Bok 2001: 378)*

So the question arises how to define "honest communication." Three points of clarification are suggested. First, we may recall that communication can involve *multiple errors* such as acoustical and visual misrepresentations, linguistic ambiguities, errors in translation, and intercultural barriers. In all these cases, communication is ethically questionable only if it is intended to mislead. (This, however, does not nullify the ethical requirement to reduce these errors as much as possible.)

> It is only when human beings purposely distort, withhold, or otherwise manipulate information reaching others so as to mislead them that we speak of *deceit* or *intentional deception*. Intentional deception may be nonverbal in form, as when messages are conveyed by gestures or false visual clues, or verbal. When a speaker makes a statement in the belief that it is false and with intention to mislead the listener, we speak of *lies*.
>
> *(Bok 2001: 379)*

Hence, an unintentional false statement is not necessarily a falsehood or a lie.

Second, further qualification is needed about making, or abstaining from, statements. Many intentionally false statements, like jokes, rhetorical flourishes, or works of fiction, are not intended to mislead listeners and, therefore, are not deceitful. On the other hand, true statements can be meant to deceive when one deliberately conveys excessive, confusing, correct, but nonetheless partial information, knowing that the listener will not be able to interpret it correctly. Also, silence can be deceitful if it conveys a message intended to mislead.

> Third, according to Bok, the term "honesty" is a broad one and

> "characterizes a person of integrity and trustworthiness who avoids, not only lies, nor only intentional deception, but also theft and other forms of betrayal. Conversely, "dishonesty" refers to the disposition to lie, deceive, steal, cheat, and defraud more generally than "deceitfulness", which concerns primarily the disposition to deceive.
>
> *(Bok 2001: 380)*

By qualifying the first guideline as "honest communication," therefore, both the "messages" and the "messengers" (be they persons or organizations) are at stake.

Given our focus on marketing ethics in China, a further question arises about how to understand "honest communication" in the Chinese cultural context that, undoubtedly, deeply influences the ways of communication. How should the characteristics of Chinese communication be taken into account?

As Ge Gao, Stella Ting-Toomy, and William B. Gudykunst point out,

> [C]ommunication is a foreign concept to the Chinese; no single word in Chinese serves as an adequate translation for the term …. The three most commonly used translations include *jiao liu* (to exchange), *chuan bo* (to disseminate), and *gou tong* (to connect). *Gou tong*, the ability to connect among people, is the closest Chinese equivalent for communication as it is usually used by Western scholars.
>
> *(Gao et al. 1996: 280 f.)*

The authors then identify five characteristics of Chinese communication (pp. 283–92): (1) Implicit communication, which is a mode of communication (both verbal and nonverbal) that is contained, reserved, implicit, and indirect, so one does not spell out everything, but leaves the "unspoken" to the listeners; (2) listening-centeredness, which reflects an asymmetric style of communication between those who are entitled to speak (parents, teachers, rulers) and those in subordinate positions who are supposed to listen; (3) politeness, which applies to all interpersonal interactions and concerns all parties involved; (4) the insider effect on communication, based on the distinction between insiders and outsiders, where communication within the group can be very personal and emotional as opposed to that outside the group; and (5) face-directed communication strategies, in which face management is essential to maintaining the existing role relationship and preserving interpersonal harmony.

Obviously, when communicating in China, these characteristics have to be taken into account. Do they redefine the understanding of honest communication outlined above? Certainly, they help specify important aspects of honest communication in China. But, in our view, they do not contradict its core meaning of refraining from intentional efforts to mislead people in order to make them act against their will. Bok's cautioning against multiple errors is particularly relevant for intercultural communication, in which misunderstandings abound. False statements are not necessarily lies. Even many intentionally false statements such as jokes and rhetorical flourishes are not intended to mislead listeners and, therefore, are not deceitful. On the other hand, true statements or even silence are no guarantee for honest communication; neither is implicit communication. They can be meant to deceive nevertheless. Also, deception is possible with listening-centeredness where subordinates tend to not voice their views. Despite politeness in language and behavior, listeners can be misled intentionally. The insider effect on communication can be honest within the group and deceitful to outsiders. Face-directed communication strategies can be pursued in order to maintain existing roles and preserve harmony, in spite of contradicting evidence.

As "honest communication" encompasses both the message and the messenger, a misleading message can shed light on the messenger and potentially disqualify him or her. In turn, a person of integrity will make sure that his or her message is not misleading. This connection between message and messenger appears particularly important in the Chinese cultural context, which greatly values interpersonal relations as distinct from anonymous market relations. It has to be taken into account when discussing the following cases.

Baidu under fire on ads

The first case is about ethics in e-commerce, a growing concern of China's rapidly expanding internet. Baidu, the nation's dominant search engine, has built its share of China's search market up to over 70 percent since Google's high-profile exit in 2010. In the last few years Chinese Central Television (CCTV) reported several stories in which Baidu was accused of unethical behavior (see sources of Baidu case):

- In 2008, CCTV aired an exposé on Baidu selling links to unlicensed medical sites with unproven claims for their products. The company's Nasdaq-listed shares subsequently fell as much as 40 percent, and its fourth-quarter revenues were 14 percent below the mid-point of the company's original forecast, prompting Baidu Chief Executive Robin Li to publicly apologize. Moreover, Baidu had overhauled its operations and sacked staff involved.
- In 2010, a report by CCTV accused Baidu of promoting counterfeit drugs through its web search engine, a promotion that duped more than 3,000 people in China. The report was aired on Sunday, July 18. Baidu declined to comment on the accusation. As a result, Baidu's shares fell as much as 4 percent on Monday.
- In 2011, CCTV aired a report asserting that Baidu continues to allow sellers of fake medicines to advertise on the site. The program showed a reporter trying to buy ads for a fake company selling weight-loss drugs – and a Baidu staffer aiding the reporter in getting around checks on pharmaceutical advertisers by registering as a machinery company and changing its keywords later. The report also asserts that Baidu's bidding system for keywords leads companies to bid more than necessary to get high-ranking search results. Since the report was broadcast, shares of the Nasdaq-listed company have lost nearly a tenth of its value, or five billion US dollars in just two days.

We now may ask whether and, if so, how, Baidu violated the guideline of honest communication. One could argue that Baidu is only a middleman between the companies who offer the medicines and the patients who seek them, and it is up to either side to take responsibility to sell safe drugs and to exercise due diligence when buying them. One could add that it is the government's role and responsibility to enact and enforce laws and regulations in order to ensure the safety of drugs and medicines. So how persuasive are these arguments?

While, undoubtedly, the sellers and buyers as well as the government bear some ethical (and legal) responsibility, this does not mean that the middleman – Baidu in this case – has no ethical responsibility at all. To the extent of its space of freedom, Baidu bears ethical responsibility as well (see Enderle and Murphy 2009: 510–13). The company was instrumental in providing false and potentially harmful information to large numbers of people; this undermined, by the way, its reputation as a trustworthy information provider. As the third incident in 2011 indicates, Baidu failed not only by negligence but also by a deficient corporate culture that did not place the needs of the customers ahead of the needs of the marketer. In addition to misleading messages, the integrity of the messenger, that is of the internet search company, was impaired. In sum, it appears fair to state that Baidu engaged in dishonest communication or, as defined above, participated in "intentional efforts to mislead people [in order to make them] act against their will" (Bok 2001: 378).

Da Vinci labeling domestic goods as foreign

As China has become the manufacturing leader of the world and "made in China" products can be found everywhere, a fashionable trend has emerged among Chinese consumers to buy products from developed countries. In particular, newly rich Chinese are eager to shop for high-end luxury goods from abroad. This trend was perceived by Da Vinci, a high-end furniture company in China, which sells very expensive furniture. A silk-covered couch, for example, is priced around 110,000 yuan (or 16,975 US dollars). Alluding to its name, Da Vinci claimed that its products were made in Italy and manufactured of rare wood (see sources of Da Vinci case).

For six months, a reporter of CCTV investigated over 100 furniture factories to find the secret of the Da Vinci code: fake production location and counterfeit products. CCTV reported that some of Da Vinci's expensive furniture labeled as foreign products was not manufactured abroad but in Dongguan, Guangdong province. Moreover, some furniture claimed to be made of rare wood was actually made from polymer and other chemicals, and some so-called "hand-carved" furniture was made by machine.

A salesman from the factory in Dongguan told CCTV that the factory has taken orders from Da Vinci since 2006 and produced three "brands" of furniture – Riva, Hollywood Homes and Cappelletti. Unknown to the owners of the Riva and Cappelletti brands, the trade totaled about 50 million yuan in 2010. The furniture manufactured for Da Vinci was shipped as "made in China" furniture from Shenzhen's harbor to Italy and later delivered to Da Vinci's storehouse in Shanghai as "made in Italy" products. As *China Daily* later learned, this salesman who blew the whistle was sacked by the factory, which stated that "he told lies to the media about our company's relationship with Da Vinci."

The Da Vinci story is a relatively clear-cut case and shows that deception can only work as long as people believe that the labeling is truthful. It is noteworthy that the factory's statement claims to tell the truth by qualifying the whistle-blower as a liar. Obviously, to learn the truth matters.

Carrefour overcharging customers

Honest communication is not only an issue for Chinese companies, but also for foreign companies in China. The French retailer Carrefour entered China in 1995 and has now more than 150 stores in various cities (see sources of Carrefour case). On January 26, 2011 the National Development and Reform Commission said in a statement that 11 Carrefour stores and some other retailers were overcharging customers and urged local authorities to take action.

The practices included referring to normal prices as sales prices, charging more than what was listed on price tags, and misleading customers with price figures typed in different point sizes. These kinds of overcharging happened all over the country: in three stores in Shanghai, three in Central China's Hunan province, two in Southwest China's Yunnan province, two in Guangzhou, and one in Beijing.

The stores were fined up to 500,000 yuan (or ca. 79,365 USD) each for violating the PRC's Price Law, a fine which was the highest ever imposed in China for such malpractice. The punishment was accompanied by a blitz of bad publicity both in the local press and on the internet.

To sum up, this case illustrates bad marketing behavior that provides intentionally misleading information on price.

Walmart labeling ordinary pork as organic

In fall 2011 the US retailer was ordered to close seven stores in the city of Chongqing in south-western China (see sources of Walmart case). A number of store managers were detained, following allegations that employees had labeled ordinary pork as organic.

Since earlier that year a scandal broke involving a toxic additive fed to pigs in China, labeling meat as organic has become a way of boosting sales. But "the problem in China is we have no central [organic] certification authorities," Mr. French, a marketing consultant in Shanghai, said. "A thousand pounds in an envelope will get you the certificate you need" (*Financial Times*, October 11, 2011).

According to Huang Bo, head of the industry and commerce bureau, Walmart has been punished 21 times in Chongqing since 2006 for violations such as false advertising and mislabeling products. In the latest episode, Walmart was fined 2.69 million yuan (423,548 USD) according to Xinhua, the official Chinese news agency.

Conclusions

As these four cases of Chinese and non-Chinese companies demonstrate, "practicing honest communication" is a first, important guideline for marketing ethics in China. The examples discussed are relatively straightforward. Although all of them occurred in China, the ethical issues at stake do not appear to be basically altered by the Chinese cultural characteristics mentioned above. Moreover, they can be legislated and they are to some extent, but the strictness and the enforcement of the legislation certainly leave room for improvement. In more complex situations, the discernment of honest communication might be more difficult and harder to legislate. The ethical commitment that is required from companies becomes even more important when regulation is not likely to occur.

Enhancing human capabilities

While communication between persons and organizations is fundamental to any business and marketing activity, it does not answer the question of its purpose itself. Communication for its own sake does not suffice. Therefore, we should ask directly about the purpose and objectives of these activities. These answers, of course, vary greatly according to the specific circumstances and levels from very specific to very general objectives. The following guidelines necessarily are quite general. They relate to the three basic categories "people," "culture," and "nature."

As for the category "people," the term "human development" will be used here, which, according to the definition of the United Nations Development Program, can be applied to any situation in developing and developed countries and, therefore, is much more operational. The short definition of "human development" is "to enlarge people's choices," which basically involves longer life expectancies and economic as well as educational improvements (UNDP 1990: 10). It takes a "humanitarian" perspective that primarily considers human beings as ends rather than mere means.

Amartya Sen's "capability approach" can further clarify the concept of human development (see Sen 1999, 2009; Enderle 2013). It is guided by the idea that each human being should have the freedom to achieve well-being. Well-being is assessed by the concept of "functionings," while freedom to pursue well-being is conceptualized by "capabilities."

> The relevant functionings can vary from such elementary things as being adequately nourished, being in good health, avoiding escapable morbidity and premature mortality, etc., to more complex achievements such as being happy, having self-respect, taking part in the life of the community, and so on.
>
> *(Sen 1992: 33)*

Living is seen as a set of interrelated functionings of persons, consisting of their beings and doings. Closely related is the notion of capability to function, which represents the various combinations of functionings and reflects the person's freedom to lead one type of life or another. In other words, the person's freedom and empowerment imply not only having the choice, but also having the capacity to exercise that choice.

The second guideline requires the enhancement of human capabilities. If the concept of marketing aims at preserving and enhancing the customer's and society's well-being (as Philip Kotler's concept of societal marketing demands; Kotler 1998), it also needs a clear and operationable understanding of well-being. The capability approach greatly helps in clarifying and strengthening this understanding.

Otis escalator safety in spotlight

Otis, the world's leading elevator and escalator manufacturer, was put in the spotlight when a 13-year-old boy was killed and 30 others injured, three seriously, because a "crowded" ascending subway escalator suddenly reversed direction (see sources of Otis case). The escalator accident occurred on July 5, 2011 at the Beijing Zoo Line 4 (Station Exit A). Since this line opened on September 28, 2009, it carried 400 million passengers until May 2011.

Photographs by witnesses posted online showed discarded shoes, bags, and flattened bottles scattered at the bottom of the escalator. Several people, lying or sitting on the bloodstained floor, were being helped and comforted by members of the public. Fu Jinyuan, one of the injured, recalled the moment when the escalator malfunctioned, while receiving treatment at Peking University People's Hospital. "First there was a crashing sound, then the rising escalator started going down. Then wave after wave of people began falling. I thought I was finished" (*China Daily*, July 6, 2011).

Based on its initial investigation, the Beijing Bureau of Quality and Technical Supervision said the Otis model (513 MPE) had design flaws and the company was inescapably responsible for the accident.

This was not the first Otis escalator accident recently in China. On March 25, 2011, 61 children were injured when an escalator suddenly stopped within the Wuxi Zoo in Jiangsu province. On December 14, 2010, 24 passengers were injured when an escalator also reversed direction in a Shenzhen subway station in Guangdong province.

As these accidents show, safety of escalators (and one may add, of elevators) has become a very sensitive issue and affects a growing urbanized population which experiences steady advances in mass transportation. People demand nothing less than zero-tolerance for failure, and companies in the escalator and elevator industry are well advised to put safety above all profit considerations (as, for example, Kone Corporation does; www.kone.com). Safety standards for escalators and elevators should not depend on particular cultural attitudes or specific levels of economic development. There are no "Chinese" standards versus "American" or "European" standards. Rather, the standards for product safety are about human life; or, in terms of Sen's capability approach, what is at stake is people's capability of being transported safely without threat of being injured or killed.

Working conditions at Foxconn led to ten suicides of young workers

From January to May 2010, Foxconn's factory in Shenzhen witnessed a rash of suicides whereby twelve workers jumped from the tops of buildings, ten of them to their deaths (see sources of Foxconn/Apple case). Taiwan-registered Foxconn is the world's largest electronics maker, with more than 920,000 employees (2010) including 300,000 in Shenzhen; it is a major supplier of Apple. The young workers (between 18 and 24 years) were desperate, feeling like machine parts in an assembly line, reliant on long hours of overtime to scrape together a meager salary. They belonged to the second generation of migrant workers who have a lower salary compared with their parents' generation (when adjusted for cost of living then and today).

For example, the breakdown of a Foxconn worker's paycheck in November 2009 was as follows (*The Other Side of Apple* 2011: 16):

- basic salary for 21.75 normal workdays: 900 yuan (ca. 135 USD);
- normal overtime 60.5 hours for overtime pay: 469 yuan (ca. 68 USD);
- weekend overtime 75 hours for overtime pay: 776 yuan (ca. 110 USD);
- total pay per month: 2,145 yuan (ca. 313 USD).

These suicides and the miserable working conditions provoked vehement and widespread reactions in the media not only against Foxconn but also against Apple. They shed a glaring light on the violation of the basic dignity of workers and their labor rights. In terms of Sen's capability approach, the workers lacked the capabilities of earning a decent livelihood, enjoying a reasonable amount of leisure time, being mentally healthy, not suffering from unbearable stress, and being respected as a human being, in addition to other capabilities.

Not only Foxconn but also Apple was held ethically responsible for these wrongdoings, the first as immediate perpetrator and the second because of its powerful position in the supply chain. Although Apple did not formally accept responsibility, it responded to the suicides at Foxconn in multiple ways, summarized in a special section of the *Apple Supplier Responsibility: 2011 Progress Report* (pp. 18–19). In June 2010, Apple COO Tim Cook and other Apple executives visited the Shenzhen factory and met with Foxconn CEO Terry Gou. In July 2010, an independent team of experts investigated the circumstances of the suicides, and in August 2010, it presented its findings and recommendations. The recommendations included psychological help such as counselors, a 24-hour care center, better hotlines, an employee assistance program, and even large nets to the factory buildings "to prevent impulsive suicides;" however, economic improvements were not mentioned.

As this case makes clear, global corporations and their suppliers share moral responsibility to ensure that the workers are able, in Sen's terms, to produce under fair and safe working conditions.

Fostering creative intercultural diversity

The third guideline further develops the second one by explicitly addressing the crucial, yet often overlooked, role of cultural diversity in international business and marketing. Based on the UNESCO Report (1995), three fundamental, culture-related features can be identified:

- Culture is *more than a mere means* to achieve economic growth. "Culture's role is not exhausted as a servant of ends – though in a narrower sense of this concept this is one of its roles – but is the social basis of the ends themselves" (UNESCO 1995: 15). Hence, it follows that marketing should not use culture merely as a means to achieve economic growth.

- Cultural *growth* needs to be promoted actively:

  > Culture is the foundation of our progress and creativity. Once we shift our view from the purely instrumental role of culture to awarding it a constructive, constitutive, and creative role, we have to see development in terms that encompass cultural growth.
  >
  > *(UNESCO 1995: 15)*

- Hence, the question arises as to what marketing can and should contribute to cultural growth.
- Although the global context includes an immense variety of cultures, the focus on economic globalization tends to ignore this rich variety and imposes a new kind of "cultural imperialism" (by flooding, for example, Asian countries with Hollywood movies). As a reaction to this trend, "cultural isolationism" arises in many countries, which rejects any influence from abroad (an extreme case being North Korea). Therefore, *both* respect for other cultures and the will to learn from them are necessary to foster creative intercultural diversity. Hence marketing faces the challenge of resisting global pressures and avoiding global neglect, which threaten the peoples' capability to define their own basic needs.

illycaffe promoting a culture of coffee in China

Since ancient times China has cherished a culture of tea so that, today, one can find hundreds of varieties of tea with an incredible range of taste – some may cost thousands of yuan for 100 grams – comparable to the abundance of types of grape vines. In contrast, the development of a culture of coffee in China is in its infancy. Only an average of 25 grams of coffee per person per year are consumed in this country, which is a huge contrast to other countries such as the United States with 8 kilograms and Finland, the leader in coffee consumption, with 13 kilograms.

Therefore, it takes a great deal of courage and entrepreneurship to build up a coffee culture in China. In fact, the Italian company illycaffe, founded by Francesco Illy in 1933, pursues the bold mission "to produce the best coffee in the world" by generating value for all the stakeholders involved (see sources of illycaffe case). Each must be able to draw satisfaction and benefits: economic, social and environmental benefits for the consumers, the customers, the collaborators, the suppliers and the community with which the company interacts and, finally, the shareholders. illycaffe exports to over 140 countries in all five continents. It established "the University of Coffee" in Trieste with branches throughout the world, including a "University" in Shanghai (in 2006). "The courses are structured in relation to the public they address: coffee growers; entrepreneurs and bar staff, restaurants and hotels; consumers and curious enthusiasts, all of them attentive and keen on increasing their knowledge of the world of coffee" (www.illychina.com). In 2001, under the name of Shanghai Fortunecaffee, illycaffe entered mainland

China and became a joint venture with illycaffe s.p.a. in 2006. It has now 16 sub-dealers around the country.

In its endeavor to spread the coffee culture in China, illycaffe does not consider Starbucks a competitor. Rather, it welcomes Starbucks with its aggressive expansion as a trail-blazer while remaining convinced that its own blend is the best in the world and will persuade more and more Chinese consumers to become users, thanks to its superior quality.

Given illycaffe's outstanding products, innovative policies, aesthetic sensitivity, sustainability focus, and ethical culture, it appears fair to say that this company makes a valuable contribution to China's cultural diversity. It respects the traditional tea culture. At the same time, it enriches the Chinese consumers' choices by offering high-end coffee produced in a sustainable fashion.

Fuda's "good people" culture with Chinese characteristics

Shanghai Fuda Group, a medium-sized company in the conveyor belt industry, was founded by Mr. Li Yuan in 1992 and has developed, under his leadership, as a successful role model of a Chinese private enterprise that has put into practice its economic, social, and environmental responsibilities in many innovative ways (see Lu *et al.* 2012). The drive for innovation has deeply shaped Yuan's understanding of the entrepreneur's mission, Fuda's strong "good people" culture, its products and processes, its well-conceived responsibilities toward stakeholders, and its organizational structures. Over the years, the company has received an impressive range of awards and recognitions.

Fuda can be seen as an outstanding example to illustrate in many respects the third guideline "to foster creative intercultural diversity." The company's culture is not only a means to achieve economic growth, but is the foundation of its identity and purpose. With foresight and persistence, it has been developed and enriched over 20 years and thus outlived by far the average 4-year life-span of Chinese private enterprises. It has successfully avoided both being "colonialized" by globalization and being "insulated" within a narrow traditional Chinese mindset.

Intercultural diversity is manifest in Fuda's promoted ethical virtues and values. According to Yuan, the entrepreneur has to be a person with a high spirit of innovation, professionalism, and a sense of social responsibility, exemplifying the four Chinese "Qis," namely magnanimity (*daqi*), loyalty to friends (*yiqi*), a sense of chivalry (*xiaqi*), and amity or harmony (*heqi*). At the same time, the "good people" culture advocates and incorporates the universal values of kindness, trustworthiness, and gratitude, which are expected from everybody in the company, from the president and the managers to the shop-floor workers.

These ethical virtues and values are specified in Fuda's responsibilities toward suppliers, customers, employees, society, and nature, and permeate its organizational structures. To be fair to suppliers entails relations based on mutual respect to ensure truthfulness in terms of pricing, purchasing, bargaining, quality, competitiveness, and reputation. With the help of "conferences of qualified suppliers", long-term and stable cooperative relations have been established. In the course of opening markets and maintaining customer relations, Fuda has gradually formed persuasive and effective marketing policies by providing high quality products and service in accordance with the requirements of customers; by launching strong after-sales services and modifying products and management strategies in a timely fashion, if needed; and by establishing stable social relations and ties with customers by family-oriented and user-friendly efforts in order to consolidate aggressively and expand steadily the customer base through forthright interactions.

As Yuan has often recalled, networking with all stakeholders is of vital importance, particularly in the Chinese context where *guanxi* (that is, relationships) play a central role. It is precisely this focus on relationships which indicates why ethical virtues and values matter so much. They have to be practiced while accounting for the characteristics of Chinese communication discussed above.

Intercultural diversity, furthermore, comes to the fore in Fuda's organizational structures. While the company is a modern private joint-stock company subject to the market forces, the people-orientation has led to the expansion of the employees' economic and social rights within the company and to the creation of a cooperative system with harmonious capital–labor relations (comparable to the "social partnership" between capital and labor in Germany's social market economy). Building up the dominant position of employees, Yuan has followed the Chinese saying that "rivers (i.e., companies) are full as long as creeks (i.e., employees) have water," which means Fuda can be rich only if its employees become rich. In other words, it is about "storing wealth into the mass." This promotes enthusiasm of the employees and motivates them to do their best to develop the enterprise actively and positively as one person.

In the pursuit of sharing wealth, several provisions were introduced: 50 percent of profit sharing with employees in the form of bonuses; general wage raises every two years; a management-buy-out to form independent affiliates with their own leaders; and a democratic procedure to elect the president of the company group.

Surprising to western and even Chinese observers is the establishment of a number of committees across Fuda, which follow some management practices of traditional state-owned enterprises (inspired by Yuan's former experience in the state-owned Shanghai Rubber Belt Factory). Although the company is a private enterprise, it has a council of worker representatives (in addition to the council of shareholder representatives), a labor union and even a committee of the Communist Party of China. The justification of this organizational structure lies in the "good people" culture. The stronger this culture is, the more decentralized the organization can be and the more employees can be empowered to participate in the company's endeavors.

In sum, Fuda represents an excellent example of using its space of freedom to the fullest extent possible and assuming its responsibilities with great imagination in order to combine Chinese traditional culture, universal values, and modern management and marketing practice.

Promoting sustainable growth and eco-efficiency

Given the increasing ecological awareness and debate around the world, it becomes almost a truism that all economic activities are intrinsically and inescapably embedded in nature. Whatever decision economic actors make and whatever action they take is related to the "environment."

Fortunately, there now exists a widely, at least theoretically, accepted general standard of environmental soundness. The World Commission on Environment and Development defines "sustainable development" as a style of progress or development that "meets the present without compromising the ability of future generations to meet their own needs" (WCED 1987: 8). Growth, then, will have to be extremely "eco-efficient," which combines economic and ecological efficiency. It is "a process of adding ever more value while steadily decreasing resource use, waste, and pollution (Schmidheiny and Zorraquin 1996: 5).

In order to operationalize sustainability and eco-efficiency, many proposals have been made, including early ones by Van Dieren (1995), Hammond *et al.* (1995), Schmidheiny and Zorraquin (1996), DeSimone and Popoff (1997), and the Sustainability Guidelines of the Global Reporting Initiative (GRI), which have been continuously improved since 1997. It is fair to say that today sustainability and eco-efficiency have become serious concerns in public debates: see, for instance, Westra (2005), Newton (2005, 2010), Rogers *et al.* (2006), DesJardins (2007), Collier (2010), Rivera (2010), and UNDP (2011). By now, a great range of environmental tools and strategies are available for those who want to commit themselves to sustainability and eco-efficiency: see, for example, McDonough and Braungart (2002), Laszlo (2005), and Esty and Winston (2006).

Baosteel and Haworth – champions of environmental responsibility

To illustrate the growing acceptance and use of the Sustainability Guidelines of the Global Reporting Initiative (GRI), two examples are presented briefly: Baosteel (or Baoshan Iron & Steel Co., Ltd.) and Haworth, in particular Haworth Asia Pacific.

Baosteel, headquartered in Shanghai, is a state-owned enterprise, founded by Deng Xiaoping in 1978, which has become the second-largest steel producer in the world in 2011 (see sources of Baosteel case). It started publishing annual environmental reports in 2003. From 2005 on it compiled the annual Sustainability Report in accordance with the GRI Sustainability Guidelines (the G3 version since 2007). It mainly addresses economic, environmental, social, and other activities of Baosteel and its 13 branches and subsidiaries.

The 2010 Sustainability Report (see www.baosteel.com) includes 18 chapters on topics such as governance structure, management improvement, anti-corruption, innovation development, harmonious development, and social responsibility. The chapter on environmental protection (pp. 38-48) is particularly relevant with regard to the fourth guideline. It begins with the statement that "our goal is to build a global leading clean steelmaker." Although the term "eco-efficiency" is never used, the idea of combining economic and ecological efficiency clearly runs all the way through the chapter regarding management guidelines, management structure and responsibilities, the systems of environmental and energy management, and education and training thereof. As for the concept of sustainability as defined by the World Commission on Environment and Development, neither this chapter nor the report in general addresses this issue. It only speaks of enhancing Baosteel's "sustainable" core competitiveness and building the company into the world's most competitive steelmaker" (pp. 3-4).

Haworth International, Inc. is a privately held global corporation, headquartered in Holland, Michigan, USA, serving the contract market with furniture and workspace interiors (see sources of Haworth case). The division of Asia Pacific, Middle East, and Latin America is located in Shanghai. Haworth has a strong sustainability vision that goes beyond eco-efficiency. Processes must be neutral or improve the environment. Haworth strives to balance economic, social, and environmental responsibilities. It describes its inspiration as "nature, science and a commitment to future generations" and defines its commitment as "our sustainability journey." "Haworth will be a sustainable corporation." "As always, there is more to do, yet we are pleased with our progress." (Haworth 2011, Sustainability Report: 1-2).

Like Baosteel, Haworth started publishing annual sustainability reports in 2005 with consideration for the GRI Sustainability Reporting Guidelines. In its 2010 Report it explicitly highlights GRI content throughout the document. In addition to social responsibility and stakeholder engagement, environmental responsibility plays a particularly important role and is explained in great breadth and depth, covering sustainable products and workplace design, energy management, green transportation, zero waste and emissions, and green building and sustainable site management. While there is certainly still room for improvement, Haworth has made great strides toward being a sustainable corporation.

Pollution spreads through Apple's supply chain

While Baosteel and Haworth can be seen as champions of environmental responsibility, sharp criticism has been raised against Apple and its suppliers in China by a group of Chinese environmental non-governmental organizations (NGOs; see sources of Apple case). As already mentioned in the Foxconn case, the IT industry investigative report *The Other Side of Apple* was published on January 20, 2011, accusing Apple of violating, in its supply chain, not only occupational safety and labor rights and dignity but also seriously harming the environment. Apple responded to those accusations, to some extent, in its *Apple Supplier Responsibility: 2011 Progress Report* (February 2011), but did not explicitly address the criticism concerning environmental wrongdoings. In August 2011, a second report *The Other Side of Apple II* followed, focusing entirely on the spread of pollution through Apple's supply chain. Ten case studies were presented that revealed the following malpractices: shocking levels of environmental pollution, causing direct harm to the community, huge amounts of hazardous waste leaving hidden dangers for China, more pollution records in Apple's supply chain, and Apple's audits covering up blood-stained production. Three months later, five Apple employees met with nine representatives of the NGOs' report in Beijing.

Although the controversy is not settled yet (as of the end of November 2011), one can already discern several ethical challenges. As Apple continues to expand, its environmental impact, outsourced to China and other countries, becomes greater and more unmanageable. At the same time, internal opposition in China is growing through aggressive environmental groups and green coalitions like the *Green Choice Initiative*, which includes already about three dozen NGOs. Apple has to decide how seriously it wants to engage in stakeholder dialogue. Given its power to control the production processes of its suppliers and its dominance over the distribution of profits, Apple has to make up its mind to what extent it should take responsibility for the environmental as well as social and economic impact in its supply chain. Having publicly stated its commitment to "driving the highest standards of social responsibility throughout our supply base" and that its suppliers "use environmentally responsible manufacturing processes wherever Apple products are made" (*2011 Progress Report*: 3), Apple bears the ethical obligation to live up to those standards. Moreover, while many other IT companies operating in China actually explicitly name their suppliers, Apple maintains a culture of "secrecy" and has refused to disclose its suppliers. The discrepancy between Apple's public commitment and actual environmental performance and the lack of transparency amount to deceiving its customers and other stakeholders, thereby violating the guideline of honest communication.

ConocoPhillips's oil spill in China's Bohai Bay

In summer 2011, an oil spill from an offshore field operated by ConocoPhillips China, a subsidiary of the Houston-based energy company ConocoPhillips, lasted three months, leaked about 3,200 barrels of oil and mud from oil, and polluted at least 5,500 square kilometers (or 2,124 square miles). It was China's worst offshore accident, although not the country's worst oil spill, which happened in 2010 in a PetroChina port facility in the city of Dalian and amounted to more than 11,000 barrels of oil (or, according to Greenpeace, to 430,000 – 650,000 barrels of oil).

To understand the backdrop of this offshore accident, one may recall a couple of circumstances. With its booming economy, China is in urgent need for new energy resources. The oil field in the Bohai Bay, discovered in 1999, is one of the largest in China. Lacking up-to-date technology, China has lured foreign companies such as ConocoPhillips, Anadarko, BP, and Husky Energy to form joint-ventures with China National Offshore Oil Corporation (Cnooc). So the offshore Peng Lai oil field is run in a venture that gives Cnooc 51 percent ownership and ConocoPhillips a 49 percent stake as operator. Because of a series of environmental disasters such as the BP oil spill in the Gulf of Mexico and the Fukushima Daiichi nuclear meltdown in Japan, environmental awareness has significantly risen in China, as in other parts of the world. Moreover, lagging somewhat behind, the state regulators have become stricter and set tougher rules for offshore drilling, and foreign companies are a ready target.

Without investigating the case in further detail, one can discern the following ethical challenges. First, it is imperative to realistically assess the extent and seriousness of the oil spill as it is unfolding in each phase. Second, the ethical responsibilities of all major actors involved in the spill have to be clearly identified as well as the ways they are to be shared in joint-ventures between majority shareowner and operator, between regulators and regulated firms and industries, between the media, academia, NGOs, and other actors in society. Third, the involved companies and regulators must disclose all the relevant facts in a timely and honest way in order to restore and maintain trust in the population. Fourth, appropriate measures have to be taken to repair the harm inflicted on community residents and natural environment and to prevent similar disasters in the future.

Conclusion

With the help of four ethical guidelines and several positive and negative concrete examples of Chinese and non-Chinese companies, we have attempted to provide a broad and timely, but far from complete, view on marketing issues in China and to discern their ethical challenges. Admittedly, most of these cases are relatively straightforward and not too difficult to address. But we hope they can help clarify some basic concepts and lay a solid foundation for further developing marketing ethics in the Chinese context.

We may conclude by indicating a few perspectives for further development. First, the very concept of marketing is of paramount importance for a well-founded understanding of marketing ethics. If marketing is conceived in a strictly instrumental way or as a body of merely logistic knowledge (that is, what Amartya Sen calls an "engineering approach"), ethical guidance can come only from "outside" the field and expertise of marketing. A more promising and more realistic concept follows an "ethics-related approach," in which intrinsic values, human motivations, and the assessment of social results play an indispensable role "within" marketing.

Second, marketing ethics cannot consist of a case-by-case approach, offering nothing more than case solutions. Rather, more systematic efforts are needed. For this purpose, "mid-level principles" should be elaborated, which are determined by both general ethical principles and practical and theoretical marketing expertise. In such a way a robust concept of marketing ethics can, so to speak, "walk on two legs," namely, a normative-ethical and a descriptive-analytical "leg." We think, for example, of human rights as proposed by the United Nations Framework for Business and Human Rights (UN 2011) and Sen's capability approach, on the one hand, and Kotler's concept of societal marketing, on the other.

Third, to understand the ethical dimension in mid-level principles, it will be crucial to distinguish three kinds of ethical obligations (De George 1993: Chap. 10); otherwise, there is confusion in talking about "ethics," demanding "ethical conduct" from companies, or blaming marketers for "unethical behavior." The first includes *basic ethical norms* such as not to deceive customers; the second involves *positive obligations beyond the minimum*, for instance, to respect and support in principle a host country's culture; and the third relates to *the aspiration for ethical ideals*, which, for example, may mean a company taking a leadership role in promoting sustainability. This distinction provides a more sophisticated understanding of "ethics and values" and is particularly relevant in international business and marketing, in which the search for both a common ethical ground and the respect for pluralism is quite complex and difficult.

Finally, marketing ethics shouldn't be content with analyzing its challenges in ethical and marketing terms. As the very understanding of ethics requires, it is about what we ought to do. Its ultimate purpose is to recommend thought-through and practice-tested solutions for the multifarious challenges of marketing ethics. Undoubtedly, like any other country, China needs this commitment.

At the end of this article, the reader may ask how this chapter relates to the overall theme of this book "Marketing and the Common Good." The short answer is, the four guidelines can provide direction for marketing toward "the common good." Of course, there is a large variety of meanings of the common good, and one can argue that the term is too nebulous in order to be helpful. In the Aristotelian and Scholastic traditions as well as in the tradition of the Natural Law, the common good is the purpose of the "polis" (or the political body) and of society, for which the government is responsible and to which the various social actors have to contribute in their own ways (Braybrooke and Mohanian 2001). On these views, the common good is the well-being of the society as a whole, which includes the well-beings of its members, but is more than the aggregate of its individual well-beings. In the history of political philosophy, the latter notion has been advocated by utilitarianism and contract theories (mostly individualistic philosophies). The former notion has been taken up by Catholic Social Teaching, particularly since the papal encyclical *Rerum Novarum* in 1891, and significantly modified up to the definition of the common good stated in the *Pastoral Constitution on the Church in the Modern World* in 1965. There, the common good is defined as "the sum of those conditions of social life which allow social groups and their individual members relatively thorough and ready access to their own fulfillment" (*Gaudium et Spes*, No. 26). It is noteworthy that this understanding applies not only to the nation states but also to the regional communities and humanity as such. The four ethical guidelines of practicing honest communication, enhancing human capabilities, fostering creative intercultural diversity, and promoting sustainable growth and eco-efficiency aim to specify, to some extent, "the common good" as it is proposed in this definition.

Notes

1   We would like to thank Pat Murphy for his idea to apply the framework for international marketing ethics to China and also for his and John Sherry's helpful suggestions.

2   In 2010, consumer retailing goods reached a total of 15.7 trillion yuan (2.47 trillion USD) according to the Bulletin on the National Economy and Social Development (www.stats.gov.cn/tjgb/ndtjgb/qgndtjgb/t20110228_402705692.htm).
3   Literature on marketing ethics in general: Brenkert, 2008; Enderle and Murphy, 2009; Laczniak and Murphy, 1993; Murphy *et al.* 2005; Singhapakdi and Vitell, 1999; Vitell, 2001.
4   Literature on business ethics in China: Enderle, 1997, 2003, 2005, 2010; Enderle and Lu, 2013; Ip, 2009; Lu, 1997, 2009, 2010; Lu and Enderle, 2006/2013; Niu, 1997; Paine, 2010; Thompson, 2009; Zhou *et al.* 2009; Zhou, 2012.

References

Bok, S. (2001) "Deceit," in L. Becker and C. Becker (eds) *Encyclopedia of Ethics*, Routledge: New York: 378–81.
Braybrooke, D. and Monahan, A.P. (2001), "Common good," in L. Becker and C. Becker (eds) *Encyclopedia of Ethics*, Routledge: New York, pp. 262–66.
Brenkert, G.G. (2008) *Marketing Ethics*, Malden, MA: Blackwell.
China Watch (2011) *China Daily*, November 10 (advertisement inserted in *Financial Times*, November 10, 2011).
Collier, P. (2010) *The Plundered Planet. Why We Must – and How We Can – Manage Nature for Global Prosperity*, New York: Oxford University Press.
De George, R.T. (1993) *Competing with Integrity in International Business*, New York: Oxford University Press.
DeSimone, L.D. and Popoff, F. (1997) *Eco-Efficiency. The Business Link to Sustainable Development.* With the World Business Council for Sustainable Development, Cambridge, MA: MIT Press.
DesJardins, J.R. (2007) *Business, Ethics, and the Environment. Imagining a Sustainable Future*, Upper Saddle River, NJ: Pearson Prentice Hall.
Enderle, G. (1997) "Ethical guidelines for the reform of state-owned enterprises in China," *University of Pennsylvania Journal of International Economic Law*, 18(4): 1177–92.
——(1998) "A framework for international marketing ethics: preliminary considerations and emerging perspectives," *Journal of Human Values*, 4 (1), 25–44 (New Delhi).
—— (2003) "What perspectives for developing business ethics in China?', in King-Tak Ip (ed.) *Market Economy and Corporate Ethics* (in Chinese), Shanghai: Fudan University Press, pp. 1–15.
—— (2005) "Business ethics in China," in P.H. Werhane and R.E. Freeman (eds) *The Blackwell Encyclopedia of Management. Volume II: Business Ethics*, 2nd edition, Oxford: Blackwell, pp. 76–80.
—— (2010) "Wealth creation in China and some lessons for development ethics," *Journal of Business Ethics*, 96 (1): 1–15.
—— (2013) "The capability approach as guidance for corporate ethics," in C. Luetge (ed.) *Handbook of the Philosophical Foundations of Business Ethics*, Springer: Dordrecht, pp. 675–91.
—— and Lu, X. (2013) "Business ethics in China," in D. Koehn (ed.) *Wiley Encyclopedia of Management. Volume Business Ethics*, 3rd edition, Hoboken, NJ: Wiley.
—— and Murphy, P.E. (2009) "Ethics and corporate social responsibility for marketing in the global marketplace," in M. Kotabe and K. Helsen (eds) *The SAGE Handbook of International Marketing*, Los Angeles: Sage, pp. 504–31.
Esty, D.C. and Winston, A.S. (2006) *Green to Gold: How Smart Companies Use Environmental Strategy to Innovate, Create Value, and Build Competitive Advantage*, New Haven, CT: Yale University Press.
Gao G., Tong-Toomy, S., and Gudykunst, W.B. (1996) "Chinese communication processes," in M.H. Bond (ed.) *The Handbook of Chinese Psychology*, Hong Kong: Oxford University Press, pp. 280–93.
Gaudium et Spes (1965) The Pastoral Constitution on the Church in the Modern World. Available at: www.vatican.va/archive/hist_councils/ii_vatican_council/documents/vat-ii_cons_19651207 _gaudium-et-spes_en.html (accessed September 12, 2012).

Hammond, A., Adriaanse, A., Rodenburg, E., Bryant, D., and Woodward, R. (1995) *Environmental Indicators: A Systemic Approach to Measuring and Reporting Environmental Policy Performance in the Context of Sustainable Development*, New York: World Resources Institute.

Ip, P.K. (2009) "The challenge of developing a business ethics in China," *Journal of Business Ethics*, 88: 211–24.

Kotler, P. (1998) *Marketing Management. Analysis, Planning, Implementation, and Control*, Upper Saddle River, NJ: Prentice-Hall.

Laczniak, G. R. and Murphy, P.E. (1993) *Ethical Marketing Decisions: The Higher Road*, Boston, MA: Allyn and Bacon.

Laszlo, C. (2005) *The Sustainable Company. How to Create Lasting Value Through Social and Environmental Performance*, Washington, DC: Island Press.

Liu, C., Jingjing, P., Yu, P., and Gu, Y. (2011) "What makes the Chinese fraud stocks listed in the U.S. so outrageous?" Research paper in the MBA course "Professional Ethics and Integrity' in June 2011, SAIF, Shanghai Jiaotong University, Shanghai.

Lu, X. (1997) "Business ethics in China," *Journal of Business Ethics*, 16: 1509–18.

—— (2009) "A Chinese perspective: business ethics in China now and in the future," *Journal of Business Ethics*, 86: 451–61.

—— (2010) *Business Ethics. A Chinese Perspective*, Shanghai: Shanghai Academy of Social Sciences Press.

—— and Enderle, G. (eds) (2006/2013) *Developing Business Ethics in China*, New York: Palgrave Macmillan.

McDonough, W. and Braungart, M. (2002) *Cradle to Cradle: Remaking the Way We Make Things*, New York: Farrar, Strauss and Giroux.

Murphy, P.E., Laczniak, G.R., Bowie, N.E., and Klein, T.A. (2005) *Ethical Marketing*, Upper Saddle River, NJ: Pearson Education.

Newton, L.H. (2005) *Business Ethics and the Natural Environment*, Malden, MA: Blackwell.

—— (2010) "Environmental ethics and business," in G.G. Brenkert and T.L. Beauchamp (eds) *The Oxford Handbook of Business Ethics*, New York: Oxford University Press, pp. 657–76.

Niu Q. (1997) "Studies of marketing ethics," *Journal of China Business and Market*, No.6, ISSN1002-8811(1007-8226) (in Chinese).

Paine, L.S. (2010) "The globe. The China rules," *Harvard Business Review*, 88 (6): 103–07.

Rivera, J.E. (2010) *Business and Public Policy. Responses to Environmental and Social Protection Processes*, Cambridge: Cambridge University Press.

Rogers, P.P., Jalal, K.F., and Boyd, J.A. (2006) *An Introduction to Sustainable Development*, Cambridge, MA: Harvard University Press.

Ryan, L.V., Gasparski, W.W., and Enderle, G. (2000) *Business Students Focus on Ethics. Praxiology: The International Annual of Practical Philosophy and Methodology*, Volume 8, New Brunswick, NJ: Transaction Publishers.

Santoro, M.A. (2009) *China 2020: How Western Business Can – and Should – Influence Social and Political Change in the Coming Decade*, Ithaca, NY and London: Cornell University Press.

Schmidheiny, S. and Zorraquin, F.J.L. (1996), *Financial Change. The Financial Community, Eco-Efficiency, and Sustainable Development*, Cambridge, MA: MIT.

Sen, A. (1992) *Inequality Reexamined*, New York: Oxford University Press.

—— (1999) *Development as Freedom*, New York: Knopf.

—— (2009) *The Idea of Justice*, Cambridge, MA: Belknap Press of Harvard University Press.

Singhapakdi, A. and Vitell, S.J. (eds) (1999) "International marketing ethics," special issue of *Journal of Business Ethics*, 18 (1) (January 1).

Thompson, M.J. (2009) "Integrity in marketing: Chinese and European perspectives," *Journal of International Business Ethics*, 2 (2): 62–9.

UNESCO (1995) *Our Creative Diversity*. Report of the World Commission on culture and development, Egoprim, France.

United Nations (UN) (2011) *Guiding Principles on Business and Human Rights: Implementing the United Nations "Protect, Respect and Remedy" Framework for consideration by the Human Rights Council*. Report of the Special Representative of the Secretary-General on the issue of human rights and transnational corporations and other business enterprises, John Ruggie. Human Rights Council. Seventeenth Session. A/HRC/17/31.

United Nations Development Program (UNDP) (1990) *Human Development Report*, New York: Oxford University Press.

—— (2011) *Human Development Report 2011. Sustainability and Equity: A Better Future for All*, New York: Palgrave Macmillan.

Van Dieren, W. (ed.) (1995) *Taking Nature into Account*. A Report to the Club of Rome, New York: Springer.

Vitell, S.J. (ed.) (2001) "Special issue on marketing ethics," *Journal of Business Ethics*, 32 (1) (July 1).

Westra, L. (2005) "Environment and environmental ethics," in P.H. Werhane and R.E. Freeman (eds) *The Blackwell Encyclopedia of Management. Second Edition. Volume II: Business Ethics*, Malden, MA: Blackwell, pp. 175-8.

World Commission on Environment and Development (WCED) (1987) *Our Common Future*, New York: Oxford University Press.

Wu, M., Zhang, J., Xiang, K., and Li, S. (2011) "Double standards in marketing practices of multinationals in China – The cases of Nestle, HP and Toyota," research paper in the MBA course "Professional Ethics and Integrity" in June 2011, SAIF, Shanghai: Shanghai Jiaotong University.

Zhou, Z. (2012) "Business ethics as field of training, teaching and research in East Asia," in D. Rossouw (ed.) "A global survey of business ethics as field of training, teaching and research," *Journal of Business Ethics*.

——, Ou, P., and Enderle, G. (2009) "Business ethics education for MBA students in China: current status and future prospects," *Journal of Business Ethics Education*, 6: 103–18.

——, Yuan, L., and Nanfeng, L. (2010) "Economic and business ethics in China: training, teaching and research," paper presented at the Third Shanghai International Conference on Business Ethics, SASS Center for Business Ethics, October 29–30.

Sources of case studies

Alibaba

February 21, 2011: "Alibaba executives resign after rise in fraud cases," *BBC*: www.bbc.co.uk/news/ business-12521833

February 21, 2011: "Alibaba.com chief executive resigns," *Guardian*: www.guardian.co.uk/business/ 2011/feb/21/alibaba-chief-resigns-over-frauds

February 22, 2011: "Alibaba execs resign over supplier frauds," *China Daily*: www.chinadaily.com.cn/china/2011-02/22/content_12053723.htm

February 24, 2011, "Alibaba's Chief Lu wants to 'fix mistakes, prevent detours'," *Bloomberg Business Week*: www.businessweek.com/news/2011-02-24/alibaba-s-chief-lu-wants-to-fix-mistakes-prevent-detours-.html

Baidu

July 19, 2011, *Reuters*: www.reuters.com/article/2010/07/19/us-baidu-idUSTRE66I1HK20100719

August 16, 2011, *Forbes*: www.forbes.com/sites/ericsavitz/2011/08/16/baidu-slides-after-china-tv-finds-ads-for-fake-meds/

August 17, 2011, *Reuters*: www.reuters.com/article/2011/08/17/us-baidu-cctv-idUSTRE77G14X20110817

August 18, 2011, CTTV: http://english.cntv.cn/program/bizasia/20110818/106379.shtml video: http://english.cntv.cn/program/bizasia/20110818/105780.shtml

November 2, 2011, CTTV: http://app1.vote.cntv.cn/viewResult.jsp?voteId=3392&score=0

Da Vinci

July 11, 2011, *China Daily*: www.chinadaily.com.cn/metro/2011-07/15/content_12913165.htm

July 12, 2011, *China Entrepreneur Magazine* (in Chinese): www.iceo.com.cn/shangye/36/2011/0712/223742.shtml

July 19, 2011, *China Daily*: www.chinadaily.com.cn/bizchina/2011-07/19/content 12930222.htm

Carrefour

February 11, 2011: "Authorities fine French retailer for using misleading price tags, fake discounts to attract customers," *China Daily European Weekly*.

February 26, 2011: "'Reselling' claims put more pressure on Carrefour," *China Daily*.

Walmart

October 11, 2011: "China shuts seven Walmart stores in pork row," *Financial Times*, p. 13.

Otis

July 6, 2011: "Subway escalator crush kills boy," *China Daily*: www.chinadaily.com.cn/usa/epaper/ 2011-07/06/content_12845709.htm

July 14, 2011: "Escalator safety in spotlight," *China Daily*: http://usa.chinadaily.com.cn/china/ 2011-07/14/content_12900424.htm

July 19, 2011: "Going down: Otis share prices fall after elevator accident," *China Daily*: www.wantchinatimes.com/news-subclass-cnt.aspx?cid=1102&MainCatID=&id=20110719000039

Foxconn/Apple

May 27, 2010: "Apple, HP and Dell investigate Foxconn," *Financial Times*, p. 1.

May 29, 2010: "Foxconn to raise staff salaries by 20% after spate of suicides," *Financial Times*, p. 1.

May 29, 2010: "Showing the strain," *Financial Times*, p. 5.

June 8, 2010: "Foxconn wants clients to share wages burden," *Financial Times*, p. 16.

June 26, 2010: "Chinese pay rises encourage move to cheaper provinces," *Financial Times*, p. 9

June 29, 2010: "Foxconn to shift Apple gadgets production," *Financial Times*, p. 1.

January 20, 2011: *The Other Side of Apple*. Report by Friends of Nature, Institute of Public and Environmental Affairs, and Green Beagle.

February 2011: *Apple Supplier Responsibility: 2011 Progress Report*: www.apple.com/supplier responsibility.

February 16, 2011: "China pays a high cost for Apple's success," *Shanghai Daily*, p. A2.

September 13, 2011: "Foxconn effect sparks change in direction," *Financial Times*, p. 3.

illycaffe

illy Branding 2009 (illy information)
illy Marketing Communication Activity 2009 (illy information)
illycaffe Questions and Answers 2010 (illy information)
illycaffe: Beauty has a Taste 2011 (illy information)

Fuda

Lu Xiaohe, Gu Xunli, and Xiangqin Chen: 2012, *Corporate Responsibilities: Searching the Standards for China's Small and Medium Enterprises.* A case study of Shanghai Fuda (Group) and a comparative study with international standards of corporate responsibilities (Shanghai Academy of Social Sciences, Shanghai).

Baosteel

Baosteel. 2011. *2010 Sustainability Report.* Baoshan Iron & Steel Co., Ltd. Better Steel, Better Environment, Better Life: www.baosteel.com.

Haworth

Haworth. 2011: *2010 Sustainability Report:* www.haworth.com.
Haworth Asia Pacific: www.haworth-asia.com.

Apple

July 6, 2010: "Clues in an iPhone autopsy. A supply chain with costs rising at each stop," *The New York Times Business,* p. B1.
October 2010: *Greening Supply Chains in China: Practical Lessons from China-Based Suppliers in Achieving Environmental Performance.* Working paper by Institute of Public and Environmental Affairs and World Resource Institute.
January 20, 2011: *The Other Side of Apple.* Report by Friends of Nature, Institute of Public and Environmental Affairs, and Green Beagle.
February 2011: *Apple Supplier Responsibility. 2011 Progress Report:* www.apple.com/supplier-responsibility.
August 31, 2011: *The Other Side of Apple II. Pollution Spreads Through Apple's Supply Chain.* Report by Friends of Nature, Institute of Public and Environmental Affairs, Green Beagle, Envirofriends, and Green Stone Environmental Action Network.
September 1, 2011: "Apple accused of using Chinese suppliers with pollution record," *Financial Times,* p. 11.
September 1, 2011: "Foxconn tackles pollution claims," *Financial Times,* p. 12.
October 2011: "Apply faces internal opposition in China," *Ethical Performance,* 13 (5):12.
November 16, 2011: "Five Chinese environmental protection groups met with Apple," *Business and Human Rights Resource Center:* www.business-humanrights.org.

Jilin

November 15, 2005: "Five dead, one missing, nearly 70 injured after chemical plant blasts," *People's Daily Online:* http://english.people.com.cn/200511/15/eng20051115_221428.html
November 23, 2005: "Toxic leak threat to Chinese city," *BBC:* http://news.bbc.co.uk/2/hi/asia-pacific/ 4462760.stm
November 27, 2005: "China's toxic shock," *Time Magazine:* www.time.com/time/magazine/article/ 0,9171,1134807,00.html
November 28, 2005: "The world's toxic waste dump choking on chemicals in China," *Spiegel:* www.spiegel.de/international/spiegel/0,1518,387392,00.html

ConocoPhillips

July 5, 2011: "China admits extent of spill from oil rig," *New York Times*: www.nytimes.com/2011/ 07/06/world/asia/06china.html?ref=asia.

July 13, 2011: "Update on Bohai Bay oil cleanup and production curtailment," ConocoPhillips Newsletter: www.conocophillips.com.cn/EN/newsroom/newsreleases/Pages/20110713.aspx.

August 9, 2011: "ConocoPhillips slow to clear up oil spill in China's Bohai Sea," *The Guardian*: www.guardian.co.uk/environment/2011/aug/09/conocophillips-oil-spill-china.

August 25, 2011: "China to sue ConocoPhillips over oil spills," *New York Times*: www.nytimes.com/ 2011/08/26/world/asia/26china.html.

August 27–28, 2011: "China hits Conoco on spill." *The Wall Street Journal*, p. B3

September 1, 2011: "ConocoPhillips: Bohai oil spill cleanup 99 percentage complete," CCTV English news: http://english.cntv.cn/program/china24/20110901/102701.shtml.

September 7, 2011: "China taking a harder line on pollution after Conoco spill," *Financial Times*, p. 19.

September 19, 2011: "Chronology-ConocoPhillips oil spill in China's Bohai Bay," *Reuters*: www.reuters.com/article/2011/09/19/china-conoco-spill-idUSL3E7K60J320110919.

PART VII
Conclusion

18

CAN WE GET THERE FROM HERE?

Charting the contours of the common good

John F. Sherry, Jr.

In their analysis of the historical interplay of commercial mythmaking and free-market capitalism, in which new market ideologies are launched to counter crises of faith provoked by critical activists, Giesler and Veresiu (2012a,b) draw upon Foucault's (1978) concept of governmentality to trace the evolution of society's recent relationship to the market: protecting the state from the market in the seventeenth century yielded to protecting the market from the state in the eighteenth century, which in turn yielded to a triumphal hybridizing of the market in search of its ideal form in the twentieth century. The progression moves from a *governing* the market through a governing *through* the market to a governing *for* the market (Giesler and Veresiu 2012b: 1). Rather than anticipate the next activist response to be precipitated by the current crisis of faith in market triumphalism, we propose a provocation straight from the heart of academic marketing thought leadership itself, which builds upon the critical scholarship of recent years. Think of it as a governing *beyond* the market phase. In this volume, we ask what marketing can do to help harness the market to work in consort with other social institutions to realize the common good.

One of the consequences of living in a brand culture is that virtue can become reframed exclusively as a product of capitalism, such that people trade in moral capital as readily as in economic or social capital, and corporate social responsibility can become a translation or embodiment of business logic, a profitable value-added (Banet-Weiser 2012: 144-45). Sociologist Donald Black (2011: 145) has characterized modern morality as a "morality of distance," wherein people prize their right to be left alone as they pursue their right of unlimited personal opportunity, expecting others to "mind their own business." Anthropologist Clifford Geertz (1988, 147) has asserted that we inhabit a world in which it is "increasingly difficult to get out of each other's way." These perspectives collide in the contemporary marketplace, where the consequences of decisions made by consumers, managers, public policy-makers and activists reverberate around the globe. Political economist Gar Alperovitz

(2011: 232–33) has challenged the polity to develop a "meaningful," "morally coherent," and "positive" politics that enhances our inexorably diminishing values of "equality, liberty and democracy" in an era of "technological abundance." Such an ambitious reformation rests upon our ability to clarify the nature of the common good, and to work comprehensively and systematically to achieve it. Each of our contributors has pulled on the marketing thread of this larger fabric, but has stopped short of making many normative pronouncements. In this concluding chapter, we consider some of the specific contours of the common good.

As early as the 1970s, the incipient Quality of Life marketing movement (hereafter QOL), known then as "sociomarketing," recognized the extraeconomic obligations of the firm, and called for the understanding of our disciplinary concepts in their "full complexity," as they bear upon the nested dimensions of well-being from the micro to the macro, envisioning marketing as the "science of positive social change," or, more succinctly, "proactive marketing" (Sirgy 2001: 6-11, 22). Managerial and public policy implications for QOL have been broached in connection with just society theory, the satisfaction of human needs, ecology, and a host of other perspectives that might inform our understanding of marketing's role in shaping the common good (Sirgy 2001).

QOL, a business practice compatible with Kotler's (1972) societal marketing orientation and intended to promote both marketing beneficence (customer well-being) and marketing nonmaleficence (stakeholder well-being), is alleged to have multiple antecedents: macro characteristics of social consciousness related to consumer well-being, industry ethical climate, commitment to organizational ethics, and long-term orientation of firms, as well as individual manager characteristics of autotelic personality, moral idealism, cognitive moral development, and caring attitude for customer well-being (Lee and Sirgy 2004: 45, 52–55). QOL seems a noble refinement of current managerial and disciplinary effort, if not an outright redirection. While the consequences of QOL are implicitly endorsed by the contributors to this volume, these antecedents pose something of a challenge to conventional marketing wisdom. In short, we believe that marketing should be tasked to help produce an intellectual and emotional climate in which these antecedents may be catalyzed. That is, a significantly different Utopian vision is required of marketing if the common good is to be realized. How can marketing foster such a reformation of its present purpose?

The brothers Skidelsky – political economist Robert and philosopher Edward – point us in a promising direction. They have recently urged society to revive a long dormant line of inquiry: What is wealth for? They lament that the Faustian bargain society has struck with the forces of wealth creation has robbed citizens of a sense of proportion or propriety, leaving individuals without a collective vision of the good life (Skidelsky and Skidelsky 2012: 68–69, 218). The Skidelskys seek to bring the idea of the good life (what our contributors have called the common good throughout this volume) back into the public forum. Believing that modern liberal theory and neoclassical economics have monopolized public discourse, leading to a world consumed with the "satisfaction of private wants" wherein the good life has become a "marginal concern," the brothers advance what they call a "non-coercive paternalism" to help correct the situation (Skidelsky and Skidelsky 2012: 87, 93, 193). Such an approach would help ensure that "the fruits of productivity are more evenly shared" and that the contemporary "pressure to consume" would be reduced (Skidelsky and Skidelsky 2012: 194).

After rehearsing a litany of familiar shortfalls, Peter Corning (2011: ix–xii), who holds an interdisciplinary doctorate in social and life sciences, adds his voice to the throng proclaiming that free market capitalism "has not lived up to its billing," and calls for a "rethinking" of the social (indeed "biosocial") contract that recognizes the anthropological insight that a sense of fairness and a concern for social justice are cultural universals. Equally critical of socialism, he proposes a revised public philosophy that embodies a new synthetic set of ground rules for a biosocial contract that includes these tenets: an unqualified commitment to meet the survival needs of all members; an equitable distribution of surplus beyond survival based on merit; and a requirement for universal (with few exceptions) contribution of equitable share to collective survival (Corning 2011: 12). He identifies fourteen primary "needs domains" – thermoregulation, waste elimination, nutrition, water, mobility, sleep, respiration, physical safety, physical health, mental health, communications, social relationships, reproduction, and the nurturance of offspring – deemed "indispensible" for the "biological adaptation/fitness" of humanity (Corning 2011: 96). His is a sustainability platform writ large.

Corning's (2011: 170) Fair Society model seeks a "proper balance" between equality in the satisfaction of primary needs, "fair recognition" of merit, and "proportionate reciprocity." His advocacy of "stakeholder capitalism" as a decisive step for achieving such balance resonates with many of the ideas proposed by the contributors to this volume (but also conflicts with a few). His advocacy of a nonpartisan "fairness coalition," a political movement designed to seek such reformation (Corning 2011: 177, 192), might be construed as a righteous intervention in public policy. Most germane to our present concern is a paraphrasing of his activist orientation: What can marketing do to "help bend the arc of the moral universe" (Corning 2011: 195), and what would the resultant society resemble?

Breaking the "addiction" to consumption and work would depend in part upon universal access to "basic goods" such as health, security, respect, personality, harmony with nature, friendship, and leisure (Skidelsky and Skidelsky 2012: 145, 154–66). The Skidelskys suggest that the state that has failed to provide all of its citizens with the material conditions of the good life might seek enlightenment from moral opinions expressed in religious traditions, citing Catholic Social Teaching and Protestant New Liberalism as potential sources of secular inspiration (Skidelsky and Skidelsky 2012: 169; 186–90). Since several of the contributors to this volume have referenced the former tradition in their analyses, and given its traction in the literature (Santos and Laczniak 2009), we employ a few of the principles of Catholic Social Teaching here in our Conclusion to suggest some secular ways that marketing might address the issue of the common good (which is itself a fundamental tenet of CST). As educators, we adopt a scholastic perspective with the notion that a spirited intellectual engagement with the discipline's perils and promises might lead efficiently to innovative, practical interventions in the marketplace. By reinvigorating the moral ties between classroom and boardroom, a marketing reformation may be catalyzed.

- *Human dignity*. One of the principal goals of marketing education at every level – undergraduate, MBA and executive – ought to be the cultivation in our students of a critical imagination capable of discerning alternative Utopias to which the marketing imagination might be applied, the outcome being actionable recommendations for creating a marketplace that serves the common good. This would be an explicitly moral undertaking (as opposed to the implicit morality which often goes unexamined in our curricula) that moves beyond the simple (but necessary) application of ethical precepts to elements of the marketing mix. Such a reformation of vision might begin with a consideration of successful contemporary alternative or "real" Utopias, the relationship between economic, social, and state power, and the hybrid strategies that might transform the marketplace toward the ends of social and political justice (Wright 2010). That public goods must in many cases supersede private goods if enlightened cultures are to survive might provide the initial premise for a critical investigation of the relationship between market and nonmarket logics. A reconsideration of the essence and nature of the gift might serve equally well. The most ancient and enduring source of social cohesion, the gift creates an energy with the potential to humanize and harness the economy in the service of community. The charge of this moral education is to get all stakeholders to examine, challenge, and reformulate foundational precepts of marketing, and use our knowledge of marketing to construct a more equitable, viable system. Hard-form stakeholder theory (Laczniak and Murphy 2012) is a promising step in this direction.
- *Preference for the poor and vulnerable*. Given the fallout of the 2008 economic meltdown (including the misalignment of moral hazard and moral panic) and the growing income disparity around the globe, one of the immediate goals of marketing education ought to be a rigorous and comprehensive elaboration of bottom-of-the-pyramid (BOP) development principles (Prahalad 2006; Yunus 2009) for impoverished and emerging markets (Santos and Laczniak 2008) and a recalibration of BOP best practices for developed markets. A detailed rethinking of the dynamics of debt (Graebner 2011) and the feasibility of sharing (Belk 2010) on a grand scale is also warranted. Each of these exercises will demand an egalitarian reconceptualization of needs and wants, such that the former might universally be met and the latter not impinge upon creation of the common good. Cultivation of an ethos of philanthropy over acquisition as a touchstone both of identity and community would be an integral component of this rethinking process.
- *Solidarity*. To the extent that capitalism becomes inimical to community, a near-term goal of marketing education might be the close examination of hybrid forms of market mechanisms that help to produce the organic solidarity requisite to authentic social life. Throughout this volume, we have emphasized that

marketers are also social architects and behavioral engineers, not merely material provisioners of society. As they help create the milieu in which they operate, they share responsibility for correcting problems of misplaced identity, cultural dislocations of income disparity, mercarigenic disease, and other dysfunctions chronicled in this book. Progress will require creative collaboration between marketers, thought leaders of other disciplines, and civic authorities. Beyond the sociological study of real Utopias, a careful consideration of a range of values-based exchange systems requires undertaking. Religion is one such potential font of insight, and the primer by Coward and Maguire (2000) contains a number of practical proposals from Catholic, Protestant, Jewish, Hindu, Islamic, Buddhist, Confucian, Taoist, and indigenous African religious traditions. Sherry (2000) has identified other religious sources (notably animist) for marketers interested in catalyzing a progressive Utopia. In a secular key, our disciplinary understanding of the dynamics of brand community (Muniz and O'Guinn 2001) might be repurposed in the service of place-making, and directed toward creating meaningful engagement with locales, whether neighborhoods, bioregions, or nations. Ron Nahser (Chapter 9 this volume) suggests a productive context for such an enterprise.

- *Stewardship*. Perhaps the most pressing goal of marketing education is to develop a discipline whose philosophy and practice are grounded in an ecological understanding of our enterprise. A planet-centric conception of marketing can no longer remain the rallying cry of critics and reformers; it must be elaborated into an actionable set of managerial practices, and practitioners must assume more responsibility for the behavioral architecture that will preserve not just the market, but the planet. Inherent in this obligation is the understanding of the sacramentality of sources presently construed as resources. A closer look at our relationship with "stuff" may help us learn to reinvest our animistic impulses in nature, and to reorient our ethos of consumption along much more sustainable lines.

By adopting and creatively applying just these few precepts, let alone plumbing the wisdom of other spiritual traditions, a reformulated marketing might have a stunning impact on the social order. Imagine a society whose:

- modal ethical agent was a distributed, communal extended self;
- measure of self-worth was decoupled from possessions and invidious comparison;
- status system rewarded charitable giving and discouraged appetitive acquisition;
- conception of the good life exalted leisure to the same level as work;
- civic agenda was an equitable redistribution of resources insuring universal thriving;
- commercial, civic, and social spheres operated in synergistic harmony;
- cultural ethos insisted that humanity inhabit the biosphere in a sustainable manner.

If such a liberal democracy (or democratic pluralism) were the Utopian vision to which our society aspired, a reconfigured marketing could facilitate the achievement, or, at least, a heroic approach.

In a recent eulogy, Donaldson (2009) problematizes Peter Drucker's lament that pluralistic societies like our own eventually crumble for lack of attention to the common good, and that the market's failure to nurture community demands volunteerism as a corrective. Donaldson (2009: 46) views the threat that corporations pose to community to be a "fault line that runs through the very structure of modern democratic capitalism," that may never be sealed. Citing consumerist movements and virtual communities of moral activism as market-based responses to this problem, Donaldson is skeptical of Drucker's incitement of business leaders to go "over the walls" in pursuit of community whose constitution is mandated by civic responsibility. If consumer-led initiatives of resistance in the service of community are to rise above the local and the reactive, the collaboration of business leaders must be enlisted. How might that collaboration be achieved?

The need to imagine models beyond investor capitalism that recognize the "legitimate economic and social interests of members of society other than stockholders," that question the "very purpose of corporate leadership," and that foster virtues such as "custodianship, duty and responsibility" is the urgent message behind Khurana's (2007: 365–66, 381) magisterial analysis of the evolution of the American business school. Khurana (2007) advocates a rehabilitation of the profession of management that would renounce the current commodification of the business degree and restore the moral sense of a "calling" to students that chartered our original foray into higher education. This reformation demands a reclamation of "cultural authority" by the professoriate, and a re-infusing of curricula with normative training related to identity beyond the cultivation of technical expertise (Khurana 2007: 370–71). We have suggested throughout this volume that a careful and comprehensive consideration of the questions "What are markets for?" and "What is the common good?" are the collective cornerstone upon which an enlightened marketing might be raised.

The critique of neoliberalism should not be relegated to departments of sociology, nor the correction of its global excesses to schools of government or public policy. Just as charity begins at home, so also must the remaking of marketing begin in the business school. The University of Notre Dame has long considered itself to be a place where the Catholic church can do its thinking. In a parallel, small "c" catholic spirit of that conviction, our faculty trusts that this volume will stimulate readers of all traditions to reimagine the nature of marketing, and begin to craft the principles necessary to its reformation. We believe a focus on the common good is the key to a righteous re-enchantment of marketing. We hope this volume advances the ball closer to the goal line of the common good.

References

Alperovitz, G. (2011) *America Beyond Capitalism: Reclaiming our Wealth, Our Liberty and Our Democracy*, Takoma Park, MD: Democracy Collaborative Press and Boston, MA: Dollars and Sense.

Banet-Weiser, S. (2012) *Authentic: The Politics of Ambivalence in Brand Culture*, New York: New York University Press.

Belk, R. (2010) "Sharing," *Journal of Consumer Research*, 36 (5): 715–34.

Black, D. (2011) *Moral Time*, Oxford: Oxford University Press.

Corning, P. (2011) *The Fair Society: The Science of Human Nature and the Pursuit of Social Justice*, Chicago: University of Chicago Press.

Coward, H. and Maguire, D. (eds) (2000) *Visions of a New Earth: Religious Perspectives on Population, Consumption and Ecology*, Albany: State University of New York Press.

Donaldson, T. (2009) "A frustrated quest for community," *Journal of the Academy of Marketing Science*, 37: 44–46.

Foucault, M. (1978) "Governmentality" (lecture at the Collège de France, 1 February), in G. Burchell, C. Gordon, and P. Miller (eds) *The Foucault Effect: Studies in Governmentality*, Hemel Hempstead, UK: Harvester Wheatsheaf, 87–104.

Geertz, C. (1988) *Works and Lives: The Anthropologist as Author*, Palo Alto, CA: Stanford University Press, 147.

Giesler, M. and Veresiu, E. (2012a) "Sustaining the invisible hand: A dialectical theory of commercial mythmaking and free market capitalism," working paper, Schulich School of Business, York University, Toronto, Ontario.

—— (2012b) "Sustaining the invisible hand: A dialectical theory of commercial mythmaking and free market capitalism," presented at the Association for Consumer Research Annual Conference, Vancouver, BC, October 5.

Graeber, D. (2011) *Debt: The First 5000 Years*, Brooklyn, NY: Melville House.

Khurana, R. (2007) *From Higher Aims to Hired Hands*, Princeton, NJ: Princeton University Press.

Kotler, P. (1972) "What consumerism means for marketers," *Harvard Business Review*, 50 (3): 48–57.

Laczniak, G. and P. Murphy (2012) "Stakeholder theory and marketing: Moving from a firm-centric to a societal perspective," *Journal of Public Policy and Marketing*, 31 (2): 1–9.

Lee, D. and M.J. Sirgy (2004) "Quality-of-life marketing: Proposed antecedents and consequences," *Journal of Macromarketing*, 24 (1): 44–58.

Muniz, A.M., Jr. and O'Guinn, T.C. (2001) "Brand community," *Journal of Consumer Research*, 27 (4): 412–32.

Prahalad, C.K. (2006) *Fortune at the Bottom of the Pyramid: Eradicating Poverty Through Profits*, Noida, India: Dorling Kindersley.

Santos, N. and G. Laczniak (2008) "Marketing to the poor: A justice-inspired approach," paper presented at the 14th Annual World Forum, Colleagues in Jesuit Business Education, International Association of Jesuit Business Schools, Business and Education in an Era of Globalization: The Jesuit Position, July 20–23.

—— (2009) "'Just' markets from the perspective of Catholic social teaching," *Journal of Business Ethics*, 89 (1): 29–38.

Sherry, J.F., Jr. (2000) "Distraction, destruction, deliverance: The presence of mindscape in marketing's new millennium," *Marketing Intelligence and Planning*, 18 (6-7): 328–36.

Sirgy, M.J. (2001) *Handbook of Quality of Life Research: An Ethical Marketing Perspective*, Boston, MA: Kluwer.

Skidelsky, R. and Skidelsky, E. (2012) *How Much Is Enough? Money and the Good Life*, New York: Other Press.

Wright, E. (2010) *Envisioning Real Utopias*, London: Verso.

Yunus, M. (2009) *Creating a World Without Poverty: Social Business and the Future of Capitalism*, New York: Public Affairs.

19

AFTERWORD

A blast from the past

John J. Kennedy

The early years

The journey to the "common good" focus within the Department of Marketing at Notre Dame was not a straight path and the seeds of this focus were sown back in those distant days of 1963. I was there. I witnessed them. Let me ruminate.

I was department head of Marketing in the College of Business Administration in 1963. The department at that time was seeking a new vision, goals, and national recognition. Tom Murphy was the dean. The assistant dean was John Malone (just stepping down as Marketing's department head). In the department were Jerry McCarthy, Yu Furuhashi, John Malone, Bill Bonwich, Ed Crain, and Wesley Bender. Back then, there were regular, heated debates about marketing and its links to materialism. The alternative economic systems rampant around the world in the thirties, forties, and fifties had served to demonize marketing. Marketing as a discipline was not universally applauded. On campus, marketing even seemed to conflict with some deeply held Catholic beliefs.

In the sixties at Notre Dame (as well as many other institutions), the business college was, in the minds of many, a trade school. It was hardly a place for substantive intellectual curiosity. It was also suspected of being a haven for less gifted students. Business schools in the sixties lacked gravitas.

The sixties were also a time of dramatic, colossal shifts in the currents of power in the world. Formalized religions that once had broad, massive, all-encompassing influence started to see the sunset of that dominance. Globalization and the increasing manifestation of businesses' "iron grip" on world events forced universities to rethink the role of the business college.

Slowly but surely, it became apparent that if there were to be a flowering of the common good, it would probably have to come partially through the influence of the world's business leaders. This was quite a contrast to the prevailing demeaning attitudes on campuses toward business people. The sixties and seventies were ripe for planting the initial seeds for what has become today a highly recognized, singularly branded Department of Marketing for the common good at Notre Dame.

The anti-marketing department

In 1963 and 1964, the Marketing Department set up workshops with a range of disciplines from the College of Arts and Letters in an attempt to bring different intellectual content into the marketing discipline and the business curriculum generally. We called this the "anti-marketing department" idea, which can be illustrated in a short tale of joint programs run with the departments of Theology, Psychology, Anthropology, and Philosophy by the Marketing Department. This tongue-in-cheek label and holistic approach were what we felt was needed in the world to counter the on-rushing train of consumerism.

The faculty had a lot of fun with this idea. The goal was to initiate thinking about all the alleged well known "evils" of capitalism, the role of business in society and more specifically, the nature and scope of the marketing discipline. The primary purpose of business was then, as now, a hot topic. Was it profit or to serve the common good? It was a natural arena for all the liberal arts departments involved. That helped create, at that time, a revised perspective of the business school, and particularly, the Department of Marketing.

The University's Catholic character

Looking back over the years that I have been associated with Notre Dame, I have observed that a common thread has been the Catholic message. That was and still is part of the University's fabric. The concern for the common good is intertwined in all the daily activities of the colleges and departments. It is the context for decisions at all levels. It states, if not overtly, the message "Let's make a difference in a really messed up world."

Thus, a subtle but significant determinant for "the common good" perspective was that it had to be a primary criterion in all the decision-making processes. It was not always visible, but it was and still is an enduring element of the life under the Golden Dome. This was a solid platform for a common good focus for the Department of Marketing.

To identify the "driving force" behind the past half-century, we would have to single out the faculty members that have devoted their careers to the cause of the "common good." This devotion too often came with the sacrifice of more trendy and rewarding academic brass rings, more rewarding salaries and, occasionally, tenure.

They were many, and I do not think at this point in time that I can identify them all, but certainly a few shine as the beacons. These included John Houck, Ollie Williams, Pat Murphy, George Enderle, Bill Wilkie, and John Sherry. They hit the home runs, but many others hit triples, doubles, and singles along the way, as readers can glean from the citations in this book.

Quite a journey

As the decades have passed, Notre Dame has focused more and more on the centrality of ethics. By the nineties, the College of Business had developed a world-class ethics program. This program was dominated by the Departments of Marketing and Management. In the new millennium, the environmental consequences of globalization, the diminishing role of formal religions, and the rising power of business institutions have all helped to create a fertile ground for a flourishing of the focus on the common good. This volume is the culmination of our long journey.

INDEX

Note: page numbers in *italic* type refer to Figures; those in **bold** refer to Tables. Page numbers followed by 'n' and another number refer to Notes.

Lightning Source UK Ltd.
Milton Keynes UK
UKOW06f0452280415

250476UK00003B/60/P